AMERICA AND THE POSTWAR WORLD

Grantchester
13 April 2018

Remaking International Society, 1945–1956

The main tide of international relations scholarship on the first years after World War II sweeps toward Cold War accounts. These have emphasized the United States and the USSR in a context of geopolitical rivalry, with concomitant attention upon the bristling security state. Historians have also extensively analyzed the creation of an economic order (Bretton Woods), mainly designed by Americans and tailored to their interests, but resisted by peoples residing outside of North America, Western Europe, and Japan. This scholarship, centered on the Cold War as vortex and a reconfigured world economy, is rife with contending schools of interpretation and, bolstered by troves of declassified archival documents, will support investigations and writing into the future.

By contrast, this book examines a past that ran concurrent with the Cold War and interacted with it, but which usefully can also be read as separable: Washington in the first years after World War II, and in response to that conflagration, sought to redesign international society. That society was then, and remains, an admittedly amorphous thing. Yet it has always had a tangible aspect, drawing self-regarding states into occasional cooperation, mediated by treaties, laws, norms, diplomatic customs, and transnational institutions. The U.S.-led attempt during the first postwar years to salvage international society focused on the United Nations Relief and Rehabilitation Administration, the Acheson–Lilienthal plan to contain the atomic arms race, the Nuremberg and Tokyo tribunals to force Axis leaders to account, the 1948 Genocide Convention, the 1948 Universal Declaration of Human Rights, and the founding of the United Nations. None of these initiatives was transformative, not individually or collectively. Yet they had an ameliorative effect, traces of which have touched the twenty-first century—in struggles to curb the proliferation of nuclear weapons, bring war criminals to justice, create laws supportive of human rights, and maintain an aspirational United Nations, still striving to retain meaningfulness amid world hazards. Together these partially realized innovations and frameworks constitute, if nothing else, a point of moral reference, much needed as the border between war and peace has become blurred and the consequences of a return to unrestraint must be harrowing.

Professor David Mayers holds a joint appointment in the History and Political Science Departments at Boston University. His previous books include *Cracking the Monolith: US Policy Against the Sino-Soviet Alliance, 1949–1955* (1986), *George Kennan and the Dilemmas of US Foreign Policy* (1988), *The Ambassadors and America's Soviet Policy* (awarded the 1995 Douglas Dillon prize from the American Academy of Diplomacy), *Wars and Peace: The Future Americans Envisioned, 1861–1991* (1998), *Dissenting Voices in America's Rise to Power* (2007), and *FDR's Ambassadors and the Diplomacy of Crisis* (2013).

Routledge Studies in Modern History

www.routledge.com/history/series/MODHIST

AMERICA AND THE POSTWAR WORLD

Remaking International Society, 1945–1956

David Mayers

Routledge
Taylor & Francis Group

LONDON AND NEW YORK

First published 2018
by Routledge
2 Park Square, Milton Park, Abingdon, Oxon OX14 4RN

and by Routledge
711 Third Avenue, New York, NY 10017

Routledge is an imprint of the Taylor & Francis Group, an informa business

© 2018 David Mayers

British Library Cataloguing-in-Publication Data
A catalogue record for this book is available from the British Library

Library of Congress Cataloging-in-Publication Data
A catalog record for this book has been requested

ISBN: 978-0-8153-7615-6 (hbk)
ISBN: 978-0-8153-7616-3 (pbk)
ISBN: 978-1-351-23844-1 (ebk)

Typeset in Bembo and Stone Sans
by Florence Production Ltd, Stoodleigh, Devon, UK

In memoriam
Anne Frank
Emmett Till

CONTENTS

FIGURES

PREFACE

This book is centered on U.S. attempts during the period immediately after World War II to remake what remained of international society. To that end, several projects were launched: to reinvigorate damaged economies, avert unbridled atomic arms race, punish Axis villains, reaffirm legal standards and norms of right conduct, and build sturdy global institutions. All of this initiative was undertaken as the war's aftershocks disrupted venerable empires and geopolitical patterns and stirred social change in the United States.

The aim here is to pull together a broad range of generally known material and present the component parts in a new whole that takes up an important but underexamined phenomenon: the U.S. role in salvaging global society after the Axis surrenders. Additionally, I try here to break free from what can be called "Cold War teleology." I want to push an interpretation independent of the dominant one, itself rooted in notions of a bipolar world centered on Washington and Moscow, and premised on that key construct of international relations scholarship and theorizing: anarchy. Inescapable and resonant, the Cold War does figure throughout the following pages but it is not the controlling plot device that many authors rely on to explain causation in post-1945 history.

Essentially a synthesis based on a reading of pertinent scholarly literatures, this study nevertheless does use primary source research, including in unpublished manuscripts and archival sources. A legion of archivists and librarians has been indispensable to this purpose. I am deeply grateful to them. Their institutional affiliations are indicated in the bibliography.

I do not mean to implicate any of the following individuals in whatever stylistic infelicities, factual errors, and interpretative deficiencies mar this book. I alone am responsible for such problems. But I do want to acknowledge and thank these people for providing moral support and practical help: Susan Abel, Nancy Ammerman, John Archer, Andrew Bacevich, Elizabeth Borgwardt, Amanda Bundy, Jonathan Bush, Rosella Cappella, Dino Christenson, David Clinton, Walter Connor, Frank Costigliola, Neta Crawford, Ann Cudd, Andrew David, Alan Dobson, Stephanie Fawcett, Luke Fletcher, the late David Fromkin, Irene Gendzier, Hata Gohei, Erik Goldstein, Akira Iriye, Robert Harry Jackson, Gaynor Johnson, Elizabeth Kirkland Jones, Peter Kenez, William Keylor, Doug Kriner, David Levering Lewis, Michael Loewe, Igor Lukes, Judith Odette Mayers, Marilyn Anne Mayers, Peter Kirkland Mayers, Peter Michael Mayers, Carol McHale, Charles Neu, Cathal Nolan, Eric Nye, Arnold Offner, Elzelien van de Paverd, Larry Plitch, Andrew Preston, Christopher Ricks, J. Simon Rofe, Gina Sapiro, James Schmidt, Karol Soltan, the late Ruth Ann Stewart, John A. Thompson, Vladimir Vulovic, Jenny White, David Widdicombe, Peter Widdicombe, Andrew Williams, Graham Wilson, Gregory Winger.

Boston University's College of Arts and Sciences granted sabbatical time and research funds to me. Without that generosity the writing of this book would have been impossible. I also appreciate the attentive audiences that allowed me to make presentations of my work as it developed and obliged me to improve it: the Foreign Policy Seminar at University of Connecticut, the School of International Relations at St Andrews University, the Society for Historians of American Foreign Relations, and the Transatlantic Studies Association.

Portions of Chapter 1 appeared as an article in October 2016 in *The International History Review*: "Destruction Repaired and Destruction Anticipated: United Nations Relief and Rehabilitation Administration (UNRRA), the Atomic Bomb, and U.S. Policy 1944–1946." Much of Chapter 3 appeared as an article in September 2015 in *Diplomacy and Statecraft*: "Humanity in 1948: The Genocide Convention and the Universal Declaration of Human Rights."

It has been a pleasure from start to finish to work with the editorial staff at Routledge. I was delighted by the encouragement and immense efficiency that Robert Langham afforded me at every step.

In 2013 I was Visiting Fellow (later a Life Member) at Clare Hall, Cambridge University. Then I enjoyed, as since, good comrades and fellowship, including that provided by the hovering spirit of Telford Taylor. This American jurist, who won fame at the Nuremberg tribunals, spoke these words to an assembly on the fortieth anniversary of the end of World War II. Although not directly addressed to me, I have taken Taylor's words to heart. They constitute a premise of this book:

> In England, near Cambridge, there is a large American air force cemetery, where lie many of those that we honor today, most of whom had flown into battle from airfields in East Anglia. I have had frequent occasion to go to Cambridge, and I have never been there without visiting that cemetery. It is, of course, a place of death. But, set as it is in the lovely green English countryside, the luxuriant lawns and foliage of the cemetery breathe life. It is a quiet place, conducive to meditation, and if the dead could speak, I think they would tell the visitor to look to the future.[1]

The book is dedicated to two people who in their early youth died in appalling circumstances: Anne Frank and Emmett Till. The significance of their brief lives, like those of servicemen commemorated at the Cambridge cemetery, still inspires.

DM
Newton, Massachusetts
30 July 2017

NOTE

1 Victory in Europe 40 Years Ago, 28 April 1985, Series 10, Folder 177, Box 7, Telford Taylor Papers.

CHRONOLOGY, 1945–1956

1945

20 January: Franklin D. Roosevelt (FDR) was inaugurated for the fourth time as president.

27 January: Soviet soldiers entered Auschwitz and liberated 7,000 survivors.

3 February: The United States launched a massive air assault on Berlin. Nearly 1,000 bombers were deployed.

4–11 February: FDR, Winston Churchill, and Joseph Stalin met at Yalta. Among other matters, they agreed that a conference should be held in San Francisco to organize an international institution: the United Nations.

13–15 February: British and U.S. air forces launched raids on Dresden.

19 February–26 March: The battle of Iwo Jima island was fought between U.S. and Japanese forces.

9–10 March: Tokyo subjected to U.S. bombing and huge firestorm.

22 March: The Arab League, devoted to fostering Arab unity, was established in Cairo and originally consisted of Egypt, Iraq, Saudi Arabia, Transjordan (later Jordan), Yemen, Syria, and Lebanon.

1 April–22 June: The battle of Okinawa island was fought between U.S. and Japanese forces.

12 April: FDR died in Warm Springs, Georgia. Vice President Harry Truman then took the oath of presidential office.

25 April: Conferees, representing fifty-one countries, met in San Francisco to found the United Nations. The Charter was signed on 26 June.

2 May: The Soviet army completed its capture of Berlin.

7 May: Germany surrendered in Rheims (France) to the Allies and war in Europe ended.

8 May: Nationalist riots against French rule erupted in Algerian cities. The Algerian war of independence did not explode full-scale until 1954. Algeria gained independence in 1962.

16 July: Atomic bomb detonated (Operation Trinity) at Alamogordo, New Mexico.

17 July–2 August: Truman, Stalin, and Churchill (then replaced by Clement Attlee after Labour's electoral victory) met at Potsdam. On 26 July the conferees reiterated Allied demands that Japan surrender unconditionally.

6 August: The United States warplane *Enola Gay* dropped an atomic bomb on Hiroshima.

8 August: The USSR declared war upon Japan and sent soldiers to invade Japanese-ruled Manchuria and occupy Korea.

9 August: A United States warplane dropped an atomic bomb on Nagasaki.

11 August: Soviet–U.S. agreement divided Korea at the 38th Parallel into two zones of military occupation.

14 August: Pacific/Far Eastern war ended with surrender announcement by Emperor Hirohito.

17–18 August: Nationalists in Indonesia declared their country free of Dutch rule. Nationalists, led by Ho Chi Minh, declared Vietnam independent of French rule.

22 August: World Zionist Congress in London demanded that the United Kingdom allow 100,000 European Jews to enter Palestine.

2 September: Formal surrender of Japan aboard the USS *Missouri* in Tokyo Bay.

2 September: Ho Chi Minh proclaimed the Democratic Republic of Vietnam.

8 September: U.S. armed forces arrived in southern Korea and began occupation duties.

20 November: The International Military Tribunal (Nuremberg) commenced and ran for the better part of a year. Administered exclusively by the United States, the subsequent Nuremberg Military Tribunals went from November 1946 to April 1949. The International Military Tribunal Far East (Tokyo) met from May 1946 to November 1948.

21 December: Moscow Agreement devised plans to reunify Korea, but was not implemented.

27 December: Representatives of twenty-four nations met in Washington to establish the International Bank for Reconstruction and Development (World Bank) in fulfillment of plans advanced by the 1944 Bretton Woods conference.

1946

10 January: The UN General Assembly held its first meeting (London). Secretary of State James Byrnes led the U.S. delegation, which included Eleanor Roosevelt.

24 January: The UN Atomic Energy Commission was established.

25–26 February: Race riots swept Columbia, Tennessee. More than one hundred African Americans were arrested, two of whom were killed in police custody.

5 March: With Truman in attendance, Churchill delivered "Iron Curtain" speech in Fulton, Missouri.

17 March: *A Report on the International Control of Atomic Energy* (Acheson–Lilienthal Report) was submitted to Secretary of State James Byrnes.

25 March: Moscow announced that Soviet soldiers in Iran would be withdrawn within six weeks, thereby resolving an East–West confrontation rooted in the August 1941 Anglo-Soviet partition of that country. According to provisions of agreement, confirmed at the 1943 Tehran conference, all Allied soldiers were to leave Iran after the defeat of Axis power. But the Soviets had lingered past the scheduled departure time and supported communists in the northern province of Azerbaijan.

29 April: An Anglo-U.S. committee of inquiry recommended against partition of Palestine and establishment instead of a single state with autonomous provinces for Jews and Arabs.

14 June: Bernard Baruch submitted a U.S. plan to the UN Atomic Energy Commission for international controls on atomic science and technology. The Soviets expressed disapproval; the Baruch proposal was not adopted.

1 and 24 July: The United States tested two atomic weapons (Operation Crossroads) at Bikini Atoll in the Marshall Islands.

4 July: The Philippines became an independent republic after forty-eight years of U.S. rule.

22 July: King David Hotel in Jerusalem was blown up by Zionist militants (Irgun); ninety people killed.

30 September: The International Military Tribunal (Nuremberg) pronounced verdicts on convicted Nazis criminals.

5 November: Elections placed the GOP in control of the U.S. Senate and House of Representatives.

23 November: French forces bombed Haiphong to suppress anti-colonial rebellion.

14 December: UN delegates unanimously voted for a resolution to prohibit production or use of atomic weapons.

19 December: Viet Minh attacked French forces in Tonkin—start of the first Indochina war.

1947

18 February: The British government declared its intention to leave Palestine and referred questions of its future to the United Nations.

20 February: The British government announced that it would transfer power and independence to India.

12 March: Truman proposed $400 million of aid to Greece and Turkey to resist the USSR and communism—the "Truman Doctrine." Congress subsequently passed the Greek-Turkish Aid Act that Truman signed on 22 May.

22 March: Truman issued Executive Order 9835 and established a loyalty program applicable to federal employees and applicants.

5 June: Secretary of State George Marshall at the Harvard commencement proposed idea for European economic recovery—the "Marshall Plan." Representatives of sixteen nations subsequently met (July–September) in Paris to devise a program in response to Marshall: the European Recovery Program, 1948–1952. More than $12 billion were eventually allocated to the countries of Western Europe.

15 August: British rule on the Indian subcontinent ended and it was partitioned amid communal violence into a Hindu-dominated India and a Muslim-dominated Pakistan.

17 September: The U.S. government referred the question of Korean independence to the United Nations.

9 October: Truman decided in favor of proposals for the Jewish and Arab division of Palestine.

18 October: The House Committee on Un-American Activities commenced investigation of alleged communist infiltration of Hollywood.

14 November: The UN General Assembly approved establishment of the UN Temporary Commission on Korea (UNTCOK) to supervise national elections leading to reunification and independence.

29 November: The UN General Assembly decided for the partition of Palestine into Jewish and Arab states, with Jerusalem to be internationalized: effective date set for 15 May 1948. Britain abstained from the voting. Arab delegations paraded out of the Assembly.

1948

1 January: In Geneva the representatives of twenty-three countries signed the General Agreement on Trade and Tariffs (GATT), aimed at reducing world trade barriers.

24 January: Soviet occupation authorities forbade UNTCOK from entering northern Korea and thus prevented national elections.

30 January: A Hindu extremist assassinated India's Mahatma Gandhi. Mohammed Ali Jinnah of Pakistan died later in the year, 11 September.

2 February: President Truman proposed a civil rights package to Congress that would outlaw lynching and establish a federal commission on civil rights.

25 February: Soviet-supported communists seized political control of Czechoslovakia.

19 March: Ambassador Warren Austin indicated that the USA no longer favored the partition of Palestine but instead preferred a UN trusteeship.

10 May: Elections held in southern Korea under UN supervision.

14–15 May: The British mandate in Palestine ended. The state of Israel was declared and quickly recognized by the USA and the USSR. Israel subsequently defeated invading Arab League armies and hundreds of thousands of Palestinian Arabs were displaced—through eviction or flight—from their homes.

June: Communist guerrilla warfare in Malaya began. It enjoyed some support from Malaya's ethnic Chinese community. Not until July 1960 did British and Commonwealth forces achieve victory.

5 June: Emperor Bao Dai was appointed by the French to head the state of Vietnam.

24 June: The USSR began its land blockade of Berlin, which was countered by an Anglo-U.S. airlift of food and fuel to the city's Western sectors.

26 July: Truman signed Executive Order 9981 to end discrimination in the U.S. armed forces and in federal employment.

3 August: Whittaker Chambers, a former communist, accused Alger Hiss of the Carnegie Endowment for International Peace (and of the State Department) of holding membership in a communist cell in the 1930s.

15 August: Republic of Korea (South Korea) was established with Syngman Rhee as president.

9 September: The Democratic People's Republic of Korea (North Korea) was established, with Kim Il Sung as president.

17 September: The UN Middle East mediator Count Folke Bernadotte was assassinated in Jerusalem by militant Zionists (Stern Gang) opposed to compromise between Jews and Arabs in Palestine. Ralph Bunche thereupon assumed the mediation role.

2 November: Truman and the Democratic party won a surprising victory in the presidential election against the GOP's Thomas Dewey. The prospects for Truman's success had been hurt by party fragmentation—the States' Rights Party (Dixiecrats), which supported Strom Thurmond, and the Progressives, who backed Henry Wallace.

9 December: The UN General Assembly approved the Convention on the Prevention and Punishment of the Crime of Genocide. It obtained force of international law in January 1951.

10 December: The UN General Assembly approved the Universal Declaration of Human Rights.

12 December: The UN recognized the Republic of Korea as the only legitimate government on the Korean peninsula.

23 December: Tojo Hideki, formerly a premier of wartime Japan, and other figures convicted as war criminals by the International Military Tribunal for the Far East were hanged in Tokyo. The U.S. Supreme Court had rejected their appeal.

31 December: Soviet occupation forces left North Korea.

1949

February–July: Armistice agreements were signed between Israel and Arab governments—Egypt, Transjordan, Lebanon, and Syria.

4 April: Twelve states pledged themselves to establishing the North Atlantic Treaty Organization (NATO), including the USA, the UK, France, Italy, the Netherlands, and Canada. The U.S. Senate approved the treaty on 21 July by a vote of eighty-two to thirteen. Turkey and Greece joined NATO in 1952. West Germany joined in 1955.

8 April: The USSR blocked the admission of South Korea to the United Nations.

12 May: The USSR ended its blockade of Berlin.

23 May: The Federal Republic of Germany (West Germany) was established.

29 June: American occupation forces left South Korea; 500 U.S. advisers remained.

5 August: The State Department released its *China White Paper* on the defeat of Jiang Jieshi (Chiang Kai-shek) and his government by Maoist revolutionaries.

29 August: The USSR successfully detonated an atomic bomb, a fact publicly confirmed by Truman on 23 September.

1 October: Mao Zedong in Beijing proclaimed the People's Republic of China. The USSR and the UK were among the countries that recognized the new regime. The United States refrained from doing so until 1979.

24 October: The UN's headquarters were dedicated in New York City.

27 December: Indonesia was proclaimed independent of the Netherlands. Achmed Sukarno became the republic's first president.

1950

12 January: Secretary of State Dean Acheson in a National Press Club speech did not include South Korea in America's East Asian defense perimeter.

31 January: Announcement made by Truman that he had authorized the U.S. Atomic Energy Commission to develop a hydrogen bomb.

7 February: Senator Joseph McCarthy declared in Wheeling, West Virginia, that he possessed a long list of communists employed by the State Department. He soon afterward made similar charges in other venues.

14 February: The Sino-Soviet treaty of friendship and alliance was signed in Moscow.

14 April: National Security Council paper 68 recommended significant increases to U.S. defense spending.

5 June: Truman signed the International Development Act ("Point Four" of his 1949 inaugural address).

25 June: The North Korean army invaded South Korea. The UN Security Council called for a ceasefire and withdrawal of North Korean forces to above the 38th Parallel. The North Korean army numbered roughly 135,000 soldiers versus a South Korean one of 98,000.

27 June: The UN Security Council—the Soviet representative being absent—called upon member states to assist South Korea. President Truman provided for U.S. air and naval support of South Korea.

28 June: North Korean soldiers captured Seoul.

30 June: Truman committed to the sending of U.S. ground forces to aid South Korea.

7 July: The UN Security Council established a unified UN Command and the next day Truman appointed General Douglas MacArthur to head it.

1 August: The USSR ended its boycott (begun in January) of the UN Security Council and Ambassador Jacob Malik returned to that body to assume its presidency.

4 August: UN forces in Korea withdrew to the so-called Pusan Perimeter.

15 September: United Nations forces landed at Inchon and the next day the U.S. Eighth Army began its offensive northward of Pusan; a retreat of North Korean armies ensued.

29 September: UN forces completed capture of Seoul and the next day South Korea's Third Army Division crossed the 38th Parallel.

7 October: The UN General Assembly authorized military operations to unite Korea and two days later MacArthur demanded that North Korea surrender. Chinese forces invaded Tibet.

19 October: Chinese People's Volunteers Army crossed the Yalu river into North Korea. South Korean forces occupied Pyongyang.

27 October: Chinese forces launched a Korean offensive but disengaged on 6 November. South Korean and UN forces reached the Yalu river/Manchuria border on 20 November.

26 November: Chinese forces launched another Korean offensive that caused overextended UN armies to retreat.

15 December: UN forces in Korea retreated to south of the 38th Parallel and the next day Truman declared a state of emergency.

31 December: Chinese forces in Korea launched an offensive south of the 38th Parallel.

1951

4 January: Chinese forces in Korea captured Seoul.

1 February: The UN General Assembly condemned China for aggression in Korea.

14 March: As a result of a limited counteroffensive, UN forces in Korea recaptured Seoul.

11 April: Truman relieved MacArthur as UN commander in Korea and replaced him with General Matthew Ridgway. MacArthur had wanted to expand Korean theater operations to include bombing actions against China.

5 July: The International Court of Justice at The Hague ruled in favor of the UK and against Iran in their dispute over Iran's nationalization of oil production and companies. Iran chose not to recognize the court's competence. British–Iranian relations were cut in October 1952.

10 July: First session of Korean truce talks began at Kaesong but was suspended on 23 August; talks resumed on 25 October at Panmunjom.

8 September: The Japanese peace treaty was signed by forty-nine countries in San Francisco. The USA and Japan entered into a mutual security pact.

25 October: Conservative party's Winston Churchill replaced Clement Attlee as UK prime minister following Labour's electoral defeat.

24 December: Formerly an Italian colony, Libya—under UN sponsorship —obtained independence.

1952

26 February: Churchill announced that the UK had developed an atomic bomb capacity. The first British atomic bomb was tested in October.

28 March: Pro-independence riots rocked Tunisia, where anti-French feeling festered.

8 April: To avert a national steel strike, Truman authorized federal seizure of steel mills in Youngstown, Ohio. This move was ruled on 2 June by the Supreme Court as unconstitutional.

8 October: Korean War truce talks suspended but resumed on 26 April 1953.

21 October: The UK government declared a state of emergency in Kenya in response to the Mau Mau campaign against colonial rule. The Mau Mau revolt ended in defeat in 1960. Kenya became an independent country in December 1963.

4 November: GOP's Dwight Eisenhower defeated the Democrats' Adlai Stevenson in the presidential election and was inaugurated on 20 January 1953.

5 December: President-elect Eisenhower visited Korea and hoped to reignite stalled truce talks.

1953

5 March: Joseph Stalin died in Moscow, precipitating a "thaw" in both Soviet cultural-political life and relations with the West.

7 April: Dag Hammarskjold of Sweden was elected to a five-year term by the General Assembly to head the United Nations. His predecessor in that office, Trygve Lie of Norway, had earlier resigned under Soviet pressure.

17 June: Anti-communist demonstrations and riots by workers erupted in East Berlin. Soviet troops were eventually used to suppress the disturbances, which grew to involve at least 200,000 people.

19 June: Convicted of treason, Julius and Ethel Rosenberg were executed in Sing Sing prison in Ossining, New York.

27 July: Korean War armistice signed at Panmunjom.

13–22 August: Iranian Prime Minster Mohammad Mossadegh was overthrown in a CIA-supported coup. Mohammad-Reza Shah Pahlavi was restored to power.

8 December: Eisenhower at the United Nations discussed his "Atoms for Peace" program.

1954

12 January: In New York City, Dulles publicly unveiled his policy of "massive retaliation," whereby the USA would defend its vital interests and strike instantly at a place of its choosing and preferred means.

26 January: The defense treaty between South Korea and USA was ratified by the Senate.

12 April: The Atomic Energy Commission reported that the security clearance of J. Robert Oppenheimer, formerly of the Manhattan Project, had been revoked. He had recently opposed the decision to develop the hydrogen bomb.

22 April: The Senate began the "McCarthy–Army" hearings.

26 April–21 July: Delegates from the USSR, the USA, the UK, France, the People's Republic of China, and other states met in Geneva to resolve Korean and Indochina matters. Agreement was reached that marked the end of French rule in Indochina; U.S. involvement effectively intensified via varieties of financial, political, and military aid.

7 May: The French fortress at Dien Bien Phu, under Viet Minh assault since mid-March, surrendered. Twelve thousand survivors were marched to prison camps. Emperor Bao Dai, meanwhile, named Ngo Dinh Diem premier of South Vietnam.

17 May: The Supreme Court in *Brown v. Board of Education of Topeka* ruled unanimously that racial segregation in public schools was unconstitutional.

18 June: CIA supported operations by anti-regime insurgents against the government of Guatemala. That government, led by Jacobo Arbenz Guzman, was overthrown on 29 June.

24 August: The communist party in the USA was outlawed and membership in it declared a crime.

8 September: The Southeast Asian Treaty Organization (SEATO) was established by the USA, the UK, Australia, New Zealand, Pakistan, the Philippines, and Thailand.

2 December: The Senate censured Joseph McCarthy for having insulted his colleagues and bringing false charges against Army officials.

1955

18–24 April: Delegates from twenty-nine African and Asian states met at Bandung, Indonesia. The conferees endorsed independence for colonies, self-determination, and universal membership in the United Nations, including the People's Republic of China. India's Prime Minister Nehru criticized NATO as an instrument of imperialism.

14 May: The Warsaw Pact was established to counter NATO and West Germany's "remilitarization." The USSR was joined in the pact by Albania, Bulgaria, Czechoslovakia, East Germany, Hungary, Poland, and Romania.

6 July: Ngo Dinh Diem repudiated plans, devised by conferees at the May 1954 Geneva conference, to hold nationwide elections in Vietnam.

18 July: The first post-World War II summit conference began in Geneva. Eisenhower attended for the USA, Prime Minister Anthony Eden for the UK, Premier Edgar Faure for France, and Premier N.A. Bulganin and First Secretary of the Communist party Nikita Khrushchev for the USSR. A "spirit of Geneva" briefly thrived.

28 August: Emmett Till, a fourteen-year-old African American from Chicago, was kidnapped while visiting relatives in Money, Mississippi. A few days later his body was retrieved from the Tallahatchie river. He was alleged to have spoken disrespectfully to a white woman.

24 October: Ngo Dinh Diem was elected president of the Republic of (South) Vietnam and Emperor Bao Dai was dethroned. Diem remained in office until assassination/coup of 2 November 1963.

1 December: Rosa Parks in Montgomery, Alabama refused to surrender her bus seat to a white man. Her subsequent arrest sparked a bus boycott by African Americans, led by twenty-seven-year-old Reverend Martin Luther King.

17 December: The USA offered a loan of $56 million to Egypt in support of building the Aswan High Dam. Dulles later revoked the offer as Soviet–Egypt connections became closer.

1956

6 February: Mob violence at the University of Alabama sparked by the (first) admission of a black student, Autherine Lucy. The university administration later expelled her for allegedly slandering the school.

14–25 February: Aspects of Stalin and the "cult of personality" were criticized at the 20th Congress of the Communist Party of the USSR, most memorably by Nikita Khrushchev in his "secret speech."

28 June: Polish factory workers in Poznan demonstrated against Communist rule. Violence between workers and Polish security forces resulted in the death or wounding of hundreds of civilians. In October, the Polish Communist party selected Wladyslaw Gomulka, a reform-minded figure, to lead the country. He improved Poland's relations with the USSR.

26 July: Gamal Abdel Nasser of Egypt nationalized the Suez Canal and closed it to Israeli shipping.

23 October–4 November: An anti-Soviet revolt swept Hungary, subsequently crushed by the Red Army. At the height of this rebellion, the government in Budapest, led by the communist reformer Imre Nagy, declared neutrality in the Cold War and sought to remove Hungary from the Warsaw Pact.

29 October–7 November: French, British, and Israeli forces attacked Egypt. The U.S. and Soviet governments, in a moment of rare unity, condemned the attack as unwarranted aggression. American pressure caused Anglo-French withdrawal from positions obtained during combat along the Suez Canal. Not until March 1957 was it reopened to maritime use.

6 November: Dwight Eisenhower won reelection to the White House, defeating the Democratic challenger, Adlai Stevenson, in a landslide. The Democrats won both House of Representatives and the Senate, however.

21 December: The bus boycott in Montgomery ended, the Supreme Court having ruled in November that racial segregation on public transport violated the Constitution.

INTRODUCTION

Despite a countercurrent, the main tide of international relations scholarship on the first years after World War II sweeps toward Cold War accounts. These have emphasized the United States and the USSR in a context of geopolitical rivalry with concomitant attention upon the bristling security state. Historians have also extensively analyzed the creation of an economic order (Bretton Woods), largely designed by Americans, the ultimate victors of World War II, and tailored to their interests but resisted by peoples residing outside of North America, Western Europe, and Japan. This scholarship—centered on the Cold War as vortex, and a reconfigured world economy—is rife with contending schools of interpretation and, bolstered by troves of declassified archival documents, will support investigations and writing into the future.[1]

My intention here is to examine a past that ran concurrent with the Cold War and interacted with it but which can also be read as separable: Washington in the first years after World War II, in response to that conflagration, sought to redesign international society. That society was then, and remains, an admittedly amorphous thing. Yet it has always had a tangible aspect, drawing self-regarding states into occasional cooperation, mediated by treaties, laws, norms, diplomatic customs, and transnational institutions. None of these practices and agencies, thrust in a setting without universally acknowledged political authority and guidelines, has checked every lurking danger in which all contend against all—Hobbesian state of nature writ large.[2] But, as some theorists ("English School") have shown, a version of "anarchical society"—rules-based, institutionally vibrant, economically entwined, diplomatically mature—does exist and, analytically speaking, complicates the picture of international politics as long imagined. This more nuanced portrayal corrects literalist depictions of post-1945 reality as a perpetual starkness and anarchy.[3]

The reformist ambition, backed by U.S. economic-military heft, stemmed from the idea that Americans and their allies—for their collective sake—had to improve upon inherited practice, its recent failure evident in war-battered Europe and Asia. This outlook during the war colored Franklin Roosevelt's January 1941 Four Freedoms, the August 1941 Churchill–FDR issuance of the Atlantic Charter, and the June 1945 founding of the United Nations.[4] Scraped of their ebullient democratic language, these frameworks were intended to reduce the intensity of international violence by adjudicating conflicts. Ridiculed by skeptics, at the time and later, for amounting to empty piety and redolent of hypocrisy, or dismissed as merely cloaking the deep structures of power, these proclamations and actions nonetheless helped shape the postwar moment. They represented a version of hopefulness against the infamies that stretched from 1937 Nanjing to the 1945 atomic bombings of Hiroshima and Nagasaki.[5]

In effect, the immediate years after World War II not only coincided with Moscow–Washington competition, plus a U.S.-dominated economic order, both of which long obtained. Other realities also appeared. They are crucial to revisit and are integral to any understanding of contemporary history. Moreover, whereas the Cold War finally ended and U.S. economic domination slackened, the postwar sensibility supportive of a global society lingers, alongside those conditions that have always vexed international life: love of power, hunger for glory, promiscuous violence.

★ ★ ★

This study rests upon a pair of intertwining themes. One, most pressed in the early chapters, concerns the reconstitution agenda set by the Allied coalition of World War II—manifested in the convening of military tribunals at Nuremberg and Tokyo, ratifications of the Genocide Convention and the Universal Declaration of Human Rights, and founding of the United Nations. None of these enterprises, though seemingly new in their time, was wholly novel or unprecedented. Individually, and as an interlocking set of standards and institutions, they built upon antecedents. What did set them apart from previous iterations and attempts to stabilize international life was that these bore an ineradicable American imprimatur—or were, at minimum, highly conditioned by U.S. behaviors, both good and ill.

The second theme concerns those material urgencies that confronted global society following Axis defeat. These pivoted on the repair of wartime damage, the spread of atomic weaponry, and the redistribution of power among the world's principal empires.

★ ★ ★

This book comprises six chapters—the last a coda—that document the recent history of international society and its anti-anarchy struggle. Each chapter, except the last, is structured along these lines. First, there is a statement of the problem. A narrative then follows. The last section of each chapter concentrates on implications plus the continuities running from the post-World War II era to the early twenty-first century. The pervading idea is that the liberal political-diplomatic world—now tattered and under severe stress in the Donald Trump/Brexit/ISIS era—crystalized in 1945–1956.

The first chapter delves into that problem which preoccupied millions of people in the war's aftermath: destruction. It had been a lived experience for countless Europeans and Asians. Naturally, they sought to restore damaged cities, plundered countryside, and weakened economies. Many Americans were comparably stimulated, for reasons ranging from humanitarian sympathy to calculations of self-interest. These mixed motives were evidenced in the part assumed by Americans in the United Nations Relief and Rehabilitation Administration (UNRRA), an experimental organization that did most of its work in 1945–1946.

While UNRRA attended to emergency needs, people also brooded about a future in which even greater harms might occur. Astonished by the fate of Hiroshima and Nagasaki, George Orwell predicted in October 1945 that "likely we all are to be blown to pieces by [the atomic bomb] within the next five years."[6] Against this prospect, Washington officialdom contemplated the potential benefits of internationalizing atomic science and technology. The 1946 Acheson–Lilienthal proposal was intended to avert a nuclear weapons race and place atomic knowledge in UN safekeeping. After that exercise failed, Americans devised elaborate strategies that if implemented would have produced unprecedented ruin, a dark game soon joined by the Soviets (1949) and British (1952).

My examination of UNRRA and the Acheson–Lilienthal project brings into conversation their drafting histories, politics, and diplomacy. Placing them in the same analytical framework, something not hitherto done in the literature, this chapter traces the saga of UNRRA and Acheson–Lilienthal and their tandem Cold War fates. As peoples and governments pick their way through the humanitarian conundrums and nuclear hazards of the twenty-first century, it is useful to reflect upon the experiences and lessons of these two long-ago initiatives.

Chapter 2 is centered on the postwar trials of Axis leaders, taking as its point of reference the International Military Tribunal (IMT) at Nuremberg, which ran simultaneously with the bulk of UNRRA's operations and the Acheson–Lilienthal effort. The IMT met from 20 November 1945 to 1 October 1946 at the Justizpalast in a broken city under U.S. Army occupation. The Nuremberg mission, and its largely forgotten contemporaneous counterpart in Tokyo, aspired—at least partly—to resuscitate meaningful standards of civilized conduct. American leaders, not least President Harry Truman, pushed this IMT idea. They and their chief legal representative at Nuremberg, Robert Houghwout Jackson, associate justice of the Supreme Court, insisted that existing positive law upheld the IMT assize. Insofar as positive law had deficiencies in this regard, so the argument went, the IMT was adequately anchored in natural law tradition and set moral-legal precedent that would apply in coming years to all countries, including the United States. In effect, at the time of commencement, Nuremberg had an explicit dual purpose: to reconfirm and advance the cause of venerable codes and to provide in future years an orientation for the conduct of nations. These qualities together amounted to a Nuremberg axiom. It has constituted one measure to assess post-1945 U.S. actions, both by the standard that Americans once set for themselves and from the perspective of a general ethic.

Undeniably, the U.S. performance at Nuremberg—that too of the British, French, and Soviets—involved procedural flaws and instances of unscrupulousness. The scale of this waywardness was serious, enough so that diverse commentators at the time condemned the IMT, calling it too flimsy a scaffold on which to erect anything substantial. The Tokyo inquest was similarly disparaged. Yet, even as Nuremberg and Tokyo failed to satisfy highest standards, plausible justice was propounded. This allowed Telford Taylor, originally a member of Jackson's prosecutorial staff, to argue in 1949 on behalf of this position that sits at the intersection of hoary realism and brighter promise:

> International morality is based, and can develop, only on a hard foundation of national self-interest. But that means an *enlightened* self-interest, for the relations between nations are growing . . . intricate and intimate even when they are at odds with one another, and, at the same time, man's capacity for race suicide has increased beyond all prior imaginings [which necessitates] a general campaign for the development and application of international law to enforce minimum standards of enlightened self-interest by punishing transgressors.[7]

In the years since Nuremberg, dissenters have gratefully repaired to it. Taylor, for one, referred to Nuremberg in the early 1970s, when he invoked its "anti-aggression spirit" to indict Washington's Vietnam War and tried by other actions (a 1972 visit to Hanoi) to heighten public awareness of the carnage then wrought by Americans in Indochina.[8] In subsequent years, and with like vigor, critics have excoriated "enhanced interrogation techniques" employed in the "war on terror," invoking the IMT spirit and citing Nuremberg's explicit prohibitions on torture.[9]

The book's third chapter concentrates on two events of late 1948. On 9 December, the UN General Assembly adopted the Convention on the Prevention and Punishment of the Crime of Genocide, a cause to which the American-based Jewish-Polish refugee, Raphael Lemkin, devoted himself. Next, on 10 December, the General Assembly ratified the Universal Declaration of Human Rights (UDHR), everlastingly tied to Eleanor Roosevelt. The Genocide Convention and the UDHR interlaced to uphold an alternative version of humanity to the atavism of 1937–1945. This third chapter, at heart, amounts to a conspectus of the Genocide Convention and the UDHR. In combination, they amounted to progress in international thought, the significance of which scholasticism and partisan wrangling over the genealogy of rights discourse and norms-making of the late 1940s have obscured, to say nothing of the slurs visited upon these two documents by guardians of public safety during the Cold War.

Like UNRRA, Acheson–Lilienthal, and the international military tribunals, the Convention and UDHR inspired sundry skeptics. Across the political spectrum from right to left, along cultural-philosophical divides, and from political leaders to pundits, the two initiatives elicited jeers, shrugs, and bafflement. After all, observed a host of commentators in 1948, the East–West split of Europe was hardening: Greek civil war, a communist coup in Prague, Soviet blockade of Berlin. While rumors of impending war circulated, the Lemkin–Roosevelt measures seemed distracting, expressions of shallow optimism and unhelpful in view of ongoing emergencies. Outside Europe, meanwhile, other regions were also roiling—sectarian mayhem in partitioned India–Pakistan, war in Palestine–Israel, revolution in China—against which the UN endorsement of Lemkin–Roosevelt's high-mindedness appeared likewise superfluous. Not given to hyperbole, the unflappable secretary of state, George Marshall, compared the world situation in 1948 to a keg of dynamite.[10]

In later decades, self-styled realists, plus less stern persons, could cite abundant evidence that challenged the purported wisdom and universalism of Lemkin–Roosevelt: the Soviet–U.S. nuclear arms race, mass slaughters in Southeast Asia and Africa, ethnic cleansings in former Yugoslavia, vaulting inequality between people living in the impoverished Global South versus residents of the affluent North. Still, against such objection, other voices have argued that affirmative ideas heaved with implications for improved conduct, a view with which Lemkin and Roosevelt concurred, even as they regarded their 1948 achievements as provisional stations leading to a better world: the sovereign state, a behemoth possessed of boundless pretension, must eventually accommodate cosmopolitan concepts of humanity.

Chapter 4 is focused on the United Nations during its fledgling years, with attention placed on two of that organization's critical undertakings: stanching of the 1948 Israeli–Arab violence and the safeguarding of South Korea in 1950–1953. From the realist standpoint, starry-eyed internationalists, American and other, have placed unwarranted confidence in the United Nations. In this case, alas, understandable desires for peace and harmony have subverted judgment about prudent policy and encouraged faith in an institution of careless design. Already in 1946, when the UN still enjoyed wide Western support, Winston Churchill worried that the UN must produce "a frothing of words" but little authentic work—a "cockpit in a Tower of Babel."[11]

Remarkably, though, and despite an uneven record and stumbling start, the UN did not break apart or become irrelevant. It coped. While Arab–Israeli enmity smoldered and the Korean War raged, Ralph Bunche, international civil servant par excellence, asserted coolly that the UN deserved consideration: "the greatest peace organization ever dedicated to the salvation of mankind's future on earth."[12]

The book's fifth chapter amounts to a change of gears and is perforce the most schematic. Centered on the dispersal of postwar power, as manifested in the chief empires, this chapter synopsizes transformative events of 1953–1956. During that time, the British and French empires lurched to their demise, a consummation devoutly wished by Asian and African attendees at the fabled 1955 Bandung Conference. A key moment, symbolically and substantively in the decline of Anglo-French presumption, occurred in the 1956 Suez Canal war. The Soviet empire, meantime, especially its East European components, was uncertain, supplying more evidence, were any needed, of Edward Gibbon's observation: "There is nothing more contrary to nature than the attempt to hold in obedience distant provinces."[13] Only by applications of brute force did Moscow check ambitions for independence among East Germans in 1953 and Hungarians in 1956.

In contrast to the fading British and French imperia or the one to which Stalin's successors desperately clung, the American empire exuded self-assurance, with tendrils attached to every hemisphere, even while eschewing the usual categories of directly ruled territory and colonies. Regime change induced by CIA operatives in 1953 Iran and 1954 Guatemala were only two obvious signals of U.S. preeminence, a fact driven home to the Anglo-French governments in 1956, when Washington's ire brought about the collapse of their Suez expedition.

Democratic in their ethos, republican in their institutions, and willfully unaware of their own imperial reflexes—an unacknowledged impulse to dominate, as Reinhold Niebuhr explained in 1952 warning against "moral mediocrity"—Americans in the mid-twentieth century stood astride the world.[14] By the end of the century, their liberal imperium was the sole remaining empire, an unprecedented accumulation of economic-military-political might. It survives intact today and will endure for indeterminate years to come, upholding the codification, spread, and enforcement of Washington-sculpted norms while deploying massive financial investments/trade, proconsuls, and air, army, and naval bases around the world.[15]

Presumably, though, America will not escape the fate that every colossus has met. These words uttered in 2003 by Tony Blair, successor to British prime ministers whose realm once girdled the globe, are apt: "All predominant power seems for a time invincible, but in fact, it is transient."[16]

Such considerations and starkness do not constitute the entire tale, however. This point is detailed in the book's concluding pages, which shift the locus of argumentation from the international setting to the internal U.S. scene, making explicit the book's underlying drive: to show the plurality of post-1945 U.S. history, in which domestic politics and questions were linked to wider global ones on human rights, race, and democracy. Enabled by the empire's raw immensity, the mark left by Washington preferences upon global society in the mid-twentieth century has radiated discernably across decades since, even touching upon the uncertain present. The affirmative core of that legacy formed a hedge along the demarcation between passing decency and relapse. Only the unfathomable future will disclose whether this arrangement, or what remains of it, will long survive. Perhaps, it will finally succumb to right-wing populism, embodied not only in Donald Trump and Brexit but also by these avatars: Geert Wilders of the Netherlands, France's Marine Le Pen, the Hungarian border fence, Greece's Golden Dawn, and Alternative for Germany. Were a decisive turn taken toward militant chauvinisms, the liberal order conceived just after World War II will appear to future generations as a thing of relative wholesomeness—implying that a version of better past practices and agencies should then be reinstituted.[17]

★ ★ ★

1

DESTRUCTION

Half of the children are totally blind. Others have lost one or more limbs.
Several of them have terribly lacerated faces. Most of the injuries were
sustained from land mines. The children have not yet accustomed
themselves to their handicaps. The little blind tots groped around until
they found someone to cling to, and then they held my hand in a
puzzled, frightened way.[1]

Herbert Lehman, July 1945 visit to children
sheltered in Rome's Quirinal Palace

★ ★ ★

The urgent problem posed by the cessation of Allied–Axis hostilities
centered on destruction. It encompassed psychic no less than physical
dimension, a result of that hallucinogenic fury rained—in engineering-
mathematical deliberation—upon Europe and Asia. None of the devastation suggested prompt recovery. The totality of violence, folly, and cruelty
surpassed calculation, reconfirming humanity's moral shortcomings, cumulatively a condition to manage but not a puzzle to resolve.

Precise casualty figures do not exist. Estimates of the war dead hover
around sixty million, the majority (two-thirds) civilian.[2] Many more people
were left maimed, others depleted by grief. By the end of 1945, refugees,
deportees, POWs, slave laborers, and internally displaced or otherwise

uprooted people in Asia and Europe numbered in the tens of millions.[3] Homelessness, diseases, and hunger gripped regions from the Netherlands to Ukraine to Bengal to China and beyond. Marauding armies, air forces, and blockading navies had inflicted damage to cities, industrial sites, transportation infrastructure, and agricultural production that dwarfed previous experience. This destruction, combined with great sums spent by the belligerent nations, left economies throughout the war zones in shambles. Whether in rural districts or urban centers—London, Rotterdam, Hamburg, Dresden, Warsaw, Leningrad, Stalingrad, Belgrade, Nanjing, Tokyo, Yokohama, Hiroshima, Nagasaki, Manila—desolation had swept victors and vanquished, righteous and guilty alike.

Only in time to come will Europeans discover, despite their material recovery, whether they can revive the spiritual dynamism and cultural genius that slipped in 1914, then was expunged, seemingly irrevocably, twenty-five years on. Eva Fahidi, a Jewish Hungarian memoirist and survivor of Nazi concentration camps, explained in 2015: "Time does not help. It only deepens the feeling that something is missing."[4] Neither music nor literature nor philosophy consoled her.

The Polish poet Czeslaw Milosz expressed comparable disconsolateness in his 1985 meditation on the difficulty of writing an analytically scrupulous history of the twentieth century:

> I still think too much about the mothers
> And ask what is man born of woman.
> He curls himself up and protects his head
> While he is kicked by heavy boots; on fire and running,
> He burns with bright flame; a bulldozer sweeps him into a clay pit.
> Her child. Embracing a teddy bear. Conceived in ecstasy.
> I haven't learned yet to speak as I should, calmly.[5]

Before members were arrested, the Munich-based White Rose student circle (1942–1943) protested the Third Reich's murder of European Jewry and delivered this alarm on behalf of Germans of conscience:

> Who among us has any conception of the dimensions of shame that will befall us and our children when one day the veil has fallen from our eyes and the most horrible of crimes—crimes that infinitely outdistance every human measure—reach the light of day?[6]

The burden of shame, alas, has lain heavy upon Germans born since 1945 or others equally innocent of Third Reich atrocities. To Sabina de Werth Neu (b. 1941 in Berlin), survivor of Anglo-U.S. bombings and rape by Red Army soldiers, the most enduring dilemma was rooted in national identity. Like many of her generation, she felt herself "a reluctant German." If not directly, she allowed in 2011, "we were the children of monsters" by association.[7]

Brutality in Asia, from 1937 Nanjing to 1945 Nagasaki, also encased perpetrators and blameless in time outside of normal time. Compliance with humanitarian tenets plunged, in the maltreatment of Allied prisoners by their Japanese captors, the massacring of Chinese civilians, and the ravishing of tens of thousands of "comfort women."

Formerly a student at a Christian-sponsored school for girls, Hata Tomoko of Hiroshima discerned "an instance of the utmost human insolence" in the atomic killing of non-combatants on 6 August 1945. Of the purported justification, reliant upon utilitarian arithmetic, that countless Japanese and Allied lives were thereby saved, she protested: "Nobody except God is allowed to do such a thing, using an uncertain calculation about the future as a basis for committing an irreparable crime in the present."[8]

That the suffering of innocents transcended geography and rival blocs also struck onetime Auschwitz inmate Primo Levi, when in 1978 he ruminated upon Anne Frank, who died at Bergen–Belsen, and an unknown Japanese girl: they belonged to the same sorrowful sorority. Before them, and the other untold dead, the Cold War wielders of modern weapons might pause.

> Nothing is left of . . .
> The Dutch girl imprisoned by four walls
> Who wrote of her youth without tomorrows.
> Her silent ash was scattered by the wind,
> Her brief life shut into a crumpled notebook.
> Nothing remains of the Hiroshima schoolgirl,
> A shadow printed on a wall by the light of a thousand suns,
> Victim sacrificed on the altar of fear.
> Powerful of the earth, masters of new poisons,
> Sad secret guardians of final thunder,
> The torments heaven sends us are enough.
> Before your finger presses down, stop and consider.[9]

Despite the annihilations or the threat of resumption, restoration was launched in 1944–1946 in several former war zones. To this cause, the United Nations Relief and Rehabilitation Administration (UNRRA) made early contribution. Under UNRRA's first director general, Herbert Lehman, aid reached millions of Asians and Europeans. Simultaneous with this attempt to repair damages, an effort was made to prevent future cataclysm of potentially larger scale, conveyed in the Acheson–Lilienthal idea of placing atomic science and technology under United Nations aegis. Both UNRRA and the proposed internationalization of atomic science supposed that a disordered world might yet be righted and cross over to safety.

UNRRA

Achievements

Varied initiatives were taken during World War II to ease the plight of peoples touched by violence. Hundreds of faith-based and secular groups were financed and staffed in Allied countries, prominently in Great Britain, Canada, and the United States. Unitarians, Quakers, Jews, Catholics, and mainline Protestants, sometimes joined to ethnic fraternal organizations, numbered in the rescue formations. These and other nongovernmental philanthropies struggled to supply sufferers with food, clothing, medicines, and other balm.[10] This last included, as provided by the New York-based Emergency Rescue Committee, safe haven for intellectuals and artists hunted by Nazi pursuers.

The U.S. government, at the behest of Treasury secretary Henry Morgenthau, established the War Refugee Board (WRB) in January 1944. Albeit little and late compared to the need, the WRB did manage to save 200,000 imperiled Jews and an additional 20,000 persons. The State Department had earlier created the Office of Foreign Relief and Rehabilitation Operations (OFRRO). The commissioning of this agency in November 1942 particularly gratified former president Herbert Hoover. He had lobbied since the outset of European hostilities for a program, modeled on his World War I relief work conducted in Belgium behind German lines, to succor trapped civilians, irrespective of where they resided or under which regime they lived.[11] As actually mandated, OFRRO, in coordination with other Allied agencies, was to deliver necessities of life to victims of

Axis power provided that they dwelt in territories liberated from Third Reich conquest.[12] This proviso, contra Hoover, stemmed from the British government's concern—voiced in August 1940 by Prime Minister Churchill—that assistance intended for people in Axis-subjugated countries would inevitably land in enemy hands, thus inadvertently supplementing German strength.[13]

A modest undertaking, crewed by only 150 staffers, OFRRO provided help to refugees (Poles, Greeks, Yugoslavs, Jews) and others in need in French North Africa, Egypt, Palestine, Spain, and Kenya. Picked by FDR to head OFRRO, Lehman later recalled its doings with pride; he regarded his ten-month-long tenure, punctuated by bruising moments in Washington's interagency warfare, as useful rehearsal for his subsequent UNRRA career.[14]

Headquartered in Washington, UNRRA constituted a unique multi-national aid effort, underwritten by forty-four Allied countries. Through combined action and pooling of resources, these "United Nations" (a moniker coined by FDR to designate the anti-Axis coalition) meant to enlarge upon OFRRO while also enlisting many of its top administrators. As originally devised in January–June 1943 by Dean Acheson, then assistant secretary of state for economic affairs, and resident Washington ambassadors—Lord Halifax (UK), Maxim Litvinov (USSR), Wei Tao-ming (China)—UNRRA proposed to help people whose countries had been overrun by Axis armies and could not yet procure adequate amounts of foodstuffs, medicines, or other essentials on the world market.[15] (As later amended, Axis lands were designated eligible for UNRRA aid, albeit restricted to supporting refugees and displaced people and providing nourishment to children and mothers.[16]) Upon signing of the UNRRA protocols in a White House ceremony on 9 November 1943, President Roosevelt delivered this mission statement:

> The sufferings of the little men and women who have been ground under the Axis heel can be relieved only if we utilize the production of ALL the world to balance the want of ALL the world. In UNRRA we have devised a mechanism, based on the processes of true democracy, which can go far toward accomplishment of such an objective in the days and months of desperate emergency which will follow the overthrow of the Axis.[17]

As stipulated by Acheson and company, UNRRA operations would be maintained by member states that had been spared Axis invasion, each doing so to the value of 1 percent of its annual national income.[18] This formula in actual practice was not realized, however; the theoretically eligible nations did not contribute at the designated levels. Nor was the burden of supporting UNRRA budgets evenly shouldered, their final total amounting to $4 billion (equivalent in 1945 dollars to nearly $55 billion in 2017).[19] The United States, at the time in possession of more than half the world's production, and largest bankroller of the Allied war, accounted for 73 percent of UNRRA funding. The remaining percentage came from the United Kingdom (16 percent), next Canada, with Brazil, South Africa, India, Australia, and New Zealand accounting for most of the rest.[20] In the event, by Lehman's estimate, twenty-five million tons of UNRRA supplies were distributed to stricken peoples.[21]

Americans should not begrudge any financial lopsidedness supporters said, such as Vice President Henry Wallace. They argued that the U.S. economy in coming years would require revitalized overseas markets, sustained by robust societies capable of absorbing U.S. investment capital and goods produced in American factories and farms. In other words, humane feeling and business concerns intertwined, ample justification for Washington's prominence in UNRRA. Clout in that organization should reinforce Washington's global leadership while fostering conditions conducive to long-term U.S. profit.[22] "It was to their own [American] interest to rehabilitate these ravaged countries," Lehman once pronounced.[23] General Dwight Eisenhower, one of the few military leaders who respected UNRRA's European operations, made this case for enlightened self-interest. "We [Americans]," he told Congress's fiscal watchdogs in November 1945, "must make our proportionate contribution to relief of the distress in Europe if our . . . victory is to have permanent significance."[24]

Regarding governance, UNRRA guidelines mandated a policymaking council, composed of delegates from each member state. The primary authority, though, resided in an executive committee—consisting of American, British, Chinese, Soviet representatives—that would in light of unfolding contingencies set priorities, allocate resources, and monitor the efficacy of specific programs. It was this executive committee that nominated Lehman to serve as general-director, that choice dutifully ratified by the wider council at its first session (10 November–1 December 1943 in Atlantic City, New Jersey). As needs required, the executive committee

Recipients of UNRRA commodity aid

	(Thousands of U.S. dollars)[25]
Albania	26,250.9
Austria	135,513.2
Byelorussian SSR	60,820.0
China	517,846.7
Czechoslovakia	261,337.4
Dodecanese Islands	3,900.4
Ethiopia	884.9
Finland	2,441.2
Greece	347,162.0
Hungary	4,386.5
Italy	418,222.1
Korea	943.9
Philippines	9,880.2
Poland	477,927.0
San Marino	30.0
Ukrainian SSR	188,199.3
Yugoslavia	415,642.0

was pledged to consult other UNRRA members, a sop not reassuring to lesser nations, specifically the Canadians, who at one point toyed with the idea of severing their UNRRA tie; they chafed at taking instruction from a cabal of big powers, allegedly devoid of finer democratic sensibility and presumptuous in their distributing of Canadian products (wheat, for example) to distant peoples not necessarily aligned with Ottawa's economic-diplomatic interests. A number of middling bodies was meanwhile created, among which were committees to advise on the purchase of supplies (often from military surplus) and implement relief programs at a pace commensurate with the retreat of Axis power from captive territories. Even more specialized committees were formed to deal with logistical dilemmas, provisioning priorities, and disbursements of health care, farm tools, food stocks, clothing, fuel, and transport.[26]

Apart from the coordinating of personnel belonging to assorted private relief agencies, UNRRA's own operations employed thousands of men and women, recognizable on assignment by distinctive gray/khaki uniforms and red shoulder patches with white lettering: UNRRA.[27] The UNRRAIDs—whose roster peaked at 20,000—were posted in missions stretching from

Western Europe to Soviet territories, the Balkans, Africa, China, and the Philippines.[28] Better than 40 percent of UNRRA employees in 1946 were female, many enrolled on the social work side and heavily recruited from the United States (often imbued with New Deal idealism), Canada, Great Britain, and Western Europe.[29] Doctors and nurses—of whom there were always shortages—hygiene experts, crops/animal husbandry specialists, engineers, accountants, and administrative support were also deployed.

The top slot in UNRRA, designated a U.S. preserve, was filled most lengthily by staid Lehman—Democratic governor of New York in 1933–1942, New Deal stalwart, civil rights proponent.[30] Immediately following Lehman's 31 March 1946 resignation, the flamboyant and voluble mayor of New York City, Fiorello La Guardia, assumed the directorship. He held the post through the end of 1946, whereupon Major General Lowell Ward Rooks of the U.S. Army accepted the post, his duty being to oversee the orderly closure of UNRRA transactions, mostly phased out in 1947 and entirely finished in summer 1948.

The position of Senior Deputy Director General originally fell to Britain's Sir Arthur Salter (an Oxford scholar), at the time over-worn, albeit dedicated to the UNRRA cause. An Australian navy man, Commander R.G.A. Jackson ("Jacko"), with a liveliness of mind, physical stamina, and a knack for disentangling bureaucratic knots, succeeded Salter.[31] Canadian, Chinese, Czech, Dutch, Polish, South African, and Soviet figures also held major posts. Canada's Mary Craig McGeachy, a veteran diplomat, became the senior ranking woman in UNRRA and the only one appointed to executive level. She headed, if not brilliantly, the sprawling welfare division.[32]

Despite admitting to a myriad glitches along the way, UNRRAIDs by their self-assessment achieved much in a brief time: they helped to control epidemics, check famines, enhance rates of agricultural/industrial production, and kindled enough spark in injured peoples that they could exercise responsibility for their own well-being. Proponents claimed that their UNRRA had created a blueprint for postwar international society.[33] George Woodbridge, a member of UNRRA's European Regional Office (London) and official chronicler of UNRRA, offered this paean in 1950:

> [UNRRA] amply justified its existence. . . . The work performed through UNRRA was a demonstration on the largest scale which the world has yet seen that nations can unite to fulfill the exhortation

voiced long ago by the prophet Ezra, "Do right to the widow, judge for the fatherless, give to the poor, defend the orphan, clothe the naked, heal the broken and weak."[34]

To support this viewpoint, Woodbridge and colleagues could, indeed did, cite cases, including the following sample.

The largest slice of UNRRA assistance went to China. There these achievements were salient, wholly compatible with Washington's interests as imagined by FDR, prone to rhapsodize about that country's future economic wallop and strategic importance.[35] Damaged dykes and levees were repaired—with new ones erected—along rivers to stanch seasonal floods, thereby reclaiming lands lost for tillage since the 1937 Japanese invasion. Several million people were fed and saved from death by starvation, even while famine stalked the country.[36] Other people were gainfully employed in UNRRA-sponsored works, such as paving highways, restoring railway roadbeds, and modernizing sanitation facilities. Medical clinics were established. Clothing, shelter, and medicines were distributed on a scale hitherto unknown in impoverished China. Education programs were inaugurated to train local youths to fill future cadres of technicians in public health, pharmaceuticals, food production, transportation, and communications. Power plants, waterworks, coal mining, fisheries, port facilities, and textile manufacturing were restored, updated, and turned from disrepair and idleness to usefulness. All this done as civil war convulsed the country— Mao's rebellion versus the fading Guomindang government.[37] In understatement, Woodbridge allowed in 1950: "How much more extensive and enduring the [UNRRA program] might have been, but for the continuing dislocation and destruction resulting from civil war, must be left to conjecture."[38] Still, Lehman believed, from a U.S. standpoint all was not forfeited, not even in the radically new circumstance of a communist People's Republic: "The Chinese people know of our record of enlightened fairness and friendship. They have not forgotten UNRRA."[39]

Even less open to doubt was the Filipino case. The UNRRA investment in the Philippines, though small compared to that in China, helped rebuild war-trampled Manila, revived agricultural production, and resurrected fisheries. Thousands of Filipino families obtained shelter and nutrition. Carlos Romulo, first foreign minister of the independent Philippines republic, testified in 1958 that UNRRA had let his countrymen thrive

FIGURE 1.1 Distribution of UNRRA rice during 1946 Chinese famine

Source: United Nations Archives

again.[40] Evidence suggests that Korea too made headway in relief and rehabilitation, despite the deepening north–south divide. In the event, the northern zone was recipient of medical supplies, locomotives, and trucks, whereas clothing items and raw materials were in the south. The benefits of such relief operations and goods on Korea were not destined to survive the bloodletting of 1950–1953, however.[41]

Of European states, Poland received the most aid. More than 16 percent of the nation's prewar population had perished. Upon first viewing Warsaw, a stunned Ira Hirschmann, while on UNRRA reconnaissance, remarked on the city's "all-embracing" wreckage.[42] Infusions of food, medical personnel, rolling stock (primarily trucks), and insecticides (DDT) enabled the Polish government to avoid massive starvation and preempt typhus and typhoid epidemics. The UNRRA "spark plug" also ignited, as a future basis for modern industry, electrical power generation, coal mining, and a semblance of self-sustaining mechanized agricultural economy.[43]

Ruin in the western republics of the USSR (Ukraine, Byelorussia) overwhelmed anything that UNRRA could deliver. Indeed, the scale of desolation and casualties—upward of 25 million dead—from Germany's invasion of the Soviet Union surpassed anything in the annals of modern warfare. Pursuant to the Nazi idea, iterated in Berlin's 1941 Hunger Plan, demography in parts of the western Soviet Union had been altered via mass executions, orchestrated starvation, and forced emigration. This elimination policy also aimed to raze cities, eradicate industries, demolish monuments of civilization, and foster a version of primitive agriculture adequate to meet the food requirements of Germans but not those of anyone else.[44] Consequently, as with other scorched areas of the USSR, the restoration of Ukraine and Byelorussia proved an epic undertaking. It consumed Soviet resources and assets into the deep postwar future. Yet UNRRA's supply of food, clothing, hospital equipment, and machinery constituted a useful grant—done at a moment when the remainder of the USSR was little able to assist.[45]

In Czechoslovakia, "Auntie UNRRA" dispensed goods and services sufficient to help reactivate the country's economy and transportation network. Czechoslovakia, in fact, became the first receiving nation to make contribution to other hungry ones via donations of fruits, vegetables, and sugar.[46] No other UNRRA-assisted country by mid-1947 was in better physical shape than Czechoslovakia, a testament to the hardihood of the people themselves but also evidence of UNRRA's impact on collective morale.[47] Neighboring Austria, by Allied fiat in 1943 accorded the status of Hitler's "first victim," received necessary supplies of food (meats, grains, fats, oils), along with fertilizers, seeds, and farming equipment. Malnourishment did not overtake the cities or the countryside, basis for the 1948 judgment of Britain's Brigadier Reginald Parminter, who had supervised UNRRA programs from his Vienna office: "There is no possible shadow of doubt that the Austrian nation owes its survival to UNRRA aid."[48]

In the Balkans, civil upheavals compounded wartime devastation, as in Greece (ELAS versus royalists), and ethnic vengeance, as in Yugoslavia (Croats versus Serbs). Nevertheless, despite unceasing violence, UNRRA mounted ameliorative campaigns. These stalled famine, contained malaria and tuberculosis, dispensed penicillin, staffed hospitals, distributed garments, and imported locomotives, trucks, tractors, and draft animals. In the absence of UNRRA in Greece and Yugoslavia, conditions of penury in those countries would have lingered for even longer decades than occurred.[49]

Shipments of UNRRA medical and food aid to mangled Italy, dubbed an Ally after defecting from the Axis in September 1943, were likewise delivered on an impressive level and ran through the end of June 1947. Cautious hope supplanted pervading gloom as a million mothers, pregnant women, and children were quickly rescued from disaster. Other categories of people were soon afterwards helped. Industrial tools, fuel, vaccination dispensaries, and agricultural machines were additionally sent.[50] Lehman later claimed that UNRRA was responsible for preventing Italy (Greece too, by his reckoning) from communist takeover.[51]

Not only did UNRRA workers assist people as they struggled to overcome economic-social paralysis. But UNRRA also, with the International Red Cross and Allied military governors, assumed responsibility for the repatriation of countless uprooted men, women, and children: displaced persons (DPs). In Europe and North Africa, DPs were congregated in improvised centers (schools, prisons, disused military encampments), mainly located in territories of the former Third Reich or Italy. Nationals of every country hit by Nazi armies, the surviving remnant of European Jewry, slave laborers, military prisoners, and orphans populated nine hundred DP camps in 1945–1947.[52] Their organization and administration were monumental tasks. So was the care required to deal with people possessed of a bewildering diversity of need—shelter, food, education, medical attention, counseling, cultural uplift, political reengagement—while properly processing their homeward return. In Germany alone, according to one estimate, UNRRA tended to the care and repatriation of 6.5 million displaced persons.[53] One UNRRAID observer of the DP scene, Milton Winn, testified in 1946: "[The affliction] that befalls these poor wanderers of all faiths and the stupidities and viciousness that pursues them cast one into a state of despair where all one can think of is man's inhumanity to man."[54]

The DP effort also subsumed attempts via the Child Search program to return to anxious parents their kidnapped youngsters who had disappeared into the maw of Hitler's *Lebensborn* program; for their Aryan qualities (blond, blue eyes), as many as 350,000 had been snatched in Nazi-occupied areas (the Baltic republics, Czechoslovakia, France, Poland, Ukraine) and taken to Germany for assimilation into the *Herrenvolk*.[55]

Not all people who were eligible wanted to return to the county of their origin. Reluctant repatriates included hundreds of thousands of Poles uneasy about living under communist rule and those Soviet soldiers who had collaborated with Hitler's war effort, such as General Andrei Vlasov's Russian Liberation Army or the Ukrainian Galician Division.[56] Also resisting were guiltless Red Army men who nonetheless came under Moscow's suspicion of disloyalty by virtue of having been captured by Germans or their allies. In the event, hundreds of thousands of unwilling Red Army personnel were obliged by Western governments in 1945–1947 to return to the USSR, in which UNRRA acquiesced and usually abetted.[57] Many Jews meanwhile longed to move to Palestine, not resettle in their native lands, where returnees were often greeted gloweringly or—as in parts of Poland—with outright malice and violent outbursts (Kielce, July 1946). Like most relief associations at the time, UNRRA did not distinguish the singularity of the Shoah from the general horror. Luckily, from the standpoint of their charges, Jewish philanthropic agencies—not UNRRA— were allowed from September 1945 onward to exercise responsibility for the welfare of Jews while facilitating the relocation of individuals to places of their preference.[58]

Criticisms

Few recipients of UNRRA aid stinted their appreciations. Britain's foreign secretary, Ernest Bevin, in January 1948 voiced a view shared by millions of people: "What sort of Europe we should have had without UNRRA, I really do not know." He thought it "too horrible to contemplate."[59] Yet the reputation of UNRRA was hardly unblemished or free of skeptics who thought the program oversold, actually pernicious.[60]

People of best caliber or competence, as Lehman occasionally fretted, did not occupy all top UNRRA echelons: "We had some bad actors."[61] He himself lacked executive drive. He was devoid of charisma. He possessed too passive a personality to navigate adroitly among Washington hazards: partisan skirmishers, bureaucracy barons, preening egos. "Not a very good fighter" was Henry Wallace's apt verdict.[62] As for the field personnel, they were in instances hastily recruited (from more than forty countries), without much orientation placed in novel and trying situations, and expected to follow orders that were not always clearly stated or understood; faulty transmission or gabled translation frazzled nerves and caused worry.[63] Exacerbating these problems, UNRRAIDs were expected to exercise considerable independent initiative. But if trends ran wrong, higher authority could repudiate the local UNNRA team, leaving it isolated and demoralized.

Allied army officers, among them the celebrated Field Marshal Bernard Montgomery, often looked askance at UNRRA. They thought it an ill-disciplined enterprise that occasionally hindered combat operations, got in the way of occupation governments, employed busybodies and do-gooders, cluttered logistics schedules, commandeered ships and planes otherwise available for military service, taxed limited food and medical supplies, and anyway was inferior to the time-tested Red Cross.[64] Even some military officers seconded to UNRRA shared this attitude, holding assignment to UNRRA a "degradation" and openly disparaged its works.[65] Case in point was Britain's Lieutenant General Sir Frederick Morgan, previously a planner of the 1944 D-Day operation. This amiable but distorted personality, who led (October 1945–August 1946) the displaced persons operation in Germany, made himself unpopular in UNRRA by not taking more seriously than he did or treat in better tone and decency the enervated Jewish DPs in his care.[66] After visiting (summer 1946) the Wolfratshausen DP camp in southern Bavaria, Morgan confided in his diary that the internees were employed in "nefarious businesses" and lived contentedly in squalor: "These people being Jews all one can notice is every evidence of a year's dilapidation and accumulation of filth."[67] A self-proclaimed expert on the "Oriental" Hebrew mind, Morgan recoiled from what he described as Semitic vengefulness, Shylock slyness, hysterical rabbis, exaggerated camp grievances, Jewish-dictated news media, and scheming Jewish staffers in UNRRA ("not one of whom do I trust").[68] But he was not fired (by La Guardia) until after he publicly charged that UNRRA was feeble in every respect but one: protecting Soviet spies and giving cover to sundry criminals involved in narcotics peddling and human smuggling schemes of Zionist–Moscow design.[69] Of his successor at UNRRA, Myer Cohen, Morgan scorned the man as slinking Jew and incompetent.[70] What a pity, Morgan reflected a few months after his dismissal from UNRRA, that Jewish restiveness in DP camps intertwined mischievously with London's attempts to counter Zionists and Jewish immigration to British-administered Palestine. "Our bureaucrats just haven't got the guts," he observed to a friend, "to shoot or gas these people as our late enemies had."[71]

Other people, not just the egregious Morgan, did wonder at the inability of Lehman, and later La Guardia, to suppress the malfeasance that swirled about UNRRA's fringes. Black-market racketeers, prostitution-ring pimps, and wily officials fed upon UNRRA bounty or swindled its intended beneficiaries. Nor was UNRRA assumed in every capital to be politically chaste or above intrigue. Soviet officials worried about the doings of British and American aid workers in Ukraine and Byelorussia, even as Moscow sought to insert its own reliable figures—not exactly intelligence agents—into senior UNRRA management. Mikhail Menshikov, assigned to duties in the Washington office (deputy director general, Bureau of Areas) and who outwardly assumed a nonpartisan role, warranted Lehman's posting a sharp outlook.[72] (Menshikov became Soviet ambassador to the United States in 1958, in which capacity he served for four years.) An UNRRAID in Yugoslavia was arrested for spying and subsequently removed from Belgrade. Albania's communist leader, Enver Hoxha, accused UNRRA of deploying saboteurs and spies in his country. In actuality, Lehman blocked OSS agents from involvement with UNRRA, thinking, quite rightly, that their detection would erode UNRRA's credibility.[73]

The severest critics of UNRRA resided in the United States. They combined fiscal conservatism with skepticism about the supposed merit of postwar involvement overseas, a viewpoint exemplified by Senator Robert Taft (R, Ohio). Having given full throttle to anxieties about government waste, from New Deal innovations onward, the GOP won the November 1946 congressional elections, gaining control of both Senate and House chambers. This political reality ensured that future UNRRA funding—not easy to secure even in the organization's halcyon days—would be hard, if not impossible, to obtain in the new regime of austerity and retrenchment.[74] Meanwhile, the GOP's grand old man, Herbert Hoover, intensified his critique of UNRRA. Despite his failed presidency, he enjoyed a reputation for expertise on international aid and good standing for his earlier deeds, notably directing the American Relief Administration in post-World War I Europe. Stung at not having been asked to head UNRRA, resentful of Lehman, persuaded that receiving countries should pay for UNRRA contributions, Hoover since UNRRA's inception had circulated blistering criticisms in Washington.[75] After FDR's death in April 1945, Hoover took advantage of his friendship with Harry Truman to pour calumny into the president's ear about UNRRA. To Lehman's shock, in March 1946 Truman asked Hoover to evaluate the food needs of Europeans and Asians.[76] Lehman resigned in consequence, a move made easier by his designs on a 1946 Senate run, which flopped. Thereupon the colorful but ailing La Guardia took command.[77] (He died in September 1947, a demise accelerated by his UNRRA exertions.)

Enthusiasm for UNRRA also withered in the State Department. Secretary James Byrnes (July 1945–January 1947) came to object to a governing council composed of diverse regimes, including communist, which presumed to decide on the size and destination of aid levied upon the United States.[78] Matters here were aggravated when, in August 1946, a U.S. transport plane was downed over Marxist Yugoslavia. In Byrnes's account, the captive crew, whose number included an UNRRA man, saw this through the gate of their Yugoslav prison:

> An American-made locomotive over at the railway depot with the letters UNRRA printed on it. They knew that 70 percent of the cost of that locomotive was furnished by the U.S. taxpayer and the thought contributed little to the comfort of their internment.[79]

Indeed, "a pretty poor return," Hoover chimed, for that aid heedlessly funneled to Tito's Yugoslavia.[80]

Will Clayton, a principal architect of the State Department's European Recovery Program (ERP or Marshall Plan), likewise damned UNRRA. He rued Washington's forfeiture of exclusive decision-making authority while Americans bore the main financial burden. He felt that vigorous unilateral policies instead would produce political-economic dividends for the United States, far exceeding anything to arise from mushy-minded multilateralism. Of the prospective Marshall Plan, he said in 1947, as the Cold War chrysalis was bursting open: "We must avoid getting into another UNRRA. *The United States must run this* [ERP] *show.*"[81]

Well after UNRRA ended, Acheson, once the organization's champion, penned this judgment, a reflection of State Department interpretation and prevailing Washington sentiment:

> Internationally administered relief had been a failure. The staff obtainable had been weak and the leadership weaker. UNRAA supplies turned up all too frequently in black markets, but, far more serious, the bulk of them, from our point of view, went to the wrong places and were used for wrong purposes.

In pique, he observed, "relief, largely supplied or paid for by the United States, [had gone] to Eastern Europe and was used by governments bitterly hostile to us."[82] Yet he took solace in this notion: where UNRRA had erred, the Marshall Plan in 1948–1951 went right; only deserving European states deemed worthy of U.S. aid had benefited, to the tune of $12.3 billion. Neither that glory nor the diplomatic advantage that accrued to Washington was dissipated or shared with others.[83] Against such appraisal, the ghost of La Guardia surely moaned, as did the living man who in 1946 reviled those security planners who wanted to "play power politics with bread."[84]

Atomic bomb

While UNRRA performed its chores, the Americans at Bikini Atoll in the Marshall Islands detonated two 21 kiloton atomic bombs, 1 and 24 July 1946.[85] Already impressed by U.S. acquisition of atomic weaponry and willingness to use it, Joseph Stalin had earlier ordered Soviet scientists to hasten their research.[86] The resultant effort, abetted by clandestine intelligence agents, yielded a Soviet atomic bomb in August 1949, before most U.S. scientists and the CIA thought probable. In January 1950, as a consequence of this Soviet breakthrough, Truman authorized development of a radically more fearsome thing, the hydrogen bomb, an addition to the U.S. arsenal made in 1952. (Elugelab of the Marshall Islands was obliterated in a November test.) In turn, Soviet scientists, whose corps included Andrei Sakharov, tested their first thermonuclear bomb in August 1953, done, in his somber telling, "to make the country strong enough to ensure peace."[87] As for Great Britain, it ascended to the atomic club with the testing of a fission bomb in 1952 and a hydrogen one in 1957. Thus the three preeminent powers joined the nuclear arms race, unaware and unembarrassed by Hata Tomoko's protest against "human insolence."

Yet attempts were made in 1945–1946, of which Hata would have approved had she known of them, to defer or halt the spread of these weapons. Before the test explosion (16 July 1945) in the New Mexico desert, a group of Manhattan Project scientists had tried to block the atomic assault on Japan. Centered at the University of Chicago—clustered around physicists James Franck and Leo Szilard—these petitioning scientists, of whom there were more than sixty, favored international control of the atom.[88] Their worry was, in Franck's words, that "mankind has learned to unleash atomic power without being ethically and politically prepared to use it wisely."[89] To speed the war's end, Franck and colleagues argued to Secretary of War Henry Stimson in June 1945 on behalf of a demonstration explosion of an atomic device, presumably on a remote Pacific island. According to this reasoning, Tokyo's civilian and military officials would be so sobered by the spectacle that they would seek surrender. An arms race would be preempted, the conditions for far-reaching agreements on atomic weaponry advanced. This Franck line, alas, made no headway among other Manhattan Project scientists—J. Robert Oppenheimer, who directed the Los Alamos laboratories, Enrico Fermi, and Ernest Lawrence—or with Stimson. None of them perceived a feasible alternative to combat use. Truman probably did not read the Chicago recommendations and was apparently uninhibited regarding Hiroshima and Nagasaki.[90]

Notions of checking atomic weaponry did not disappear, however. They rode upon cresting anxiety, a feeling Stimson shared.[91] Though he never disavowed the ostensible wisdom of launching the Hiroshima and Nagasaki strikes, indeed defended them in print and speech, he had been eager in late summer 1945 to find an exit from the nascent atomic dilemma. To this end, and despite his dislike of Stalinism, he urged Truman to reach an understanding with the Kremlin. "In effect," Stimson wrote in a memorandum,

> to enter an arrangement with the Russians, the general purpose of which would be to control and limit the use of the atomic bomb as an instrument of war and so far as possible to direct and encourage the development of atomic power for peaceful and humanitarian purposes.[92]

Bold cooperation could avert an arms race, Stimson stated in the September days just before he retired from government service: "Our objective must be to get the best kind of international bargain we can—one that has some chance of being kept and saving civilization not for five or for twenty years, but forever."[93] In the event, no such initiative won endorsement by Truman or his cabinet officers, who, excepting Henry Wallace (then of the Commerce Department), viewed the USSR with mounting impatience, if not abhorrence.

Clear-eyed about Stalin, and mindful of problems that had thwarted arms control since time immemorial, backers of atomic control nevertheless dared to hope. Solution might reside in a type of custodianship. To this end, Acheson, by then State Department undersecretary, concentrated his attention from January 1946 to midyear. Previously he had supported

Stimson's idea of negotiating directly with Kremlin authorities.[94] Thereafter, Acheson, not yet a confirmed Cold Warrior—in early 1946 he still favored more UNRRA aid to Soviet territories and thought a generous loan to Moscow doable—labored for atomic cooperation within a United Nations framework.[95] The occasion for his work rested in a resolution, 24 January 1946, of the UN General Assembly to establish the Atomic Energy Commission (AEC). It was charged with making recommendations on the sharing of scientific knowledge, eradicating atomic weaponry, and fashioning safeguards to protect the complying states from violators and evaders.

To advise the government on this bundle of complications, Byrnes chose Acheson to head a committee to sketch a U.S. position. Other members were Vannevar Bush (senior science adviser, head of the Carnegie Institution), James Conant (president of Harvard University), Major General Leslie Groves (Manhattan project director), and John McCloy (former assistant secretary of war). To assist this committee, Acheson organized a body of consultants led by David Lilienthal, the strong-willed chair of the Tennessee Valley Authority; other consultants were Chester Barnard (president of New Jersey Bell Telephone), Charles Thomas (vice president and technical director of Monsanto Chemical Company), and Harry Winne (vice president in charge of engineering policy for General Electric Company). The most prominent of Acheson's consultants was Oppenheimer, a man by then unsettled by his role in the incinerations of Hiroshima and Nagasaki.[96] He confessed to Truman, himself possessed of more remorse than he publicly admitted: "Mr. President, I have blood on my hands."[97]

In early March 1946, the consultants submitted their ideas and findings—*A Report on the International Control of Atomic Energy*—to Acheson and his committee. They, in turn, despite quibbles and qualms (Groves notably), endorsed the recommendations. Remembered since as the Acheson–Lilienthal Report, it was mainly the product of Oppenheimer's pertinacity.[98] His sensibility suffused the document: "We are not dealing simply with a military or scientific problem but with a problem in statecraft and the ways of the human spirit."[99]

The report distinguished between safe operations and "intrinsically dangerous" ones. The former were to be left to the control of individual sovereign governments, the latter to reside in an agency of unique prestige, prospectively named the Atomic Development Authority (ADA) and to be housed in the UN's Security Council. Presumptively safe activities pointed to peaceful uses of atomic science, for example the generation of electrical energy for domestic heating and light or the use of radioactive tracers in medical studies. Designated dangerous activities hinged on the making of atomic bombs, the collecting of raw materials, and the producing of plutonium and uranium-235.[100] Only the ADA could conduct dangerous operations. It alone would enjoy access to the planet's uranium and thorium caches; it would build, own, and run reactors and separation plants; its expert personnel would license and inspect activities in every country that undertook nuclear work. In effect, the United States would divest its atomic monopoly, expected anyway to be temporary, and place trust in an international institution and mechanisms of joint control. Thus the atomic arms race should be foreclosed before it gained unstoppable momentum.[101]

Additional benefits from the program were predicted to be equally profound, perhaps leading to a version of perpetual peace. The new scheme, if properly executed, could "establish patterns of cooperation among nations, the extension of which may even contribute to the solution of the problem of war itself." To that optimism, and its intimations of establishing a world federation, the authors added this flourish:

> When the plan is in full operation there will no longer be secrets about atomic energy. We believe that this is the firmest basis of security; for in the long term there can be no international control and no international cooperation which does not presuppose an international community of knowledge.[102]

Henry Wallace welcomed the Acheson–Lilienthal idea. To him and like-minded progressives, it was a wholesome shift away from blunt power politics or a showdown with Moscow. He declared that FDR would have applauded—who, incidentally, by the time of the 1945 Yalta conference entertained the idea of sharing atomic science with the USSR.[103]

To skeptics, neither the ghost of FDR nor the preachment of Wallace was reassuring: the premises and practicality of the Acheson–Lilienthal plan—which excluded inspection of Soviet security sites—indicated superficial reasoning, thus risking the surrender of tangible advantages for the sake of a nebulous future based on degrees of cooperation never before attained. Besides, doubters said, the United Nations was a fledgling affair. Established only in June 1945, scattered in makeshift quarters around New

York City, it was an unproven institution, hardly substantial enough to ensure U.S. security or host the contemplated ADA. The Soviets, in any event, were making trouble—not vacating northern Iran, playing crudely in those European countries occupied by the Red Army, running atomic spies in Canada—and seemed less than reliable partners. Kremlin denizens were not, in short, the sort of people with whom to share scientific findings of potential military application. Stalin's tough radio address (9 February) added further to this outlook, reinforced by tutorials from George Kennan ("long telegram," 22 February) and Churchill ("iron curtain" speech, 5 March). If executed, the Acheson–Lilienthal proposal would give away too much, too soon—a patently premature move, one Bernard Baruch warned, constituting an unprecedented compromise of U.S. security.[104]

Byrnes asked Baruch to present Washington's atomic energy case to the AEC, a request that reflected White House ambivalence on the merit of reposing confidence in UN agencies or trust in Stalin.[105] Wealthy, vain, and obstinate, Baruch was a self-styled counselor to presidents, from Woodrow Wilson onward. Still feisty, despite the passing years (b. 1870), the prospect of a UN appearance flattered his *amour propre*. Before that event, 14 June 1946, he and his aides—business associates of conservative bent, plus a recruited scientist, Richard Tolman of the California Institute of Technology—modified the Acheson–Lilienthal proposal.[106] They shrouded it in sterner spirit, much to the chagrin of Oppenheimer, Wallace, et al.[107] The concept of Atomic Development Authority was retained, but states that violated the agreement on atomic controls would be quickly punished, in ways not clarified but severely.[108] Moreover, in a swipe against Moscow, no veto-wielding member of the UN Security Council could skirt the prohibitions on making atomic weapons: "There must be no veto to protect those who violate . . . agreements not to develop or use atomic energy for destructive purposes."[109] Baruch told AEC delegates that the United States would naturally cease building atomic weapons once all conditions were met.

The Soviet representative to the AEC, Andrei Gromyko, responded on 19 June to Baruch with a counterproposal. This stressed a comprehensive ban on atomic bombs: they should not be produced, not stockpiled, not used. All existing atomic weapons must be dismantled once a convention was agreed upon; signatory states would punish any delinquent regime—for which potential designation only the USA, with its nine bombs in 1946, could possibly qualify—that refused to abolish its atomic arsenal.[110] In the ensuing months, an intense discussion developed, one not eased by modest adjustments adduced by each side. Choleric feeling expressed within AEC conclave inevitably spilled over into the General Assembly, where the implacable Vyacheslav Molotov defended Moscow's position.

The entire exercise to internationalize atomic science fizzled by year's end. The AEC did approve (ten votes for, with Poland and the USSR abstaining) a draft of the Baruch plan. But it lacked hope of realization in the face of Soviet objection armored with Security Council veto. An unresolvable problem held: Kremlin comrades distrusted the United States and were determined to achieve atomic equivalence, lest the USSR be permanently relegated to second-class status and vulnerability. Indeed, Soviet atomic researches were never constrained by any version of pending international control, not even the more forgiving Acheson–Lilienthal one.[111] To Baruch and his allies, meanwhile, only feckless U.S. statecraft would forego the security advantage inherent in atomic monopoly, no matter how fleeting. At a minimum, the United States should not jeopardize its head start on weapons research or nuclear findings, such as those obtained at Bikini in July by the test explosions (done days and with much controversy after Gromyko first addressed the AEC).[112] By late 1946, both parties perceived that the atomic arms race had its own ineluctability, unimpeded by UN negotiations, soon lost anyway in the miasma of propaganda war.[113]

Each side in time accused the other of acting in bad faith. Dripping in sanctimony, both scrambled for the moral high ground. They exchanged platitudes about the desirability of global understanding. Marxist jargon collided with U.S. narcissism. Clichés about democracy and the human future were solemnly intoned. The Soviets charged the Americans with coy subterfuge to propagate their atomic hegemony and impose capitalist enslavement over all peoples. The Americans rejoined that the logic of Moscow policy was to subvert world peace.[114] Heedless of Primo Levi's imperative—"stop and consider"—the two sides achieved rhetorical parity, nothing more.

★ ★ ★

The question of how to mend destruction-past and avert destruction-future focused thoughtful minds, U.S. and other, as they pondered this paradox:

the force necessary to defeat Axis monstrosity also begat another evil. The dilemma, to France's Léon Blum, was that Hitler's Germany had created a situation which obliged otherwise undepraved people to behave ferociously. Although he lived to see Nazi power beaten, Blum sensed that Berlin's method and idolatry of military might would remain supreme. "You [Nazis]," he said during the war,

> are already conquerors in this sense: you have breathed such terror all about that to master you, to prevent the return of your fury, we shall have no other way of fashioning the world save in your image, your laws, the law of Force.[115]

In an echo of Blum, Oppenheimer in early 1947 vented this anguish about what was done at Hiroshima and Nagasaki:

> The only justification for our action is our complete acceptance of the Nazi philosophy which we were fighting against, and which asserts that anything, no matter how brutal, and whether directed against non-combatants or not, is justified if it helps to win a war.[116]

Even earlier, contemplating Vishnu's words in the *Bhagavad-Gita*, Oppenheimer already knew that World War II-past and atomic bomb-future were cast in the same infernal moment: "Now, I am become Death, the destroyer of worlds."[117]

However unexpected, a "sublime irony" (Churchill's phrase) did subsequently hold. The prospect of mutually assured destruction in the Cold War years encouraged the exercise of restraint by Washington and Moscow. The deterrent power of nuclear weapons can be credited, at least in part, with having averted a third world war. "Safety," Churchill again, became "the sturdy child of terror, and survival the twin brother of annihilation."[118]

Needless to elaborate, the willingness and preparation to kill millions of people in an instant—intrinsic to U.S. and Soviet strategic doctrines—denoted not only a deviation from the spirit that animated the Acheson–Lilienthal proposal but also moral collapse. Under the trailing shadow of nuclear war, Cold War populations lived apprehensively for decades. William Faulkner captured that mood when, in his 1950 Nobel Prize acceptance speech, he asked: "When will I be blown up?"[119] Moments of nuclear swagger were disconcerting, as when in 1953 President Dwight

FIGURE 1.2 Atomic bomb test at Bikini Atoll, 24 July 1946

Source: U.S. National Archives

Eisenhower implied atomic usage to hasten a Korean armistice or threatened similarly to break the impasses during the 1955 and 1958 contests centered on the offshore islands (Jinmen, Mazu). In the 1956 Suez Canal war, Nikita Khrushchev warned of the lethality of Soviet nuclear-tipped missiles should they rain upon London, Paris, or Israel.[120] Faulkner's question resounded during the Cuban missile events of October 1962.

After Cuba, the Soviets and Americans took affirmative, albeit tentative, steps: emplacing safeguards to prevent war by accident or miscalculation, monitoring the environmental-health hazards associated with thermo-nuclear tests, checking the spread of doomsday weapons, capping the size of arsenals. Admittedly, none of the ratified instruments—White House–Kremlin "hot line," the limited test ban, SALT or START treaties, the nuclear nonproliferation regimes—ended the Cold War, in which case they shared kinship with the Acheson–Lilienthal initiative. This had not fenced nuclear science within UN quarantine or forestalled the Cold War. The latter purpose, of course, was not part of the Acheson–Lilienthal aim; to assert otherwise would invite a category mistake. The atomic question, contributory though it was, explained neither the origins of the Cold War nor its duration. For such explanation, one must probe the geopolitical rearrangement caused by World War II, intensified by East–West ideological competition.

The nuclear problem preceded the Cold War, the U.S. possession of the bomb in 1945 being a function of the atomic race against Nazi Germany. Correspondingly, nuclear dangers have bided past the fall of the Berlin Wall and splintering of the USSR. That the collapse of the Cold War order did not inaugurate abandonment of nuclear arms is underscored in the numbers below, their sum measuring the increase of danger first addressed by Acheson–Lilienthal, when the world possessed only a handful.

Total nuclear warheads in 2015[121]

United States	4,764
Russia	4,300
China	250
France	300
United Kingdom	225
Pakistan	120
India	110
Israel	80
North Korea	10

Plainly, as an experiment in multistate cooperation, UNRRA could claim more success than the 1946 attempt, blending quixotic with exigent, to corral atomic science. Unconnected either to the revitalization of postwar Germany or Japan—supplanted in popular memory by ERP, that most creative Cold War project knitting Western economies to the burgeoning United States—UNRRA nevertheless functioned worthily. Like Henry Wallace, Lehman and La Guardia resisted the pull of anti-Soviet mentality and defended UNRRA against faultfinders. "Let us stop talking cynically about the next war and think sincerely about future peace," La Guardia urged. He lamented that UNRRA, like Wallace (forced from Truman's cabinet in September 1946), became a Cold War casualty.[122]

Born of wartime aspiration, tinged with something of the expectancy that attached to Acheson–Lilienthal thinking, UNRRA presupposed a continuing of Allied cooperation that, in the event, ceased. Still, retrospectively viewed, UNRRA as internationalized relief work suggested that an alternative to Cold War once existed. Further, before UNRRA folded ("assassinated" in the judgment of Ira Hirschmann), it compiled a record demonstrating that hardships can be ameliorated via multilateral collaboration—an achievement worth noting in the twenty-first century, when problems of global distributive justice and dilemmas faced by millions of forcibly displaced people have reached emergency level.[123] Significantly, too, UNRRA's legacy encompassed more than a tantalizing outline of that path not taken to exit from Cold War irreversibility. Numerous UNRRA veterans and property were eventually transferred to institutions that assumed honorable roles in mitigating misery. In palpable ways, UNRRA inspired, if not actually spawned, the Food and Agriculture Organization, the International Refugee Organization (later renamed the United Nations High Commission for Refugees), the World Health Organization, and the Children's Emergency Fund (UNICEF).[124]

In the final analysis, World War II not only placed patches of earth and nations in extremis. The war also injected into history—beyond retrieval—new categories of crime, such that people would thenceforth only feel shame that fellow human beings in a torrent of ethical capitulation had done the things.[125] Neither conscience nor memory could be unstained, not after the applications of perverted science traced in emptied Zyklon-B canisters or mushroom clouds or any of the other inerasable evidences. Only faith would allow for anything so fanciful as a better future.[126] However distinctive in their ways, UNRRA as succor and Acheson–Lilienthal as plausibility were indissolubly linked: they testified to faith's irrepressibility against irrefutable experience and dismal odds.

★ ★ ★

2

JUSTICE

We must never forget that the record on which we judge these defendants today is the record on which history will judge us tomorrow. To pass these defendants a poisoned chalice is to put it to our lips as well.[1]
Justice Robert Jackson, Nuremberg, 21 November 1945

★ ★ ★

As a result of wartime operations and the 1945 capitulation of Germany and Japan, high-ranking Axis officials, civilian and military, fell into Allied captivity. To the victors this situation posed a dilemma that, though anticipated, had not been fully resolved during the period of hostilities. What should be done with surviving Axis leaders? Might they be summarily executed, just retribution for the misery they had caused? Might they instead, in the spirit of magnanimity, have their freedom restored and be allowed to reenter whatever passed for normality in their war-torn societies? Or might these people in solemn assembly be held to public account, in which case an intelligent and discriminating evaluation should be made of their misdeeds? From this last approach, so Supreme Court Justice Robert Jackson believed, a semblance of sane order could arise. The Nuremberg tribunal's "value to the world," he stated in 1949, will depend less on how faithfully it interpreted the past than on how accurately it forecast the future. It is possible that strife and suspicion will lead to new aggressions and that the nations are not yet ready to receive and abide by the Nuremberg law. But those who gave some of the best effort of their lives to this trial are sustained by a confidence that in place of what might have been mere acts of vengeance we wrote a civilized legal precedent and one that will lie close to the foundations of that body of international law which will prevail when the world becomes sufficiently civilized.[2]

To critics, Jackson's apologia was deficient. It did not rectify the wrong perpetrated at Nuremberg and, by extension, in Tokyo. In both instances, the objection ran, triumphant states had inflicted victor's justice and retroactive laws while labeling as singular the wartime transgressions of vanquished people.

Nuremberg

Of handsome cities in pre-World War II Germany, few rivaled Bavaria's Nuremberg. Dresden alone might have surpassed it. Nuremberg had been residence to composers, bards, and artists, the most renowned of whom was Albrecht Dürer. The city once caused the poet Henry Wadsworth Longfellow to enthuse: "Everywhere I see around me the wondrous world of Art." Pillar of the Holy Roman Empire, center of the German renaissance, site of Baroque architectural masterpieces, laced by stone bridges, and backdrop to Richard Wagner's *Die Meistersinger*, moated Nuremberg even shone in Leni Riefenstahl's propaganda film, *Triumph des Willens*.

Hitler's 1935 convening of the Reichstag in Nuremberg to approve anti-Semitic legislation, the holding of Nazi jamborees and neo-pagan rites, and the building of grandiose pavilions, congress halls, and stadia were torments to sensibility. However demoralizing these were to some Nuremberg residents, nothing prepared them for war's whirlwind. Allied air raids in early 1945 smashed the city's medieval core, killed thousands of civilians, and wounded or displaced many times more. Nuremberg subsequently fell to the U.S. Army after tough fighting inflicted more casualties and widened the field of desolation. By the time of Germany's May surrender, the city, previously home to 400,000 souls, had been reduced to rubble. Beneath mountains of debris lay 30,000 corpses, making for malodorous air and a sanitation hazard.[3]

FIGURE 2.1 Palace of Justice and American guards, Nuremberg, 1945

Source: U.S. National Archives

Nuremberg's inhabitants had to manage without potable water. They were plagued by food, fuel, and medicine shortages. Francis Biddle, who served as principal U.S. judge at Nuremberg, later recalled upon assumption of duties in autumn 1945: "Faceless ghosts poked about the ruins, looking for refuse that could be eaten."[4]

Amid the city's wreckage stood the Justizpalast, an imposing complex, constructed in 1909–1916, of courtrooms, offices, and detention cells. These had sustained relatively light damage. Allied authorities selected Courtroom 600, a commodious space located in the eastern wing of the Justizpalast, to host the International Military Tribunal (IMT) as it pronounced upon Germany's senior civilian and military figures.

The idea of taking German officials to task had evolved fitfully.[5] Churchill and FDR occasionally broadcast that Nazis responsible for heinous acts would be punished in accordance with Anglo-American writ. The Allies issued a pledge at the 1943 Moscow meeting of foreign ministers:

captured German leaders would be subjected to punishment for any atrocities they commissioned. Fastidious legality, though, was not foremost in the minds of Roosevelt, Churchill, or Stalin. At one time or another, each of them entertained the idea that after Berlin's surrender the chief culprits should promptly be executed.[6] Such a procedure would emphasize to Germans the comprehensiveness of Allied victory and exact justice against men whose malevolence had spawned wide suffering. Among FDR's cabinet ministers, Secretary of Treasury Henry Morgenthau favored this approach, compatible with his deindustrialization idea for Germany. He once allowed: "We didn't ask for this war; we didn't put millions of people through gas chambers. We didn't do any of these things. [The Germans] have asked for it."[7]

The War Department housed the main opposition to unqualified punitiveness. Secretary Stimson and his lieutenant, John McCloy, campaigned against measures that might invite mistakes, cause unintended results (the creation of Nazi martyrs), and would, in any case, run counter to conventional ideas of due process. Furthermore, presumably, a trial would edify people in Germany—elsewhere, too—about the multiple malignancies of Hitler's regime, while buttressing international law and norms.[8] Their restoration should help ensure an orderly future for Americans and Europeans alike. Thus, according to the Stimson–McCloy line, the twin aims of peacemaking and conflict prevention would be enhanced.[9] This reasoning seems to have impressed FDR. It certainly persuaded his successor, Harry Truman. By the time of the Potsdam conference in July 1945, Churchill and Stalin had been prevailed upon to accede to the War Department preference, itself hedged with this corollary: nothing like the feeble 1921 Leipzig exercise, convened to examine alleged German criminals of World War I, would be permitted. Thus, in effect, the Americans assumed the roles of principal sponsors and executants of what came to be the Nuremberg tribunal.[10]

After wrangling in individual Allied governments and between them, their company expanded to include Charles de Gaulle's provisional French regime, the London Agreement was issued on 8 August 1945, along with the Charter of the IMT. These two documents itemized the IMT's governing procedures and charges against the defendants, defined as "major" players whose presumed offenses were without particular geographical location, as distinct from persons who were charged with committing depredations in specific countries and should be brought to justice in them.

The defendants inter alia would be allowed counsel of their choosing while facing an indictment encompassing varied crimes (enumerated below).[11]

Berlin functioned as the IMT's de jure headquarters, which designation gratified Soviet occupation authorities, and would have been the site of subsequent trials had they not been canceled owing to Cold War stresses.[12] At a comfortable remove from the Soviet zone, squarely in the area of U.S. Army control, Nuremberg suited the Americans and their British and French colleagues. Nuremberg's Justizpalast and the city's Grand Hotel, another survivor of bombings and battle, promised better working/ living conditions than anything afforded in the third contending city and incubator of Nazism: bomb-crumpled Munich. Of surpassing symbolism, said apologists, the IMT would contribute to the purging of Nazi mentality from the collective life of Germans by meeting in Hitler's celebrated Nuremberg.

The American settlement in Nuremberg in 1945–1946 included two judges (the same number allotted by charter to the UK, the USSR, and France): Biddle, a journeyman lawyer whose career had included service as solicitor general and attorney general, and his alternate, husky John Parker of the Fourth Circuit Court of Appeals (Richmond, Virginia). Justice Jackson—earthy, ambitious, eloquent—led the U.S. prosecutorial team. This counted two dozen lawyers, a number of whom were competitive with one another and teetered on reciprocal enmity, case in point Colonel (later Brigadier General) Telford Taylor versus Thomas Dodd, Jackson's number two and executive trial counsel.[13] Jackson, by the example he set and his poor managerial skills, bore partial responsibility for this unpleasantness. He and William Donovan, of OSS renown, early collaborators at Nuremberg, had squabbled. Disagreement over the kind of evidence to be used provoked a breach; Donovan preferred witnesses and testimony, while Jackson emphasized compiling heaps of incriminating documentation. The remainder of difficulty arose from clashing egos, culminating in flashes of Jackson's imperiousness, then Donovan's leaving Nuremberg in late 1945.

Before the trial began, American psychologists administered IQ exams/ Rorschach ink-blot tests to the Nuremberg defendants, whose published results excited conversation among them. The psychiatric staff also closely monitored the internees' emotional response to subsequent legal hearings and political events.[14]

Alternately scooping and cooperating with each other, eighty U.S. correspondents took assignments of varying duration to cover the IMT while immersing themselves socially with journalists of other countries, such as Britain's discerning Rebecca West (who enjoyed a brief romantic fling with Biddle).[15] Nearly three hundred members of the world press were on hand during the trial's first day. The American reportorial pool included such talents as John Dos Passos, Walter Cronkite, William Shirer, and Howard K. Smith.[16]

Security at the Justizpalast was provided by a garrison of young GIs—commanded by Colonel Burton Andrus—who yearned to return to U.S. shores and strained against prohibitions, ever weakening, on fraternization with local frauleins. Brawls between white and black soldiers in and around Nuremberg occurred, which caused Major General Ernest Harmon, chief of the American constabulary, later to comment: "Our greatest problem in Germany was our own soldiers."[17] The fault in his view lay overwhelmingly with the African American men, who committed most—90 percent, he claimed—of the havoc and serious crimes: rape, assault, looting.[18]

Shortly after VE Day, Harmon had shared with a fellow officer this notion: African American soldiers in Germany, as elsewhere in Europe, presumed more than they ought and enjoyed license from the locals:

> The timber of the negro as I have observed it is not good. I am sure we have got to kill a few of them to make them stand to heel, particularly since white women of all the allied countries, as well as the occupied countries, don't seem to draw any color line, which makes it difficult to enforce our normal attitude toward the negro with respect to white people.[19]

Harmon afterward authorized his constabulary to shoot unruly blacks, instanced in this episode concerning a battalion in the southern sector of the American occupation zone: "He [a constabulary trooper] went down there alone and soon was required to shoot a colored soldier in line of duty. We immediately court-martialed him, cleared him, and had no more trouble with that battalion."[20]

While General Harmon unabashedly applied his version of propriety and order to GIs in Bavaria, the Nuremberg proceedings unfolded slowly.[21] Novelty yielded to tedium. Linguistic and technological problems of simultaneous translation (English, Russian, French, German) annoyed everyone. The difficulty of meshing diverse legal systems—continental, Anglo-American, Soviet—compounded procedural misunderstandings and delays. Courtroom revelations of cosmic horror heightened the disconcertedness of living in a pulverized city. In these trying circumstances, the U.S. community struggled to maintain morale. Yet all was not bleak, especially for the higher echelons, who mingled cordially with their British and French counterparts. These included equable Lord Justice Geoffrey Lawrence, president of the tribunal, and his alternate, the gifted Sir Norman Birkett. The lead UK prosecutor was Sir Hartley Shawcross, recently made attorney general in Clement Attlee's Labour government. The bulk of British responsibility actually fell to the imperturbable Sir David Maxwell Fyfe, later raised to the peerage as Lord Kilmuir. Led by Judge Henri Donnedieu de Vabres and, as alternate, Robert Falco, the French contingent was somewhat diffident, perhaps due, observers guessed, to the lingering daze of 1940 defeat and Vichy ignominy. In the event, a diligent Francois de Menthon and Auguste Champetier de Ribes led the French prosecutors. Collectively, these Anglo-U.S.-French juridical groups enjoyed an intense existence, one not devoid of privilege, a chasm away from that borne by the pauperized indigenes. In reminisces, flecked with embarrassment, both Biddle and Taylor likened Allied life in Nuremberg to that of nabobs in colonial settings.[22]

Mutual wariness shadowed the interaction between Westerners and Soviets, despite vodka-lubricated lapses into conviviality. Even the sartorial divide seemed to indicate tension, Soviet judges wearing their military uniforms in court appearances versus Western tribunes donning conventional robes. The Soviet judges, Major General Iona Nikitchenko and (alternate) Lieutenant Colonel A.F. Volchkov, and lawyers, headed by Lieutenant General Roman Rudenko, were reserved. This was understandable, as NKVD agents, answerable to a morbidly suspicious Kremlin, monitored conversations and doings. The immediate boss, who kept his charges on tight rein, was Andrei Vyshinsky, at the time deputy foreign minister but formerly public prosecutor in the 1930s purge trials. Incidentally, both Soviet judges at Nuremberg had assisted in those undertakings, through which Stalin had liquidated the Bolshevik old guard. And Rudenko, in equally sensational trials in 1936–1938, had prosecuted Ukrainian engineers and mine administrators for their "sabotage."[23] The Anglo-American-French jurists nevertheless got on satisfactorily with their Soviet comrades.[24] All parties sought cooperation, in contrast with escalating Moscow–Washington recriminations elsewhere.[25]

East–West discord at the time pivoted on unbudging Red Army units in northern Iran, Soviet pressure on the Dardanelles, the sharing of spoils of victory in Germany, and NKVD machinations in Eastern Europe. Cumulatively these alarums encouraged the Nuremberg prisoners and their lawyers to think a Soviet–U.S. war might soon erupt.[26] Then Washington and London would, they bet, dispense with the trials and make common cause with Germans against the Soviet menace. This fleeting German hope did nothing to lift the awkwardness that marked social contact between the defense counsel and Anglo-U.S.-French lawyers and judges, however. Fourteen of the German advocates (from a total of thirty-five defense counsel) had held Nazi party membership and were disinclined to renounce it. They and other colleagues, only slightly less obdurate, repeatedly challenged the IMT's legitimacy.[27]

Crimes and punishments

The accused at Nuremberg were brought up on four charges, which were in brief as follows:

1. The defendants were involved in a conspiratorial and well-organized plan that subsumed three additional counts. In the language of the indictment: "All the defendants, with diverse other persons, during a period of years preceding 8th May 1945, participated as leaders, organizers, instigators or accomplices in the formulation or execution of a common plan or conspiracy to commit, or which involved the commission of, Crimes against Peace, War Crimes, and Crimes against Humanity."[28]

2. Crimes against peace were defined as "planning, preparation, initiation or waging of a war of aggression, or a war in violation of international treaties, agreements or assurances, or participation in a common plan or conspiracy for the accomplishment of any of the foregoing."

3. War crimes were defined as "violation of the laws or customs of war." Said violations included "murder, ill-treatment or deportation to slave labor [of POWs], killing of hostages, plunder of public or private property, wanton destruction of cities, towns or villages, or devastation not justified by military necessity."

4. Crimes against humanity were specified as "murder, extermination, enslavement, deportation, and other inhuman acts committed against any civilian population before or during the war, or persecutions on

political, racial or religious grounds in execution of or in connection with any crime within the jurisdiction of the Tribunal, whether or not in violation of domestic law of the country where perpetrated."[29]

The prosecution's case corresponded to this rough-and-ready division of labor. The Americans took the lead on the first count, the British on the second, the French on counts 3 and 4 as applied to Western Europe, and the Soviets on counts 3 and 4 as applied to the East. To the delight of men in the dock and the consternation of Soviet counsel, Churchill delivered (5 March 1946) his "iron curtain" peroration just as Rudenko finished his recital against the accused.

The German legal side mobilized several rebuttals to charges lodged against its clients: the IMT operated without precedent and amounted to an extravagant innovation in international law. The IMT was a front for the Allied military services and by its nature could produce only drumhead justice—the tribunal serving as source of new law, prosecution, judge, and jury. The IMT subverted the venerable tradition against imposition of ex post facto law.

The defense added that the waging of war was an ancient right of sovereign states, in which case the Third Reich was no guiltier than other national governments, especially those that had to make safe passage through 1930s European turbulence. Besides, no sovereign power had ever made aggressive war a crime; no universally agreed or binding definition existed of aggressive war; no penalty had ever been attached to its commission; no court had ever been convened to examine offenders. Individuals had never before been held legally accountable for deeds committed by their state. Persons who had sworn oaths of obedience to the Führer had merely complied with Third Reich law and unexceptional notions of patriotism. Finally, Soviet legality occupied an unfit position to judge German actions, given Moscow's deviation from normal standards and complicity with Berlin in 1939–1941.[30]

Not every Third Reich personage, albeit qualified in the Charter's terms, appeared in the Nuremberg courtroom. A few prospective candidates escaped via suicide during the war's last days or immediately afterward, a category that embraced not only Adolf Hitler but also Heinrich Himmler (minister of the interior) and Josef Goebbels (minister of information/propaganda). Other ranking officials mysteriously vanished, for instance Martin Bormann (head of Nazi party chancellery/secretary to the Führer) and Adolf Eichmann (head of the Gestapo's department of Jewish affairs). The industrialist Gustav Krupp, once identified by the Americans as a person of interest, was upon close investigation deemed unfit for trial because of physical-mental infirmities of old age, then dropped from the list of Nuremberg inductees. Of those people who were taken to Nuremberg, one managed to die by his own hand before the trials began: Robert Ley (minister of labor).[31]

Ultimately, twenty-two men were tried. Twelve earned the death penalty. Three were sentenced to life. Four were given prison sentences of varying lengths. Three persons were let go. On count 1, twenty-two charges had been leveled, of which eight were sustained. On count 2, sixteen charges had been leveled, of which twelve were sustained. On count 3, eighteen charges had been leveled, of which sixteen were sustained. On count 4, eighteen charges had been made, of which sixteen were sustained. See Appendix B.

The IMT also considered the alleged criminality of certain organizations under Article 10 of the Charter, which meant inter alia that an individual's membership in any of them was a chargeable offense: the Reich Cabinet, the Leadership Corps of the Nazi party, the SS including SD (intelligence agency of the SS), the Gestapo, the SA ("Brownshirts"), the General Staff and High Command of the German Armed Forces. In their final verdict, the tribunes judged that only the Reich Cabinet and General Staff were not legally culpable.

Capital punishments, done by hanging, were meted out during the wee hours of 16 October 1946. Men given terms of imprisonment were assigned to the Allied-run prison in Spandau.

Only the Soviet side offered opinions dissenting from the IMT verdicts and sentences. Favoring greater stringency, Nikitchenko reproved the acquittals of Hjalmar Schacht (economics minister, Reichsbank president), Franz von Papen (vice chancellor, ambassador to Turkey), and Hans Fritzsche (director of radio propaganda). The Soviets also protested the sparing of the life of Rudolf Hess (deputy to the Führer and once heir apparent to Hitler) and believed that the Reich Cabinet and General Staff should have been declared criminal. Stalin and Molotov were furious at IMT "leniency."[32] They had always endorsed this wish relayed by Vyshinsky in November 1945 to Western interlocutors at a Nuremberg reception: "I propose a toast to the defendants. May their paths lead straight from the courthouse to the grave!"[33]

Needless to elaborate, the foregoing synopsis does scant fairness to the range of personalities and human interest featured at Nuremberg. The parade of Nazi bigwigs filing into court riveted the attention of spectators, even though the former were as a group by then wan and devoid of swagger. While weeks turned into months, certain men stood out. Hess did by virtue of his dementia, punctured by unexpected bursts of lucidity, his contribution to Western philosophy being that National Socialism amounted to "applied biology."[34] Hermann Goering (head of Luftwaffe, designated heir to Hitler), weaned by an American medical team of his drug addiction and shed of his corpulence, had returned to mental alertness. He was articulate, unrepentant, the dominant personality among the prisoners.[35] On the stand, subject to grilling, he outwitted Justice Jackson, leaving him flustered and resentful of the bench, which he thought derelict in not better supporting him.[36] To Janet Flanner, who covered the trial for *The New Yorker*, Goering was "a brain without a conscience."[37] Field Marshal Wilhelm Keitel, obedient soldier and self-professed stoic, groused about what he regarded as inferior prison conditions, then whimpered about the disgrace of having to be hanged instead of shot by firing squad, which form of execution upheld traditional forms of military honor.[38] A prison-convert to Roman Catholicism, Hans Frank (governor-general of Poland) memorably declared in reference to the murdered Jews of Europe: "A thousand years will pass and still this guilt of Germany will not have been erased."[39] Albert Speer (head of armaments and war production), seemingly overcome by contrition, won sympathetic notice from Western jurists, thereby commencing his shrewd career in reputation salvaging. Julius Streicher (editor/publisher of *Der Stürmer*) was notable for his pornographic and anti-Semitic obsessions.[40] Other defendants sought to cling to vestiges of dignity, such as Schacht and von Papen, who protested as unwarranted their being lumped together with Nazi diehards.

Occasionally lethargic or bored, sometimes overcome by self-pity or filled with rancor against erstwhile colleagues, the defendants did not inspire pride in humanity. The Nazi catalog, meanwhile, as detailed in previously confidential Third Reich papers and depicted in German-made documentary films, upset anyone who reviewed it. Upon watching one movie clip that showed corpses of Jewish children and mounds of their belongings in Auschwitz, Fyfe thought of his youngest daughter, Miranda (b. 1939), stiffening this resolve:

When one sees children of [Miranda's] age and younger in this horrible place and the clothes of infants who were killed, it is worth a year of our lives to help register forever and with practical result the reasoned horror of humanity.[41]

Credible witnesses amplified the archival evidence. A veteran of the French resistance and survivor of German torture, Vaillant Couturier looked as if she would rip out Goering's eyes as she passed by the prisoners' dock, but for an MP who escorted her from the witness stand.[42] Rudolf Hoess, commandant at Auschwitz (May 1940–December 1943), provided the most chilling moment. When called upon by the lawyer of Ernest Kaltenbrunner (chief of security police and security services), Hoess gave a matter-of-fact account of homicidal procedures that had claimed count-less innocents, from newborns to elders.[43] "There was no end to the horrors of the testimony," Biddle later wrote.[44] Yet Nuremberg did involve brighter moments, enough to convince so unvarnished a realist as Walter Lippmann. He prophesized to his readers in June 1946 that the emergent Nuremberg principles would command future admiration comparable to that accorded to the Magna Carta, habeas corpus, and the Bill of Rights.[45] Britain's Sir Harold Nicolson,

FIGURE 2.2 Justice Robert Jackson addresses the IMT at Nuremberg

Source: U.S. National Archives

another unsentimental thinker, also credited the IMT: "The inhuman is being confronted with the humane, ruthlessness with equity, lawlessness with patient justice."[46]

Courtroom statements made by the prosecution merited this Lippmann–Nicolson praise. After rehearsing German rapacity, Shawcross spoke crisply on the need to return decency to the society of nations via respect for the sanctity of international obligations.[47] De Menthon talked incisively about Germany's past contributions to European culture, obscured but not erased by race idolatry or the elevation of bestiality to civic virtue or other "crimes against the spirit."[48] Jackson's speech of 21 November 1945 possessed equal parts indignation, invoking of standards applicable to victors and vanquished alike, and a soaring brief on behalf of natural law when existing positive law is too pinched to satisfy the moral order. He exclaimed with an eye to future generations of Americans and Europeans:

> The wrongs which we seek to condemn and punish have been so calculated, so malignant and so devastating, that civilization cannot tolerate their being ignored, because it cannot survive their being repeated. . . . The real complaining party at [the bar] is Civilization. In all our countries it is still a struggling and imperfect thing. It does not plead that the United States, or any other country, has been blameless of the conditions which made the German people easy victims to the blandishments and intimidations of the Nazi conspirators. But it points to the dreadful sequence of aggressions and crimes . . . it points to the weariness of flesh, the exhaustion of resources, and the destruction of all that was beautiful or useful in so much of the world, and to greater potentialities for destruction in the days to come . . . to start or wage an aggressive war has the moral qualities of the worst of crimes. The refuge of the defendants can be only their hope that International Law will lag so far behind the moral sense of mankind that conduct which is crime in the moral sense must be regarded as innocent in law. Civilization asks whether law is so laggard as to be utterly helpless to deal with crimes of this magnitude by criminals of this order of importance. It does not expect that [right judgment at Nuremberg] can make war impossible. It does expect that [right] judicial action will put the forces of International Law, its prospects, its prohibitions and, most of all, its sanctions, on the side of peace.[49]

Criticisms and doubts

Nuremberg in 1946 made some Americans cringe. They held that Jackson's verbal artistry and jurisprudential acrobatics—those of Shawcross and de Menthon too—could not possibly exonerate the IMT enterprise.

Prominent lawyers and politicians numbered among the denigrators.[50] The Supreme Court's chief justice, Harlan Stone, derided Jackson's undertaking as a "lynching expedition," embroidered by sanctimony.[51] Justice William O. Douglas, also of the Supreme Court, believed the IMT substituted power for principle. He professed to see in Jackson's zeal evidence of ambition to win elected office and the currying of favor with Jewish voters.[52] To Senator Robert Taft, Nuremberg represented the application of retroactivity and pulsed with instincts antithetical to impartial justice. The trappings of legality were observed, he told an audience at Kenyon College in 1946, but not the substance: the verdicts were fixed in advance and contrary to existing codes and protocols of punishment (*nullum crimen sine lege, nulla poena sine lege*). He disparaged the IMT proceedings as overly determined theater, consonant with ancient shabbiness—condemning defeated parties for varieties of turpitude.[53] Some mainstream publications, including *Fortune* magazine, and Robert McCormick's Chicago *Tribune*, as well as the syndicated columnist Westbrook Pegler, agreed with Taft.

Restrained by custom from giving public comment, senior army and naval officers, among them General Eisenhower and Admiral William Leahy, were nevertheless discomfited by Nuremberg. They were particularly bothered that the IMT condemned their German equivalents for adhering to the soldier's universal duty: obedience to orders.[54]

Just how, other U.S. servicemen wondered aloud, would contingent security plans appear to persons outside the Pentagon's walls? Justice Jackson, upon visiting the National War College (NWC) in December 1946, was peppered with hard-hitting questions from students (promotion-bound field-grade military officers): "Is it a crime to make plans to defend the United States against attack?" Alluding to arguments by defense counsel at Nuremberg along the logic of preemptive war, one student pressed with this: "Would the right of self-defense include the right to attack another country if we believed that the other country was preparing to attack us?" Asked another anxious NWC officer: "How may I know what makes a war one of aggression?" Still another student queried:

Decisions as to war or peace are usually made by the political branches of Government, so I am wondering whether merely helping to make military plans for the conduct of a war becomes a crime if those who are in authority later declare or engage in a war which may be considered one of aggression.

To these concerns, Jackson spoke reassuringly. Yet doubts persisted. Many NWC students (and faculty) felt that their German counterparts had been treated unfairly, without regard to mitigating circumstance: their subordinate status within the Third Reich's hierarchy. Had the Allies lost the war, might their ranking officers have wound up in a courtroom administered by Axis judges and required to justify severe operations against Germany, a country surrounded by enemies and outnumbered? And how, should such a theoretical possibility ever materialize, would Soviet judges likely evaluate Anglo-U.S. commanders in the event of their defeat in World War III?[55]

Critics were also unsettled by Soviet representation at Nuremberg. That the Soviets, bolstered by Western acquiescence, had succeeded in preventing certain topics from being reviewed by the IMT did not obviate their gravity. The Berlin–Moscow pact had allowed the Wehrmacht to master continental Europe in 1939–1941. The USSR's record during that period suggested that Moscow officials had authorized crimes comparable to those charged against Berlin: Red Army invasion of Poland in September 1939, aggressive 1939–1940 war against Finland, absorption of the Baltic republics (Estonia, Latvia, Lithuania), suspected massacre of Polish military officers at Katyn forest, wholesale mistreatment of German and other Axis POWs contra the Hague and Geneva conventions.[56] To this litany, skeptics added that what passed for justice inside the USSR was tarnished by the Stalinist show trials and the Siberian penal system. Meanwhile, plain to Western analysts in 1945–1946, the civilian population in the Soviet zone of Germany endured afflictions aplenty as marauding Red Army soldiers pillaged and murdered.[57]

Even the oral presentations of Rudenko at Nuremberg raised questions. In contrast to the precise language of his Western colleagues, his rhetoric belonged to an alien jurisprudence. He referred to "Hitlerite brigands," "hangmen" endowed with "the morals of cannibals and the greed of burglars," "cutthroats," "German barbarians."[58] Predictably, averred critics, the Soviets at Nuremberg dissented from the granting of acquittals, the recognition of gradations of guilt, or moderation in the sentencing of Hess and others. Albeit wholly committed to his Nuremberg duty, Dodd confided to his wife in July 1946:

> Everything—and I mean everything—that we have charged the
> Germans with in this case has been done, and worse, is being done
> by Russia. . . . They are terrorizing all of Eastern Europe. . . . The
> Achilles heel of this great trial is the Russian participation in it.[59]

Dissenting scholars at the time included the Protestant theologian
Reinhold Niebuhr. He warned that the trials could only further depress
the Germans; they were in desperate need of moral uplift, not fresh censure
by peoples possessed of retributive compulsion and wielding absolute power
over a prostrate nation. He regretted that the Allies allowed themselves to
be judges in their own case.[60] Robert Maynard Hutchins, legal expert and
president of the University of Chicago, thought that the United States,
hobbled by its legacies of bigotry and lynching, had long since forfeited the
ethical authority to judge at Nuremberg.[61] How much better the trial should
have been, added still others, were it administered by judges from countries
neutral in 1939–1945, and were the victors subjected to scrutiny as rigorous
as that applied to the humbled Germans. In this vein, doubters posed these
questions: How would unbiased international law have evaluated British
plans (canceled in the event) to invade Norway in 1940 to preempt the
Germans? How about the American-led invasion of French North Africa
in 1942, at a time when Washington maintained diplomatic relations with
Marshal Pétain's Vichy regime? How might the law have viewed the U.S.
bombing of Romanian oil fields in 1943, when Washington was technically
at peace with Bucharest? In sum, the trial dishonored core concepts of
Anglo-U.S. legality and rested on a double standard.

Other reservationists counted the political scientist Hans Morgenthau.
This avatar of "realism" held that German leaders had by their monstrous
deeds lost rights to due process; justice demanded the execution forthwith
of ringleaders. The diplomat George Kennan, unhappy with what he later
identified (in 1951) as the "legalistic-moralistic approach to international
problems," would have preferred to dispense with Nuremberg, in which
case Nazi leaders ought to have been summarily shot.[62]

Even though Jewish opinion in the United States supported the IMT,
discontent did bubble to the surface. Editorial writers in Jewish news media,
prominent rabbis too, criticized the acquittals of Schacht, von Papen, and
Fritzsche. Penalties that demanded less than capital punishment generated
puzzlement. There was also incredulity that the tribunal, inconsistent with
other findings involved with crimes against humanity, chose not to punish

the defendants for persecution of minorities unless related to the waging of aggressive war; in effect, the agony of prewar German Jewry went unremarked by the IMT. In later years, Elie Wiesel, Nobel peace laureate and Shoah survivor, was stupefied to learn that Nuremberg paid less attention to the German assault on European Jewry than to Berlin's waging of offensive warfare.[63]

Despite these many and varied objections, U.S. opinion polls in 1945–1946 indicated overall approval (around 75 percent) of the IMT.[64] It seemed compatible with concurrent denazification programs, the conviction of thousands of German officials by Anglo-French authorities, and arraignments of people in victimized nations (for instance, Hoess convicted in a Polish court). This support, even as public interest gradually waned, buttressed the second round of Nuremberg trials, November 1946–April 1949, whose principles and procedures derived from the preceding assize. Held under exclusive U.S. supervision, the trials were presided over by thirty-two jurists of uneven competence recruited from the United States (state supreme courts, law school deans, practicing attorneys). Telford Taylor led the prosecution.[65]

Second Nuremberg Trials

Operating under Control Council Law Number Ten of 20 December 1945, the Nuremberg Military Tribunals (NMT) involved twelve sets of charges against 185 defendants and heard testimony from 1,300 witnesses. These trials were no less dramatic than the IMT. They were also important for the development of international criminal law and equally astonishing for what they revealed of Hitler's Germany.

The Medical Case centered on Nazi doctors and scientists accused of conducting experiments on concentration camp inmates and supervising euthanasia programs. The Milch Case scrutinized forced labor practice and human experiments at Dachau. The Justice Case involved abuses by senior Third Reich jurists. The Pohl Case investigated SS officers who administered concentration camps and used slave labor in various economic schemes. The Flick Case dealt with "aryanization" by industrialists of Jewish property and their employment of forced labor. The I.G. Farben Case explored offenses committed by leaders of a chemical conglomeration against slave laborers and with advocating aggressive war plans. The Hostages Case probed the mistreatment by defendants of civilians in

FIGURE 2.3 Telford Taylor, front on right, and his staff at the NMT

Source: U.S. National Archives

southeastern Europe, including the killing of hostages and reprisal murders. In the RuSHA Case, members of the SS Race and Settlement Office were connected to policies of forced evacuation, "Germanization," and "racial reorganization" in German-occupied countries. The Einsatzgruppen Case investigated SS defendants charged with the killing of racial and political "undesirables." The Krupp Case examined directors from Krupp and their use of slave labor and aid to Nazi war planning. The Ministries Case took aim against figures from the foreign office and other departments who helped design the Third Reich's "New Order" in Europe, which, said the indictment, also meant crimes against peace and humanity. In the High Command Case, top Wehrmacht officers were accused of atrocities against civilians in occupied territories and against POWs (as at Malmedy in December 1944), and the devising of aggression.

Like the IMT, the NMT recognized gradations of individual responsibility and foreswore notions of collective guilt while aiding the denazification policy. The NMT likewise produced a range of verdicts, punishments, and acquittals. Thirty-five defendants were cleared of legal, if not moral, culpability. Another nineteen were released on miscellaneous grounds. Capital punishment was imposed on twenty-four defendants. Twenty received life imprisonment. Eighty-seven received jail terms of varying length.[66]

To its critics, the NMT amounted to yet another misconceived undertaking, most regrettable in the context of a looming Soviet threat. Congressman George Dondero (R, Michigan) and Senator William Langer (R, North Dakota) were among the outspoken. They claimed that left-wingers, intent on undermining capitalism and the military profession, ran the NMT "charade," with gratuitous damage to German resuscitation and U.S. safety.[67] Congressman John Rankin (D, Mississippi) argued that the NMT amounted to a Jewish-orchestrated "Saturnalia of persecution," driven by a disloyal religious minority in America against a traumatized nation in need of sympathetic understanding.[68]

Unlike Dondero, Langer, or Rankin, John McCloy, U.S. high commissioner for Germany in 1949–1952, occupied a position to implement his objection to the NMT. McCloy pursued a species of radical clemency, justifiable he felt to ensure the rehabilitation of Konrad Adenauer's Federal Republic of Germany and its integration into the Western coalition.[69] To the gratification of German petitioners, McCloy paroled sixty convicted war criminals in 1949.[70] Many more followed. During the Korean War, he commuted the sentence—twelve years and forfeiture of real estate and personal property—of Alfried Krupp (son of Gustav). A wholehearted Nazi since his early twenties, he had been convicted of war crimes and crimes against humanity related to plunder and the Krupp firm's reliance on slave labor.[71] Following the restitution of his liberty and possessions, Alfried returned to the family business and the manufacturing of weaponry, thenceforth used to stock NATO arsenals. *Time* magazine pictured him on its cover in 1957 and identified him as one of the wealthiest men in the world. McCloy also reduced the sentences of, or paroled altogether, doctors who had conducted experiments on concentration camp prisoners. He did the same for incarcerated Einsatzgruppen officers, Nazi judges, and the industrialist Friedrich Flick. Had McCloy his druthers, he would have liked an Allied commission to grant reprieves for Hess and Speer in Spandau, a suggestion odious to the Soviets, who vetoed it.

Exponents of the NMT, such as Churchill and Shawcross, disapproved of McCloy's amnesties for going too far. The eminent Cambridge University legal theorist Hersch Lauterpacht, who had defined crimes against humanity in the IMT Charter, railed against the indignity done to millions of victims by the release of convicted Nazi killers.[72] (The murdered included Lauterpacht's parents, siblings, and most of their children, all of whom had resided in Poland.) As for Telford Taylor, he charged that McCloy's actions had rendered his efforts superfluous; he called the commutations misguided, born of imprudent political calculation.[73] Commiserating with Taylor, Jackson grumbled: "The policy of winning German support against Communists by releasing Nazis, goes on apace. Apart from the matter of principle, I cannot help but doubt the expediency of giving so dramatic a demonstration for propaganda uses."[74] Had Jackson (d. 1954) lived long enough, he would have been further disquieted when in 1958 the last NMT offender was released from detention in Landsberg Prison.[75]

Tokyo

As in Europe, Japanese civilian and military leaders were charged with trespass and cruelty. These counts were leveled before the International Military Tribunal for the Far East (IMTFE) in Tokyo, which ran from 3 May 1946 to 4 November 1948. Twenty-two hundred national courts— Soviet, American, Chinese, Dutch, Australian, British, Australian, French, Filipino—and military commissions also met to review "B" and "C" war crimes cases brought by Allied prosecutors.[76] A majority of Americans accepted, as with Nuremberg, the East Asian/Pacific trials as credible.

Still, some people at the time (and many more since) doubted the legitimacy of what was done, an example being the October–December 1945 trial in Manila of General Yamashita Tomoyuki. A U.S. military commission held him derelict for failing to exercise command responsibility as Japanese soldiers in Manila and environs went on a rampage during the closing violence of World War II. This culminated in thousands of fatalities and rape victims. Yamashita was hanged on 23 February 1946, General Douglas MacArthur, America's senior Army officer in the Pacific, having confirmed the findings and sentencing.

The proceedings were a miscarriage of justice, freighted with reflexive retribution, said two Supreme Court justices, Douglas Murphy and Wiley Blount Rutledge. They were persuaded by this line: Compelled by invading forces to retreat to a remote mountain redoubt in northern Luzon, his means of communication with subordinates in Manila severed by relentless U.S.

military action, Yamashita at the critical time had neither knowledge of the outrages suffered by Filipino civilians and POWs nor the ability to stop them. He had not ordered or condoned the mayhem.[77] One American Army attorney, A. Frank Reel, who served on Yamashita's defense counsel, excoriated the trial as hurried and irregular. It mocked Allied ideals: "Having fought and won a war against totalitarianism . . . we could have shown the world just what we meant. Instead of that, we fell to the level of our enemies. We adopted their judicial techniques."[78] Of the subsequent IMTFE proceeding, Douglas declared that it too lacked fairness and due deliberation.[79]

Like the Nuremberg trials, the Tokyo tribunal detailed charges of conspiracy, crimes against peace, war crimes, and crimes against humanity. A bench composed of eleven judges met at the Tokyo headquarters (Ichigaya) of the Japanese army. The court president, appointed by General MacArthur, was Australia's irascible Sir William Webb, chief justice of the Queensland Supreme Court. Jurists from Allied states recently at war with Japan joined Webb. In addition to Australia and the USA, these were Canada, China, France, India, the Netherlands, New Zealand, the Philippines, the UK, the USSR.[80] President Truman selected a stud poker chum as the chief prosecutor: tipsy and mercurial Joseph Keenan, assistant attorney general in charge of the Justice Department's Criminal Division at the time of appointment. His mismanagement of the prosecutorial team resulted in disorganization and a number of well-publicized resignations.[81] His interrogation of General Tojo Hideki was inept, worse than Jackson's fumbled examination of Goering at Nuremberg.[82]

More than four hundred witnesses testified at the IMTFE. Nearly eight hundred affidavits were submitted; 4,300 exhibits were run. This was conducted through the haze of translations (English, Japanese, Chinese, Russian, French), diverse legal traditions, and aggravated in summer months by smothering heat and drenching humidity—all played against the backdrop of bombed Tokyo ruins.[83] Upon first viewing the city, Keenan, who enjoyed his creature comforts in Japan, confessed to an acquaintance: "The area of Tokyo is demolished beyond my power of description."[84] Each day, roughly 1,000 people entered the courtroom, a company that included not only judges/lawyers and the accused (housed at Sugamo prison) but also representatives of the world press, banks of translators, and U.S. Army guards.[85]

FIGURE 2.4 General Tojo and guard at the IMTFE

Source: U.S. National Archives

Twenty-eight once exalted Japanese figures, categorized as class A war criminals, were charged, the most prominent of whom was Tojo. A mix of Japanese and American lawyers defended them. As at Nuremberg, not all the Tokyo defendants survived the trial. Before its termination, Matsuoka Yosuke, formerly foreign minister, and the naval minister Admiral Nagano Osami died from natural causes. The nationalist theoretician Okawa Shumei was declared mentally unfit to stand trial, then committed to psychiatric care.

The remaining defendants provoked the scorn of Keenan. Except Tojo, whom he grudgingly respected, Keenan thought the defendants "craven or snarling. They lie like pirates and give childish explanations and denials of matters that are proven beyond peradventure through Japanese documents, some of which they compiled."[86] None of the defendants was found innocent. All were sentenced either to death or prison. See Appendix C.

Whereas Soviet tribunes at Nuremberg signaled unhappiness with putative leniency, several IMTFE judges thought the verdicts and sentencing excessive. The Philippines judge, Delfin Jaranilla, once a victim of Japanese incarceration and survivor of the Bataan "death march," did hold that numerous defendants got overly light treatment. But Webb in contrast wondered—in a separately filed opinion—about the deterrent effect of capital punishment, was unconvinced about the basis in international law of "naked conspiracy," and questioned the absence of Emperor Hirohito while a collection of his minions sat in the dock. The Dutch judge, B.V.A. Roling, believed that Baron Hirota Koki (prime minister) was guiltless and should have been spared the death penalty. Roling also felt that Field Marshal Hata Shunroku (war minister), Marquis Kido Koichi (Lord Keeper of the Privy Seal), and Shigemitsu Mamoru (foreign minister) should have been cleared. The French judge, Henri Bernard, fired that the IMTFE was so procedurally erratic that it could not possibly pass responsible judgment. Like Webb, Bernard was troubled by that immunity from prosecution enjoyed by Hirohito.[87]

Most controversial was the Indian judge, Radhabinod Pal, who reasoned on behalf of the Japanese defendants and thought their treatment at Tokyo suffused in ex post facto legislation. On every charge, the men should have been acquitted, he stated.[88] Sound evidence had not been adduced to support a case of Japanese conspiracy from the late 1920s onward to wage aggressive wars.[89] Nor did Pal believe that Japanese forces had with premeditated malice, or systematically, committed atrocities beyond the admittedly regrettable but usual run of such happenings that mark all wars. In the case of 1937 Nanjing, he was not persuaded by what he read as "distortions and exaggerations" produced by "excited" and "prejudiced observers."[90] He asserted too that use of atomic bombs against Hiroshima and Nagasaki qualified as monumental atrocity; this instance of "indiscriminate destruction of civilian life" belonged to a category of methods preferred by Nazi Berlin.[91] In dropping atomic bombs, he contended, Americans had denied themselves any right to judge persons who against white imperialism had resorted to defensive war, provoked in the first place by Allied economic sanctions and building of Pacific fortifications, as at Pearl Harbor. Pal's denunciation of what he called the victor nations' "pretense of legal justice," pursuit of "vindictive retaliation," and hypocrisy eventuated in his lauding by latter-day Japanese nationalists. A commemorative memorial in his honor was erected in 2005 at the Yasukuni war shrine.[92]

★ ★ ★

Few Japanese closely followed the IMTFE or other Asian courtrooms in which former leaders were prosecuted. Those people who did monitor the trials found little that was instructive beyond this jaded wisdom: *Vae victis* ("Woe to the vanquished").[93] A surgeon at the Red Cross Hospital in Hiroshima who had treated hundreds of atomic bomb victims, Terufumi Sasaki, meditated: "I see that they are holding a trial for war criminals in Tokyo just now. I think they ought to try the men who decided to use the bomb and they should hang them all."[94]

To a people absorbed with finding ways to survive in a land controlled by foreign occupiers, the IMTFE seemed remote.[95] People were quietly pleased when, after the 1951 Japanese peace treaty and the U.S.–Japan security alliance were adopted, detained men were paroled, a measure of Washington's new regard for Tokyo premised on Cold War need.[96] Similarly, in Germany, most citizens were not attentive to the Nuremberg proceedings or related other trials. The minority who had the temperamental wherewithal to follow them was not, in any event, inclined to ascribe all blame to the Axis and every virtue to the Allies, especially given the predatory nature of Red Army occupation, the influx of millions of harried German expellees—from Poland, Czechoslovakia, Hungary, Romania—and German ruins. Besides, the ghastly images and testimonies produced at the IMT initially struck many Germans as fantastical inventions of Allied propaganda.[97] Collective awareness among Germans of the viciousness enacted in their name did not quicken until the 1960s, with the trial of Eichmann in Jerusalem (1961) and the Auschwitz trials (1963–1965).[98] Before then, only a minority, which counted the Heidelberg philosopher Karl Jaspers, detected in the IMT signs of reborn morality or admitted to anything worthwhile at Nuremberg.[99]

Not just from the standpoint of hard-pressed survivors in Germany and Japan or contemporaneous critics but also from a twenty-first-century perspective the case for the Nuremberg/Tokyo inquests is difficult to make. The taint of retroactive law was not satisfactorily removed, not even by Justice Jackson's heroic effort.[100] Even if one accepts the 1928 Kellogg–Briand outlawry of war as constituting positive law against which the Axis powers rebelled, even if one suspends skepticism to allow that a workable definition of aggressive war actually existed in the World War II era, even if one accepts that Anglo-American conceptions of conspiracy as applied in domestic law have wider applicability, even if one excuses the sometimes hasty choosing of defendants (exemplified by the Gustav Krupp confusion), and makes allowance for the rush to judgment of Yamashita and the racialist assumptions that tinged that officer's trial as regrettable but understandable functions of wartime passion, one must still pause.[101]

Most disturbing in retrospect, as to critics at the time, is the fact that Soviet lawyers and judges at the IMT evaluated German actions that paralleled ones taken by Stalin's government. Apart from those noted above, these included the mounting of unprovoked war against Japan in 1945 (contra the 1941 Tokyo–Moscow pact), the annexing of Romania's Bukovina, and the terrorizing or deporting of millions of unarmed civilians in Eastern Europe. Indeed, the Soviet presence, as Dodd recognized, threatened to impeach the IMT as a travesty of justice. This despite the earnestness with which Jackson and other principals had approached their tasks or the moral and practical impossibility of excluding Moscow jurists from Nuremberg, Allied victory having been won at astronomical cost to Soviet lives and treasure.

The silence of the Nuremberg/Tokyo tribunals on the saturation bombing of cities (and unrestricted submarine warfare) is also disquieting, even if taken for practical reason, namely to prevent the defendants from mobilizing *tu quoque* arguments. As eagerly waged by the Allies as by the Axis, and to more devastating effect, the aerial war against cities claimed hundreds of thousands of civilian casualties in Germany and Japan. The Anglo-U.S. air campaigns, like those conducted by the Axis, ignored distinctions between combatant and noncombatant, between legitimate and illegitimate targets, and exacted levels of "collateral damage" that made nonsense of any "double effect" defense but belonged to long-defined categories of criminality. "It is difficult to contest the judgment that Dresden and Nagasaki were war crimes," said Telford Taylor years after the war, despite his willingness to accept the leveling of those cities as "tolerable in retrospect only because their malignancy pales in comparison to Dachau, Auschwitz and Treblinka."[102] The main point stands, however. Judgment was withheld at Nuremberg and Tokyo on one of the war's reprehensible stratagems.

Other dubiousness also hurt the Tokyo/Nuremberg attempt to stamp the Allied war with unalloyed righteousness. The absence of German/ Japanese judges and ones from neutral countries (say, Switzerland or Sweden) undercut the trials' claims to scrupulousness—as did the decision not to hold trials in a neutral setting (say, Geneva or Stockholm). Instead, the victorious powers tried the defeated in territories held by the Allies whose own dirty hands were protected from inspection. Nothing was allowed against the accusers, whose license to prosecute might have been inhibited by reference to atomic bombs, Soviet diplomacy, or Red Army misbehavior. Roling made the point succinctly: "The defense counsel [at Nuremberg and Tokyo] were forbidden . . . to mention the war crimes which were committed by the countries sitting in judgment."[103]

Omissions related to the gathering Cold War further sullied the claim of the tribunals to fairness. On MacArthur's authority, Japanese medical practitioners in Surgeon General Ishii Shiro's Unit 731 in Manchuria, which had experimented upon thousands of captive Chinese to determine the effect of biological weapons, were spared from prosecution. The assumption was that the findings of Unit 731 would benefit U.S. medical science and military technology. This consideration trumped all else—a viewpoint, incidentally, in line with the ongoing Tuskegee syphilis study conducted (1932–1972) on African American sharecroppers by the U.S. Public Health Service and experiments conducted (1946–1948) by that same agency on Guatemalan prisoners and mental patients, deliberately infected with venereal diseases.[104]

More than 1,600 German scientists and engineers received immunity (Operation Paperclip) in exchange for data generated by their work. Rocket experts, not least Werner von Braun (SS officer) and Arthur Rudolph (SA member), were brought to the United States to work on defense projects. This exemption from indictment was obtained despite previous Braun/ Rudolph work that had employed thousands of slave laborers forced to live in appalling conditions, where rates of mortality leapt high. Moreover, thousands of former high-ranking Nazi officials, whose wartime activity connected them to heinousness, were recruited into the counter-intelligence agencies of the United States, Great Britain, and France. Western intelligence services actually smuggled potentially useful "assets" into Latin

America for safekeeping, while these same people were tracked by Allied teams to bring them to trial.[105]

Finally, the Nuremberg/Tokyo exercise did little to slow the great powers from doing as they wanted in the decades after World War II. The main judging nations conspicuously deviated from the anti-aggression principle espoused by their representatives at the IMT and IMTFE. French colonial wars in Indochina and Algeria, the 1956 Anglo-French invasion of Egypt, the Soviet crushing of liberation movements in 1956 Hungary and 1968 Czechoslovakia, the 1979 Soviet incursion into Afghanistan, and U.S. ventures in Southeast Asia, Latin America, and the Middle East were indefensible by Nuremberg and Tokyo standards, as well as undeterred by them. (On such episodes, more in Chapter 5.)

Yet however glaring the deficiencies—however the Allies strayed from principles they once grandly commended—Nuremberg, Tokyo, and the rest were good enough. They were useful for helping to salvage—redemption far beyond their power—the postwar moment, as when in December 1946 the UN General Assembly affirmed the principles of the IMT as international law.[106] Moreover, as Stimson had supposed, the trials did qualify (eventually, at least) as ethical and historical edification. Justice Jackson and Telford Taylor had themselves during the war viewed tales of German outrage with reserve. But their incredulity vanished as they encountered incontrovertible evidence that convicted Nazism of immeasurable evil.[107] These words of Lord Kilmuir, published in 1964, are still apt:

There is in each of us a sundial facet of our mentality. We are inclined only to count the sunny hours. Moreover, after exhausting wars men tend to suffer from a weariness of mind. This lassitude can make them shrink from facing the limitations of human nature. It can produce a facile skepticism about their evil deeds. New generations dislike reading the history of gas chambers, and so the fact that men claiming to be civilized put millions to death in the gas chambers slips from history. Further, every devil has his advocate. We have seen apologists for everything. It is, therefore, just as well that in respect of Nazi war crimes the apologist of the future will be confronted by the admissions of the many accused found guilty, and the mass of incriminating documents produced at the trials, whose authority had been established by the very men who wrote them. Both devil and advocate are faced by an unscalable barrier of truth.[108]

The retailing in Far Eastern hearings of extreme Japanese misbehavior, from 1937 Nanjing onward, was equally important in building reliable accounts based on facts. These have continued to confound deniers and apologists.

Nor did Nuremberg and Tokyo amount to sham justice whereby defendants were browbeaten by shrill prosecutors, harassed by unrestrained judges, or forbidden from explaining themselves. In contrast with Nazi (or Stalinist) legal practice, both tribunals allowed for acquittals, degrees of guilt, and calibrated penalties. By concentrating on specific Axis individuals, the Allies also resisted the seductive but destructive idea of attributing collective guilt to all Germans and Japanese, which if done would have made less feasible the rehabilitation of these two peoples and their return to respectable place in global society.[109]

What is most striking from a long-term perspective about the trials is that the sovereign state's prerogative and presumption were forthrightly contested. The state as cold monster (Friedrich Nietzsche's term) was, if not tamed, at least forced to acknowledge a countervailing concept rooted in cosmopolitanism conducive to community and moral maturity. In regard to statesmen, this upheld claims of responsibility superior to national or other parochial loyalties. For military officers, it meant that compliance with orders could no longer constitute a sufficient defense. In the IMT's language: "Individuals have international duties which transcend the national obligations of obedience imposed by the individual state."[110]

The Allied participants at Nuremberg and Tokyo consciously built upon philosophical foundations set by just war theorists: Augustine, Thomas Aquinas, Francisco de Vitoria, Francisco Suarez. Allied jurists drew upon and elaborated the achievements of international law advocates: Hugo Grotius, Emmerich de Vattel. Ideas advanced by the proponents of laws of war, including America's own Francis Lieber, were additionally refined upon. Further, the sanctity of modern multilateral agreements was reconfirmed—of the kind associated with The Hague in 1899 and 1907, Paris in 1928, and Geneva in 1929. In surpassing them, the Nuremberg and Tokyo trials created usable precedent while advancing an outlook based on minimally defined humane standards and the inadmissibility of aggressive war. World politics thus nudged past the degradations of World War II to create, as Jackson once phrased the matter, a wall against civilization again losing control itself.[111] As investments in the moral environment, the IMT and IMTFE were defensible, if hardly perfect. The international tribunals that in subsequent decades passed judgment on events in Rwanda, Yugoslavia, Sierra Leone, Cambodia—plus the establishment in July 2002 of the International Criminal Court—built on Nuremberg/Tokyo and continued to implicate justice with manipulations of power.[112]

Moreover, critics of post-World War II American foreign policy have periodically reminded audiences of pronouncements made by Jackson: codes and proper axioms pertaining to the start or conduct of wars apply to the United States as to other powers.[113] To dissenters, a disastrous infraction occurred during the 1960s with Washington's Indochina intervention. They responded by enlisting Nuremberg's outlawry of aggressive war to discredit U.S. policy. The war crimes "trial" held in 1967 in Stockholm and Copenhagen, promoted by Bertrand Russell (honorary president) and Jean-Paul Sartre (executive president), found that the United States and its partners—Australia, New Zealand, South Korea—had committed aggression against Vietnam, indulged in unconscionable bombardment of civilian targets (hospitals, schools, dams), recklessly rained napalm and herbicides on the country, and mistreated POWs, all in accordance with the logic of mercenary capitalism. Russell pronounced: "Nazism emerged from a nation unable to stabilize itself and degenerated to unforeseen limits of depravity. The policy of aggression in Washington has brought a comparable degree of scientific extermination and moral degeneracy."[114] Dissenters, including Telford Taylor, cited the Yamashita case as basis to investigate senior U.S. military officers (Generals William Westmoreland, Creighton Abrams) for the My Lai massacre and dereliction of duty in command responsibility.[115] Father Robert Drinan, the Jesuit dean of Boston College Law School, exclaimed that antiwar demonstrators on university campuses were duty bound by Nuremberg's precepts to protest.[116]

The shadow cast by the post-World War II tribunals has reached into the twenty-first century. Thomas Dodd's son, Senator Christopher Dodd (D, Connecticut), unhappy with the turn taken by the so-called war on terror, charged in 2007 that the relaxation of prohibitions on torture, use of "renditions," and resort to sequestered detention facilities amounted to reversals of rectitude:

> If, for sixty years, a single word, *Nuremberg*, has best captured America's moral authority and commitment to justice, unfortunately, another word now captures the loss of such authority and commitment:

> *Guantanamo.* . . . In a mockery of justice, we lock away terrorism suspects for years and give them no real day in court. We deny the lessons of Nuremberg, of universal rights to justice.[117]

To this, in words that he had used decades earlier, Jackson would surely have added that Washington must shun temptations born of haste or fear that "would not sit [well] on the American conscience or be remembered by our children with pride."[118]

One can also imagine Jackson's likely response to findings in a December 2014 report by the Senate Intelligence Committee, headed by Dianne Feinstein (D, California). These detailed post-9/11 CIA techniques approved at highest Washington levels: waterboarding, rectal rehydration, walling. Consistent with such revelations, Eric Fair, former interrogator at Abu Graib, said the following, unselfconsciously expanding upon Jackson on the penalty paid for abandoning Nuremberg tenets:

> I was an interrogator at Abu Graib. I tortured. . . . In some future college classroom, a professor will require her students to read about things this country did in the early years of the 21st century. She'll assign portions of the Senate torture report. . . . There will be essays and writing assignments. The students will come to know that this country isn't always something to be proud of.[119]

★ ★ ★

3

HUMANITY

When will our consciences grow so tender that we will act to prevent human misery rather than avenge it?[1]

Eleanor Roosevelt, 16 February 1946

★ ★ ★

Adopted in the anxious watches of the Cold War night, both the Convention on the Prevention and Punishment of the Crime of Genocide and the Universal Declaration of Human Rights originated in the experience of 1937–1945 warfare. The UN General Assembly, by approving these two documents in December 1948, challenged the presumption of sovereign state reason and promoted an alternative. The human person, in collective and private life, was deemed—momentarily by concession of diverse national regimes—to have rights rooted in inalienable dignity and intrinsic worth that existed prior to the state and were independent of anything conferred in its gift. What had, in effect, been advanced in the Nuremberg/Tokyo tribunals against the untouchable state was further extended. In the case of exterminating states, exemplified by Nazi Germany, they would thenceforth find no security, at least in theory, but would live under censure and sanction.

The redoubtable Raphael Lemkin was decisive in formulating the Genocide Convention, then in urging its passage by the General Assembly. He coined the neologism *genocide*.[2] The Universal Declaration, by contrast, was a composite document, conceived and drafted in committee, chaired by the widow of FDR, Eleanor Roosevelt. Sometimes celebrated, other times traduced, Lemkin and the former First Lady sponsored, albeit separately and in opposition, ideas that dominated the postwar human rights moment. They live still in legal and ethical thought.

Genocide: the word

The preoccupation of Lemkin with the extinction of groups via violence arose during his youth. Born in 1900 to a Jewish farming family, he was reared in the Russian zone of partitioned Poland, subject to pogroms and otherwise layered in latent danger. To this background was added the weight of Armenian reports upon his thinking, first as an adolescent, then while a student (philology, law) at the University of Lwow, where he decided that state sovereignty could not justify the killing of innocents.[3] Later, despite professional success—practicing attorney, public prosecutor, prolific author, law professor—in interwar Poland, he endured anti-Semitic taunts and edicts. Then, during the Shoah, Lemkin suffered searing loss: his parents and more than forty members of his extended family perished (Treblinka).[4] He thereafter crusaded for the legal protection of existentially threatened peoples.[5]

Some commentators before Lemkin had despaired of normal language to categorize instances of catastrophe meted out by victimizers. Theodore Roosevelt in 1916 decried Turkish acts against the Armenian population as so gruesome that they defied words.[6] In similar fashion in August 1941, Churchill reported on Nazi doings in Soviet territories invaded by the Wehrmacht. These beggared available vocabulary: "We are in the presence of a crime without a name."[7]

Several pre-Lemkin critics did grope or experiment with the puzzle of naming. Reviewing their country's African colonial wars, German writers spoke of *Volkermord*: "murder of a nation."[8] Woodrow Wilson's ambassador to Constantinople, Henry Morgenthau (senior), referred to Armenian suffering in the Ottoman empire as "race murder." Franz Werfel in his estimable *The Forty Days of Musa Dagh* called this same the "extirpation" of a people.[9] Ukrainians labeled Stalin's killer famine (1932–1933) with its millions of victims the *holodomor*: "hunger extermination."

British prosecutors in the 1945–1946 International Military Tribunal (IMT) did refer to *genocide*, but only hesitantly and inconsistently. Unsurprisingly, they failed to press or win convictions with it. Nor did the tribunes in their final judgment directly mention *genocide*.[10] Telford Taylor at the subsequent Nuremberg Military Tribunal (NMT), though familiar with Lemkin and his terminology, was not fully confident about the legal standing of *genocide* or its wider implications.[11] Consequently, Taylor sometimes used other language to denote German programs: for example, thanatology, "the science of producing death."[12] Nevertheless, a number of NMT defendants (in the RuSHA Case) were convicted of genocide when it involved German military aggression, the first ever such judgment.[13] Despite a shaky start, *genocide* did seep into usage—not only at Nuremberg but elsewhere too, as when Poland's Supreme National Tribunal used the term against Auschwitz's Rudolf Hoess and accused other senior figures, Arthur Greiser and Amon Goeth, of launching genocidal assault upon the Polish nation.[14]

Albeit less frequently used or approved than he desired, Lemkin read the deployment of *genocide* in Nuremberg and Poland as partial vindication.[15] Like other people, he had struggled to create language apposite to communal homicide. Years before he devised (1943) *genocide*, he had championed a resolution at the International Conference for the Unifi-cation of Criminal Penal Law—convened October 1933 in Madrid—to approve condign punishment for *barbarism* and *vandalism*. The expunging by violence or economic discrimination of ethnic, social, and religious groups constituted *barbarism*, he said. He defined *vandalism* as the obliterating of those customs-traditions and cultural-artistic monuments (archives, churches, museums, literature) that embodied a people's creativity or legacy, often entailing too the physical demolition of the society's cultural bearing stratum. Lemkin contended that instances of *barbarism* and *vandalism*—vivid against a backdrop of refugees fleeing the Third Reich, mounting pressure upon Jews in Poland, and Assyrian Christians assailed in Iraq—should expose perpetrators to the principle of universal jurisdiction, warranting legal action by responsible states (as for crimes of piracy, slavery, human trafficking, narcotics dealing). It should take form in the arrest and trial by any country of alleged offenders, irrespective of the crime sites or the nationality or domicile of the presumed culprits.[16]

In the event, the Polish government prevented Lemkin from attending the Madrid conference. There his proposed resolution, read by proxy delegate, triggered Nazi demonstration; the president of the University of Berlin and the head of the German Supreme Court exited the conference hall as Lemkin's plan was outlined.[17] It thereafter languished, never brought forward for vote.[18] In 1934 the Warsaw government disavowed the 1919 multilateral Minorities Rights Treaty, whose purpose had been to guarantee the welfare of Poland's ethnic and smaller religious groups. That same year, Foreign Minister Jozef Beck engineered Warsaw's nonaggression pact with Berlin, eventually undone by the invasion of 1 September 1939.

The German–Polish war shoved Lemkin into military service (and wounding), a wrenching farewell to his parents, then a harrowing flight via Lithuania and Latvia to Sweden.[19] Through the intercession of friends in the Swedish justice ministry, he gained asylum and employment as a lecturer at the University of Stockholm law school. From thence, after trans-Siberian journey and Pacific passage, he made his way in spring 1941 to North Carolina and a professorial assignment at Duke University law school, arranged by an American colleague, Malcolm McDermott, with whom he had collaborated in the 1930s (translating/publishing Polish criminal statutes).[20] Although disturbed by the Jim Crow regime, and sympathetic to African Americans, whose plight he likened to that of Jews in Eastern Europe, Lemkin eagerly entered into New World life.[21] He viewed the United States as a place "born out of moral indignation against oppression."[22]

While at Duke, Lemkin aided the interventionist cause via public lectures. He warned audiences that the United States must join the Allies lest the Axis powers conquer Europe and place their seal upon world politics. He also emphasized the radical nature of Nazi ambitions: to reconfigure the demographic composition of Europe in favor of Germans, with concomitant devastation to the Polish (plus other Slavic), Jewish, and Roma populations.[23] After Pearl Harbor, continuing to sound the alarm that these peoples were in imminent peril, he directly appealed to FDR and Vice President Henry Wallace, but without noticeable effect.[24] "The Nazi plan was so outrageous," Lemkin later reflected, "that nobody believe[d] it."[25] He meanwhile relocated to Washington, where he advised the Board of Economic Warfare, obtained a position in the War Crimes Office of the Judge Advocate General's Office, worked with the War

Department on foreign affairs, and in 1945 helped Justice Jackson draft the IMT's indictment of German leaders.[26]

The main feat of Lemkin during these war years was his November 1944 publication of a tome, *Axis Rule in Occupied Europe*, sponsored by the Carnegie Endowment for International Peace and later cited in the Nuremberg assizes. This study rested upon copious documented evidence— collected by Lemkin in Stockholm and at Duke—of ongoing Nazi policies in Berlin-dominated countries. "The objective," he wrote, "is to destroy or to cripple the subjugated peoples in their development so that [Germany] will be in a position to deal with other European nations from the vantage point of numerical, physical, and economic superiority."[27]

In *Axis Rule*, Lemkin fastened his philological imagination to the fast-moving emergency. He wanted *genocide* to startle people, to concentrate their minds, if possible to prod the Allied governments into taking steps to prevent cultural and biological extinguishments. His new word, he explained, melded the Greek term for race or tribe, *genos*, with the Latin word for killing, *cide*.[28] In elaborating upon this, he drew upon ideas earlier advanced in his *barbarism* and *vandalism* formulae:

> Generally speaking, genocide does not necessarily mean the immediate destruction of a nation, except when accomplished by mass killings of all members of a nation. It is intended rather to signify a coordinated plan of different actions aiming at the destruction of essential foundations of the life of national groups, with the aim of annihilating the groups themselves. The objectives of such a plan would be disintegration of the political and social institutions, of culture, language, national feelings, religion, and the economic existence of national groups, and the destruction of the personal security, liberty, health, dignity, and even the lives of the individuals belonging to such groups. Genocide is directed against the national group as an entity, and the actions involved are directed against individuals, not in their individual capacity, but as members of the national group.[29]

Lemkin acknowledged that his lexicographical innovation applied to phenomena that were centuries old and without geographical limits. He held that the scale of Nazi murder of Poles, Jews, Roma, and others was neither unique to Europe nor to the twentieth century. On this subject, he hoped to publish (but never finished) a scholarly treatise, *History of Genocide*. Its projected compass, global and comparative, was to include Emperor Nero's campaign to eradicate Christian communities, Jews slaughtered in the Middle Ages, Mongol cruelties in Russia, Moors expelled from Spain, peoples of the Americas and Australasia crushed by Europeans, Huguenots executed on St. Bartholomew's Day in 1572, Roman Catholic converts annihilated in seventeenth-century Japan, Belgian-meted suffering in the Congo, German liquidation of Herero tribesmen in South West Africa during the reign of Kaiser Wilhelm II, and the killing of Armenian and Greek subjects on Ottoman authority before and during World War I.[30]

As detailed in *Axis Rule*, two distinct stages marked Lemkin's *genocide*. In the first, the victims' national modalities and conformation were destroyed. In the second phase, those of the oppressors were imposed. Pursuant to these ends, highly coordinated actions were taken, as in the illustrative case of Nazi policies:

> Genocide is effected through a synchronized attack on different aspects of life of the captive peoples: in the political field (by destroying institutions of self-government and imposing a German pattern of administration, and through colonization by Germans); in the social field (by disrupting the social cohesion of the nation involved and killing or removing elements such as the intelligentsia, which provide spiritual leadership); in the cultural field (by prohibiting or destroying cultural institutions and cultural activities); by substituting vocational education for education in the liberal arts, in order to prevent humanistic thinking, which the occupant considers dangerous because it promotes national thinking; in the economic field (by shifting the wealth to Germans and by prohibiting the exercise of trades and occupations by people who do not promote Germanism); in the biological field (by a policy of depopulation and by promoting procreation by Germans in the occupied countries); in the field of physical existence (by introducing a starvation rationing system for non-Germans and by mass killings, mainly of Jews, Poles, Slovenes, and Russians); in the religious field (by interfering with the activities of the Church, which in many countries provides not only spiritual but also national leadership); in the field of morality (by attempts to

create an atmosphere of moral debasement through promoting
pornographic publications and motion pictures, and the excessive
consumption of alcohol).[31]

Lemkin ended his *genocide* dissertation by calling for a treaty of
prohibition, along the lines that he had urged in 1933 upon the Madrid
conferees. Only through multilateral agreement and enforcement mechanisms, he reiterated, would every nation, with its indispensable contributions
to world society, be guaranteed into the future and would-be persecutors
inhibited. Justice and humanity's splendid diversity demanded legal
protection.[32] The UN General Assembly (UNGA), reeling under the
Nuremberg revelations and spurred by Lemkin, agreed. The delegates of
India, Cuba, and Panama, assisted by the United States, sponsored a resolution adopted by the UNGA in December 1946; this declared genocide
an international crime and instructed the UN's Economic and Social
Council (ECOSOC) to devise a binding text. In turn, ECOSOC looked
to the UN Secretariat, headed by Trygve Lie, to aid the cause. That office
employed consultants, of whom Lemkin was one—plus Romania's
Vespasian Pella and former Nuremberg tribune Henri Donnedieu de
Vabres—to compose the Convention's preliminary draft. This was finished
by June 1947.[33]

As approved by the UNGA on 9 December 1948, the Genocide
Convention parted in places (reviewed below) from Lemkin's original
concepts. Yet Lemkin regarded it as a defensible improvement over previous
injunctions and laws.[34] Relentless lobbying for it destroyed much of his
emotional equilibrium and physical well-being. Depleted, veering toward
nervous collapse, he wept uncontrollably on learning that the UNGA,
meeting in Paris, had unanimously passed the Convention—verifying to
him that his parents and numberless other people had not died futilely.[35]

Genocide Convention

The final text of the Convention condemned genocide as having racked
all eras. It was henceforth, whether in peace or war, in domestic circumstances or abroad, a punishable and extraditable offense under international
law. Anyone, private person or public official, who committed or attempted
genocide, or was complicit through incitement or conspiracy, would be

subject to prosecution, either in the territory in which said crime was committed or in other suitable jurisdiction, including international penal tribunal. See Appendix D.

Article II contained the heart of the Convention:

> Genocide means any of the following acts committed with intent to destroy, in whole or in part, a national, ethnical, racial, or religious group, as such:
>
> (a) Killing members of the group;
> (b) Causing serious bodily or mental harm to members of the group;
> (c) Deliberately inflicting on the group conditions of life calculated to bring about its physical destruction in whole or in part;
> (d) Imposing measures intended to prevent births within the group;
> (e) Forcibly transferring children of the group to another group.

That the Convention distinguished genocide from general crimes against humanity and designated it as unpardonable in peacetime as in war—a switch from Nuremberg rulings that had placed genocide only within the context of aggressive war—gratified Lemkin. He was also pleased that the Convention resisted the idea, once endorsed by Pella and de Vabres, to recognize lethal attack on political groups as a variant of genocide. The violent persecution of partisan parties, Lemkin agreed, was reprehensible, but it did not constitute intended obliteration of an entire people.[36] The major flaw in the Convention, he felt, was its silence on cultural genocide— what he had earlier phrased as *vandalism*—and failure to recognize that a people could disappear into a cauldron of enforced homogeneity, no less fatal to a group than biological decrease.[37] Here too he had disagreed with Pella and de Vabres. Neither of them doubted the centrality of physical destruction to genocide, but they were undecided about the cultural aspect.[38]

Between the first drafting of the Convention and the UNGA's endorsement, Lemkin functioned as a cross between impresario and one-man pressure group. He cornered and badgered UN delegates, representing fifty-eight countries in 1948. To John Humphrey, Canadian lawyer and director of the Secretariat's Human Rights Division, Lemkin seemed to have besieged United Nations headquarters—temporarily housed in Lake Success

New York—and then in Paris, where the UNGA convened at the Palais de Chaillot: "He could be seen everywhere in the committee-rooms and, by common consent, was accorded privileges denied to other private individuals. But he was a very difficult man who looked for enemies under every bench."[39]

Lemkin had to overcome wary delegations, not exactly personal foes as he frequently imagined, but potentially recalcitrant, of whom the British, French, and Soviet were most obvious. Their reservations sprang from doubts that a genocide convention would have efficacy or, more damaging, it might be used as a tool to investigate the fate of subject peoples within the vast domains controlled by London, Paris, and Moscow.[40] Moreover, the Soviets, led in the UN by Andrei Vyshinsky, wished to link genocide narrowly to racialism of the fascist type.[41] Anxious Arab representatives suspected that the proposed convention might be used as a basis to prop up the Zionist cause in Palestine. A French delegate on ECOSOC sniffed that *genocide* was a clunky Greek and Latin bastard.[42]

Against this opposition, Lemkin recruited disparate allies and fused them in common cause. His coalition included activists from Protestant denominations, Eastern Orthodox rites, and Roman Catholicism. He successfully courted the papal nuncio in Paris, Cardinal Roncalli, the future Pope John XXIII. Lemkin enlisted Jewish figures and organizations to whom, in the wake of Nazi darkness, the Convention equaled belated enlightenment. Ecumenical associations, such as the National Council of Christians and Jews, gravitated toward Lemkin as well. He meantime solicited literary personalities, for example two obliging Nobel laureates: Pearl S. Buck and Gabriela Mistral, plus novelist Aldous Huxley. Lemkin circulated petitions in the Americas and Europe among political elites, celebrities, and public intellectuals. He engaged women's organizations, labor unions, chambers of commerce, and editorial writers, all in the fervent hope of shaping UN decisions. His was a singular performance, its energy matched only by its effectiveness.[43]

Following the UNGA's voting, Lemkin threw himself into ensuring the Convention's ratification by UN member states, for which a minimum of twenty signatories was needed. As during the UNGA deliberations, he petitioned, testified, orchestrated letter-writing drives, sought to mollify critics, persuaded agnostics, and beseeched parliamentarians and heads of state. This campaign helped lead to the UN's formal signing ceremony in October 1950, by which time the requisite number of instruments of ratification had been deposited in New York. The Convention assumed force of international law on 12 January 1951, "the most beautiful day in my life," exulted Lemkin.[44] By 1959, the year he died (heart failure), almost sixty governments had ratified the treaty.[45] Ironically, though, his country of refuge proved hard to convince, despite President's Truman's advocacy.

Lemkin feared that for so long as Washington lay outside its framework, the Convention would lack prestige and vitality, consigned to limbo with other pious-sounding but hollow covenants. To prevent this, he had with usual alacrity leapt into action, but determined adversaries and Cold War circumstances conspired against him.

Resistance to the Convention arose in several groups, each nervous about the prospect of having international law legislate for the United States. White Southern Democrats counted heavily here, especially their insistence upon the Constitution's supremacy clause. They also worried that the Convention would permit domestic troublemakers and foreigners— including from the USSR—to scrutinize, pontificate, and meddle in segregated Dixie, taking as points of reference random lynchings and the language in Article II about "mental harm." Notable in this regard were Tom Connally (D, Texas) and Alexander George (D, Georgia) of the Senate Foreign Relations Committee.[46] They interrogated the phrase in Article II on the killing of members of a group: "intent to destroy, in whole or in part." Did the violent death of one person indicate genocide? Or ten? Or a hundred, or a thousand, or a million? What percentage of a group? Or did genocide, in fact, elude quantitative definition? In the absence of precision lay a Pandora's box of theoretical murkiness and mischief.

Upon this reasoning the arch-conservative American Bar Association (ABA) elaborated.[47] It denounced the Convention—so also did Senator Bourke Hickenlooper (R, Iowa)—as trespassing on national sovereignty and inviting hostile regimes to embarrass the United States by lodging frivolous suits against Washington. If nothing else, Moscow and Maoist Beijing would wield the Convention as a cudgel to thump the United States on behalf of African Americans, Native American tribes, and assorted screwballs.[48]

Such was obviously the case, said irate Dixie senators and ABA stalwarts, when in December 1951 left-leaning black activists William Patterson (in Paris) and Paul Robeson (in New York) presented to UN offices a petition, signed by W.E.B. Du Bois among others, from the Civil Rights Congress: *We Charge Genocide*. It enumerated thousands of racist-motivated homicides and rapes. It detailed Jim Crow repression and pleaded for UN investigation into, and levies against, the U.S. government.[49] Nothing less would relieve a people who had suffered grievously since the founding of colonial settlements: "Three hundred years is a long time to wait."[50]

To draw the sting from the affronted South, Lemkin hastened to distance himself (as had the NAACP) from the Patterson/Robeson petition. In public prints and private correspondence with Patterson, Lemkin extolled the virtues of gradualism (e.g., the July 1948 executive order that ended discrimination in the armed forces) as the surest corrective to racial injustice.[51] Besides, he argued, as prospects for Senate ratification faded before Dixie fury and ABA implacability, the situation faced by black Americans belonged to another category than that faced by the victims of Ottoman malice or Hitler's hatred: "Genocide implies destruction, death, annihilation, while discrimination is a regrettable denial of certain opportunities of life. To be unequal is not the same as to be dead."[52] This argument left Patterson unmoved; he remained convinced that the United States constituted the most despotic and bloody-minded society ever built.[53] Professor Oakley C. Johnson, another signatory of *We Charge Genocide*, held that Lemkin let a version of hyperpatriotism blur his judgment of racial murders in America and ignore reams of irrefutable complaint.[54]

As white Southerners stampeded away from the Convention, other matters injurious to Senate ratification developed. For one, Lemkin and several allies fell out among themselves, most disruptively in the case of James Rosenberg, who served with the American Conference of Christians and Jews and as president of the United States Committee for a Genocide Convention. How best to counter opponents or woo undecided senators were the primary causes of disagreement. Old-fashioned bigotry meanwhile attached to Lemkin, whose Jewishness, accented English, and other alien markers fed suspicion that he was weirdly exotic, probably disloyal, definitely a nuisance—a creature more akin to Du Bois, Robeson, and Patterson than to decent folks. Senator H. Alexander Smith (R, New Jersey), once remarked, after hearing Lemkin testify on Capitol Hill, that unfortunately the "biggest propagandist" for the Convention was a "a man who comes from a foreign country and who speaks broken English." The Jewish element, Smith moaned, was in any case overly represented in the anti-genocide movement.[55]

Hoping to burnish his American bona fides, Lemkin played to pervasive anticommunism. He never hesitated to portray ratification of the Convention as a potentially useful propaganda move.[56] He also embraced as a matter of genuine conviction the cause of East European émigrés. Together with ethnic organizations—Polish, Hungarian, Czech, Lithuanian, Estonian, Latvian, Ukrainian—he charged Stalin's USSR with being a genocidal syndicate: "Russia is killing small nations."[57] Even so, the South, with its treaty-busting representation in the Senate, would not yield, or the ABA bend. Lemkin complained to supporters that Dixie senators were forfeiting their chance to display compassion while the Convention's opponents fell into Stalin's hands, witlessly abetting deportations and murder.[58]

Adding irreparable damage to Lemkin's campaign, the post-Truman White House withheld support from the Convention. President Eisenhower and Secretary of State John Foster Dulles declared in 1953 that they had no desire to entangle the United States in extravagant agreements.[59] Sacrifice of the Convention, the administration evidently felt, would calm the frenzy behind the Bricker Amendment— supported by Senators Robert Taft (R, Ohio) and Joseph McCarthy (R, Wisconsin) plus ABA president Frank Holman—which sought to curtail the chief executive's ability to approve treaties. Lemkin protested to Dulles, but to no avail.[60]

Weakened by shaky health and other misfortunes, Lemkin in the mid-1950s slowed his push for U.S. ratification. He did acquire adjunct professorial jobs (Yale, Rutgers), teaching courses on international law and the United Nations, but landed nothing permanent. He produced works— autobiography, history of German homicide programs—that were refused by publishers because they judged the potential readership too small for commercial viability.[61] Just as when the Institute for Advanced Study (Princeton) had not found a niche for Lemkin in 1947 when he cast about for an institutional perch, so during the last year of his life the Rockefeller Foundation chose not to grant funds to aid his *History of Genocide* researches.[62] In his application to the Rockefeller, Lemkin gave what amounted to a final testament of his lawyerly faith:

> A degree of civilization by itself cannot be taken for granted as remedy against genocide. A certain help can be provided by international law appealing both to the feeling of shame and to the tendency to conform, even outwardly, to established standards.[63]

Increasingly ill-tempered and self-preoccupied, Lemkin lived on the margins of society, doing so without consolations of intimacy or deep friendship, for which he had neither knack nor interest.[64] Yet, despite

FIGURE 3.1 Raphael Lemkin

Source: United States Holocaust Memorial Museum

isolation and crowding adversity, he could not cease from "consecrating" his life—an oblation, he said, to a divinely ordained mission: "God must have chosen me in some way to contribute what I can to humanity."[65]

For years, the saga of Lemkin and the Genocide Convention hardly touched public imagination in America or elsewhere.[66] Not until 1986 did the Senate pass a resolution making the United States party to the Convention, thanks to the Herculean effort (from 1967 onward) of William Proxmire (D, Wisconsin), for whom the treaty had become an imperative.[67] The Reagan government in November delivered to the United Nations the instrument of ratification, binding upon Washington as of February 1989. Thus the United States became the ninety-eighth country—Ethiopia in July 1949 being first—to ratify the Convention. This event was, at its best construction, a posthumous victory for Lemkin, whose last years were blighted by impecuniousness (auctioning of his belongings), overwhelmed by illness, and veiled by obscurity.[68] The Senate attached enough conditions in 1986 to the Convention, the so-called Sovereignty Package, to cast doubt at home and abroad on the seriousness of U.S. adherence.[69] Two years earlier, James Martin, a Holocaust denier, had published an execrable book that mocked Lemkin and ridiculed his labors.[70]

Universal Declaration of Human Rights

Of the postwar fixations of Lemkin, few equaled his disdain for the Universal Declaration of Human Rights (UDHR) and its authors, specifically Eleanor Roosevelt. He certainly had her in mind, when, in 1949, he attacked, in private correspondence, those people whose "confusion" and "intellectual vanity" led them to "prefer global generalities more than [the] concrete realities of international life."[71] He thought the UDHR high-blown rhetoric, collapsible under its own flimsiness.[72] A hortatory declaration, it made no contribution to formal code but lacked seriousness, a view also shared by that day's most renowned human rights jurist, Hersch Lauterpacht.[73] To Lemkin, moreover, the UDHR was pernicious for standing at philosophical loggerheads with the Genocide Convention, the former emphasizing individual rights versus the latter's focus on collectivities. That Roosevelt was born to privilege, lived in comfort and safety, and enjoyed lofty status must also have nettled the scrambling Lemkin, to say nothing of his anxiety that the UDHR—a confection blending sanctimoniousness with triviality, in his view—would steal the limelight that the Convention deserved.[74]

To its champions, naturally, the UDHR was quite another matter. Upon studying the text of the UDHR as passed by the UNGA on 10 December 1948, the luminous Helen Keller declared: "My soul stood erect, exultant, envisioning a new world where the light of justice for every individual will be unclouded."[75]

References to human rights peppered the UN Charter of June 1945 and virtually required (Article 68) ECOSOC to devise language and means to extend them. From that effort came instructions to John Humphrey's Human Rights Division to assist the newly established Human Rights Commission (HRC), assigned the task of devising a statement and institutional machinery of rights. Representatives of the five Security Council powers—USA, USSR, UK, France, China—sat as permanent HRC members. These were supplemented by rotating delegates from other UN missions: Australia, Belgium, the Byelorussian SSR, Chile, Egypt, India, Iran, Lebanon, Panama, the Philippines, the Ukrainian SSR, Uruguay, Yugoslavia. Elected by unanimity at the HRC's first session (27 January–10 February 1947) at Lake Success, Roosevelt chaired the HRC until 1951, while also performing additional duties on America's UN delegation, to which Truman had appointed her in December 1945. Chang Peng-chun, a polymath and leader of the Chinese UN delegation, was elected vice chair of the HRC. Lebanon's Charles Malik, Christian apologist-turned-diplomat, served as rapporteur.[76]

The HRC's membership also came to include René Cassin of France, a Jewish member of Charles de Gaulle's official family and astute lawyer. Charles Dukes (Lord Dukeston), an intellectual mediocrity but a Labour Party crony of Foreign Secretary Bevin, represented Great Britain. Bevin, incidentally, had resisted the idea of appointing Lauterpacht, despite his prior service on the British War Crimes Executive, advising Shawcross at Nuremberg, and having published in 1945 a pertinent book: *An International Bill of the Rights of Man*. (Lauterpacht's Jewishness and foreign—Polish—roots were perhaps disqualifying in Bevin's view.[77]) Of successive Soviet representatives connected to the HRC, the most spirited was Alexi Pavlov, champion of the impeccably democratic 1936 "Stalin constitution" and a worthy opponent of Malik, against whom he argued the case for scientific materialism. Australia's representative, Colonel William Hodgson, wanted the UDHR to have strong "teeth." Hernan Santa Cruz of Chile proved a tireless proponent for the inclusion of socioeconomic rights. Two people from newly independent nations also played important roles: Carlos Romulo of the Philippines and Hansa Mehta, the latter of whom brought to bear her perspective as feminist and veteran of India's independence movement.

The HRC split its effort among three undertakings. Led by Roosevelt, a subgroup—whose main members were Chang, Malik, Cassin, Hodgson, Santa Cruz—took responsibility for composing a statement on rights of the person. To run parallel to it, as originally envisioned, there was to be a binding instrument of rights, its writing assumed by a second HRC subgroup. A third subgroup was to design strategies to implement the prospective declaration and covenant.

In the case of the proposed covenant, as matters evolved, the decision came about (1951) to divide the project into two. One was termed the Covenant on Civil and Political Rights, corresponding roughly with liberal ideas focused on the individual person, per the Western philosophical canon and embodied in such documents as the American Bill of Rights and France's Rights of Man. The second—the Covenant on Economic, Social and Cultural Rights—pivoted on concepts associated with socialist ideals related to economic freedom and welfare. By virtue of its intended legal heft, each instrument was reckoned by Roosevelt to be difficult of obtaining UNGA endorsement; presumably, ratification by UN member states would be rougher still. Events proved her correct. The HRC did not finish the two covenants until 1954.[78] The UNGA did not approve them until 1966; they came into force in 1976, with the United States delaying its endorsement, as with the Genocide Convention. Anticipating such obstacles, the HRC in 1947–1948 concentrated its effort on drafting a more readily acceptable agreement of broad definition, christened after quibbling the Universal Declaration of Human Rights. The ultimate aim was that a coherent set of norms and laws would inhere within these interlocking documents. But until each was finished and put in place, as constituent parts of an International Bill of Rights, the UDHR would stand alone, point of moral reference for citizens and governments everywhere and pledge of better things to come.[79]

A daunting difficulty for the UDHR authors was to devise a statement that would satisfy the ethical perspectives and intellectual traditions of the diverse UN membership, exemplified by, but not wholly encompassed in, rival Cold War ideologies. By 1948, the UN counted more than thirty-five states anchored in Judeo-Christian legacy, eleven in Islamic, six in Marxist, and five in Buddhist or Hindu.[80] Unsurprisingly, several observers and groups doubted that a useful declaration with putatively worldwide application could be crafted.

The Executive Board of the American Anthropological Association (AAA) fired in 1947 that the forthcoming declaration would most likely insult the customs cherished since time immemorial by people residing outside the West. In themes evocative of Lemkin's *vandalism* and *barbarism*, and foreshadowing latter-day attacks on the UDHR as sticky with Western conceit, the AAA enjoined the HCR against ethnocentrism.[81] In its "Statement on Human Rights" (authored by Melville Herskovits, an

Africanist at Northwestern University), the AAA charged that Western ideas in the past had dignified imperialism and fostered calamity for entire collectivities:[82]

> In the history of Western Europe and America . . . economic expansion, control of armaments, and an evangelical religious tradition have translated the recognition of cultural differences into a summons to action. This has been emphasized by philosophical systems that have stressed absolutes in the realm of values and ends. Definitions of freedom, concepts of the nature of human rights, and the like, have thus been narrowly drawn . . .
>
> Doctrines of the "white man's burden" have been employed to implement economic exploitation and to deny the right to control their own affairs to millions of people over the world, where the expansion of Europe and America has not meant the literal extermination of whole populations. Rationalized in terms of ascribing cultural inferiority to these peoples, or in conceptions of their backwardness in development of their "primitive mentality," that justified their being held in the tutelage of their superiors, the history of the expansion of the western world has been marked by demoralization of human personality and the disintegration of human rights among the peoples over whom hegemony has been established.[83]

The AAA urged the HRC to treat seriously all cultural forms, each a manifestation of complex psychology and its yearning to understand human purpose in a mysterious cosmos. To avert the risk of causing new harm, the HRC had to appreciate that individuals realized their personalities through the culture into which they were born and lived. From this angle, it followed that the HRC must respect human differences, not drive them—inadvertently or with presumed best intentions—into sterile homogeneity. Moreover, as no hierarchy of civilizations could be said to exist, and as morals were relative to each culture, the HRC should proceed cautiously lest it privilege in statement the West over the rest. Tolerance had to discipline unreflecting hubris.[84]

African American activists also harbored reservations about the HRC project, thinking it absurd to involve the U.S. government or South Africa, where in 1950 apartheid took legal effect. People along a wide spectrum, from the NAACP's tactful Walter White to firebrands of the William Patterson ilk, cited lists of miscarried justice and identified a cataract of racial evils. Like those later mentioned in the 1951 *We Charge Genocide* petition, numerous infamies must cumulatively void U.S. participation in the UDHR: voter disenfranchisement in the former Confederacy, miscegenation bans that existed in a majority (thirty in 1950) of the forty-eight states, segregated housing and education, church fire-bombings, white vigilante rule, police misconduct, and atrocities in 1943 Detroit and 1946 Columbia, Tennessee. The anxieties of Du Bois about U.S. insincerity were confirmed for him in 1947: Roosevelt, in her capacity as HRC chair, refused to accept or introduce to UN consideration the NAACP petition, *An Appeal to the World* (assembled under Du Bois's editorial supervision), that lambasted U.S. racial practices.[85] The HRC explained that its remit did not extend to the investigation of violations as charged by individuals or private associations against state actors.[86]

A member of the NAACP's board of directors and plucky civil rights advocate, whose activities drew FBI sleuthing and the baleful watch of Senator Theodore Bilbo (D, Mississippi), Roosevelt nonetheless balked at criticism useful to America's communist rivals.[87] Of this, consonant with prevailing liberal opinion (per Americans for Democratic Action, of which she was a member), she had become irritated, despite her normal forbearance. She had already learned in HRC meetings to parry Moscow's jabs regarding U.S. racial strife and the "dominance" of the Ku Klux Klan. She cleaved to this position, despite being mortified by the Waldorf-Astoria's denial of lodging to black UN delegates (Ethiopian, Liberian, Haitian), to say nothing of slights visited on Roosevelt's compatriot and UN Secretariat official, Ralph Bunche, with whom she enjoyed cordial relations.[88] Still, she said publicly and in confidential communications to White and Du Bois, the United States, if flawed, was making progress with more on the way, evidenced in the 1947 Truman-commissioned report, *To Secure These Rights*.[89] Surely, therefore, the country need not stoke further denunciation by totalitarian regimes, themselves possessing stained rights records.[90] Du Bois read Roosevelt's response to the NAACP petition as proof that Truman's diplomats would always block African American presentations of grievance in international fora: nothing else should be expected from an administration in thrall of "reactionary, war-mongering colonial imperialism."[91] When a conciliatory Roosevelt later asked the NAACP leadership for advice to forward to the HRC, Du Bois icily refused to play along, leaving Walter White—at the time conferring with the U.S. delegates at the UN—to improvise a set of anodyne suggestions.[92]

Another organization in 1947 to approach the HRC, uninvited like the AAA and NAACP, came from within the UN body: the United Nations Educational, Scientific and Cultural Organization (UNESCO), directed by the evolutionary biologist Julian Huxley. This time, however, the unsolicited ideas were buoying. Huxley assembled a study group, the Committee on the Philosophic Principles of the Rights of Man, to determine on what intellectual basis, if any, an international bill of rights might be erected. Britain's E.H. Carr, historian and international relations theorist (who bore slight resemblance to realist caricature), chaired the committee.[93] Richard McKeon, a talented philosopher at the University of Chicago, was recruited as rapporteur. Other members included Pierre Auger, atomic physicist at the University of Paris, and Harold Laski of the London School of Economics.[94]

The Carr group originally hoped to canvass a variety of thinkers, their allegiances stretching from Confucianism to Hinduism to Islam to Christianity to contending schools of European thought. In the end, though, people actually solicited were of, or largely slanted toward, the West.[95] The list of more than sixty respondents counted Italian philosopher Benedetto Croce, British penal reformer Margery Fry, Hungarian physiologist and Nobel laureate Albert Szent-Gyorgyi, Muslim Indian poet-philosopher Humayun Kabir, American literary critic Lewis Mumford, French Jesuit and paleontologist Pierre Teilhard de Chardin, Soviet professor of law Boris Tchechko, F.S.C. Northrop of Yale University's philosophy department, and political scientist Quincy Wright of the University of Chicago.

The most famous respondent was Mahatma Gandhi, his India then being devoured by communal violence.[96] The person most impassioned by, and intimately involved in the study, was Jacques Maritain, French Catholic theologian, and at the time ambassador to the Vatican. He later wrote an eloquent introduction to a compendium of the UNESCO essays—*Human Rights: Comments and Interpretations*—distributed at a time when the UDHR was still a work in progress.[97]

Somewhat surprising to its UNESCO sponsors, the Carr-led investigation concluded that peoples of different philosophical and religious backgrounds could agree upon a workable set of civil-political and economic-social rights.

This finding, stressing pragmatic convergences rather than the chimera of deep conceptual agreement, was politely received by the HRC, despite feeling by members that UNESCO had tramped on turf not its own.[98]

Even while the AAA, the NAACP, and UNESCO sought the attention of Roosevelt, she and company faced perplexities of another kind: namely, the principal drafters of the UHDR held views that did not all tug in the same direction. Loyal to the China of Chiang Kai-shek, Chang Peng-chun said that Confucian wisdom should not be absent from whatever was finally written.[99] Chang pushed for the inclusion of venerable notions of political order and private conduct, while simultaneously despairing as Mao's armies gained firmer grip on China; he predicted that fully fledged Soviet–U.S. war would explode by autumn 1949.[100] Of a decidedly secular/pluralist type, Chang also sparred with Malik over the essence of human nature—immutability ("original sin") versus protean adjustments mediated by civilizations located in scattered times and places. Malik and Cassin, meanwhile, disagreed over Palestinian–Israeli affairs. A spokesman for the Arab League, the former protested Palestinian dispossession and dispersal. Cassin, once hounded by Vichy pursuers, and whose sister (plus other members of his extended family) had died in the Shoah, believed that new Israel held the key to Jewish revival.[101]

As for Roosevelt, she was a deft and preeminently fair chair, as well as a "practical idealist" (her phrase). Alas, by her own admission, without rudimentary university education, she felt ill at ease as her theoretically versed colleagues spun intellectual cobwebs or disputed arcane points. Lest the drafting committee crumble beneath inconclusive argumentation, be rent by disagreements over Middle East dilemmas, or be paralyzed by conflicting personalities, Roosevelt decided to subcontract the writing of the UDHR's first draft. This task fell to Humphrey and his aides in the Division of Human Rights, hitherto seconded to the HCR but not assigned primary roles.

A former professor of law at McGill University and unswerving social democrat, Humphrey was superficially self-effacing, as befit a UN civil servant (and from the New Brunswick outback). He completed a draft declaration in winter 1947, drawing for his study upon hundreds of proffered texts. Submissions came from Western organizations and individuals, among which Lauterpacht, the American Law Institute, the American Association for the United Nations, the American Jewish Congress, Latin American socialists, and the Institut de Droit International.[102] Humphrey's annotated draft listed forty-eight articles and upheld the significance of economic-social rights as no way inferior to civil-political ones.[103]

Shortly after Humphrey's document reached the HRC drafting committee, Cassin was instructed to review, streamline, and polish. This labor he did, while leaving the majority—75 percent—of Humphrey's work intact.[104] Thereafter, the whole HRC, in lengthy meetings and in consultation with UN delegations, debated definitions, haggled over the precise wording of phrases, drafted and redrafted provisions, and careened between imploding and going grimly forward. Roosevelt, never querulous or abrupt, kept the HRC from derailment by disputation.

As finally propounded, the UDHR was sufficiently elastic to accommodate a broad range of ideological preferences. It was rhetorically elegant. It enshrined key principles connected to the democratic West and collectivist East. It could even be read as manifesto for emergent national welfare states. See Appendix E.

To the generation that first read it, the UDHR was a tribute to compromise, timely at a moment when Soviet–U.S. tensions ran high, particularly in Berlin.[105] Above all, by virtue of being a declaration rather than a legal instrument, the UDHR did not obviously threaten anyone or any country.

The delegations of forty-eight UN states voted in support of the UDHR. None voted against. The delegates of two countries were absent from the proceedings: Honduras and Yemen. Eight delegations did ostentatiously abstain, however: the Byelorussian SSR, Czechoslovakia, Poland, Saudi Arabia, the Ukrainian SSR, the USSR, the Union of South Africa, Yugoslavia. The Soviet-organized states and Marxist Yugoslavia (defiant in 1948 of Stalinist dictate) abstained because the UDHR failed to mention fascism and Nazism as the main enemies of humanity and (implicitly) allowed political space for their recrudescence. Moreover, as Vyshinsky expounded, proletarian lands, by virtue of having overcome class injustice, exemplified human rights in action; in this circumstance, the workers' states were actually co-terminus with—the primary agents and guarantors of—human rights, in which case the UDHR was superfluous. From a Saudi perspective, the UDHR position on equality of marriage rights and freedom to change religion invited licentiousness and apostasy, plainly antithetical to Islamic society and redolent of crusader imperiousness. To bolster white prerogative and budding apartheid, South Africa's delegates dismissed the

FIGURE 3.2 Eleanor Roosevelt with a copy of the Universal Declaration of Human Rights

Source: Franklin D. Roosevelt Presidential Library

UDHR as insufficiently alive to the qualifications required of citizens to move within national territory or participate conscientiously in politics.[106]

Of course, eight abstentions hardly constituted defeat. The UNGA tally delighted Roosevelt and the rest of the HRC. After the results were announced, UNGA president Herbert Evatt (Australia) praised Roosevelt, seated with her U.S. colleagues. A standing ovation from UN representatives followed Evatt's words.[107] Other congratulations rushed in, including from the White House.

However much Roosevelt appreciated the approbation, she perceived the UDHR in 1948 as the start, not the finish, of human rights affirmation: much depended upon the design and adoption of political-civil and social-economic covenants, whose path the UDHR was meant to prepare.[108] To this cause, she devoted herself for the remainder of her UN tenure. But, as mentioned, completion of the proposed International Bill of Rights was elusive. She died in 1962, years before either the UN or United States endorsed the two covenants.

Roosevelt had seethed as the same elements that thwarted U.S. ratification of the Genocide Convention blocked progress beyond the UDHR: Dixiecrats, ABA leaders, UN defamers, guardians of the equipoise between federal authority and the forty-eight constituent states, and Eisenhower–Dulles caution. Opponents charged that, as a stalking horse for communists and other enemies, the pending covenants had to be rejected. The United Nations was arrogating so much power to itself that U.S. independence must finally vanish, before which day, said Senator John Bricker (R, Ohio), the country would become ensnared in a Moscow-dictated "Covenant on Human Slavery."[109]

Roosevelt wrote in an April 1953 *My Day* column: "We have sold out to the Brickers and McCarthys."[110] By that time, Eisenhower had replaced Roosevelt on the HRC with an appointee of contrasting sensibility and lesser competence, Mary Pillsbury Lord.[111] She at first labored under the misimpression that the United States had refused the UDHR because its emphases on social-economic rights were lopsided and contradicted U.S. ideals.[112] In the meantime, international problems had intensified beyond those of 1948, further postponing the future for which Roosevelt campaigned: the nuclear arms race had accelerated and war had engulfed the Korean peninsula.

★ ★ ★

Liberals circa 1948 were disappointed that the HRC did not tilt the UDHR more sharply away from the prerogatives of states in favor of the individual's welfare and dignity. These critics downplayed the upholding of nations' sovereignty in the UN Charter (Article 2.7) and emphasized its favorable references to human rights.[113] Lauterpacht, foremost in this party, wrote scathingly of the UDHR's avoiding references to states' obligations and the absence of mechanisms to enforce rights of the person.[114] He regretted too that the UDHR made no provision for private men and women or organizations to petition the UN—as the NAACP had attempted in 1947—for redress against violators.[115] How pathetic also that the UDHR failed to address the protection or support of linguistic, racial, and religious minorities. Lauterpacht's only concession was that the UDHR's inadequacies might become so apparent that new initiatives would arise in the UN or elsewhere to correct the glaring defects: "The realization of the ineffectiveness of the Declaration per se must tend to quicken the pace of less nominal measures for the protection of human rights."[116] To such complaints, Roosevelt and Humphrey tartly replied: mindful of stubborn political realities, the HRC had to prevent perfectionism from thwarting the achievable.[117]

Of Americans contemporaneous with Lauterpacht and equally unconvinced by the UDHR, two were most withering: the revolutionary humanist Du Bois and the contrarian George Kennan. Sympathetic to Stalin ("few men in the twentieth century approach his stature") and offended by Truman ("ranks with Adolf Hitler as one of the greatest killers of our day"), Du Bois also recoiled at the UDHR's saturation with European/North American claims to virtue.[118] Such speciousness could not redeem the past or mold a desirable future.[119] The truth stood stark: "There was no Nazi atrocity—concentration camps, wholesale maiming and murder, defilement of women or ghastly blasphemy of childhood—which the Christian civilization of Europe had not long been practicing against colored folk in all parts of the world."[120]

Kennan, an architect of early Cold War strategy, and intellectually far removed from the passions of Du Bois, thought the UDHR too ambitious for the U.S. polity:

> [I have] great misgivings as to the wisdom of . . . negotiating declarations of this nature setting forth ideals and principles which we are not today able to observe in our own country, which we cannot be sure of being able to observe in the future, and which are in any case of dubious universal validity. It seems . . . that this invites charges of hypocrisy against us.

Better, he advised his State Department superiors, to forswear highly pitched proclamations unconnected either to American society or to the unforgiving global competition for power.[121]

African and Asian champions of decolonization from 1948 onward regretted the UDHR's silence on national self-determination, even as they summoned its authority—as at the 1955 Bandung conference of non-aligned countries—in anti-imperialism and liberation struggles (more in Chapter 5). Explicit reference to the need of economic development and modernization was also missing from the UDHR, charged first-generation leaders of emergent states. Not until 1986 did the UNGA adopt the

Declaration on the Right to Development, an integral part of a proposed
New International Economic Order, itself unimagined by the authors of the
UDHR (though not as remote an idea to them as would have been rights
language referring to gay, lesbian, or transgender persons). Such lacunae were
hardly surprising, said African and Asian critics. To them, Western ideology
and thinly veiled interests clogged the UDHR. Chang and Malik, moreover,
were themselves members of Westernized elites, severed from their natal
traditions and, consciously or not, helping to effect a suffocating uniformity
of cultures.[122] How contemptible, some thought during the Algerian war
of independence, that Cassin (then president of the Conseil d'Etat) uttered
not a word against notorious internment centers, where torture was
commonplace, and kept quiet about other French misdeeds.[123] Subsequent
Western sermonizing on moral-political failings in African and Asian
settings—related to corruption or tyrannies of the Idi Amin type—did not
advance adherence to UDHR norms but instead triggered charges of
double standard and calls (2001 Dublin conference) for reparations for past
sins against the Global South: slavery, imperialism, untold killings.[124] In tune
with Du Bois's earlier excoriation, an Indian scholar, Arvind Sharma, noted
in 2006 the West's tendency to bask in its own self-approval: "Human rights
discourse will continue to attract the charge of being 'Western' until it faces
up to the question of the righting of historical wrongs."[125]

Despite these doubts, the UDHR has displayed a tenacity of life, moving
gradually into the realm of customary law. Although Roman Catholic
observers, at the moment of the UDHR's unveiling, regretted the document's failure to mention God or the divinely ordained nature of the moral
sphere, such qualms were dispelled when (Easter 1963) Pope John XXIII
issued his *Pacem in Terris*. Like the ecumenical World Council of Churches
earlier, this hailed the UDHR as a step toward the reform of global society
and affirmation of the worth of all human persons.[126] That same year, at
the behest of Jomo Kenyatta of Kenya, Kwame Nkrumah of Ghana, and
Julius Nyerere of Tanzania, the Organization of African Unity wove
adherence to the UDHR into its charter. Similar references to it wended
their way into constitutions of newly independent countries, from Indonesia
to northern and sub-Saharan Africa.[127] Testimonials indicate that oppos-
itionists in South Africa, Eastern Europe, Franco's Spain, and the USSR
to gain support within their own lands recited the UDHR's maxims.
The UDHR also nourished the morale of beleaguered resisters, as Nelson
Mandela once explained, reminding them that they were not alone but

lived in solidarity with strugglers everywhere. In effect, it was a document that radiated transcultural values and enabled activists to hurdle the obstacles emplaced by tyrannies to frustrate unwanted legal probes and enforcement.[128]

On its twentieth anniversary, the UDHR was likened by the Nobel Committee (in conferring the Peace Prize upon Cassin) as comparable to the Ten Commandments in shaping ethics discourse and conduct.[129] World leaders, religious figures, and unbowed dissenters likewise celebrated the golden anniversary (1998) of the UDHR. Mary Robinson, then UN High Commissioner for Human Rights, spoke for most when she called it a landmark document in human history.[130] Similar tributes came from Kofi Annan, Aung San Suu Kyi, Tony Blair, Jimmy Carter, the Dalai Lama, Mikhail Gorbachev, Václav Havel, Helmut Schmidt, and Lech Walesa.

Surviving Cold War and other vicissitudes, the UDHR in the 1950s and beyond helped inspire conventions on refugees (1951), the status of women (1952), the treatment of prisoners (1955), the elimination of racial discrimination (1965), and the rights of children (1989). Nongovernmental organizations such as Amnesty International (est. 1961) and Human Rights Watch (est. 1978) incorporated UDHR language into their missions.[131] The UN's heralded twenty-first-century initiative, the Responsibility to Protect (RtoP), is also partly traceable to the UDHR: the idea being that the world community should act to safeguard any civilian population endangered by an abusive government via mediation, economic sanction, diplomacy, or, in last resort with approval by the UN Security Council, intervention with military force.[132]

The authors of RtoP hoped to check regimes guilty of perpetrating atrocities, specifically war crimes, crimes against humanity, ethnic cleansing, and—back to Lemkin—genocide.[133] Indeed, the Genocide Convention and the UDHR, encapsulated by RtoP, are two sides of the same human rights coin: the Roosevelt side earnestly hopeful, the Lemkin side a prohibition on infernal policies. The UNGA's decision in December 1948 to circulate this new currency reflected indignation with reason-of-state doctrine, its legitimacy nullified by the recent war in which defenseless civilians had been routinely targeted. Institutionalization of antistate feeling certainly did not progress fast enough to please critics. But establishment (2002) of the International Criminal Court (ICC) in The Hague to provide impartial evaluation of political leaders charged with offenses, including genocide, may have satisfied those people otherwise unsettled by the "victor's justice" of Nuremberg/Tokyo. Even Lauterpacht might have appreciated the ICC as a place where, in words he once used in another context, "the mystical sanctity of the sovereign State . . . is arraigned before the judgment of the law."[134] Thus, though not at once but eventually, a thickening of dedication arose after 1945—prominently the Council of Europe—against political regimes, previously sheltered by ancient code that upheld the internal arrangements of a state as its exclusive affair.

As Europe's age of catastrophe passed into history, finalized by the extinction of Marxist–Leninst regimes in 1989–1991, the U.S. record remained exposed. An example of that being the White House condoned use of "enhanced interrogation techniques" against terrorist suspects during the panic years following the 9/11 attacks, contra Article 5 of the UDHR: "No one shall be subjected to torture or to cruel, inhuman or degrading treatment or punishment." In domestic affairs, despite Barack Obama's White House incumbency, the "routine disadvantage" of being black (historian John Hope Franklin's words) was meantime not excised. This fact would doubtless have disheartened Patterson and Du Bois. Even if they persisted in viewing the UDHR as deficient, they would have cited—as they did in their lifetimes—its chapters against entrenched wrongs in the United States.[135] The "Double V" of 1941–1945, victory against fascism abroad and racism at home, remained unfinished business into the twenty-first century, hence the Black Lives Matter movement.

As for Lemkin, American by necessity, what might he have thought of the career of his genocide idea, both as analytical concept and protest against types of violence that have shattered millions of people? He surely would have been incensed by wanton use of the word in popular parlance, threatening to trivialize the term's power to register outrage and denting its status in theory and law.[136] This concern was evidenced by his response to Patterson's *We Charge Genocide* that, whatever its shortcomings as perceived by Lemkin, was more serious than numerous instances in which *genocide* has been casually used in subsequent decades. Conversely, Lemkin, despite pride of authorship, would have approved attempts by other thinkers to theorize *genocide* further, though not necessarily agreeing with their every amendment.[137]

One can imagine the satisfaction Lemkin might have felt had he learned (no evidence suggests that he did) of considered comments by Roosevelt in 1948 that referred to German kidnapping of Polish children and deportation to the Third Reich for assimilation: "a dreadful kind of genocide."[138] Incidentally, he did not acknowledge her publicly expressed support in 1950 for Senate approval of the Genocide Convention, though privately he must have felt vindicated.[139]

Had he lived into the 1960s, Lemkin would have had to contend with those anti-Vietnam War protestors who labeled U.S. military actions as genocidal. At that time, Jean-Paul Sartre, involved in the 1967 "trials" of U.S. military/civilian leaders (reviewed in Chapter 2), conjured Lemkin. Taking him as reference, Sartre declared Washington guilty of committing genocide in Vietnam: torching villages, subjecting civilian populations to heavy bombing, killing livestock, destroying vegetation and crops by defoliants, indiscriminately shooting.[140] How Lemkin would have reacted to Sartre's broadcast of horrors must remain a matter of conjecture, his visceral anticommunism pulling in one direction, his dread of unconstrained violence in another.[141] Less open to doubt, though, would be Lemkin's reading of events in Bangladesh, Biafra, Bosnia, Burundi, Cambodia, Darfur, Rakhine State (Myanmar), Rwanda, and Tibet. These would, at minimum, have been treated in his projected *History of Genocide*. Lemkin then would have acknowledged the continuing relevance of words that he penned during India's 1948 upheavals: "There is too much genocide in the world today. We cannot afford to be lulled to sleep on this burning question."[142] He meanwhile would have experienced relief that the Genocide Convention, albeit unevenly applied and sharply debated, came to occupy the center of discourse about wholesale murders, methods to deter them, and means to bring *genocidaires* to justice.[143]

The events related in this chapter hardly clinch the case made by John Stuart Mill: "improvement in human affairs is wholly the work of the uncontented characters."[144] Yet Lemkin, churning genius, does fit.[145] So does the questing Roosevelt. Righteousness drove her to expand the ambit of human rights, once ridiculed as simply a feminine field.[146] Created by states but not a tool of them, the UDHR, like the Genocide Convention, earned a place in international society. They have enriched the repertoire of commonly held ideas and even inflected practice.[147]

★ ★ ★

4

UNITED NATIONS

I have a bias against war; a bias for peace. I have a bias that leads me to believe in the essential goodness of my fellow man; which leads me to believe that no problem of human relations is ever insoluble . . . I have a strong bias in favor of the United Nations and its ability to maintain a peaceful world.[1]

Ralph Bunche, 9 May 1949

★ ★ ★

By embracing the UDHR and prohibitions on genocide, the United Nations in 1948 upheld a theory premised on the centrality of people, both in their collective and individual capacities, which enjoyed primacy over the claims of the sovereign state. This endorsement of human rights dovetailed with the UN's earlier approval of the Nuremberg principles with their emphasis on personal accountability. The melding of privileges and responsibilities gestured toward, though it did not fully encompass, that philosophical line strenuously espoused by Hersch Lauterpacht: the state is not a sanctified end but merely the custodian of the welfare and ultimate purpose of human beings.[2] Such tilting in the direction of rights did not undo the essential nature of the UN, however. By the intent of its founders and modes of operation, the UN was foremost an assembly of governments, not peoples. Its proponents hoped that the UN, the comity of nations institutionalized, could foster conditions for peaceful interstate relations while checking instances of aggression when they flared. In this context UN human rights measures were understood as constrained, subordinate to state supremacy, marginally related to the contest of wills among rival countries.

In the late 1940s, Soviet–U.S. competition threatened to undo the UN's viability, an outcome congenial to hardliners in the Kremlin and on Capitol Hill. At the same time, beneath the crust of great-power confrontation, two other seemingly intractable problems developed. Though they collided with it, their origins lay not in the Cold War but in two seismic shifts occasioned by World War II: the contraction of British imperial power; the disintegration of Japan's empire. The resultant Israeli–Palestinian and Korean dilemmas outlived Soviet–U.S. antagonism while confounding generations of diplomats, UN and other.

International parliament

The 1941 Churchill–FDR Atlantic Charter contained wording on the desirability of establishing a global security system to replace the discredited League of Nations. This matter received further attention in October 1943 at the Moscow foreign ministers conference, featuring America's Cordell Hull, Britain's Anthony Eden, China's Foo Ping-sheung, and the USSR's Vyacheslav Molotov. The following year their delegates, under the chairmanship of the perennially optimistic Edward Stettinius, met (21 August– 7 October) at the Dumbarton Oaks estate, located in the Georgetown neighborhood of Washington. The conferees examined ways to organize the political machinery of the prospective United Nations and defined its scope. Drawing upon ideas advanced by the State Department's Leo Pasvolsky, provisions were made for institutionalizing democracy between governments, eventually provided in the General Assembly (UNGA).[3] A Secretariat-General, the administrative branch of the proposed UN, and an international court of justice were also mandated. Most crucially, the major players in the anti-Axis war—their postwar cooperation presumed—were to consult in exclusive conclave, realized in the Security Council (UNSC). To it six lesser powers would be admitted on a rotating basis. But their prerogatives and responsibilities would not match those of the permanent members: USA, USSR, UK, China. In their combined wisdom, the Big

Four should guide the UN on international security and in coordination, exemplified by an envisioned joint military advisory committee, police the peace. To limit encroachments on freedom of action, each permanent UNSC state was armed with an action-nullifying veto, to be used with discretion as circumstances required. In effect, the proposed UN was to be an improved League of Nations wherein the status and advantages of the great powers, as in the League, were underscored.

Stalin, Churchill, and FDR at the February 1945 Yalta meeting made refinements to this blueprint. These included attempts to resolve knotty questions on voting procedures/veto exercise in the Security Council. No less than the Soviets, the Americans would not countenance a denial to themselves of veto over action that might touch inimically upon their interests.[4] A permanent seat on the Security Council was confirmed for France, its place earlier provisionally allotted. Additionally, a compromise was struck on what had been an irksome matter connected to Soviet representation. Andrei Gromyko, chair of the Soviet delegation at Dumbarton Oaks, had averred that all sixteen republics in the USSR enjoyed absolute autonomy. Each deserved UN representation.[5] In the event, "independent" Byelorussia and Ukraine were granted UN membership. Running between 25 April and 26 June 1945, the San Francisco convention of officials from fifty-one countries—self-designated as "peace-loving"—approved the UN Charter. To stirring effect, its preamble, composed by Jan Smuts of South Africa, contained this iteration of the UN's irenic mission: "to save succeeding generations from the scourge of war, which twice in our lifetime has brought untold sorrow to mankind." See Appendix A.

Soon after San Francisco, a majority of the signatory governments ratified the Charter, the U.S. Senate voting on 28 July overwhelmingly in favor: eighty-nine to two. The Charter went into effect on 24 October 1945. The first session of the General Assembly convened in London on 10 January 1946. The bipartisan U.S. delegation, headed by Secretary of State James Byrnes, included Eleanor Roosevelt and two GOP foreign policy aficionados, John Foster Dulles and Senator Arthur Vandenberg (R, Michigan). They and delegates from other countries were welcomed to Central Hall in Westminster by Prime Minister Clement Attlee, who exhorted them: "The United Nations Organization must become the over-riding factor in foreign policy. . . . We desire to assert the pre-eminence of right over might and the general good against selfish and sectional aims."[6]

The Executive Committee's Preparatory Commission had meanwhile settled the question of where to site UN headquarters—somewhere in the United States. This choice should, it was reasoned, inhibit any future disassociation that Washington might contemplate, as with the League of Nations. Eager municipalities vied for the honor to host the new organization. Chicago, Denver, Boston, Philadelphia, San Francisco, and Atlantic City were among the cities mentioned, their manifold distinctions touted by lobbyists.

Once New York was selected, the question next arose of where in that metropolis to place the UN facilities. This problem was solved by the largesse of the Rockefeller family, buying for the UN at a cost of $8.5 million a then-slummy strip (Turtle Bay) of Manhattan along the East River. Building began in 1948 of a complex—designed by celebrated architects—to house the Secretariat, the General Assembly, the Security Council, the Economic and Social Council, and assorted commissions and agencies. Underwritten by a non-interest-bearing U.S. loan ($68 million), this construction was made functional in stages, fully finished by October 1952.[7] Until then, the offices and meetings of the UN were improvised in spots scattered around metropolitan New York. The Security Council took a Hunter College (Bronx) gymnasium into service. The Secretariat sheltered in the Sperry Gyroscope factory at Lake Success (Long Island). The General Assembly met in a retrofitted Flushing Meadows skating rink (Queens), which dated to the 1939 World's Fair.[8] Between these locations, and their own domiciles and makeshift chancelleries, UN delegates shuffled, braving snaps of inclement weather, traffic jams, and sundry exasperations of urban commuting.

Despite the inconveniences, UN business got conducted satisfactorily, in the judgment of the UN's first secretary-general, Trygve Lie. Jowly, blunt, and temperamental, this Norwegian politician won appointment by the General Assembly on 1 February 1946. A man of the labor left, he had served competently as foreign minister of King Haakon's government in its London exile during the war years. Lie had a genius for alienating UN colleagues, legendarily in the case of capable but emotionally brittle Herbert Evatt, president of the General Assembly in 1948–1949. A compromise candidate of indifferent talent but inoffensive to Soviet and Western constituencies, Lie was chosen over better-known persons. Stettinius actually referred to him as a "dud."[9] Names floated before Lie's appointment included Anthony Eden, Eelco van Kleffens (Netherlands), Jan Masaryk

(Czechoslovakia), Lester Pearson (Canada), Paul-Henri Spaak (Belgium), and John Winant (FDR's wartime ambassador to London). Alger Hiss had his advocates too, not only among the Soviets for reasons disingenuous but also among British Foreign Office personnel who appreciated his efficient directing of the 1945 San Francisco conference.[10]

The election of Lie set a precedent that has persisted: the secretary-general should not be a national of any of the great powers but recruited from a lesser. As to Lie's tenure, during it the UN scored a number of modest successes in the late 1940s. Soviet forces withdrew in spring 1946 from their positions of occupation in northern Iran (Azerbaijan), an evacuation aided by Security Council hearings. The UN helped to end violence, August 1945–December 1949, between the rising new Indonesia of Achmed Sukarno and Dutch overlordship.[11] Similarly, the UN fostered mediation and a cessation to clashes begun in May 1945 between French armed forces and liberationists in Syria and Lebanon, culminating in the latter's independence in 1946. The UNGA facilitated the launching into statehood in 1949 of two former Italian colonies—Somalia and Libya. Evidence suggests that UNGA monitoring in 1946–1949 of the Greek civil war helped prevent it from spreading into a wider Balkans conflict.[12] Even the 1948 Berlin crisis—Soviet blockade and Anglo-U.S. airlift—was calmed somewhat by the UN's good offices. In New York, acting upon Stalin's subtle encouragement (to Western journalists), Philip Jessup of the U.S. delegation pursued the USSR's Jacob Malik on whether the Berlin impasse could be broken, which initiative contributed to the blockade's lifting in May 1949.[13]

Not individually or cumulatively did the above instances vindicate the hopes for which the UN's votaries prayed. Reconciliation between adversaries did not everywhere bloom. Regularly scheduled meetings of the Security Council's Military Staff Committee, ostensible command center for UN police forces, degenerated into nonsensical ritual.[14] An ambitious peace plan, the "Twenty Year Program," that Lie formulated and circulated in 1950 to Soviet, British, French, and U.S. heads of state never thrived.[15] It died when the Korean fighting commenced on 25 June.

Nor was the UN consulted in advance about, or invited to comment upon, or allowed involvement in, momentous happenings in the late 1940s. The UN's efforts to promote peace flopped in Algeria and Indochina, where France sought to solidify colonial administrations. The United Nations could not check the Hindu–Muslim violence that blanketed India, ending in its partition after Britain's 1947 withdrawal from the subcontinent. Equally unaffected by the UN or Lie, the Chinese civil war climaxed in Mao Zedong's triumph and the Guomintang retreat to Taiwan. Subventions to Greece and Turkey (the Truman Doctrine), implementation of the Marshall Plan, and acceleration of the Soviet–U.S. atomic arms race also proceeded with negligible reference to the United Nations. Establishment of NATO in 1949 did provoke Soviet denunciations in the General Assembly, but that body never inquired into whether the alliance violated UN proscriptions.[16] Stalinist puppet regimes meanwhile were imposed in Eastern Europe, where the Red Army and NKVD reigned. On Moscow's insistence, the Security Council declined to investigate charges brought by Czechoslovakia's UN representative, Jan Papanek, that foreign agents had instigated the February 1948 Prague coup.

Throughout these tension-filled years, the White House publicly hailed the UN for its potential promise. At the October 1949 laying of the cornerstone at the UN's New York building, Truman predicted: "The United Nations will endure and will bring the blessings of peace and well-being to mankind."[17] To reinforce his faith, subject to slippage, Truman reportedly carried in his wallet for years this passage from Alfred Tennyson's *Locksley Hall*.[18]

> Till the war-drum throbbed no longer,
> and the battle-flags were furled
> In the Parliament of Man, the Federation
> of the World.
> There the common sense of most shall hold
> a fretful realm in awe,
> And the kindly earth shall slumber
> Lapt in universal law.

Contrary to such sentiment, Dean Acheson, secretary of state (January 1949–January 1953), found the UN tedious, inadequate, irrelevant. It could not possibly realize its aim of everywhere spreading peace and was too frail a thing in which to invest U.S. security. The UN at its best was an aid to Washington statecraft, but no substitute for economic-military wherewithal or diplomatic adeptness or a properly functioning balance of power.[19] Acheson belittled the "impracticable" Charter. He held that "its presentation to the American people as almost holy writ" must result in sullen

FIGURE 4.1 United Nations headquarters in New York City

Source: U.S. National Archives

disappointment. "The perverse ingenuity of man" would, as with every utopian scheme, conquer the UN and dissolve its dreams.[20] When in April 1950 Lie shared his "Twenty Year Program" with Truman and Acheson, and boasted of UN achievements in checking communist advances (Greece, Korea, Indonesia), the foreign minister inwardly balked: "I did not say, but I thought, that [Lie] had left out the most important element, which was American economic and political and military help."[21]

George Kennan, head of the State Department's Policy Planning Staff in 1947–1949, nursed doubts similar to Acheson's. To Kennan, the UN was one of several theaters in the Cold War, but nothing more—certainly not a framework for foreign policy, not an initiator of action, not a court of resort to which Americans should risk their fate. He reckoned too that U.S. influence in the UN would plummet in future years. Washington would commit a grave error by pegging national security to ephemeral voting majorities in the General Assembly. Given his druthers, he would have involved Americans in an alternative association restricted to countries that shared Washington's perspective on global affairs, thus ensuring institutional coherence.[22]

Acheson and Kennan could have cited the findings of prominent social scientists that damned the United Nations as ineffectual. In April 1947, Professors James Burnham and Tarak-nath Das, both of New York University, told the annual meeting of the American Academy of Political and Social Science that the UN's record to date was one of blinding ineffectiveness/incompetence: "100 percent negative."[23]

To faultfinders, the case for the United Nations was additionally diminished by the quality of U.S. representation at Lake Success and Flushing Meadows. Ambassador Warren Austin, who led America's delegation from late 1946 to January 1953, was not dynamic, a condition exacerbated by advancing years (b. 1877) and uncertain health.[24] Prostate surgery in autumn 1948 prevented his attending that UNGA session when the Genocide Convention and UDHR were adopted. A stroke in 1950 affected his speech.[25] Moreover, dismaying to Cold Warriors, he clung too long to the idea that Soviet–U.S. discord could be harmonized. Not until the Korean War did he convert to the security credo, but too late to recoup Acheson's regard.

To Truman, the appeal of Austin rested on their acquaintance dating to joint service in Congress. Austin had there represented his native Vermont and joined the Senate Foreign Relations Committee. A member of the GOP's internationalist wing, his appointment to the UN post was meant to buttress bipartisanship and reassure Republicans like Senator Taft, who denounced what they saw as an overactive foreign policy.[26] Austin liked the UN job, at least initially: "It is the greatest challenge I ever felt."[27] Even so, GOP personalities who shared Austin's foreign policy orientation— Eisenhower, Dulles, Vandenberg—thought him too phlegmatic and worried over his reluctance to grapple verbally with Moscow's UN delegates. The overtly nonpartisan George Marshall considered Austin a person of "slight ability."[28] Gimlet-eyed Sir Gladwyn Jebb, British ambassador to the UN (1950–1954), considered him a spent force, even "ludicrous."[29]

To reinforce Austin, Truman sent a pair of intellectually nimble lieutenants, expert in legal-political matters, to the UN embassy. Philip Jessup and Ernest Gross performed yeoman service in the difficult circumstances of parliamentary diplomacy.[30] Yet these men, irrespective of their flair, struggled vainly to devise durable solutions to the Israeli–Palestinian feud and the Korean civil war, frustrations amply shared by the UN's senior staff.

Lie forwarded a well-worn United Nations flag to General MacArthur upon his designation in July 1950 as chief of UN forces in Korea. Sweden's Count Folke Bernadotte, UN Mediator for Palestine as of 21 May 1948, had previously flown it at his Rhodes headquarters and as he shuttled determinedly between Amman, Beirut, Cairo, Damascus, and Tel Aviv.[31] Following Bernadotte's 17 September 1948 assassination in Jerusalem by militant Zionists (Stern Gang), this banner and peace mission passed to his deputy, Ralph Bunche (head of the UN's trusteeship department for non-self-governing territories). Behind the symbolism of this weathered flag lay Lie's conception: the warrant of the United Nations ran far, its geographical stretch congruent with the world's postwar moral compass. Matters, alas, were not so simple to Jews and Arabs in Palestine or to Koreans living on either side of the 38th Parallel. Their grievances festered into the twenty-first century.

Palestine and Israel

Zionism

Predating the United Nations, the Zionist idea melded the diaspora's ancient desire to return to Jerusalem with European Jewry's wounding experience. Only in a land of their own would Jews flourish, pronounced Moses Hess, Hirsch Kalischer, Yehuda Leib Pinsker, and Theodor Herzl. Backdrop to this proposition lay the reality of anti-Semitism, variously codified or informal but always lurking. Age-old defamation—deicide, blood libel, usury, perfidiousness—fueled persecution and exclusion while blending with newer toxins: national chauvinisms, race mythologies. In Western Europe, the promise of Jewish emancipation, abetted by relief presumed to lie in assimilation, was shown to be false: the Dreyfus Affair. That misfire of French justice agitated Herzl's presidency (1897–1904) of the World Zionist Organization and authorship of the 1896 primer on building a Jewish safe place, *Judenstaat*.

Throughout Eastern Europe, lethal anti-Semitism periodically erupted, the 1903 Kishinev pogrom being but an example. Murder and pillage in the czarist realm created waves of Jewish emigration. Hundreds of thousands of people sought refuge in the Americas. Fewer numbers went to the Palestinian provinces of the Ottoman empire, where Zionist pioneers had already purchased property and built settlements.

The colony of Jews in Palestine at the end of World War I may have counted 60,000 people, slightly more than 8 percent of the area's total population of 660,000. The number of Jews in Palestine then rose rapidly as their situation in Germany and elsewhere in Europe became untenable. The Palestinian Jewish population in 1936 approached the 385,000 mark. A decade later, Jews composed about 30 percent of the population: 543,000 out of 1,810,037 inhabitants. In the subsequent four years, Jewish/non-Jewish demographics altered abruptly. The Jewish share in 1950 equaled more than 87 percent of the Palestine–Israel population: 1,203,000 Jews versus 167,100 others, mainly Arabs.[32]

After demolition of the Ottoman empire, and sanctioned by the League of Nations, the British government exercised to May 1948 responsibility for Palestine—corresponding with latter-day Israel, the Gaza Strip, and the West Bank. This entailed, among other complications, the Foreign Office's November 1917 "Balfour Declaration." It signaled British sympathy for Zionist aims and, though without reference to territorial definitions, placed the government in "favor" of "the establishment in Palestine of a national home for the Jewish people." To this end, London pledged its "best endeavors," qualified by a stipulation: "nothing shall be done which may prejudice the civil and religious rights of existing non-Jewish communities in Palestine." Desultory attempts by Zionist and Arab leaders to advance collaboration between their communities, exampled by the 1919 Faisal–Weizmann agreement, did not create Zionist–Arab amity. Relations were marred by suspicion and, despite British policing, punctuated by bloodshed. Anti-Zionist riots in the 1920s rocked Jerusalem, Jaffa, Hebron, and other Palestinian towns.

Arab nationalist violence escalated in the 1930s. It flamed into full revolt, sparked in 1936 by the Peel Commission that contained a partition plan, judged later by the cabinet to be unworkable. To help quell the disorder, His Majesty's Government took steps in 1939 to curb the transfer of lands from Arab sellers to Jewish buyers. The government also decided to reduce Jewish immigration to 75,000 during the next five years, which proposed trickle coincided, albeit unforeseen by practically everyone, with the Shoah. Even Amin Al-Husayni, the anti-Jewish mufti of Jerusalem, who in November 1941 met with Nazi officials in Berlin and implored Hitler to rid Palestine of Zionists, did not fully grasp the scope of Germany's homicidal Judaeophobia.[33] Whether Al-Husayni would have much cared remains a matter of conjecture, though his bloodcurdling speech of March

1944 makes one wince: "Kill Jews wherever you find them, for the love of God, history and religion."[34]

No trace of ambiguity attached to the thinking of Saudi Arabia's monarch, King Ibn Saud. He told FDR in February 1945 that the Jewish survivors of Nazism should be compensated in Germany with the homes and other property of Hitler's people. Their transgressions against Jewry should not be paid by the dispossession of innocent Arabs, however.[35]

Civil war sundered post-1945 Palestine. Arabs and Zionists attacked each other. They also turned upon British authority. Units of the Royal Navy intercepted ships laden with Jewish refugees that sought to unload their straitened passengers in Palestine, notoriously in the case of the *Exodus*, which tried unsuccessfully to land 4,500 people at Haifa. In spring 1946, Truman pressed Attlee and Bevin to allow 100,000 Jews, recently freed from Nazi clutches, to enter Palestine—a number disallowed by existing British quotas, anyway filled. The Foreign Office meanwhile griped that neither the president nor Congress was willing to admit an equivalent number of Jews to the United States: Washington panted a cloying sympathy for victims but restrictive immigration laws and anti-Semitism ruled in America.[36]

Jewish underground fighters in July 1946, linked to the Irgun, blew up Jerusalem's King David Hotel, which housed Britain's administrative headquarters in Palestine. Ninety people were killed, others maimed. Seven months later, Attlee's government—rickety, financially exhausted, stung by recriminations from Arabs and Zionists—announced its intention to surrender the unruly territory to the United Nations, thereby incidentally making good on London's 1939 pledge that Britain would relinquish the mandate within ten years. The UN General Assembly on 29 November 1947, ignoring the preference of a majority of residents in Palestine, voted (thirty-three to thirteen, ten abstentions) to divide the land into two states—one Jewish, the other Arab—and with plans for economic union and Jerusalem internationalized. Thereafter, outrages between Jews and Arabs multiplied, as when in February 1948 more than fifty civilians, primarily Jewish, were killed by bomb explosions in downtown Jerusalem (Ben Yehuda Street), evidently in reprisal for a deadly Irgun attack upon Arabs in a Ramlah market. Thus, Jews and Arabs became trapped in what Edward Said, Palestinian scholar-activist, later called an "iron circle of inhumanity."[37]

As Britain's mandate ended on 14 May 1948, and High Commissioner Sir Alan Cunningham departed by warship from Haifa harbor, the Jewish Agency's David Ben-Gurion in Tel Aviv proclaimed a new state: Israel. Thereupon, Egyptian, Jordanian, Iraqi, Lebanese, Syrian, and Saudi forces invaded. They did so on behalf of indignant Palestinian Arabs, threatened in their ancestral homeland by disinheritance; alien and hostile, the Zionist entity had to be dislodged lest it grew to uncontainable strength and arrogance. In the event, Arab armies, except the Jordanian officered by British nationals, gave a lackluster performance. Their rout by Haganah formations coincided with the exile of 750,000 Palestinian Arabs via flight and expulsion. Episodes of Israeli terror accelerated this displacement, foreshadowed by the Irgun's April 1948 murder of civilians at Deir Yassin.[38]

Not until 1949 did warfare cease and Israel with its Arab League enemies enter (February to July) into armistices. By the end of combat, Israelis had secured borders much superior to those originally envisioned in UN guidelines. To Palestinian Arabs, the combination of rapine and ejection was devastating. The Israeli freezing of bank accounts belonging to absent Arabs, unwillingness to pay compensation to people whose property was lost or confiscated, and refusal to repatriate uprooted Palestinians biding in refugee camps compounded the trauma—all conveyed by the word *nakba* (catastrophe). Approximately 160,000 Palestinian Arabs—mostly Muslim, some Christian—remained behind in new Israel. Of them, a fourth were homeless, many of their villages abandoned and residences bulldozed.[39]

To Israelis, whose military units fielded Zionist residents of longstanding and Shoah survivors, their triumph seemed a miracle of deliverance.[40] "A millennial dream" fulfilled (Abba Eban's imagery), Israel gained UN admission in May 1949, by which time the Jewish state had also been recognized by fifty-four countries.[41] At this time too, hundreds of thousands of Jews began to stream into Israel from displaced persons camps in Europe and from Arab countries where long-established Jewish communities were thenceforth unwelcome and harassed.[42] The adjustment of these newcomers to Israel was partially eased in the early 1950s by reparation payments from West Germany, an expiation for Third Reich crimes.

The defeat and banishment of Arab Palestine invites one to enter, in Said's imagery, "the highly sensitive terrain of what Jews did to *their* victims, in an age of genocidal extermination of Jews."[43] Indeed, the depopulating of Arab Palestine, and replacement by another human group, lands one in that thicket of concepts pioneered by Raphael Lemkin (see Chapter 3). His notions concerning *barbarism* and *vandalism*, as he presented them in 1933, lie near to the lived experience of Arab Palestinians during Israel's first post-Shoah years. Ideas that Lemkin developed in his *Axis Rule in Occupied Europe*, and that the United Nations validated in the 1948 Genocide Convention, also have relevance, especially those points in Article II of the Convention that pertain to inflicting bodily or mental harm on a distinctive group or undermining it by applying drastic conditions.

This is not to say that Israel was a genocidal endeavor in 1948–1950. It was not. The intention was absent. Yet disturbing elements were at play, of the kind Lemkin once identified. These revolutionized the demographic picture of Palestine during a compressed moment. None of this obviates Israel's many cultural, political, and economic achievements since 1948, or its significance as sanctuary from continuing anti-Semitism, as Edward Said himself admitted. Yet the suffering inflicted on a people without responsibility for Jewish persecution in Europe cut deep. Constituting Israel's original sin, questions remain that are uncomfortably close to those once examined by Lemkin.

Recognition and mediation

Before the Arab–Israeli dispute hardened into insolubility, the Truman administration had sought a resolution, doing so with the United Nations as its primary ally. Divided counsel within the president's inner circle, though, produced patchy policy and puzzlement abroad about the constancy of Washington.[44] Shifting popular opinion and different preferences expressed by pundits and activists of varying stripe aggravated this unsettledness.

Supporters of an Israeli state were nestled in the liberal wing of the Democratic party, among GOP electoral strategists, civil rights groups, much of American Jewry, philanthropic agencies, and Truman's confidential advisers. Prominent individuals in this company included former vice president Henry Wallace, Rabbi Stephen Wise, Reinhold Niebuhr, the NAACP's Walter White, W.E.B. Du Bois, 1948 GOP standard-bearer Thomas Dewey, the White House's specialist on minority affairs David Niles, and Eddie Jacobson, one of Truman's few Jewish friends and his former partner in Missouri haberdashery.

To special counsel Clark Clifford, emergent Israel should be scrutinized from various standpoints. First, it behooved Truman, as the 1948 presidential election neared, to stay mindful of those Jewish voters in key states—New York, Illinois, California—to whom Palestine–Israel had become a vital concern. To alienate their confidence or traditional Democratic allegiance could result in Truman's defeat in what was promising to be an excruciating campaign season. Second, Clifford viewed Israel as a moral cause that gave the West a chance to atone for past misdeeds against Jewry. Third, he believed that angry Arab leaders would not hazard their societies or personal survival by embracing Stalinism or allowing Moscow to command the Middle East. In essence, the accumulation of Arab wealth into the foreseeable future, irrespective of anything that occurred in Palestine, depended on the selling of oil to Western economies. How preposterous, he counseled Truman, for the United States to tremble because of the "threat of a few nomadic desert tribes" either to embrace Moscow or bar affordable oil exports.[45] Finally, Clifford argued—as did other advocates, including Trygve Lie—that a resurrected Jewish state in the Holy Land would be an agent of modernization in a region depressed by antediluvian attitudes and failed economies. Truman proved particularly susceptible, as did subsequent presidents, to this line argued by Chaim Weizmann (British national, Zionist sage) during White House visits in which he conjured visions of vacant deserts transformed into fecundity and blossom.[46]

Against U.S. support of Israel stood resolute opinion and formidable influence. The dominant view in the State Department and the Pentagon held that a Zionist-aligned policy would be improvident and must exact prohibitive costs. Contra Clifford's bromides, it risked estranging the Arab countries, plus much of the Islamic world besides, from the United States and its allies. Affordable Arab-produced oil bound for Western Europe, crucial to the Marshall Plan's success, would instantly be jeopardized. Over the longer-run, future concessions to Western-based oil-extracting companies must be undone. Soviet grubbing in Arab/Muslim resentments would, moreover, produce tangible strategic benefits for Moscow. The balance of Middle East power could irrevocably slide to Soviet advantage, giving lie to Clifford's assurances but too late to correct. Secretary of State George Marshall, a person whom Truman esteemed, said emphatically that the United States risked losing rich oil fields for the sake of a Zionist venture that lacked viability, while paving the way for Soviet penetration into a critical zone.[47]

Undersecretary of State Robert Lovett shared Marshall's objection, as did other department officials: Dean Acheson, George Kennan, Dean Rusk (who directed the office of UN affairs), and Loy Henderson (head of the Near Eastern affairs division, whose attitude was colored with anxiety about the purported leftist allegiance of Jewry).[48] Presidential adviser Admiral William Leahy and Secretary of Defense James Forrestal were no less adamant. The latter declared: "Oil—that is the side we ought to be on."[49]

The State Department-Pentagon outlook complemented that of U.S. petroleum company executives, the directors of Standard Oil of New Jersey, Caltex, and Gulf Oil, for instance. James Terry Duce, spokesman for Aramco, warned in 1948 against a fatal danger to Western enterprises should a Jewish state take hold in Palestine. Thereafter, still on behalf of Aramco, he became involved in private assistance programs to alleviate Palestinian hardships.[50] Likewise, mining engineer Karl Twitchell, who once scouted for the American Eastern Corporation in Saudi Arabia, warned that the establishment of Israel would presage the ringing down of an "iron curtain" on the Middle East, "leaving the West and U.S. starved for the vital oil which is located in that area."[51] He would have preferred that Zionists investigate alternative sites to found a homeland, perhaps in the remoter reaches of Ethiopia, Brazil, or British Guiana. In any case, he said that the creation in Palestine of a Jewish commonwealth would be unjust to local Arabs, even gratuitous since New York City, he wisecracked, already qualified as such.[52]

During the last months of British mandate, this diplomatic–military–commercial alliance held firm. Its principals lobbied Truman to circumvent the General Assembly's November 1947 vote to partition Palestine and advocated a bi-national state with equal rights for Jews and Arabs. Should this fail, Palestine might properly pass into UN supervision and trusteeship. Once Israeli–Arab hostilities started in May 1948, Marshall et al. argued against sending matériel to any of the belligerents, opposed dispatching U.S. soldiers to impose or guard a truce, and urged that diplomatic distance be kept from Israel while at the same time assuring Arab parties of Washington's solicitude.

After dickering and inadvertently sending contradictory messages, Truman decided, over Marshall's protest, to support the UN partition scheme. Despite annoyance with Zionists and their champions, having refused at times to meet with them, Truman extended de facto recognition to Israel just minutes after David Ben-Gurion proclaimed (14 May) the new state.[53] Truman thereby stole a march on the Kremlin, which with alacrity also recognized Israel, an action calculated by Stalin to undermine Britain's Levant bulwark.[54]

The Washington debate on Palestine–Israel, occasionally intemperate, created hesitancy and annoyance in America's UN delegation. Of those delegates in favor of a fully fledged Jewish state, Eleanor Roosevelt was the most unreserved. Her thinking had been shaped by internees whom she had met in displaced persons camps and voiced desires to leave the European charnel house for life in Palestine. When Truman seemed likely to give way to Marshall's preference for a UN trusteeship, Roosevelt threatened to resign from the delegation; the president quickly sought to reassure her. Contra Roosevelt, Ambassador Austin originally preferred a bi-national Arab-Jewish state in Palestine, but not so strongly that he considered leaving the delegation when Washington indicated otherwise. He faithfully stuck to the shifting White House line, even when this required making awkward adjustments or obliged him to abandon his expectation that Arabs and Jews could find ways to reconcile differences in—Austin's locution— "a true Christian spirit."[55]

After accepting and then defending Truman's endorsement of a two-state plan, Austin had to reverse course in March 1948. The administration had decided, the State Department having gained fleeting ascendancy, that a UN trusteeship made sense. Trygve Lie, then contemplating an international force to guarantee partition, was so embarrassed for Austin and himself that he opined that they resign their offices.[56] Even more startling to America's UN delegates, they were unaware of Truman's later decision to recognize the newly formed Israeli government.[57] The U.S. delegation at the General Assembly in Flushing Meadows, in anticipation of a pending vote, was reciting the virtues of a UN-administered Palestine trusteeship when word arrived that Israel was born and Washington had de facto recognized its provisional government. This unexpected announcement discombobulated the Americans present and stirred bedlam among the gathered UN delegations. Jessup had to improvise a statement at the rostrum, Austin having slipped out of the UNGA meeting before that moment, apparently too rattled (he had received advance notice) to advise his colleagues.[58] Gromyko scolded the Americans for "unprincipled conduct." Lebanon's Charles Malik thundered that Washington had acted in bad faith and duped the United Nations.[59]

Not until 31 January 1949 did the United States grant de jure recognition to Israel. The first American ambassador to the country, James Grover McDonald, presented his credentials in late March, by which time the Arab–Israeli fighting had ended.

To Lie, the Arab war on Israel tested the fledgling United Nations. He feared that it would sink into inconsequence if proved too irresolute to halt this "flagrant aggression."[60] He expected that the Bernadotte mediation, commissioned by the Security Council on 20 May 1948, could devise a formula satisfactory to all Palestinian interests, but especially to the Jews whose purpose Lie judged compelling. He maintained as self-evident that they deserved a state of their own, a conviction fortified by sorrow for the Nazi herding of 760 Norwegian Jews into oblivion—nearly 50 percent of his little country's total Jewish population.[61] "This history of suffering naturally affected my conscience," Lie later wrote.[62]

Bernadotte presented proposals to Arab and Israeli belligerents on 28 June 1948, a moment of uneasy lull. His main point entailed an economic union of Jordan with Palestine; therein, a Jewish entity and an Arab entity would exercise control over their respective foreign and domestic/immigration affairs. The borders of the two national entities would be clarified by negotiation. Religious and minority rights in each would be protected in law and custom—so too would holy sites and religious buildings. People displaced by Jewish–Arab fighting would be allowed to return to their abodes and live in safety. On the subject of boundaries, Bernadotte favored placing all or most of the Negev in Arab jurisdiction and the western Galilee in Jewish territory. Jerusalem, he believed, should be put in Jordanian custody with provision for guaranteeing the municipal autonomy of resident Jews.

Upon rejection of these ideas by Zionists and Arabs, along with the resumption of hostilities, Bernadotte devised a second set of ideas. It was finalized on 16 September, the day before his assassination in Jerusalem (for which nobody was convicted, although Israel made indemnity of $54,000 to the UN and issued regrets). Bernadotte's second plan kept much of the original but with these critical amendments. Two independent states were envisioned, premised on Israel's security needs and the right of individuals to be repatriated or properly compensated if they chose not to return to their homes. Jerusalem, moreover, should be placed under UN supervision, with autonomy guaranteed for the local Arab and Jewish communities.

This second Bernadotte plan also did not persuade Arabs and Zionists. Rejection was followed by reintensified violence and a string of Israeli military victories, most notably in the Negev. This led to an Egyptian decision in early January 1949 to enter into armistice talks with Israel. These unfolded on the island of Rhodes in negotiations presided over by chain-smoking Ralph Bunche. Owing in fair measure to his tact and perseverance, a series of truce agreements—supposedly interim, pending permanent peace—were signed by Israel and the front-line states: Egypt, Lebanon, Syria, Jordan.[63] This ended the fighting and established demarcation lines, but left the matter of uprooted Palestinians unresolved. "The hapless refugees," Bunche rued, were "still on the hook. They are the *real* victims of the affair."[64]

Seventy-eight percent of mandatory Palestine was incorporated into the frontiers of Israel, including access to the Gulf of Aqaba. Gaza went to Egypt, the West Bank and east Jerusalem to Jordan. Israel's existence was thus ratified—albeit unrecognized as legitimate by Arabs—and UN champions declared a moral-practical victory, a view reaffirmed in 1950 when Bunche, dubbed by admirers the "new Colossus of Rhodes," received the Nobel Peace Prize for his feat of arbitration.[65] Upon acceptance on 10 December of the award in Oslo, he saluted the spirit of Bernadotte and added this self-effacement: "I am but one of many cogs in the United Nations."[66]

Korean years

War

Half a globe away from Oslo, while Bunche addressed Nobel dignitaries, overextended UN forces in Korea staggered under blows struck by Chinese "volunteer" armies. A third world war seemed imminent, darkening Bunche's mood: "The future of all mankind hangs fatefully in the balance."[67] On 4 January 1951, Chinese and North Korean soldiers captured Seoul and prepared to drive farther south. MacArthur consequently proposed enlarging the scope of military operations to include bombing of supply depots in China. Truman considered as an option the deploying of atomic weapons.

This Korean drama had been in the making since the collapse of the Japanese empire. Annexed by it in 1910, Korea had been subjected to cultural assimilation and economic-political cooptation. A prized province, an object of Tokyo's industrial-strategic attention, Korea was loosed from Japan's control by Allied armies in the final days of World War II. Upon agreement (11 August 1945) by Soviet and U.S. negotiators, a temporary division of the country was drawn at the 38th Parallel. Subsequently approved (mid-November 1947) by the UN General Assembly, the country was supposed to be unified under an all-Korean government via future elections.

The southern part of the country was organized under U.S. auspices, the American proconsul being Lieutenant General John Hodge. His massively bad relations with Syngman Rhee, a conservative nationalist who came to dictate Seoul politics, were outshone only by his suspicion of communists and the USSR. Simultaneous with Hodge's doings, Soviet occupation authorities in the north, centered in Pyongyang, aligned with Kim Il Sung, who consolidated his standing among competing Marxist factions to become premier of the Democratic People's Republic of Korea. Because the north balked, the scheduled all-national elections were aborted, even though UN-supervised balloting took place in May 1948 in southern precincts. This led to the election of Rhee to the presidency and the General Assembly's designating his administration as the only freely chosen and lawful government in Korea. Thus, in their respective sectors, Washington and Moscow had installed ideologically congenial elites who continued in place even after Soviet and U.S. garrisons departed (December 1948–June 1949) from the peninsula.

Each Korean regime wanted on its own terms to unify the country, ambitions that begat border skirmishing and guerrilla warfare, plus the suppression of dissent in both zones. The number of fatalities climbed into the thousands, a stalemate of sorts that ended in June 1950. With blessings from Stalin and Mao, earlier objections abraded by Kim's categorical assurances, North Korean invaders spilled over the 38th Parallel, capturing Seoul on 28 June. They drove the southern armies toward total defeat, barely averted by Truman's introduction into the conflict of U.S. land, air, and naval forces and the holding of the Pusan perimeter in southeastern Korea. Labeled by Truman a "police action," the fighting of 1950–1953 was for Koreans on either side of the 38th Parallel a disaster, their civil war swept into the Cold War whirl. Powerful armies collided, fielded by the People's Republic of China (furnished with Soviet matériel and warplanes/pilots) versus the militarily preeminent United States, aided by fifteen additional countries operating under UN aegis. As many as three million Korean civilians and servicemen—10 percent of the country's population—ended the war as casualties: killed, wounded, captured, missing. Five million people were displaced with family members dispersed by the 1953 ceasefire line. More than a million homes were destroyed and the industrial infrastructure smashed, north and south. The residents of Seoul, Pyongyang, and other cities had to eke out pitiable existence.[68] As for the cost borne by China, the sacrifice included nearly 400,000 soldiers killed (among them Mao's son) or wounded. Roughly 34,000 Americans died; 100,000 were wounded. Among other UN forces, the casualty rates were highest among British, Canadian, Australian, and New Zealand units.[69]

The human and material price notwithstanding, Lie never questioned the justice of the UN's Korean intervention. Nor did he deplore taking the side of one Cold War protagonist against another. Until his cooperation with America's Korean effort, he had wanted to maintain impartiality between Moscow and Washington, a stance for which he paid dearly on Capitol Hill, where many legislators viewed him askance. They took umbrage at his criticism of the Truman Doctrine and his publicly stated worry that the creation of NATO must weaken the UN's collective security mission. His calls for the admission to the UN of mainland China at the expense of the Nationalists on Taiwan were said to show him for what he was: communist stooge or fellow traveler. Washington should disavow him and disengage from the United Nations.[70]

Lie's part in obtaining the Security Council's decision to aid South Korea—possible because of Soviet boycott under way in support of Beijing's UN admission—remade his reputation.[71] He became a darling, even if the UN did not, of congressional hardliners, while Kremlin officials, who had hitherto tolerated him, castigated him as a tool of imperialist warmongers and worked to remove him from office. Soviet pressure ultimately resulted in his resignation, announced in November 1952 (effective April 1953).[72]

Lie cooperated with members of the U.S. delegation. He shared Ambassador Austin's assumption that the Kremlin had commissioned the North Korean attack. Lie helped ensure continuing UN support, notably the Uniting for Peace formula (devised by Washington), approved on 3 November 1950. This moved the authority for waging the war from the Security Council to the General Assembly, thus circumventing Moscow's obstruction via veto, threatened once Ambassador Jacob Malik reactivated Moscow's UN embassy in August 1950. Following the Inchon landings,

15 September 1950, Lie also backed the American-led crossing of the 38th Parallel and proposed reunification of Korea under Seoul. After China's intervention in late autumn 1950, he was content for a restoration of the Korean status quo ante bellum. He went along uncomplainingly when in April 1951 Truman ousted MacArthur from command in Korea and instated General Matthew Ridgway, the latter described by Lie as "a good United Nations man."[73] Lie labeled communist charges of U.S. germ warfare in Korea as repugnant fabrication.[74] He supported the U.S. side throughout the protracted truce talks that culminated in the July 1953 Panmunjom armistice, by which time Sweden's Dag Hammarskjold had replaced him as secretary-general.

The alternative to a defense of South Korea, Lie frequently reiterated, would have meant diminution of the UN's stature and the onset of that atrophy which crippled the League of Nations. Fortunately, he taught, the UN passed its test, vindicating the principle of global security. Upon learning that the Korean armistice had finally been signed, he exclaimed from his Norwegian retirement haven:

> As much as any man, I have been gripped by the tragedy of the Korean War. But I am also conscious of the nobility and surpassing significance of the United Nations police action in Korea. . . . It has been the first determined stand against international lawlessness and aggression which the peace-loving governments of the world have taken. . . . Korea proves that aggression does not pay.[75]

Investigations

Lie's triumphalism did not everywhere ring true, certainly not in America, where impatience with the United Nations grew during the months of Korean stalemate and sputtering truce talks. An expression of this feeling occurred in 1952 with U.S. investigations into the Secretariat's personnel practices. Even before the Korean crisis, security zealots had wondered whether disloyal Americans in the Secretariat's employ were cooperating with Soviet agents at the UN and dragging the United States to perdition. For example, in 1948, the Young Men's Business Club in New Orleans, with assistance from Representative F. Edward Hébert (D, Louisiana), protested the appointment of Mitchell Franklin to the legal staff of the Secretariat. They alleged that this Tulane University law professor, active in Henry Wallace's presidential bid, was intent on harming the United States.[76] The fact that recruitments to the Secretariat were solely the responsibility of the UN Bureau of Personnel—unlike U.S. diplomatic posts, subject to Senate approval—only heightened the alarm felt by Hébert et al. What dangerous nonsense to them was this statement from Austin's embassy regarding Franklin and the vetting of international civil servants:

> In accordance with obligations undertaken by all Member nations in signing the United Nations Charter, the United States Government must respect the independence of the United Nations in making appointment to its own staff, even when the appointees are citizens of the United States. . . . The Bureau of Personnel of the United Nations carefully checks the technical qualifications of those individuals it is considering appointing to its staff and compares them carefully with those of other applicants. In accordance with the Charter, the Bureau of Personnel does not request the approval of the respective Member governments for the employment of nationals of those governments by the United Nations Secretariat. In accepting appointment to the Secretariat, individuals pledge themselves to discharge their functions with the interest only of the United Nations in view.[77]

In the event, to Hébert's chagrin, Franklin did serve as a legal officer in the Secretariat, later returning to Tulane, where he taught until his 1967 retirement. Still, a roused and unhappy constituency had not vanished but meant to make its preferences felt at the United Nations.

Satisfaction came in the form of hearings begun in October 1952 by the Senate Judiciary Subcommittee on Internal Security, chaired by Patrick McCarran (D, Nevada), and a federal grand jury. These sought to expose and purge any American communists employed by the Secretariat, from file clerks upward. A handful of U.S. staffers either pleaded their rights against self-incrimination, permitted in the Fifth Amendment but often read in Washington as an admission of guilt, or confessed to once having flirted with communism. None of these people was ever charged with taking action injurious to the United States, but they were cited as evidence that the UN had become, in common with Korean battlefields, a place of Kremlin-sponsored hazard.[78]

After protesting on behalf of the Secretariat's prerogative in selecting its own personnel, ridiculing the idea that the UN was a sturdy platform from which anyone could launch espionage against the United States, and certain that he had never knowingly hired an American communist, Lie abased himself and his office. He declared that American communists had no place at the UN. He cashiered administrative staffers who previously had failed to convince U.S. investigators of their reliability. He agreed that American citizens in any international agency—those already hired and those recruited in future years—were appropriate subjects of U.S. scrutiny, in which case the personnel apparatus of the UN would cooperate. Anything less, he reckoned, would invite the loss of Washington's confidence and whatever remained of public support for the UN.[79]

In early 1953, at the behest of Washington's new ambassador, patrician Henry Cabot Lodge, FBI investigators at UN headquarters commenced to fingerprint and interrogate the many hundreds of U.S. nationals on the UN payroll.[80] By late July, only one woman had refused to cooperate with this security regime; her services were (Lodge's vocabulary) "terminated."[81] None of this happened, though, before Abraham Feller, an American lawyer who headed the UN's legal counsel and enjoyed Lie's respect and affection, committed suicide (13 November 1952) by defenestration from his twelfth-floor apartment.[82] This he did in a stupor of fatigue and gloom over the UN's surrender on staff policy, in which matter he had been closely involved. The resurfacing of old questions, never substantiated, about his alleged Marxist–Leninist sympathies may also have unnerved him.[83] Neither chastened nor remorseful, McCarran blurted on learning of this honorable man's death: "If Feller's conscience was clear, he had no reason to suffer from what he expected from our committee."[84]

Upset by the spectacle of FBI prying on UN premises and damages to morale, Hammarskjold, after becoming secretary-general (10 April 1953), forbade continued use of UN facilities for investigatory purposes, which decision strained his relations with Lodge. Hammarskjold also took steps to regularize the conditions by which any staff member could be dismissed and erected safeguards to protect employees from slander or unwarranted suspicion by snoops.[85]

Even so, the red-baiting of UN officials did not soon abate but only slowly petered out. One such investigation brought forward against a Secretariat member transpired in 1953–1954, focused on Ralph Bunche.

Not only was he by then a Nobel laureate. He was also a decorated veteran of OSS operations and State Department service.[86] He was, additionally, a respected scholar and author: Harvard Ph.D., professor (Howard University), president of the American Political Science Association, and major contributor in 1939–1940 to the researches of Gunnar Myrdal's seminal *An American Dilemma: The Negro Problem and Modern Democracy*.[87] Moreover, Bunche was fast becoming Hammarskjold's indispensable chief lieutenant (appointed undersecretary-general in 1954).[88]

Undeterred by this renown, members of the Senate Internal Security Subcommittee, William Jenner (R, Indiana) and Herman Welker (R, Idaho), inquired (March 1953) of Bunche whether he had ever been a communist. Or, in his OSS days in Africa, had he consorted with Soviet agents? Eventually, the subcommittee produced (January 1954) fourteen allegations of disloyalty that were examined by the International Employees Loyalty Board. Had Bunch joined the CPUSA? Perhaps he had become a "concealed" communist? Or he lived in the "control" of communists? What exactly had he been up to with the National Negro Congress (NNC), in whose founding in 1936 he had assumed a part and whose roster included known communists, specifically John Davis and James Ford? To these interrogatories and innuendo, Bunche penned detailed answers. He submitted thirty-seven exhibits of correspondence and other documentation. He testified in hearings. He explained inter alia that notions he entertained in the 1930s of racialized class oppression in Dixie did not mask a Soviet outlook or treasonous vocation. He detailed his disillusionment with the NNC and resignation (1940) from membership once that organization fell to the dictate of Stalinist hacks.[89] He quoted from his frequent denunciations of communist party activities in America and labeling of James Ford as "an utter ignoramus." Bunche cited his record of decades-long public duty and intercession in the Arab–Israeli war, a conflict, he stated, from which only the USSR and its clients could benefit: "I may be pardoned for asking what manner of Communist it could be who would act as I did in Palestine?"[90] He cited his opposition to a broad range of Soviet foreign policies. He underscored his support of the UN effort in Korea. In the end, a lack of credible witnesses or evidence undid the case against Bunche. He was cleared of all charges in May 1954, but for years afterward remained a target of aspersion by reactionaries and conspiracy theorists.[91]

Though glad of exoneration and supportive testimony by luminaries (Hammarskjold, Eleanor Roosevelt, Walter White), Bunche's having to

FIGURE 4.2 Ralph Bunche with Nobel Peace Prize
Source: Ralph Bunche Institute for International Studies, City University of New York

explain himself against spurious charges and the willful misreading of his career infuriated him. Nothing in his experience, he felt, surpassed this ordeal—melancholy realization from one orphaned in youth, who beat the odds against black men on mean Los Angeles streets, tempted fate in Dixie with Myrdal to take the measure of race relations, and in execution of public trust had stomached uncouthness in Jim Crow Washington.[92] He wrote in heat:

> I must express my indignation and protest that . . . presumably informed public officers, charged with responsibility for the investigation of such matters, have not themselves found the open

record of my conduct over the years so complete a refutation of any possibility of Communist Party membership or pro-Communist attitudes as to make quite unnecessary any denial by me of such association.[93]

He meantime wondered whether the country had lost its sense altogether; strands of fear-mongering and bigotry had webbed into an environment permissive of demagoguery.[94]

Aware that the charges against Bunche were outlandish, and, luckily for his later reputation, uninvolved with the inquiry, Lodge nevertheless was gratified when U.S. and UN personnel procedures came to align. He wagered that this would give cover to Eisenhower against extremists in the GOP while encouraging ordinary citizens to repose greater faith in the UN.[95] Suspension of UN employment practices, to whose inviolability Washington had once vouchsafed, and the sacrifice of people's careers if necessary, constituted acceptable price to retain U.S. commitment to the United Nations. Without blanching, Lodge broadcast (1956) his part in appeasing the Korean-era guardians of public safety:

> Of the 3,000 employees of the United Nations, 1,800 are Americans, and the first thing I did on becoming U.S. representative was to arrange for the fingerprinting of every one of these 1,800 and for having them screened by a special U.S. commission in accordance with Civil Service and FBI procedures. . . . When there are so many good Americans to choose from there is no excuse whatever for employing one single American Communist.[96]

★ ★ ★

That the United Nations withstood State Department critiques and congressional reputation seekers, and did not crumble in Palestine or Korea, testified to a quality of grit unimagined by even the most ardent Dumbarton Oaks conferees. Yet to Americans, plus other peoples, the litany of UN sins of omission and commission ran unceasingly, well past the end of the twentieth century.

From a U.S. standpoint, the admission of new African/Asian states to the General Assembly in the mid-1950s onward signaled a dilution of Western influence in that body.[97] This untoward condition provoked a corresponding dip in Washington's interest and spikes of dismay as in 1975, when the General Assembly adopted Resolution 3379, which equated Zionism with racism.[98] Withdrawal in 1984–2003 from UNESCO, in part for its putative anti-Israeli bias, and consternation in Congress after UNESCO in 2011 permitted Palestinian membership, reflected continuing U.S. displeasure. So too did blistering public comments by ambassadors to the UN: Daniel Patrick Moynihan (1975–1976), Jean Kirkpatrick (1981–1985), John Bolton (2005–2006). They waxed livid in defense of Israel. They portrayed the Secretariat as a bloated bureaucracy riddled with wastefulness and corruption, the General Assembly as a talk shop mired in hypocrisy. Congress chose in 1985 not to authorize full payment on U.S. fees owed to the United Nations. A decade later, the United States was $1.4 billion in arrears, with corresponding disruption to UN operations, including peacekeeping.[99]

Only Voltaire's Pangloss could have credited the UN during the Cold War or after with success in realizing its primary mission: ensuring the peace, abolishing warfare. From a Washingtonian angle, the UN record in international policing and deterring aggression was deficient, particularly regarding crises linked to Moscow machinations. Not until 1990–1991 were Americans able, for the first time since the Korean War, to involve the UN in a U.S. military operation considered urgent by the White House: liquidating Iraq's occupation of oil-rich Kuwait.

Despite its shortcomings, real and imagined, the UN in its auxiliary functions since 1945 has made genuine contributions to human security broadly defined.[100] The UN has led attempts to improve public health (WHO), enhance the welfare of children (UNICEF), protect refugees (UNHCR), and safeguard civilization (UNESCO). Since its founding in 1949, UNRWA has worked to ameliorate the suffering of disinherited Palestinians.[101]

Consequential matters have also appeared on the agendas of specialized UN agencies and been aired in General Assembly deliberations: economic development, urbanization, oceanic regulation, climate change, environmental degradation, gender equality, and illegal narcotics. Operating under UN auspices, peacekeepers ("blue helmets") and emergency responders to natural catastrophes (floods, earthquakes, famines) have at times shone brightly. The office of the secretary-general has meanwhile approached the equivalent status of secular pope, sanctified by martyrs: Hammarskjold, killed in the Congo in 1961. The pronouncements of secretaries-general have commanded periodic attention and their good deeds have been lauded, as when in December 1954 Hammarskjold went to Beijing to win the release of fifteen U.S. airmen taken captive during the Korean War—an errand that helped thaw the frost between him and Lodge.[102]

In the weighing of UN virtues and defects, the unsung Austin was as cogent as anyone when he uttered these words late in his ambassadorship. As Korean fighting blazed along, he said in language that, if pedestrian, was true and remains apt. Against anarchy, "the United Nations has not achieved perfection, but it has taken steps in the right direction."[103] Observers meanwhile, assigned to the UN Truce Supervision Organization, were reporting violations committed by Arabs and Israelis. Yet a version of the Bunche-promoted armistice held, surviving until the June 1967 war (when Israel gained territories that included the whole of Jerusalem, Gaza, and the West Bank). None of these happenings, of course, altered the longstanding Middle East dilemma, succinctly summarized by Philip Jessup: "We have an obligation both to see that Israel is not exterminated and to see that it behaves itself."[104]

★ ★ ★

5

EMPIRES

The crisis will not soon be resolved, nor can its outcome be predicted. It may culminate, as I hope it will, in a reassertion of the traditional values, in a renewed awareness of the creative power of the American example. Or it may culminate in our becoming an empire of the traditional kind, ordained to rule for a time over an empty system of power and then to fade or fall, leaving, like its predecessors, a legacy of dust.[1]

Senator J. William Fulbright, 13 December 1967

★ ★ ★

History is replete with dramatic shifts in the distribution of power, as triggered by World War II, which led to British departure from Palestine and Japanese ejection from Korea and the emergencies that ensued upon those territories. Both of those imperial retreats manifested reconfigured global power. They also instanced the ultimate fate awaiting every empire, refrained dolefully in Rudyard Kipling's *Recessional*:

Lo, all our pomp of yesterday
Is one with Nineveh and Tyre![2]

Repositories of economic-military vigor, empires have constituted the chief players in international society.[3] In that function, even while competing among themselves, they have defended their collective primacy against challengers, among them states of Westphalian inspiration or trans-sovereign organizations, such as the United Nations. Yet if any law of political science can be said to apply everywhere and at all times, it is that each empire, irrespective of its splendor, eventually collapses, either supplanted quickly by other dominating powers or birthing long periods of uncertainty and disorder.[4] The replacement of Third Reich mastery by that of the Soviets in post-1945 Eastern Europe illustrates the former case. The second is exemplified by the instabilities that have plagued the Middle East since the 1922 dissolution of the Ottoman domain.

The Ottoman provinces had been connected by uninterrupted land bridges. Similarly constructed empires at the beginning of the twentieth century included Romanov Russia and ramshackle Austria-Hungary. Although possessing overseas colonies, Hohenzollern Germany and the republican United States were mainstays of might that spread their writs across contiguous zones. The other empires of that day, keeping in thrall diverse colonies and peoples, were assembled along sea routes and, except for Japan, were centered on Western Europe: France, Great Britain, Italy, the Netherlands, Belgium, Portugal, Spain.

World War I not only erased the Ottoman and Austro-Hungarian empires and "unmixed" their subject peoples but also shrank the territories of Russia and Germany.[5] Russia and Germany, moreover, lost sizable population by transfer to other places and underwent regime change. The French and British imperia, albeit technically victorious in the war and despite augments to the number of their far-flung holdings, were wounded, more gravely than either the political class in Paris or London cared to admit or impartial observers knew. Only the United States and Japan emerged from the 1914 holocaust in comparative good health. On the eve of hostilities, the United States had been an international debtor but by war's climax stood as the foremost creditor. Japan, little engaged in military operations, collected Germany's concession in China (Shandong) and Pacific island properties.

Renewed by totalitarian leaders and chiliastic doctrines, Germany and Russia resurfaced as formidable empires in the interwar period. Their cooperation in 1939–1941 resulted in Germany's subduing of continental Europe and Soviet recovery of most of the czarist patrimony. The subsequent war between Nazi and Soviet power broke Germany but elevated Russia to levels of status and influence unmatched since Czar Alexander marched his army through Paris after Napoleon's 1814 defeat.

Even more than in 1814, France in the aftermath of World War II amounted to cumulative injury: bled white in 1914–1918; defeated in 1940; disoriented by Vichy collaboration. France, too, had been insulted by Axis usurpation of parts of the empire, notably Indochina, which fell to Japanese suzerainty (1940–1941), then (March 1945) to total control. Elsewhere in Asia/Pacific, other European and U.S. colonies—from British Burma to Dutch Indonesia to America's Philippines—were captured by Japanese forces, operating under Tokyo's guise of redeeming the East from white trespass. Following its 1945 defeat, Japan forfeited its hard-won empire, stretching from island nations to Chinese mainland districts. Still, the damage done to white pretensions and claims to superior morality ran deep. While the capitals—Paris, The Hague, Brussels—of ancient empires had been occupied by Germany, its Japanese ally demonstrated by conquests that white preeminence need not be a permanent condition in the Asia/Pacific or, implicitly, in Africa.

Despite colonial contraction after 1945, exemplified by the British Raj's abdication in India and Dutch evacuation from Indonesia, this hope controlled in metropolitan centers: to retain traditional prerogatives. Consequently, successive French and British administrations waged rearguard actions. Their futility was highlighted at Suez, when (19 October– 7 November 1956) Anglo-French collusion to save privileges failed, chiefly to opposition by the United States, the twentieth century's paramount empire.

Washington officials by 1956 sat atop a sprawling scheme: wealth, well-patrolled spheres of influence, client states, access to crucial natural resources. This immensity—imperial in content, liberal in form—eclipsed the dimming French and British empires. It enjoyed advantages over that of the Soviet in Eastern Europe, which Moscow kept via suppression and coils of dependency.

Decolonization

As watched in America, the collapse of French and British colonialism seemed abrupt, despite portents of gathering weakness, easier read in retrospect than at the time. Late in his life, Dean Acheson conveyed this sense of startlement felt in post-1945 Washington:

It didn't really strike home to us that the British Empire was gone, the great power of France was gone. . . . I still looked at the map and saw that red on the thing, and, by God, that was the British Empire, the French Senegalese troops in East Asia and in Germany—all this was gone to hell.[6]

The dismantlement of the French–British colonial regimes had advanced by the day Acheson left his State Department office to John Foster Dulles. But, as mentioned, the ceding of imperial entitlements was hardly viewed across the political spectra in Paris and London as inevitable or warranted.

France held in 1953 to distant areas, despite the 1946 forfeiting of Syrian/Lebanese possessions or the material and moral costs borne by the war on rebels in 1947 Madagascar. In Vietnam and against mounting doubts about chances for success, French naval-air-military forces sought to reimpose their version of order against a national-communist revolt, led by indefatigable Ho Chi Minh and that self-taught strategist, General Vo Nguyen Giap. The former in September 1945, proclaiming the Democratic Republic of Vietnam, invoked two august documents: the 1776 Declaration of Independence, the 1789 Declaration des droits de l'homme et du citoyen. Even earlier, Ho had attempted—vainly, in the event—to contact White House incumbents, first Woodrow Wilson during the 1919 Paris Treaty negotiations, then, years afterward, Franklin Roosevelt.

President Roosevelt had not relished the return of the French to Southeast Asia. He had, in fact, labored to prevent France from reclaiming Indochina. He preferred its relinquishment or, if political apprenticeship seemed appropriate, a period of UN trusteeship for the three entities: Laos, Cambodia, Vietnam. Roosevelt's idea along these lines must have been colored by the military effort of Ho and his Viet Minh. Their cooperation with the OSS during anti-Japanese campaigns showed to better effect than anything undertaken by Marshal Philippe Pétain's Vichy or General Charles de Gaulle's Free French, each of which FDR anyway disparaged. Yet these sentiments did not translate into Roosevelt's espousal of Ho Chi Minh or his cause.

In October 1945 and February 1946, Ho appealed to President Truman to support a Vietnamese bid for independence.[7] This démarche yielded silence and unavailability in Washington, despite Truman's misgivings (similar to FDR's) about the French empire and its role in future international society.

Doubts aside, Truman arranged for the transfer of varied aid to France in support of its Indochina holdings, doing so for reasons grounded in this calculation: France was needed as a reliable player in the European balance of power and to check the USSR. The restoration of the Indochina possessions, with corresponding boost to Paris's morale, seemed therefore logical. Conversely, failure in Indochina must dispirit the French and shake their positions elsewhere, particularly in North Africa: Morocco, Tunisia, Algeria (the last designated as a department of France).[8] A palsied France, one could have surmised, would be worse for Washington than having no ally at all.

This Truman orientation trumped scruples about the application of rights of self-determination to peoples, who French colons insisted anyway lacked competence for self-rule. Modest at first, the volume of U.S. assistance swelled after the June 1950 start of Korean hostilities. In the meantime, Moscow and Beijing accorded diplomatic recognition to Ho's regime, which also won receipt of Chinese matériel and military advisers.[9]

In line with Truman's policy, the Eisenhower–Dulles government furnished France with military equipment, logistics, and funding. The United States underwrote roughly 78 percent of French financial costs in Indochina by 1954; the overall U.S. investment for 1950–1954 approximated $3 billion.[10] At the same time, France created the fiction of a politically sovereign South Vietnam (Republic of Vietnam), presided over by Emperor Bao Dai, to whom Washington extended diplomatic status. This supposedly independent entity, along with Laos and Cambodia in les Etats Associes de l'Indochine, gained membership in the French Union.

The battle of Dien Bien Phu, under way in spring 1954, tempted Eisenhower to intervene directly in Vietnam.[11] This could have entailed the dispatching of U.S. soldiers to rescue the beleaguered French fortress or the heavy bombing, possibly with tactical nuclear weapons, of communist armies laying siege to it.[12] Yet any such action, the White House decided, hinged on the British also contributing to Dien Bien Phu's relief. Prime Minister Churchill and Foreign Secretary Eden thought any likely venture imprudent, however. It might activate an otherwise avoidable and expensive war against China (with loss of British Hong Kong) or the USSR. Besides, said Churchill, ongoing negotiations convened in Geneva—involving delegates from France, China, UK, USA, USSR, India, Laos, Cambodia, and Vietnamese parties—should resolve the Indochina knot, obviating the need for Anglo-U.S. military adventure. This British balking not only irked Washington officials but quashed their taking steps on behalf of Dien Bien Phu.

French troops surrendered on 7 May 1954 to Giap and thereupon trudged through steamy jungle and hazard to confinement.[13] French recovery from this debacle proved impossible. Despite Dulles's remonstrance and cajoling, the coalition government of Pierre Mendes France perceived no alternative to accepting the July 1954 Geneva formula: first, temporary partitioning of the country at the 17th parallel; second, allowing national elections in 1956, at which time the Viet Minh-controlled north and the noncommunist south (increasingly guided by the Catholic mandarin Ngo Dinh Diem) ought to unify as a single free state.

While Americans became entangled in the post-Geneva web of provisional Indochina solutions, the French empire encountered further untenableness. Algerian nationalists, restive since the Sétif massacres (May 1945) and encouraged by the example of Ho-Giap victory, instigated a full revolt in November 1954. This engulfed an Algerian population of nearly one million people of European descent, politically privileged and fairly affluent, and nine million estranged Arabs, stuck in poverty and relegated to second-class status.[14] The violence strained the Fourth Republic's forbearance, shoved France to the brink of civil war, and ended only in 1962 with the conferring—by de Gaulle's government—of independence upon Algeria. Its first president, Ahmed Ben Bella, had played a part in the career of the Front de Liberation Nationale, which fought pitilessly, albeit defended as redemptive and regenerative by Jean-Paul Sartre and the theorist/psychiatrist Frantz Fanon.[15] Countermeasures adopted by French forces, particularly paratroopers and Foreign Legionnaires, were even more drastic. Broadly reviled, they blotted France's reputation. Arab fatalities reached roughly 300,000 versus 25,000 French deaths. Billions of francs were expended.[16] Overall, the Algerian conflict fed French bewilderments, a bundle of trauma almost on par with the 1940 surrender to Germany.

Coincident with revolutionary strife in Indochina and Algeria were the troubles that rocked British standing in Malaya and Kenya. In the so-called Malaya emergency, authorities managed to defeat a communist uprising, many of whose adherents came from the country's ethnic Chinese community. Lieutenant General Sir Rawdon Briggs and Field Marshal Sir Gerald Robert Templer retailed methods of counterinsurgency later familiar to

Americans in Vietnam: forced relocations, use of herbicides, establishment of fortified villages, arrests of suspects unmediated by formal charges or regular trials, and "nation building" measures pegged to the winning of "hearts and minds." British confidence eventually rested in Tunku Abdul Rahman, who, though viewed by Americans as weak, proved robust, serving as the original prime minister (1957–1970) of independent Malaya (later Malaysia).[17]

British efforts in Kenya to suppress the Mau Mau rebellion, 1952–1960, were draconian. Sweeping military campaigns, squalid internment camps, fierce interrogations, imposition of capital punishment following flimsy judicial reviews (abetted by mobile gallows and public spectacle), and uprooting of village populations (the entire male population of Nairobi in "Operation Anvil") caused desolation. Tens of thousands of Kenyans died, perhaps as many as 200,000—versus those of 1,800 black loyalists and fewer than a hundred European fatalities by Mau Mau.[18] The Kikuyu people, from which sprang such rebel leaders as Dedan Kimathi, suffered inordinately. So too, protestors gasped, did British compliance to international laws of war and Nuremberg maxims. Senior figures in the Anglican Church, famously the Archbishop of Canterbury, featured among the enraged.[19]

To revolutionists, the colonial world's twilight entailed not only regrettable violence. Diplomacy and elation at a presumed inexorableness were also involved, memorably at the conference (18–24 April 1955) in the verdant Indonesian city of Bandung.

Possessing equal parts jamboree and iron will, the Bandung meeting was organized by the governments of five newly freed states: Burma (Myanmar), Ceylon (Sri Lanka), Indonesia, India, Pakistan. Participating delegates, roughly 1,000, came from twenty-nine Asian and African nations and claimed to speak on behalf of 1.5 billion people, inhabitants of almost a fourth of the planet's land surface. Apart from the sponsoring ones, the following countries sent representatives to Bandung: Afghanistan, Cambodia, the People's Republic of China (PRC), Egypt, Ethiopia, the Gold Coast, Iran, Iraq, Japan, Jordan, Laos, Lebanon, Liberia, Libya, Nepal, the Philippines, Saudi Arabia, Sudan, Syria, Thailand, Turkey, North Vietnam, South Vietnam, Yemen. Of the parties invited, only the Central African Federation declined to attend.

Not all Asian and African states were asked to the Bandung gathering. Conspicuously absent were the Republic of China (Taiwan), Israel, both

Koreas, apartheid South Africa, Outer Mongolia, and the USSR (whose Asian expanses, Soviet pedants reminded, ran from the eastern Urals to the Pacific).

Sympathetically disposed people without delegate status also descended upon Bandung. These men and women came from such associations as the African National Congress and the South African Indian Congress and places such as Australia, Cyprus, French North Africa, Malaya, and Yugoslavia. A few prominent African Americans (about whom more later) were present too. In addition to these observers and invitees came numerous diplomats on reportorial assignments. Into this mix also poured hundreds of journalists from practically every country, largest press contingents arriving from the British Commonwealth, the PRC, the USA, and the USSR.

Peoples admissible of Bandung representation lived in disparate political conditions. These encompassed refractory colonial regimes, vulnerable states that enjoyed mere formal sovereignty, and entities that had good claim to authentic independence. The delegates also represented in their persons a kaleidoscope of cultural traditions, economic arrangements, political preferences, ethnicities/races, and religious creeds. A multiplicity of languages was featured, too, a potential problem averted, paradoxically, by resort in official transactions to the imperialists' transcending tongues: English primarily but also French. Nor, despite moments of stylized political choreography and paeans to unity, could all dignitaries overcome suspicions of each other—illustrated by the sullen reticence, occasionally undone by volcanic outbursts, that marred Indian–Pakistani interactions, to say nothing of the mutual loathing between the two Vietnamese delegations. Despite the virtuosity of PRC participants, several Bandung countries, namely those with security links to the West or whose national boundaries contained large Chinese minorities (such as Indonesia), regarded Beijing warily. The Japanese presence was also viewed uneasily by persons from those countries occupied a decade earlier by Imperial armies. This was so despite publicly expressed remorse by Tokyo's envoy, Tatsunosuke Takasaki, and his government's willingness to pay reparations. The victims, though, judged the amounts proposed risible. Lapses of decorum and judgment also occurred, as when the Grand Mufti of Jerusalem, Amin Al-Husayni, attached to the Yemeni delegation, excoriated not only Israel but all Jewry, which purportedly dominated the United Nations and its finances. Petty jealousies, too, did not help, as in the case of Ceylon's Sir John Kotelawala. He could not abide India's Prime Minister Jawaharlal Nehru, whom he thought pompous—the self-christened "great statesman of Asia." Compounding the strain and flashes of fury was that apprehension related to armed phalanxes of soldiers, detailed to protect the conference from Darul Islam, a sect desirous of overthrowing the Indonesian regime, led by President Sukharno, and replacing it with Sharia law. Ensconced in the mountains surrounding Bandung, Darul Islam guerillas vowed to attack conferees and otherwise disrupt their proceedings. In the event, no such event materialized, but the threat of bloodshed hung heavy.[20]

Despite security and other distractions, the conference rested on this premise: colonialism, already receding, belonged to a wicked past; once-subjugated peoples should henceforth create their own destiny, unfettered by former masters or the meddling of the self-designated great and good in Washington and Moscow. Sukarno declared in words of welcome to the delegates: "A *New Asia* and a *New Africa* have been born!"[21] Bandung luminaries—among whom the PRC's dexterous Foreign Minister Zhou

FIGURE 5.1 Zhou and Nehru at the Bandung Conference

Source: U.S. National Archives

Enlai, Egypt's charismatic Colonel Gamal Abdel Nasser, and the persevering Nehru—refined upon this theme with differing inflections but unwavering enthusiasm.

The conferees sought to stimulate economic, cultural, and political cooperation in the African-Asian world, to which end they devised recommendations of varying feasibility and ambition. Racial equality was proclaimed, as was the legal parity of all states, whether large or small. The virtues of the United Nations were also extolled and the cause of human rights upheld, with particular reference to the Universal Declaration of Human Rights as a standard of achievement for every person and government. The conference designated as especially vile French rule in Algeria, Morocco, and Tunisia; policies of racial discrimination in white-ruled African lands, particularly South Africa; the plight of Palestine's routed and disenfranchised Arabs; the existence, stockpiling, and testing of thermonuclear weapons (as danger not only to humanity but to all life forms and the natural environment); and the continued exclusion from the United Nations of various countries (Cambodia, Ceylon, Japan, Jordan, Libya, Nepal, and a prospective united Vietnam). Significantly, the delegates crafted this injunction, too: Asian and African nations ought not affiliate with alliance systems centered on the interests of any great power, a rebuke of those countries (Iraq, Iran, Pakistan, Turkey) joined to the Western-centered Baghdad Pact, the Southeast Asian Treaty Organization (Pakistan, Philippines, Thailand), and Japan for its 1952 security tie to America.[22]

Moscow officialdom charily viewed the Bandung doings. Already concerned in 1955 about the fraying of relations with Beijing, Khrushchev's circle feared that Zhou would so ingratiate himself with African and Asian personalities that they would spurn Moscow. Zhou's Bandung performance also underscored just how fleeting China's continued political subordination to the USSR could prove. His silence at Bandung in the face of charges against alleged Soviet colonialism (a matter explored below) and support for the admission to the United Nations of states whose applications Moscow had previously vetoed undercut comradely solidarity.[23]

The Eisenhower administration's stance bordered on contempt. The president suggested facetiously (at a National Security Council meeting) that Bandung worthies could be bought with a few thousand dollars and that he would gladly approve action short of assassination to stymie unfriendly delegations.[24] Neither the White House nor State Department sent greetings to the conference—in contrast with the Soviets' conveying fraternal salutation to Asian and African toilers struggling against Western oppression. Dulles worried that the Chinese delegation would bend Bandung in Beijing's direction; the gravitational pull of decolonization anyway slanted against the West and toward Sino-Soviet rhetorical advantage. To counter this, Dulles mobilized U.S. information agencies and wondered whether to sponsor an alternative conference, in which Asian-African states oriented toward the West would command attention and primacy.[25] CIA master-minds in East Asia suggested a far more desperate idea, but rejected in Washington: destroy the airplane carrying Zhou to Bandung.[26] In fact, just a week before the meetings convened an Indian chartered plane, the *Kashmir Princess*, transporting PRC delegates and foreign correspondents to Indonesia crashed in the South China Sea, prompting Beijing's charges that Taiwan and the United States had conspired to bring about the air disaster. The preponderance of evidence at the time—subsequently confirmed—indicated that clandestine Guomindang operatives based in Hong Kong were the culprits and had employed a hidden bomb, but U.S. agents apparently were uninvolved.[27]

Malice aforethought did not afflict the Americans who attended Bandung. These included three renowned black figures drawn in "colored" solidarity against white conceit: Mississippi-born novelist Richard Wright (*Native Son*), by 1955 expatriated in Paris; journalist Carl Rowan, then with the *Minneapolis Tribune*; and Congressman Adam Clayton Powell (D, New York).

Wright lauded Bandung as a conclave where the "rejected" and "the underdogs of the human race" affirmed their identity as new players on the world scene, never again to be trifled with or ignored.[28] Gratified that the Bandung nations had acquired tangible liberty at the expense of European overlords, Rowan won accolades for his writing on the conference.[29] He also enjoyed a conversation with Zhou (the contents of which Rowan shared with the CIA director, Allen Dulles) about ways in which the simmering Sino-U.S. confrontation over Taiwan's future might peaceably end.[30]

At his own expense, Powell went to Indonesia as eager witness. He garnered attention—plus plaudits in America—for press interviews in which, to the surprise of onlookers, he defended Western political ideals and declared that racism and restricted citizenship were disappearing in the United States. Black gains were irreversible, he said.[31] Once back in Washington, he met with Allen Dulles, then Eisenhower. Powell tried to impress upon them the value of cultivating friendships with the political elites of rising Africa and Asia, the majority of whom, he emphasized, wanted good relations with Americans.[32] This assessment, incidentally, dovetailed with that of Ambassador Hugh Cumming, head of Embassy Jakarta. He did not detect anti-U.S. bias at Bandung or a pro-communist surge, on which score he meant to reassure Eisenhower.[33] Cumming, like Powell, did not dissent from this post-conference evaluation made (31 August 1955) by the National Security Council: "Instead of Bandung['s] . . . becoming a neutralist or pro-communist vehicle for the condemnation of the Western powers . . . it provided a forum in which a number of champions of democracy fearlessly expressed [opposition] to communism."[34]

More than their counterparts in Moscow or Washington, foreign office personnel in Paris and London viewed the Indonesian confab anxiously. Publicly they faced it with impassivity and indulgent, if slight, curiosity. Damnations of France in North Africa and Britain in Kenya elicited either silence or terse retort about political responsibility and duties borne. Beneath this imperturbability, though, churned feelings of injured innocence and achievements slighted. Indications of this piling resentment were occasioned when Nasser nationalized the Suez Canal (opened in 1869 and run by French–British combinations). The eventual assault upon Egypt sprang not only from a wish to rescue an Anglo-French enterprise hijacked by an allegedly piratical regime, but also to counter Cairo's militancy and that liberationist imperative touted by Nasser at Bandung: "Egypt . . . stands in defense of the cause of freedom."[35]

Interred figuratively at Bandung, the French and British empires then came apart at Suez (reviewed in later pages). General André Beaufre, commander of Paris's soldiers in the 1956 war, observed that it simultaneously tarnished the Anglo-French escutcheon and signaled "the end of empire, the end of an epoch."[36]

Soviet imperium

Few questions aired at Bandung provoked more feeling than whether the USSR constituted an imperial project hostile to international society's survival.[37] Albeit resisted by many attendees, those from countries joined to the West backed this line: the Soviet position in Eastern Europe entailed tragedies, no less than those experienced by Asians and Africans trapped in the British/French empires. Mohammad Fadhil Jamali (Iraq) exclaimed that the USSR and communists were agents of "a new form of colonialism, much deadlier than the old one."[38] Carlos Romulo (Philippines) warned against "super-barbarism, a new super-imperialism" emanating from Moscow.[39] Fatin Rustu Zorlu (Turkey), Mohammed Ali (Pakistan), Wan Waithayakon (Thailand), and Kotelawala spoke similarly. The conference's final communiqué, perforce an exercise in compromise, did not explicitly fault the USSR. The communiqué nevertheless conveyed solidarity with Moscow-dominated nations, from the annexed Baltic republics to those of compromised independence (Albania, Bulgaria, Czechoslovakia, East Germany, Hungary, Poland, Romania): "Colonialism in all its manifestation is an evil which should speedily be brought to an end."[40]

Acquired as a result of wartime operations against Nazi Germany, the Soviet zones in Eastern Europe at the time of Bandung—except for Marshal Tito's renegade Yugoslavia—disallowed escape.[41] The rigor of this empire had not lessened when Stalin, Genius Leader of Progressive Mankind, died in March 1953, which event allowed cautious cultural, political, and penal reforms in the USSR and the promulgation of "peaceful coexistence." But this "thaw," and concomitant "new course," did not quickly radiate outward or cause the Soviet grip on subject nations to slip. Stalinist satraps remained in place. Red Army garrisons still paraded. Secret police agents prowled. The boots of the NKVD protruded everywhere (Czeslaw Milosz's imagery), while censors upheld a stifling Index.[42] Moscow-sanctioned courts enforced what passed for proletarian legality. Always vigilant, Soviet guardians foiled capitalists, Western spies, Titoists, Zionists, and other reprobates.

The temperament of the post-Stalin imperium showed plainly in mid-June 1953, when protests by construction workers occurred in East Berlin. These triggered sympathetic actions throughout East Germany that involved hundreds of thousands of people. Calls then sounded for a general strike, multi-party politics, free elections, and the resignation of East German leaders. Tremors of this political earthquake registered elsewhere—Hungary, Czechoslovakia, prison camps in the USSR—even as elements of the Red Army and Volkspolizei reestablished order.[43] Meanwhile, broadcasts from U.S. propaganda radio, located in West Berlin, beamed moral support,

FIGURE 5.2 East Berlin protestors and Soviet tanks, 1953

Source: U.S. National Archives

which led some protestors to conclude that American military formations would march. Washington, though, never seriously thought to mount a rescue mission, underscoring the hollowness of GOP talk in the 1952 presidential campaign about the "immorality" of containment and obligations to "rollback."[44] Only later did figures in the Republican government suggest exceptional steps, as when in March 1954 C.D. Jackson, psychological warfare maven, urged this plan upon the CIA: "Clandestine terroristic pressure should be organized against members of the Soviet regime in East Germany, and if a [Walter] Ulbricht [communist party leader in Berlin] or two didn't show up at the office some morning, few would weep."[45]

The tally of people killed and injured in the 1953 uprising, or incarcerated, reached several thousand.[46] When East German authorities scolded their compatriots for losing self-control, manipulated by Western "fascist" plotters, the poet-playwright Bertolt Brecht dropped his Leninist compunction and mused:

. . . the people
had forfeited the confidence of the government
and could regain it only through redoubled efforts.
Wouldn't it be simpler under these circumstances
for the government to dissolve the people
and elect another one?[47]

More disturbing than East Germany to tranquility in Moscow's empire, demarcated by the Warsaw Pact (est. May 1955), were Polish agitation in 1956 and Hungarian daring. Unchecked, Khrushchev knew, these would unmake the Kremlin-designed order.[48] To preserve it, he and colleagues threatened Warsaw with military action. Later, after hesitation, they trounced the progressivist regime in Budapest, led by Imre Nagy, a man enamored of Bandung ideals, particularly the right of lesser powers to navigate unmolested between the Cold War blocs.[49]

Emboldened by the Kremlin's partial repudiation of the Stalinist record—per Khrushchev's February 1956 "secret speech" at the 20th Congress of the CPSU—reformed minded officials in Warsaw and Budapest sought to loosen Moscow's tethers.[50] In this, they were heartened by Kremlin conciliatoriness toward Yugoslavia, signaled by the April 1956 dissolution of the Cominform (which organization had earlier excommunicated the "deviationist" Yugoslavs from Stalin's fold). Prospective Soviet–Yugoslav rapprochement seemed to imply Moscow's openness to a version of East European autonomy.

Labor unrest in Poland, concentrated in Poznan during summer 1956, reflected nationwide discontent and stimulated wide dissent. To dispel the mood of defiance, Warsaw comrades removed (October) the unpopular defense minister, Marshal K. Rokossovsky. At the expense of the equally disliked incumbent First Secretary of the Polish party, Boleslaw Bierut, they installed Wladislaw Gomulka, a survivor of previous purges and incarceration. He, in turn, managed to persuade edgy Soviet chiefs (Khrushchev, Anastas Mikoyan, V.M. Molotov) that he would reestablish domestic discipline and not upset Poland's political-military alignments. This remarkable diplomatic feat transpired even while Soviet tanks and infantry were poised to move against the Polish capital. Still, a stark fact loomed behind this "Polish October." In the absence of the hastily improvised Gomulka solution, demonstrated to Soviet satisfaction in subsequent months, the Red Army would have crushed Poland. Reforms to that country's internal economic arrangements and governance, in effect, could (if just barely) be brooked by post-Stalin Moscow. But the primacy of communist party rule remained sacrosanct, as did the security architecture of the Soviet imperium; degrees of permissibility remained slight.[51]

In contrast with Gomulka, who grasped Soviet resolve to uphold Marxist–Leninist institutions and empire integrity, Budapest reformers deceived themselves. They mistook Kremlin passivity and apparent lenience at popular shows of unity with Poland—staged by university students who issued sixteen demands and toppled an enormous statue of Stalin in Budapest's municipal park—for a clean break from the hardline. No such conversion to moderation had occurred, however. Soviet belatedness, late October 1956, in disciplining Hungarian waywardness simply reflected uncertainties on the method to employ. A Hungarian equivalent of Gomulka, nationalist face on a regime otherwise dependent upon Soviet power, would probably have won grudging Kremlin approval. Yet when Nagy, hitherto a Moscow loyalist (rehabilitated after a period of rustication and disgrace), allowed himself to be carried away by citizens' enthusiasm for Cold War neutrality, secession from the Warsaw Pact, competitive party politics, free press, and similar heresies, the Kremlin acted.[52] With Hungary forfeit, the Warsaw Pact would have dissolved, along with Soviet mastery.[53] Even Mikoyan, the most liberal-minded member of the Kremlin elite, felt this necessity: "We cannot let Hungary be removed from our camp."[54]

Fighting in Budapest and environs, earnestly joined on 4 November, between national resistance—factory workers, youths, professionals, peasants—and Soviet military units resulted in the deaths of 2,700 Hungarian fighters and seven hundred Red Army soldiers. Approximately 19,000 Hungarians were wounded.[55] Twenty-two thousand "counter revolutionaries" were subsequently imprisoned, their sentences running to five or more years. Thousands of additional souls were jailed for briefer durations. Other people lost their jobs, were placed under surveillance, or subjected to intimidation.[56]

Janos Kadar, dependable from a Soviet standpoint, established a new government, while Nagy and closest associates sheltered (until 22 November) in the Yugoslav embassy. Upon leaving it, with assurance of safe conduct, they were abducted by Soviet security forces (apparently with the connivance of Tito) and put into KGB detention.[57] Cardinal Jozef Mindszenty, primate of Hungary, found haven in the U.S. legation. There he, symbolic heir of Lajos Kossuth (of the 1848 revolution) and exemplar of Vatican opposition to Sovietism, resided until 1971.

Roughly 200,000 Hungarians, 2 percent of the nation's population, fled their country in 1956. Exiting at the Austrian frontier, they took sanctuary in transit camps and, in most instances, sought permanent refuge in Western countries. The United States accommodated 80,000 persons, many of whom, as in the earlier East German case, had been buoyed by U.S. broadcasts (Radio Free Europe, Voice of America) that suggested Washington would aid anti-Soviet insurrectionists, perhaps along the lines of the earlier enunciated "liberation policy."[58] In fact, as in 1953, the Americans had neither the aim nor means—save at inciting general war—to shape events in a sector of the Soviet imperium.[59] A bitter survivor of the Budapest combat later said that the United States was willing to fight Marxism and the USSR to the last Hungarian.[60] But then neither, as this person must have understood, did the United Nations or Secretary-General Hammarskjold make a fuss in the darkest hours, despite Hungarian pleading.

That the subduing of Hungary constituted a public relations fiasco for the USSR was obvious to most people, irrespective of where they stood along the Cold War divide. Only a few agreed with Sartre when he, parroting Moscow's line, condemned the "rightest spirit" that allegedly animated the Hungarian uprising.[61] But unprejudiced observers realized that Moscow had suffered a blow in the competition for popular allegiance.[62] Astute commentators discerned an existential victory in the Hungarian rebellion, hence this statement by Albert Camus: "Hungary conquered and in chains has done more for freedom and justice than any people for twenty years."[63] Certainly, the Kremlin's crackdown vindicated those Bandung participants, in their own thinking at least, who earlier had issued jeremiads against Soviet imperialism. Krishna Menon, member of the Indian entourage at Bandung, and profoundly innocent of pro-Western feeling, commented shortly after Nagy's execution (June 1958) by hanging: "Whoever remains silent today about the suffering in Hungary not only helps in the acceptance of what has happened but also becomes an accomplice in the suppression of the Hungarian people."[64]

The Anglo-French imperial reprise at Suez offset the propaganda benefits to the West, otherwise accruable from the Soviet Goliath smashing Hungarian David. The simultaneity of the Egyptian crisis with the one that overcame Hungary stunned Washington officials while threatening to break NATO.

United States empire

Although a minority had questioned the wisdom of such an undertaking, Americans in the nineteenth century had created an empire.[65] Their modus operandi conformed to that of other imperial practitioners. Americans obtained their empire by purchase, exampled in 1803: Louisiana territory. They did so by declaration, as in 1823: Monroe Doctrine. They did so via population repatterning (internal colonialism) per the 1830 Indian Removal Act. They did so through conquest, as in 1846–1848: war against Mexico. Subsequent iterations of purchase, declaration, demographic reshuffling, and capture included Alaska (1867); Manifest Destiny, Open Door notes (China); tribal reservations (administered by the Bureau of Indian Affairs and enforced by the Army); the 1898 war against Spain.

By the mid-twentieth century, Americans had not only leapt their continental borders, having gained Caribbean islands and the Hawaiian and Philippine archipelagoes.[66] But also the United States had become first among empires. Its territorial core, in contrast with European and Asian ones, had escaped wartime ravage. The industrial base and agricultural economy were vast, the dollar currency dominant, U.S. air-military-naval forces supreme, and the popular culture invincible. Though denying the applicability of such terminology to their country, Americans enjoyed, too, an informal empire. This touched New World, European, Middle East, and Far East reaches. As that unsparing critic, Reinhold Niebuhr, observed: Americans of his generation averted their gaze—"frantically avoiding recognition of the imperialism which we in fact exercise."[67] Irrespective of whether they admitted or preferred other explanation, Americans after World War II policed their realms with an intensity of purpose not inferior to that of the French, British, or Soviets in their respective zones. Cold War crusade constituted a shorthand definition of the national interest and entailed an imagination at play in earlier empire-building experience: Marshall Plan as purchase, Truman Doctrine as declaration, nuclear bomb strategy as prospective depopulation, the CIA's Iranian and Guatemalan ventures (here briefly summarized) as conquest.

Iran, 1953

Previously an object desired by the Soviets and British, Iran fell to U.S. sway in 1953. That year Eisenhower authorized the CIA to cooperate with the domestic enemies of the Tehran regime, led by the democratically selected Prime Minister Mohammad Mossadegh, alternately described by Western detractors as idiosyncratic or entombed in an "imponderable Oriental mind."[68] The aim was to emplace a regime impervious to communist blandishments, dangled by the Tudeh party, and synchronized to Western purpose: unimpeded access to abundant and affordably priced oil reserves.[69]

Difficulties arose in April 1951, when Mossadegh nationalized the Anglo-Iranian Oil Company (AIOC), of which the British government owned a majority share. The British impulse was to use military force (Plan Buccaneer) and protect the huge refinery at Abadan.[70] Even though Prime Minister Attlee decided to scuttle the gunboat option, retaliation in alternative form did follow: AIOC and six additional petroleum companies mounted a boycott against Iranian-produced oil. Iran's resultant economic corrosion obliged Mossadegh in early 1953 to appeal to the United States for relief, either by helping to lift the boycott or provide financial aid to his country. The White House refused, saying that the crisis was of Tehran's own making; the sooner Mossadegh struck a deal with AIOC, the better for all parties concerned. Given these circumstances, the White House elaborated, Washington must withhold revenue aid, the continuing shortfall remediable by AIOC's reversion to the pre-nationalization status quo. To Iranian officials, Eisenhower also communicated—dissemblingly—that the British government, by then returned to Tory leadership under Churchill and Eden, was offering a package of sound ideas on the sharing of oil profits that promised just solution to the AIOC snarl.

No less oblivious of popular preference than the Soviets in 1953 East Germany, Eisenhower and Churchill in July approved plans once developed for contingency purposes by the CIA and Britain's SIS/MI6: undermine Mossadegh; replace him with people congenial to the West.[71] Thereupon dispatched to Iran, CIA operative Kermit Roosevelt met with potential conspirators: the SIS/MI6 station chief in Tehran, disgruntled army officers, notably Major General Fazlolla Zahedi, and internal security personnel. With the aid of General H. Norman Schwarzkopf (commander during World War II of the U.S. Gendarme Mission in Iran), Roosevelt also established a working relationship with the young (b. 1919) and feckless Mohammad-Reza Shah Pahlavi.[72] In collaboration with local agents, and distributing cash to support their efforts, Roosevelt assembled mobs and coordinated with anti-regime soldiers. These groups in mid-August demonstrated in Tehran and assaulted Mossadegh's followers, which included members of Iran's leftist community. Perhaps three hundred people died in street violence, larger numbers injured.[73]

A bungled start nearly undid the Roosevelt action, causing the Shah briefly to leave Iran. Yet the anti-Mossadegh forces managed to rally by 19 August, on which day Zahedi assumed power. The Shah subsequently returned to home and throne. Mossadegh left office, was detained, then imprisoned, and finally put in house arrest. "My only crime," he protested to the tribunal that charged him with subversion, "is that I nationalized the Iranian oil industry and removed from this land the network of colonialism and the political and economic influence of the greatest empire on earth."[74] Mossadegh's anti-royalist foreign minister, Hussein Fatemi, faced trial for treason, then execution (November 1954). Secretary Dulles meantime advised cabinet colleagues that the restoration of the Shah and defeat of his enemies gave the United States a much-needed "second chance" in Iran.[75]

Funds were quickly sprung ($5 million) from CIA coffers to help ease Iran's economic woes, followed by a sizable U.S. grant in September 1953 ($45 million).[76] A year later the Majlis (Iranian parliament) approved a revised oil regime. It ended the AIOC monopoly, supplanted by an international consortium charged with thenceforth developing Iranian oil reserves and selling the products. Six U.S. companies obtained 40 percent of the shares in this new petroleum order.[77]

Guatemala, 1954

Before the first anniversary passed of Mossadegh's downfall, Eisenhower's government again acted—June 1954—on behalf of imperial needs. This time: Guatemala. Chuffed after the Iranian adventure, the CIA once more served as principal instrument.

Whereas in Iran U.S. power penetrated a country historically outside Washington's ambit, in Guatemala the Americans struck a regime determined to shred longstanding neocolonial arrangements. The Guatemalan episode corresponded with empire protection against riled national feeling, a category of dilemma familiar to the Anglo-French in Asia and Africa and the Soviets in Eastern Europe.

Like Mossadegh in Tehran, Jacobo Arbenz Guzman in Guatemala City assumed executive responsibility in 1951, legitimized by democratic ballot. President of a small (2.8 million inhabitants, 53.6 percent Maya) and impoverished country, Arbenz promoted reforms begun by his predecessor, Juan Jose Arevalo.[78] These aimed at eradicating the feudal economy, delivering the peasantry from precarious subsistence, and building strong democratic institutions. Attempts to improve the educational system and raise the status of manual workers were pursued with fanfare, to an approving chorus of left-leaning (but hardly Soviet-controlled) labor unions.[79] Arbenz meanwhile took measures detrimental to the American-owned United Fruit Company (UFC) that for decades had been the organizing principle of economic life in Guatemala. To critics, the UFC ran the country like a plantation (bananas, coffee) while it paid paltry wages, circumvented the tax system, debauched domestic politics, and enjoyed handsome profits repatriated to the United States. Arbenz's minister of labor and economy, Alfonso Bauer Paiz, voiced a common opinion when he leveled this charge: "The United Fruit Company is the . . . enemy of the progress of Guatemala, of its democracy and of every effort directed at its economic liberation."[80]

Adopted in June 1952, Arbenz's Decree 900 expropriated fallow lands from private estates, doing so with variable compensation in government bonds. The unused but arable lands (1.4 million acres) were then distributed among the peasantry, benefiting half a million people (mainly Maya), who also received financial credit to develop their newly acquired possessions.[81] Applied to the UFC, Decree 900 meant that 85 percent of that company's holdings were exposed, then seized (400,000 acres). To reformers, the company's demise heralded a bright dawn.

The expropriation involved levels of compensation inferior to market value, according to UFC stockholders and publicists, who lobbied Congress and the White House (first Truman, then Eisenhower) for redress.[82] Incidentally, Secretary Dulles and his brother Allen enjoyed an association with the UFC—dating to their legal work on the staff of Sullivan and Cromwell in which they facilitated UFC deals—and were astonished by the presumption of confiscation, behind which they inferred nefarious Marxism.[83]

Already worried by Arbenz's acceptance of support from indigenous communists, critics were further distressed by Czechoslovakia's May 1954 shipment of weapons (2,000 tons of light arms and artillery) to Guatemala: the country could become wholly reoriented toward Moscow.[84] To forestall that possibility and reinforce the Central American flank, Eisenhower ordered naval patrols to intercept and search merchant ships of any country that approached Guatemalan ports. Even earlier, he had instructed the CIA to provide money, training (in camps located in Nicaragua and Honduras), and arms to groups of Guatemalan exiles, of whom Lieutenant Colonel Carlos Castillo Armas was one.

In coordination with air raids on Guatemala City (rebel warplanes supplied by the United States), and encouraged by radio broadcasts transmitted from the Voice of Liberation, hundreds of Castillo Armas's fighters invaded (18 June) from Honduran hideaways. What passed for the Guatemalan army failed to offer meaningful defense. Arbenz's appeals to the UN were also unavailing, despite Soviet support for an investigation into the funding and background of the anti-Arbenz fighters. In the event, Ambassador Henry Cabot Lodge prevented the Security Council from launching any inquiry, warning the Soviets to desist.[85]

Arbenz resigned on 27 June. The Mexican embassy granted him political asylum, from which followed a lonely life of wandering exile.[86] As for Castillo Armas, he helped organize a military junta, approved and recognized by the United States in mid-July. Castillo Armas outlawed political parties. He disposed of labor unions. He disbanded peasant associations. On his command, hundreds of people were executed by firing squads. In October, he was elected president with—in the Soviet style—99 percent of the people's vote. He also obtained financial bolstering ($80 million in 1954–1957) from attentive Washington, along with backing from the Army officer corps and local Catholic hierarchy.[87] In turn, he restored lost properties to the UFC and its pride of place in Guatemala's political economy. He sojourned to Washington in October–November 1955, where officialdom feted him.

To Eisenhower, a disquieting moment during the Guatemalan episode arose when French and British officials intimated skepticism to Washington about the legitimacy of U.S. action. Not only were they unsupportive; they at one point intended to allow the UN Security Council to delve into the Guatemala tangle. However unlikely in normal circumstances, a Soviet–French–British combination in the UN against the United States might have formed. This did not happen, though, as the White House threatened to use the American veto and issued reminders that U.S. support of the Anglo-French in African and Asian locales implied reciprocal forbearance.[88] In the end, neither the French nor British made a commotion at the UN about Guatemala. They certainly never joined publicly with the Soviets on a question affecting U.S. economic-political interests in a region dear to Washington. Would that the Americans were equally indulgent, Eden and French Premier Guy Mollet surely prayed in 1956 as they, with Israeli accomplices, lumbered toward finale at Suez.

Suez, 1956

The Anglo-French assault turned on a place that successive Paris and London leaders thought vital, having far greater significance than negligible Guatemala. Roughly two-thirds of the oil consumed in energy-ravenous Europe passed through the Suez conduit.[89]

Advocates claimed that an invasion should ensure the efficient and economical transport of Middle Eastern oil to Europe. Held as an article of faith in the Quai d'Orsay (under Christian Pineau), Nasser's expiry would also conduce to Algerian peace by stanching the flow of Egyptian aid to anti-French rebels.[90] Additionally, French and British leaders discerned in Nasser the makings of a dictator; his dethronement would spare Egyptians, and many more people besides, from a horrid future. Eden occasionally likened him to Hitler or Mussolini. At a minimum, said the Briton, Nasser wanted to be "a Caesar from the Gulf to the Atlantic, and to kick us out of it all."[91]

To fair degree, Anglo-French goals meshed with Washington's.[92] In communications (foreign office exchanges, ambassadorial confidences, presidential pronouncements), the Americans in 1955–1956 expressed scorn for Nasser. To them, his oft-spoken pledges of fidelity to Bandung nonalignment sounded false. Even if earnest, these were slight comfort, as neutrality in the Cold War, Secretary Dulles preached, amounted to an ethically inexcusable position. Unsurprisingly, Egyptian purchase (September 1955) of Soviet-bloc weaponry via Czechoslovakia and recognition (May 1956) of the People's Republic of China led the Americans to renege (July 1956) on offers to help finance Nasser's vaunted modernization scheme: construction of the Aswan High Dam on the Nile.[93] Moreover, as they told French and British interlocutors, the Americans looked forward to Nasser's substitution—by CIA stealth, perhaps—by a Western-oriented crowd.[94] Yet a caveat applied, repeatedly sounded to London and Paris: nothing in the wake of Bandung should be done that was diplomatically premature, militarily reckless, or demeaning to the West.[95]

FIGURE 5.3 Nasser in Cairo after announcing that he would nationalize the Suez Canal

Source: U.S. National Archives

American reproof of the Suez expedition shocked Mollet and Eden. Currents of anti-Americanism swept through swathes of the French and British (not Labour Party leaders) populations.[96] Few anywhere had guessed that Eisenhower would lend his voice to the indignation that rang in the Middle East and beyond. Bandung's former conveners, who had lobbied for a nonviolent resolution, probably constituted the most livid onlookers. "I cannot imagine a worse case of aggression," Nehru uttered during the first hours of reported battle.[97]

In a matter of days, 3,000 Egyptian lives were lost versus two hundred British, French, and Israeli fatalities, statistics that strengthened Nehru's contention while underscoring the disproportionality between European and anti-colonial armies. Spectators at the United Nations, meanwhile, accustomed to debate between Soviet and U.S. representatives, heard both delegations at the Security Council decry the tripartite invasion of Egypt. More upsetting still to Paris and London ministers, Eisenhower readied penalties: reductions on the exporting to France and Britain of U.S.-produced oil, just as the availability from Middle East sources came into question; withholding support from the pressured British pound, as London's reserves of dollars and sterling plummeted by $279 million in a handful of Suez days.[98]

As the run on sterling quickened and Britain's economy teetered, the Anglo-French declared (7 November) a ceasefire. Before Christmas, all British and French forces decamped from Suez. Physically and emotionally unwell, Eden resigned from office on 9 January 1957. His sense of betrayal by Washington, saturated with enmity for John Foster Dulles, knew no limit.[99] In France, some people, including de Gaulle (primed from World War II onward to distrust the Yankees), concluded that the United States as guarantor of West European safety was demonstrably undependable; in this case, Parisian statecraft should revise its security/foreign policy and shift from Washington, logic that reinforced the idea of France's nuclear *force de frappe* and 1966 disassociation from NATO's integrated command structure.

Of the invaders, only the Israelis achieved any of their goals. The number of Egyptian-sponsored raids by the fedayeen against Israeli civilian targets fell. After Israeli forces withdrew (March 1957) from Sinai, the Egyptians, as part of broader agreement, lifted their blockade (dating to 1951) of the Gulf of Aqaba, important to Israeli maritime commerce and the port city of Eilat. Thousands of Jewish Egyptians, meanwhile, stigmatized as treacherous by their erstwhile compatriots chose to leave their country or were expelled by Nasser.

Under Egyptian managers and pilots, the canal reopened in April 1957 to international shipping (not Israeli). The new supervisors ran it competently, confounding the expectation of taunting British doubters. Basking still in the afterglow of Bandung benediction, Nasser emerged from the Suez war as anti-imperialist hero and pan-Arab champion. This sentiment peaked in 1958, when Egypt and Syria combined briefly into the United Arab Republic (disbanded in 1961) with Nasser as president. At the same time, though frustratingly, Eisenhower sought to identify, cultivate, and build up a plausible popular Arab/Muslim alternative to Nasser.[100]

The Suez misadventure not only killed Eden's political career and damaged NATO but caught the White House unawares. Eisenhower's reelection bid against the Democrats' Adlai Stevenson was in its final days—polling conducted on 6 November. The president could ill afford the diversion of a Middle East war, heedlessly waged, as he perceived it, at Anglo-French initiative, done without consulting Washington: this must provoke Arab and Muslim wrath and generate opportunities for the Kremlin, trawling hopefully in Western–Egyptian turmoil for whatever advantage could be had.[101] An irate Eisenhower wondered aloud to his cabinet: "How can we possibly support Britain and France if in doing so we lose the whole Arab world?"[102] At all costs, he felt, the United States ought not be associated in Asian or African minds with the intrigues of notorious European empires.[103] Compounding these problems, Washington appeared cramped when it should otherwise have concentrated world attention on the Soviet trampling of reformist Hungary.[104] Richard Nixon, vice president in 1956, later recalled: "We couldn't, on one hand, complain about the Soviets intervening in Hungary and, on the other hand, approve of the British and the French picking that particular time to intervene against Nasser."[105]

The untoward consequences to Western power of Suez did not last long. Anger in Washington over the war's timing and secrecy proved more ephemeral than suggested by Eisenhower's fuming. The United States propped up sterling: the International Monetary Fund made $561.47 million available (10 December) to Britain, with a stand-by commitment of $738.53 million; the U.S. Export–Import Bank approved (21 December) a $500 million line of credit, extended to London in February 1957. Neither did NATO collapse, its power anyway augmented in May 1955 by West Germany's joining. A post-Suez axiom of British foreign policy was that it should adhere to the main Washington line. From that viewpoint, even the affronted French under de Gaulle did not sharply dissent in practice— rhetoric, though, being another matter. As for Arab and Muslim suscepti- bility to Soviet wooing, this did not deepen, despite Moscow's ballyhooed support of Egyptian improvement schemes, notably at Aswan.

Ultimately, Suez was important for what it laid bare: the prerogative and majesty of the French and British empires belonged to a bygone day, beyond reviving. In the new era of Washington dispensation, neither conglom- eration was allowed to assert itself contrary to U.S. preference. Not two years had passed after Suez before the Americans, under cover of the Eisenhower Doctrine (ostensibly pointed at communist aggression), injected themselves into the Middle East. As brazenly as France and Britain at Suez, 14,000 marines were put ashore in summer 1958 in Lebanon to pacify civil strife and contain the spread of Nasserite influence.[106] Anglo-French pundits cried hypocrisy. Eden's successor, Prime Minister Harold Macmillan, jested but tellingly to Eisenhower: "You are doing a Suez on me."[107] Fervent Soviet diplomats at the UN protested. But no state or international body could force the overweening empire to abandon or alter course, confirming ancient Thucydides once again: the strong do as they like.[108]

* * *

Of the empires that survived both World Wars, then were tested in the 1956 imbroglios, only the United States emerged unscathed. It retained incontestable vitality, evidenced by quantitative data and every other measure.[109] America's giant industrial-agricultural economy, military prowess, and confidence contrasted markedly with the rest: the Soviet image tarnished—not rubbed clean in the 1957 Sputnik success—by deploying force to save Moscow's Hungarian assets; the Anglo-French chastened at Suez.

In the decade following, the Soviets again resorted to coercion (1968 Czechoslovakia) to keep hold on East Europeans, retroactively justified by the so-called Brezhnev Doctrine that sought to justify repression by invoking principles of socialist solidarity.[110] The remainder of French and British overseas possessions meanwhile passed into fully fledged independence, anticipatorily celebrated by the 1955 Bandung delegates. One can only guess how scandalized those conferees would have been had they been able to glimpse the 1960s future. There the once hopeful nonaligned movement came a cropper on age-old human frailties and perversity, hence such happenings as the Sino-Indian border war, sanguinary Indonesian civil strife, flailing African states (Nigeria–Biafra), and resentments in East Pakistan that kindled the 1971 Bangladesh war.

In the 1960s aftermath of empire, French attention turned increasingly to Europe, foreshadowed by accommodation with the hereditary German foe and building of institutions constitutive of the European Community (EC)—European Coal and Steel Community (1952), European Economic Community (1957), European Atomic Energy Community (1957). After initial hesitation, two Gaullist vetoes (1963, 1967), and despite persistent qualms, post-imperial Britain joined the EC in 1973, which evolved into the European Union (EU), advanced by the far-reaching 1991 Maastricht Treaty. The EU, from its outset, has contained the sinews of potential empire: space, wealth, population, economic depth, and security aims.

FIGURE 5.4 USS *George H.W. Bush* and destroyer escorts in the Atlantic, December 2013

Source: U.S. National Archives

Whether such a coherent entity ever emerges—surmounting secessionist referenda, immigration anxieties, populist passions, financial vicissitudes—only the future will disclose. But if an EU empire does take shape, Britain, on whose imperial compass the sun once never set, may one day function as an offshore province, a thing harnessed to continental (German–French) dynamism—or, following the 2016 Brexit vote, a patch of social-political discordance and shriveling economic-diplomatic relevance, less influential "outside" than "in" embryonic Europe.

Should an EU empire actually arise—in defiance of heavy odds—it would draw into ever-closer cooperation Moscow's onetime Warsaw Pact dependencies plus parts of the former Soviet core (not only Estonia, Latvia, Lithuania) such as Ukraine. Should such a scenario come about it would render Russia even more forlorn and marginalized than in 1991 when the USSR imploded, leaving the United States as the twentieth century's sole surviving empire.

Critics of the U.S. empire registered worries and complaints during the immediate post-Cold War years. Mikhail Gorbachev, the last head of the USSR, protested that everyone had lost the Cold War, boastful Americans included. He chided them for their hubris; he resented their lecturing about human rights and freedoms while failing to ensure such protections at home.[111] Russia's first post-communist foreign minister, Andrei Kozyrev, stated that neither he nor his countrymen should be counted upon to fall in line with whatever fancifulness engrossed Washington.[112] French Foreign Minister Hubert Védrine referred to the United States as *hyperpower* (a term attributable to a British commentator, Sir Peregrine Worsthorne[113]). Védrine thought America an unprecedented colossus that must in its conceit inflict abuses and pursue voracious self-aggrandizement.[114]

Observers in the Global South also felt unease, if not absolute dread or disdain. America as embodiment of human rights rectitude elicited scoffs in Beijing, which derided Washington officials for sanctimoniousness while ignoring U.S. deficiencies.[115] Samir Amin, an Egyptian economist (and student of the Bandung exercise), declared that under the mantle of morality, law, and justice, the U.S.-organized north would continue to pillage southern nations, extracting their resources and consigning the peoples to poverty and despondency.[116]

The charges issued by Gorbachev, Beijing's spokesmen, Amin, etc. in the 1990s belonged to a well-worn catalog of accusations. Decades earlier, Frantz Fanon rehearsed them while ranking the United States of Eisenhower and Truman in odiousness equal to that of Europe. The diplomatic record of America, he argued, and its domestic history, mocked claims to noble purpose in an emergent global society. Instead of Thomas Jefferson's "empire of liberty," steadily widening the scope of people's contentment, Fanon perceived this: "A former European colony decided to catch up with Europe. It succeeded so well that the United States of America became a monster, in which the taints, the sickness, and the inhumanity of Europe have grown to appalling dimensions."[117]

Any elaboration of Fanon's indictment, centered on the U.S. empire sketched in this chapter, had substance from which to draw, even without reference to Iran or Guatemala. Prodded by security zealots, this included hysteria about internal dangers and disloyalty: McCarthyism. Spawned by anti-New Deal partisans and populist resentment of northeastern elites (Ivy League-educated know-it-alls of dubious political orientation and doubtful personal uprightness), extravagant anticommunism spurred irregular legality, bullying, and expurgation of government and university rosters. The unhealed wound of slavery meantime festered. Dixie's codified racial segregation interlocked with de facto discrimination elsewhere in America. Among the humiliations wrought, few were more infamous or fateful than the arrest of Rosa Parks in December 1955. This black seamstress and NAACP activist in Montgomery was arrested after forcible removal from her bus seat, having refused to vacate it for a white patron. Bursts of racially motivated violence also disturbed what passed for the domestic tranquility—persuading Fanon not only that America had assumed a grotesqueness like Europe's but that U.S. claims of fitness to lead democratic humanity were insupportable. Just a few months before Rosa Parks's arrest, fourteen-year-old Emmett Till, an African American from Chicago, was murdered during holiday in Money, Mississippi. He had the temerity to speak, maybe flirtatiously, with a local white woman (Carolyn Bryant).[118]

★ ★ ★

6

AMERICA

The U.S. continues to be a place which makes you want to weep one day and reveals itself the next in ways that are quite impressive.[1]

George Kennan, 22 July 1957

★ ★ ★

Lillian Smith was a Southern white woman, memorable for trenchant writing on racial matters and sexual mores. Reflecting upon the Till homicide, spates of lynching, and Jim Crow code, and aghast at McCarthyism, she frequently refrained (unselfconsciously) Frantz Fanon in her publications. She once made this comparison between her home state of Georgia, led by Governor Herman Talmadge, and Stalin's Caucasian republic: "We remember that Georgia, USA still has a lot in common with Georgia, USSR. Totalitarianism is an old thing to us down home." She added:

> The unquestioned authority of White Supremacy, the tight political set-up of one party, nourished on poverty and ignorance, solidified the South into a totalitarian regime under which we were living when communism was still Russian cellar talk and Hitler had not even been born.[2]

Yet Smith harbored the idea that some type of "empire of liberty"—a thing expansive and more bracing than Thomas Jefferson had imagined—could be realized.[3] She adhered to an optimistic credo, despite all that she unblinkingly admitted about the United States or the history of other imperia. A different type of empire and spirit might yet ascend, universal but not flinty. She once wrote:

> Every creative act, every poem, every painting, every honest question or honest dissent, every gesture of courage and faith and mercy and concern will count; every new awareness will count; every time we defend the human spirit it will count; every time we turn away from arrogance and lies, this, too, will count.[4]

Less lyrical but equally committed, other Americans contemporaneous with Smith also yearned for a grander conception. That their empire not constitute just another ransacking power that flitted across existence, devoid of affirmative purpose. Among people so intent, featured in this book, were Herbert Lehman, Eleanor Roosevelt, Ralph Bunche, and Telford Taylor. None fled controversy or debates, although occasionally tempted, and shared Smith's determination for a twentieth-century America unencumbered by cascading injustice but useful to international society.

Following UNRRA, as senator from New York (1950–1957), Lehman supported prohibitions—by federal action as needed—on lynching, poll taxes, the thwarting of black voters, and discrimination in employment, services, and accommodation. He cheered the Supreme Court's 1954 decision to outlaw school segregation (*Brown v. Board of Education of Topeka*). He tried energetically, against the Southern wing of his own Democratic party, to introduce a strong civil rights plank at Chicago's 1956 presidential nominating convention.[5]

Championing what he called the "decencies of public life" against anticommunist vigilantes, Lehman also waged a spirited defense of victims of smear, including Dean Acheson, George Marshall, Professor Owen Lattimore, and Ambassador Charles Bohlen.[6] Lehman's verbal jousting with McCarthy once nearly culminated in fisticuffs on the Senate floor. With abundant gratification, Lehman joined with more than sixty-five other senators in December 1954 to censure McCarthy for misconduct.[7]

After the 1948 Universal Declaration of Human Rights, Roosevelt (idolized by Lillian Smith) persisted, as a member of the NAACP board of

FIGURE 6.1 Rosa Parks and Dr. Martin Luther King, Jr.

Source: U.S. National Archives

directors and in other capacities, to condemn forms of prejudice: ethnic, religious, gender, and, above all, racial. She said that discrimination "sears" human souls: Americans who had fought fascism must not allow it at home.[8] In radio broadcasts and public prints, she reviled the Ku Klux Klan, emphasizing the "similarity between a white nightshirt and a Nazi brownshirt."[9] In cooperation with Rosa Parks and Reverend Martin Luther King, she solicited funds to aid the 1956 Montgomery bus boycott and in private messages offered heartfelt encouragement.[10] She spoke on behalf of fair housing, lobbied for federal civil rights legislation, celebrated black students who wanted admission to Southern universities, and praised the courage of white and black Freedom Riders as they crisscrossed portions of the former Confederacy.[11] Her words and doings, to say nothing of socializing with activists, were confirmatory to detractors, among whom the FBI's J. Edgar Hoover, who speculated that "Negro blood" ran through Roosevelt's veins.[12]

Like Lehman, Roosevelt fought the Red-baiters. She had first tangled with them in 1939, when taking the side of the American Youth Congress against Martin Dies's House Special Committee to Investigate Un-American Activities (HUAC). She urged that HUAC be abolished (not done until 1975): "The Un-American Activities Committee seems to me to be better for a police state than for the USA."[13] She also defended Alger Hiss (wrongly in light of later evidence) as innocent of treason. She backed the Voice of America and overseas libraries against scurrilous right-wing charges. She abhorred attacks on free speech and inquiry in educational institutions. Roosevelt worried that the proliferation of loyalty boards and oaths stemmed from a U.S. citizenry that had lost its mental moorings and self-assurance. She admitted to despising McCarthy. She never forgave Richard Nixon in his 1950 brass-knuckles campaign for the U.S. Senate (from California) against Helen Gahagan Douglas, besmirching her as a communist.[14]

Acquainted with Roosevelt since before their respective UN careers, Ralph Bunche appeared to carpers more inhibited than she in expressing himself on American racial matters. Certainly, his position as an international civil servant was obstacle to his commenting upon the internal conditions of any country, including his own. This circumspection irritated Adam Clayton Powell and (later) black firebrands—Malcolm X, Stokely Carmichael—who scolded Bunche as an "Uncle Tom." Still, while he chafed under UN constraints, Bunche did find opportunities to speak about "the Negro's burden and the nation's shame." An admirer of Gandhi, Bunche gravitated to the moral force mobilized by Martin Luther King, first deployed in the Montgomery bus boycott, which Bunche hailed. The landmark 1963 rally in Washington witnessed him as a speaker at the Lincoln Memorial. With King, he walked in the front line in the 1965 Selma march. Bunche attended King's 1968 Atlanta funeral, as in 1963 he had interrupted UN chores to participate in memorial services held in Jackson (Mississippi) for the martyred Medgar Evers. No less than apartheid South Africa, Bunche volunteered that Mississippi merited the UN's attention.[15]

The harm that habitual prejudice inflicted on U.S. world standing vexed Bunche as professional diplomat. (He had refused, he explained at a 1949 White House press conference, a Truman offer to serve as assistant secretary of state because he did not want to reside in segregated Washington.[16]) This sorry condition, Bunche told NAACP and other audiences, bore implications:

> We need many friends to win this [Cold War] struggle, and we seek friends. We would be shortsighted if we ignored the fact that the preponderance of the world's people are non-white, and that the vast millions of Asia, Africa, the Middle East, the Caribbean, and Latin America are extremely sensitive to our undemocratic racial practices. In our design for democratic living by a free people we have something of compelling appeal for all peoples. But we must first demonstrate that this design can be applied to peoples of all colors.[17]

Regarding anti-communist fundamentalists, Bunche felt even more constrained than on civil rights questions in publicly showing dismay. He did lament as inexcusable the pressures brought to bear against Abraham Feller of the UN legal counsel, which contributed to his dejection and 1952 suicide (see Chapter 4).[18] As one who drew HUAC's attention in the early 1950s and additional security interest into 1960, Bunche savored the few occasions that came his way to lash out in print and speech, specifically against maligners of the UN who would demolish it or hasten U.S. disengagement.[19]

Unlike Lehman, Telford Taylor did not have the satisfaction of casting a vote in congressional chambers to censure McCarthy. Nor did Taylor enjoy a public following comparable to Roosevelt's or Bunche's. Yet this former Nuremberg prosecutor was forthright in reproaching the Wisconsin senator and his cronies. A practicing attorney in New York City during the 1950s (then professor of law at Columbia University), Taylor also criticized the Eisenhower government. It did not, in his brief, frankly confront the nation's "domestic totalitarians," preferring instead a mealy-mouthed approach to demagogues, who trucked in hackneyed slogans and censoriousness.[20] Taylor especially rued the maiming of the Foreign Service, intelligence agencies, philanthropic foundations, Hollywood, and scholarly communities, including key scientific ones.[21] Soon after Eisenhower's Atomic Energy Commission suspended (1954) the security clearance of

J. Robert Oppenheimer, Taylor testified: "To have exiled him under stigma from the atomic world which he had done so much to shape was an unforgivable and shameful blunder, of which the Kremlin is likely to be the ultimate beneficiary."[22]

Impressed by that handful of GOP figures, such as Maine's Senator Margaret Chase Smith, who disowned McCarthy, Taylor nonetheless marveled that so few responsible Republicans followed her example.[23] He urged them, for the sake of their party's integrity, to confront extremists within their ranks.[24] In any event, every American, he avowed against the floodtide of right-wing radicalism (in both Republican party and Dixiecrat variants), must aim to preserve an intact democracy. In this connection, the 1954 outlawry of the American communist party was even more injurious to an enlightened polity than the antics of Representative Martin Dies (D, Texas), Senator Patrick McCarran (D, Nevada), Senator William Jenner (R, Indiana), McCarthy, and so forth. Americans had allowed themselves to fall into "a state of cold civil war," Taylor stated in 1955. It threatened, as much as any external enemy could hope, to destroy U.S. well-being:[25]

> It is not only our plains and mountains and rivers and lakes, beautiful as they are, that we arm ourselves to defend; even more it is the traditions by which we live in and among them. The spirit of free inquiry and free enterprise; tolerance for differing beliefs within the framework of ordered government; enforcement of the law without fear or favor—these things may not be sacrificed even in the face of great national peril, because without them our national existence loses its meaning.[26]

Nothing that followed after McCarthy warranted a lowering of the guard against—in George Kennan's words—"the mountebanks, the blackguards, and philistines" who sought assiduously to recapture the scene.[27] A character witness for John Paton Davies and other Foreign Service officers hounded in the 1950s, Kennan discerned in the Cold War just another occasion for obnoxious elements in the political class (military also) to flap about. He blamed the perennial defects of U.S. political culture. By this reckoning, the USSR was hardly free of blame, but the Cold War was largely a function, practically an invention, of American deficiencies. He meditated in 1975:

The Cold War was dear to the hearts of many public and political figures in our country for what might be called purely rhetorical reasons. The devil-image of a great international opponent is a God-send to politicians, insofar as it makes it possible for them to conceal behind clouds of patriotic bombast their various timidities and poverty of ideas with respect to internal problems. And then, you always the generals, for whom tension with the Soviet Union is the very staff of life.[28]

★ ★ ★

The nature of the U.S. empire has long defied tidy classification, fostering among Americans that ambivalence conveyed by Kennan in this chapter's epigraph. Indeed, nothing remotely like a consensus among Americans, or other peoples, can be said to have existed in the immediate post-World War II years, or subsequently, about the character and aims of the U.S. empire. Only its economic, military, and political preeminence has been obvious—from 1956 (Suez), through 1991 (Soviet disunion), and since.

How long into the future the United States will retain this top position is, naturally, impossible to know, as are the factors that will bring about that condition which no empire has escaped: reduction. Maybe, another empire—say, the People's Republic of China—will by virtue of dynamism and purpose bump past, then supersede, the United States, just as its social fabric frays, political institutions atrophy, civic discourse coarsens, and vigor is sapped by demoralizing neocolonial wars of the Vietnam, Afghanistan, and Iraq ilk. Perhaps accelerating environmental decline will spawn such calamities that the United States will suffer irremediably, along with other portions of the globe: scorching temperatures, droughts, desertification, rising seas, unbreathable air, undrinkable water. Before any such foreshortening of power, or a dramatic diminution, the United States will necessarily cope with other challenges—shadowy cyber warriors not clearly aligned with any state, resurgent Russia, unpredictable North Korea, nebulous terrorist groups that anchor their nihilism in deformed interpretations of Islam. Resentments will also stay in play, as nursed by an aged but obstinate Fidel Castro in March 2016. Alert lest his Cuba were swept by a tidal wave of U.S. commercialism and democracy-spouting tourists, he proclaimed: "We do not need the empire to give us anything."[29]

What will be the legacy of this U.S. empire? Perhaps future historians will view it as just another amalgamation of dominance, existing for the profit and safety of its privileged classes. This in effect would be a version of that indictment of America, from colony to super empire, put forward by Fanon—a system of control that has brimmed with evictions and despoliation (native tribes), kidnappings and slavery (Africans), external aggression, atavistic behaviors (legalized torture), and morbid suspicion (Salem witch hunts onward).[30] Or, maybe, other sentiments will prevail, at least contend, such as this one captured by that Swedish observer of mid-twentieth America, Gunnar Myrdal. He published these lines during the last phase of World War II, which if read by Lillian Smith surely caused her again to reflect upon the chasm between U.S. theory and practices:

> America feels itself to be humanity in miniature. When in this crucial time the international leadership passes to America, the great reason for hope is that this country has a national experience of uniting racial and cultural diversities and a national theory, if not a consistent practice, of freedom and equality for all. What America is constantly reaching for is democracy at home and abroad.[31]

Seven decades after Myrdal wrote, a U.S. president offered this upbeat assessment of his country's post-World War II striving. Barack Obama commented in September 2015:

> Out of the ashes of the Second World War, having witnessed the unthinkable power of the atomic age, the United States has worked with many nations . . . to prevent a third world war . . . [support] the steady emergence of strong democracies . . . [build] an international system that imposes a cost on those who choose conflict over cooperation, an order that recognizes the dignity and equal worth of all people.[32]

In defense of the hopeful Myrdal–Obama interpretation one could cite the record—if blemished and ambiguous—of U.S.-led attempts during the first postwar years to salvage international society: UNRRA, Acheson–Lilienthal plan, Nuremberg/Tokyo tribunals, Genocide Convention, Universal Declaration of Human Rights, the United Nations. Needless to elaborate, none of these initiatives was transformative, not individually or collectively. Yet they had an ameliorative effect, traces of which have touched the twenty-first century—in struggles to curb the proliferation of nuclear weapons, oblige war criminals to account, create laws and norms supportive of human rights, and maintain an aspirational United Nations, still striving to retain usefulness amid world hazards. Together these partially realized innovations and frameworks constitute, if nothing else, a point of moral reference, much needed as the border between war and peace has become blurred and the consequences of a return to unrestraint must be harrowing.

★ ★ ★

APPENDICES

APPENDIX A

Preamble to the Charter of the United Nations, 26 June 1945

WE THE PEOPLES OF THE UNITED NATIONS
DETERMINED

to save succeeding generations from the scourge of war, which twice in our lifetime has brought untold sorrow to mankind, and

to reaffirm faith in fundamental human rights, in the dignity and worth of the human person, in the equal rights of men and women of nations large and small, and

to establish conditions under which justice and respect for the obligations arising from treaties and other sources of international law can be maintained, and

to promote social progress and better standards of life in larger freedom,

AND FOR THESE ENDS

to practice tolerance and live together in peace with one another as good neighbors, and to unite our strength to maintain international peace and security, and to ensure, by the acceptance of principles and the institution of methods, that armed force shall not be used, save in the common interest, and to employ international machinery for the promotion of the economic and social advancement of all peoples,

HAVE RESOLVED TO COMBINE OUR EFFORTS TO ACCOMPLISH THESE AIMS

Accordingly, our respective Governments, through representatives assembled in the city of San Francisco, who have exhibited their full powers found to be in good and due form, have agreed to the present Charter of the United Nations and do hereby establish an international organization to be known as the United Nations.

★ ★ ★

APPENDIX B

International Military Tribunal (Nuremberg): Defendants, Verdicts, Sentences—October 1946

In order of indictment, these people in Allied captivity sat the IMT exercise from start to finish. Charges against them, findings, and penalties were as follows.

- Hermann Goering (head of the Luftwaffe; designated heir to Hitler) was accused on counts 1, 2, 3, and 4 and found guilty in each. He was sentenced to death but cheated the gallows by hours via suicide (cyanide).

- Rudolf Hess (deputy to the Führer and designated heir to Hitler after Goering—until the 1941 "peace" mission to Scotland) was accused of 1, 2, 3, and 4 but found guilty only on 1 and 2. He was sentenced to life imprisonment.

- Joachim von Ribbentrop (foreign affairs minister) was accused of 1, 2, 3, and 4 and found guilty on each. He received a sentence of death.

- Field Marshal Wilhelm Keitel (armed forces chief of staff) was accused of 1, 2, 3, and 4 and found guilty on each. He received a sentence of death.

- Ernst Kaltenbrunner (chief of security police and security service) was accused of 1, 3, and 4 and found guilty only on 3 and 4. He received a sentence of death.

- Alfred Rosenberg (head of eastern occupied territories) was accused of 1, 2, 3, and 4 and found guilty on each. He received a sentence of death.

- Hans Frank (governor-general of Poland) was accused of 1, 3, and 4 but found guilty only on 3 and 4. He received a sentence of death.

- Wilhelm Frick (interior minister; protector of Bohemia and Moravia) was accused of 1, 2, 3 and 4, but found guilty only on 2, 3, and 4. He received a sentence of death.

- Julius Streicher (editor/publisher of *Der Sturmer*) was accused of 1 and 4 but found guilty only on 4. He received a sentence of death.

- Walther Funk (minister for economics; Reichsbank president) was accused of 1, 2, 3, and 4, but found guilty only on 2, 3, and 4. He was sentenced to life imprisonment.

- Hjalmar Schacht (minister of economics; Reichsbank president before Funk) was accused of 1 and 2. He was acquitted on both counts.

- Grand Admiral Karl Doenitz (commander of U-boat fleet; head of Navy; actual successor to Hitler) was accused of 1, 2, and 3 but found guilty only on 2 and 3. He was sentenced to ten years' imprisonment.

- Grand Admiral Erich Raeder (chief of Navy) was accused of 1, 2, and 3 and found guilty on each. He was sentenced to life imprisonment.

- Baldur von Schirach (head of the Hitler Jugend) was accused of 1 and 4 but found guilty only on 4. He was sentenced to twenty years' imprisonment.

- Fritz Sauckel (director of conscript labor) was accused of 1, 2, 3, and 4 but found guilty only on 3 and 4. He received a sentence of death.

- Colonel General Alfred Jodl (operations chief of the armed forces) was accused of 1, 2, 3, and 4 and found guilty on each. He received a sentence of death.

- Franz von Papen (vice chancellor; ambassador to Turkey) was accused of 1 and 2. He was acquitted on both counts.

- Arthur Seyss-Inquart (commissioner for the Netherlands) was accused of 1, 2, 3, and 4 and found guilty only of 2, 3, and 4. He received a sentence of death.

- Albert Speer (head of armaments and war production) was accused of 1, 2, 3, and 4 but found guilty only on 3 and 4. He was sentenced to twenty years' imprisonment.

- Konstantin von Neurath (foreign affairs minister before Ribbentrop; governor of Bohemia and Moravia in 1939–1941) was accused of 1, 2, 3, and 4 and found guilty on each. He was sentenced to fifteen years' imprisonment.

- Hans Fritzche (director of radio propaganda) was accused of 1, 3, and 4. He was acquitted on all three counts.

- Bormann, tried in absentia, was accused of 1, 3, and 4 but found guilty only on 3 and 4. He received a sentence of death.

★ ★ ★

APPENDIX C

International Military Tribunal Far East (Tokyo): Defendants, Verdicts, Sentences—November 1948

These people in Allied captivity sat the IMTFE exercise from start to finish. Charges against them, findings, and penalties were as follows.

Like General Tojo Hideki (hanged in 1948), three defendants had been prime ministers: Baron Hiranuma Kiichiro (life imprisonment; paroled in 1955), Baron Hirota Koki (hanged in 1948), General Koiso Kuniaki (life imprisonment; died in 1950).

Two men had been foreign ministers along with Matsuoka Yosuke: Shigemitsu Mamoru (sentenced to seven years; paroled in 1954), Togo Shigenori (sentenced to twenty years; died in 1948).

Four people had served as war ministers: General Araki Sadao (life imprisonment; paroled in 1955), Field Marshal Hata Shunroku (life imprisonment; paroled in 1954), General Itagaki Seishiro (hanged in 1948), General Minami Jiro (life imprisonment; paroled in 1954). Admiral Shimada Shigetaro served as minister of the Navy (life imprisonment; paroled in 1955).

Six Army generals were charged with offenses: Doihara Kenji, commander of the 5th Army in Manchuria (hanged in 1948); Kimura Heitaro (hanged in 1948); Matsui Iwane, commander of Japanese forces in Nanjing and central China during 1937–1938 (hanged in 1948); Muto Akira (hanged in 1948); Sato Kenryo (life imprisonment; paroled in 1956); and Umezu Yoshijiro (life imprisonment; died in 1949).

Two ambassadors were charged: Oshima Hiroshi, posted to Hitler's Berlin (life imprisonment; paroled in 1955), and Shiratori Toshio, posted to Mussolini's Rome (life imprisonment; died in 1949).

Three economic/finance leaders were charged: Hoshino Naoki (life imprisonment; paroled in 1955), Kaya Okinori (life imprisonment; paroled in 1955), and Suzuki Teichi (life imprisonment; paroled in 1955).

Marquis Kido Koichi had been Lord Keeper of the Privy Seal and closest adviser to Emperor Hirohito (life imprisonment; paroled in 1955). Admiral Oka Takasumi was given life imprisonment (paroled in 1954). Colonel Hashimoto Kingoro, member of the Diet and energetic propagandist, was also given life imprisonment (paroled in 1954).

★ ★ ★

APPENDIX D

Convention on the Prevention and Punishment of the Crime of Genocide, 9 December 1948

Approved and proposed for signature and ratification or accession by General Assembly resolution 260 A (III) of 9 December 1948

Entry into force: 12 January 1951, in accordance with article XIII

The Contracting Parties,

Having considered the declaration made by the General Assembly of the United Nations in its resolution 96 (I) dated 11 December 1946 that genocide is a crime under international law, contrary to the spirit and aims of the United Nations and condemned by the civilized world,

Recognizing that at all periods of history genocide has inflicted great losses on humanity, and

Being convinced that, in order to liberate mankind from such an odious scourge, international co-operation is required,

Hereby agree as hereinafter provided:

Article I

The Contracting Parties confirm that genocide, whether committed in time of peace or in time of war, is a crime under international law which they undertake to prevent and to punish.

Article II

In the present Convention, genocide means any of the following acts committed with intent to destroy, in whole or in part, a national, ethnical, racial or religious group, as such:

(a) Killing members of the group;
(b) Causing serious bodily or mental harm to members of the group;
(c) Deliberately inflicting on the group conditions of life calculated to bring about its physical destruction in whole or in part;
(d) Imposing measures intended to prevent births within the group;
(e) Forcibly transferring children of the group to another group.

Article III

The following acts shall be punishable:

(a) Genocide;
(b) Conspiracy to commit genocide;
(c) Direct and public incitement to commit genocide;
(d) Attempt to commit genocide;
(e) Complicity in genocide.

Article IV

Persons committing genocide or any of the other acts enumerated in article III shall be punished, whether they are constitutionally responsible rulers, public officials or private individuals.

Article V

The Contracting Parties undertake to enact, in accordance with their respective Constitutions, the necessary legislation to give effect to the provisions of the present Convention, and, in particular, to provide effective penalties for persons guilty of genocide or any of the other acts enumerated in article III.

Article VI

Persons charged with genocide or any of the other acts enumerated in article III shall be tried by a competent tribunal of the State in the territory of which the act was committed, or by such international penal tribunal as may have jurisdiction with respect to those Contracting Parties which shall have accepted its jurisdiction.

Article VII

Genocide and the other acts enumerated in article III shall not be considered as political crimes for the purpose of extradition.

The Contracting Parties pledge themselves in such cases to grant extradition in accordance with their laws and treaties in force.

Article VIII

Any Contracting Party may call upon the competent organs of the United Nations to take such action under the Charter of the United Nations as they consider appropriate for the prevention and suppression of acts of genocide or any of the other acts enumerated in article III.

Article IX

Disputes between the Contracting Parties relating to the interpretation, application or fulfillment of the present Convention, including those relating to the responsibility of a State for genocide or for any of the other acts enumerated in article III, shall be submitted to the International Court of Justice at the request of any of the parties to the dispute.

Article X

The present Convention, of which the Chinese, English, French, Russian and Spanish texts are equally authentic, shall bear the date of 9 December 1948.

Article XI

The present Convention shall be open until 31 December 1949 for signature on behalf of any Member of the United Nations and of any non-member State to which an invitation to sign has been addressed by the General Assembly.

The present Convention shall be ratified, and the instruments of ratification shall be deposited with the Secretary-General of the United Nations.

After 1 January 1950, the present Convention may be acceded to on behalf of any Member of the United Nations and of any non-member State which has received an invitation as aforesaid.

Instruments of accession shall be deposited with the Secretary-General of the United Nations.

Article XII
Any Contracting Party may at any time, by notification addressed to the Secretary-General of the United Nations, extend the application of the present Convention to all or any of the territories for the conduct of whose foreign relations that Contracting Party is responsible.

Article XIII
On the day when the first twenty instruments of ratification or accession have been deposited, the Secretary-General shall draw up a procès-verbal and transmit a copy thereof to each Member of the United Nations and to each of the non-member States contemplated in article XI.

The present Convention shall come into force on the ninetieth day following the date of deposit of the twentieth instrument of ratification or accession.

Any ratification or accession effected subsequent to the latter date shall become effective on the ninetieth day following the deposit of the instrument of ratification or accession.

Article XIV
The present Convention shall remain in effect for a period of ten years as from the date of its coming into force.

It shall thereafter remain in force for successive periods of five years for such Contracting Parties as have not denounced it at least six months before the expiration of the current period.

Denunciation shall be effected by a written notification addressed to the Secretary-General of the United Nations.

Article XV

If, as a result of denunciations, the number of Parties to the present Convention should become less than sixteen, the Convention shall cease to be in force as from the date on which the last of these denunciations shall become effective.

Article XVI

A request for the revision of the present Convention may be made at any time by any Contracting Party by means of a notification in writing addressed to the Secretary-General.

The General Assembly shall decide upon the steps, if any, to be taken in respect of such request.

Article XVII

The Secretary-General of the United Nations shall notify all Members of the United Nations and the non-member States contemplated in article XI of the following:

(a) Signatures, ratifications and accessions received in accordance with article XI;
(b) Notifications received in accordance with article XII;
(c) The date upon which the present Convention comes into force in accordance with article XIII;
(d) Denunciations received in accordance with article XIV;
(e) The abrogation of the Convention in accordance with article XV;
(f) Notifications received in accordance with article XVI.

Article XVIII

The original of the present Convention shall be deposited in the archives of the United Nations.

A certified copy of the Convention shall be transmitted to each Member of the United Nations and to each of the non-member States contemplated in article XI.

Article XIX

The present Convention shall be registered by the Secretary-General of the United Nations on the date of its coming into force.

★ ★ ★

APPENDIX E

Universal Declaration of Human Rights, 10 December 1948

Universal Declaration of Human Rights Preamble

Whereas recognition of the inherent dignity and of the equal and inalienable rights of all members of the human family is the foundation of freedom, justice and peace in the world,

Whereas disregard and contempt for human rights have resulted in barbarous acts which have outraged the conscience of mankind, and the advent of a world in which human beings shall enjoy freedom of speech and belief and freedom from fear and want has been proclaimed as the highest aspiration of the common people,

Whereas it is essential, if man is not to be compelled to have recourse, as a last resort, to rebellion against tyranny and oppression, that human rights should be protected by the rule of law,

Whereas it is essential to promote the development of friendly relations between nations,

Whereas the peoples of the United Nations have in the Charter reaffirmed their faith in fundamental human rights, in the dignity and worth of the human person and in the equal rights of men and women and have determined to promote social progress and better standards of life in larger freedom,

Whereas Member States have pledged themselves to achieve, in cooperation with the United Nations, the promotion of universal respect for and observance of human rights and fundamental freedoms,

Whereas a common understanding of these rights and freedoms is of the greatest importance for the full realization of this pledge,

Now, therefore, The General Assembly, proclaims this Universal Declaration of Human Rights as a common standard of achievement for all peoples and all nations, to the end that every individual and every organ of society, keeping this Declaration constantly in mind, shall strive by teaching and education to promote respect for these rights and freedoms and by progressive measures, national and international, to secure their universal and effective recognition and observance, both among the peoples of Member States themselves and among the peoples of territories under their jurisdiction.

Article 1
All human beings are born free and equal in dignity and rights. They are endowed with reason and conscience and should act towards one another in a spirit of brotherhood.

Article 2
Everyone is entitled to all the rights and freedoms set forth in this Declaration, without distinction of any kind, such as race, colour, sex, language, religion, political or other opinion, national or social origin, property, birth or other status. Furthermore, no distinction shall be made on the basis of the political, jurisdictional or international status of the country or territory to which a person belongs, whether it be independent, trust, non-self-governing or under any other limitation of sovereignty.

Article 3
Everyone has the right to life, liberty and security of person.

Article 4
No one shall be held in slavery or servitude; slavery and the slave trade shall be prohibited in all their forms.

Article 5

No one shall be subjected to torture or to cruel, inhuman or degrading treatment or punishment.

Article 6

Everyone has the right to recognition everywhere as a person before the law.

Article 7

All are equal before the law and are entitled without any discrimination to equal protection of the law. All are entitled to equal protection against any discrimination in violation of this Declaration and against any incitement to such discrimination.

Article 8

Everyone has the right to an effective remedy by the competent national tribunals for acts violating the fundamental rights granted him by the constitution or by law.

Article 9

No one shall be subjected to arbitrary arrest, detention or exile.

Article 10

Everyone is entitled in full equality to a fair and public hearing by an independent and impartial tribunal, in the determination of his rights and obligations and of any criminal charge against him.

Article 11

1. Everyone charged with a penal offence has the right to be presumed innocent until proved guilty according to law in a public trial at which he has had all the guarantees necessary for his defence.

2. No one shall be held guilty of any penal offence on account of any act or omission which did not constitute a penal offence, under national or international law, at the time when it was committed. Nor shall a heavier penalty be imposed than the one that was applicable at the time the penal offence was committed.

Article 12
No one shall be subjected to arbitrary interference with his privacy, family, home or correspondence, nor to attacks upon his honour and reputation. Everyone has the right to the protection of the law against such interference or attacks.

Article 13
1. Everyone has the right to freedom of movement and residence within the borders of each State.

2. Everyone has the right to leave any country, including his own, and to return to his country.

Article 14
1. Everyone has the right to seek and to enjoy in other countries asylum from persecution.

2. This right may not be invoked in the case of prosecutions genuinely arising from non-political crimes or from acts contrary to the purposes and principles of the United Nations.

Article 15
1. Everyone has the right to a nationality.

2. No one shall be arbitrarily deprived of his nationality nor denied the right to change his nationality.

Article 16
1. Men and women of full age, without any limitation due to race, nationality or religion, have the right to marry and to found a family. They are entitled to equal rights as to marriage, during marriage and at its dissolution.

2. Marriage shall be entered into only with the free and full consent of the intending spouses.

3. The family is the natural and fundamental group unit of society and is entitled to protection by society and the State.

Article 17

1. Everyone has the right to own property alone as well as in association with others.

2. No one shall be arbitrarily deprived of his property.

Article 18

Everyone has the right to freedom of thought, conscience and religion; this right includes freedom to change his religion or belief, and freedom, either alone or in community with others and in public or private, to manifest his religion or belief in teaching, practice, worship and observance.

Article 19

Everyone has the right to freedom of opinion and expression; this right includes freedom to hold opinions without interference and to seek, receive and impart information and ideas through any media and regardless of frontiers.

Article 20

1. Everyone has the right to freedom of peaceful assembly and association.

2. No one may be compelled to belong to an association.

Article 21

1. Everyone has the right to take part in the government of his country, directly or through freely chosen representatives.

2. Everyone has the right to equal access to public service in his country.

3. The will of the people shall be the basis of the authority of government; this will shall be expressed in periodic and genuine elections which shall be by universal and equal suffrage and shall be held by secret vote or by equivalent free voting procedures.

Article 22

Everyone, as a member of society, has the right to social security and is entitled to realization, through national effort and international co-operation and in accordance with the organization and resources of each State, of the economic, social and cultural rights indispensable for his dignity and the free development of his personality.

Article 23

1. Everyone has the right to work, to free choice of employment, to just and favourable conditions of work and to protection against unemployment.

2. Everyone, without any discrimination, has the right to equal pay for equal work.

3. Everyone who works has the right to just and favourable remuneration ensuring for himself and his family an existence worthy of human dignity, and supplemented, if necessary, by other means of social protection.

4. Everyone has the right to form and to join trade unions for the protection of his interests.

Article 24

Everyone has the right to rest and leisure, including reasonable limitation of working hours and periodic holidays with pay.

Article 25

1. Everyone has the right to a standard of living adequate for the health and well-being of himself and of his family, including food, clothing, housing and medical care and necessary social services, and the right to security in the event of unemployment, sickness, disability, widowhood, old age or other lack of livelihood in circumstances beyond his control.

2. Motherhood and childhood are entitled to special care and assistance. All children, whether born in or out of wedlock, shall enjoy the same social protection.

Article 26

1. Everyone has the right to education. Education shall be free, at least in the elementary and fundamental stages. Elementary education shall be compulsory. Technical and professional education shall be made generally available and higher education shall be equally accessible to all on the basis of merit.

2. Education shall be directed to the full development of the human personality and to the strengthening of respect for human rights and funda-mental freedoms. It shall promote understanding, tolerance and friendship

among all nations, racial or religious groups, and shall further the activities of the United Nations for the maintenance of peace.

3. Parents have a prior right to choose the kind of education that shall be given to their children.

Article 27

1. Everyone has the right freely to participate in the cultural life of the community, to enjoy the arts and to share in scientific advancement and its benefits.

2. Everyone has the right to the protection of the moral and material interests resulting from any scientific, literary or artistic production of which he is the author.

Article 28

Everyone is entitled to a social and international order in which the rights and freedoms set forth in this Declaration can be fully realized.

Article 29

1. Everyone has duties to the community in which alone the free and full development of his personality is possible.

2. In the exercise of his rights and freedoms, everyone shall be subject only to such limitations as are determined by law solely for the purpose of securing due recognition and respect for the rights and freedoms of others and of meeting the just requirements of morality, public order and the general welfare in a democratic society.

3. These rights and freedoms may in no case be exercised contrary to the purposes and principles of the United Nations.

Article 30

Nothing in this Declaration may be interpreted as implying for any State, group or person any right to engage in any activity or to perform any act aimed at the destruction of any of the rights and freedoms set forth herein.

★ ★ ★

NOTES

Introduction

1   For examples of the range of scholarship and interpretations on the Cold War, see Melvyn Leffler and Odd Arne Westad, Eds., *The Cambridge History of the Cold War* (Cambridge: Cambridge University Press, 2010), 3 vols. See also the multifaceted treatment in Wested's *The Cold War: A World History* (New York, NY: Basic, 2017). For Bretton Woods and its consequences, see Benn Steil, *The Battle of Bretton Woods: John Maynard Keynes, Harry Dexter White, and the Making of a New World Order* (Princeton, NJ: Princeton University Press, 2013).

2   Hobbes's famed 1651 account of unrestrained conflict:

> *Out of civil states, there is always war of every one against every one.* Hereby it is manifest, that during the time men live without a common power to keep them all in awe, they are in that condition which is called war; and such a war, as is of every man, against every man . . . and the life of man, solitary, poor, nasty, brutish, and short.
>
> > Michael Oakeshott, Ed., Thomas Hobbes, *Leviathan or the Matter, Forme and Power of a Commonwealth Ecclesiasticall and Civil* (New York, NY: Collier, 1973), p. 100.

3   See Hedley Bull's durable *The Anarchical Society: A Study of Order in World Politics* (London: Macmillan, 1977) and Robert Harry Jackson's *The Global Covenant: Human Conduct in a World of States* (Oxford: Oxford University Press, 2000). A probing assessment—evaluating strengths and weaknesses of

Hedley Bull and company is in Hidemi Suganami, Madeline Carr, and Adam Humphreys, Eds., *The Anarchical Society at 40: Contemporary Challenges and Prospects* (Oxford: Oxford University Press, 2017).

4   FDR touted the Four Freedoms in his 6 January 1941 State of the Union message: freedom of speech, freedom of religion, freedom from want, freedom from fear of aggression. These "essential human freedoms," as he phrased them, were incorporated into the Atlantic Charter.

The Atlantic Charter also supported, with slight modification, these principles: renunciation of territorial and other aggrandizement; national self-determination; free trade and access to raw materials; fair labor standards and social security; freedom of the seas; world disarmament and abandonment of the use of force with promise of a multilateral organization to ensure international security.

5   In a sense my book is a response to Ira Katznelson's *Desolation and Enlightenment: Political Knowledge After Total War, Totalitarianism, and the Holocaust* (New York, NY: Columbia University Press, 2003) and to Pankaj Mishra's *Age of Anger: A History of the Present* (New York, NY: Farrar, Straus and Giroux, 2017). Katznelson traces a type of liberal reaction to World War II, at once cautious, wary, and unsparingly aware of the frailties and flaws centered in human nature. Mishra charges Western imperialism and dissemination of Western ideas with creating a world of violence, bleakness, and chaos.

6   George Orwell, "You and the Atomic bomb," *Tribune*, 19 October 1945.

7   Telford Taylor, "Wisdom, Not So-Called 'Morality,' of A-Bombing Held Up as Our Guide," *Washington Post*, 13 November 1949.

8   Telford Taylor, *Nuremberg and Vietnam: An American Tragedy* (New York, NY: Bantam, 1971), pp. 203, 207; "Judging Calley Is Not Enough," *Life*, 9 April 1971, p. 23.

In a company of war resisters who included Joan Baez, Taylor visited Hanoi in December 1972, when that city was a target of heavy U.S. bombing. At that time, he detailed in newspaper articles the damages done and the response of North Vietnamese officials and ordinary citizens. He ended one article this way: "As in Britain thirty years ago, so today in Hanoi there is lots of 'London pride.'" See Taylor's "Hanoi Under the Bombing: Sirens, Shelters, Rubble and Death," *New York Times*, 7 January 1973, p. 3.

9   Stephen Holmes, "Is Defiance of Law a Proof of Success? Magical Thinking in the War on Terror" in Karen Greenberg, Ed., *The Torture Debate in America* (Cambridge: Cambridge University Press, 2006), pp. 124–125.

10 Allida Black et al., Eds., *The Eleanor Roosevelt Papers: The Human Rights Years, 1945–1948* (Detroit, MI: Thomson Gale, 2007), Vol. I, p. 759.

11 Winston Churchill, *Never Give In! The Best of Winston Churchill's Speeches* (New York, NY: Hyperion, 2003), Speech of 5 March 1946, p. 415.

12   On the Occasion of the Presentation of the Nobel Peace Prize, 10 December 1950, Box 415, Ralph Bunche Papers, UCLA.

13   Edward Gibbon approvingly cited by George Kennan in *Memoirs: 1925–1950* (Boston, MA: Little, Brown, 1967), p. 130.

14   Reinhold Niebuhr, *The Irony of American History* (Chicago, IL: University of Chicago Press, 1952, 2008), p. 160.

15   The United States as liberal empire is a contested concept and the literature extensive. A fair sample of the theorizing can be found in Lloyd Gardner, Walter LaFeber, and Thomas McCormick, *Creation of the American Empire: U.S. Diplomatic History* (Chicago, IL: Rand McNally and Company, 1973), Michael Doyle, *Empires* (Ithaca, NY: Cornell University Press, 1986), Michael Mann, *Incoherent Empire* (London: Verso, 2005), chapters 1 and 2 of Odd Arne Westad, *The Global Cold War: Third World Interventions and the Making of Our Times* (Cambridge: Cambridge University Press, 2007), Richard Immerman, *Empire for Liberty: A History of American Imperialism from Benjamin Franklin to Paul Wolfowitz* (Princeton, NJ: Princeton University Press, 2010), Paul Kramer, "Power and Connection: Imperial Histories of the United States in the World," *American Historical Review*, December 2011, Julian Go, *Patterns of Empire: The British and American Empires 1688 to the Present* (Cambridge: Cambridge University Press, 2011), Anthony Pagden, *The Burdens of Empire: 1539 to the Present* (Cambridge: Cambridge University Press, 2015), Duncan Bell, *Reordering the World: Essays on Liberalism and Empire* (Princeton, NJ: Princeton University Press, 2016), and Krishan Kumar, *Visions of Empire: How Five Imperial Regimes Shaped the World* (Princeton, NJ: Princeton University Press, 2017).

16   Quoted in Niall Ferguson, *Colossus: The Rise and Fall of the American Empire* (New York, NY: Penguin, 2004), p. 302.

17   Timothy Snyder, *Tyranny: Twenty Lessons from the Twentieth Century* (New York, NY: Tim Duggan, 2017), pp. 10–12.

Chapter 1: Destruction

1   Quotation in Allan Nevins, *Herbert H. Lehman and His Era* (New York, NY: Charles Scribner's Sons, 1963), p. 264.

2   Richard Bessel, "Death and Survival in the Second World War" in Michael Geyer and Adam Tooze, Eds., *The Cambridge History of the Second World War* (Cambridge: Cambridge University Press, 2015), Vol. III, p. 252; Gerhard Weinberg, *A World at Arms: A Global History of World War II* (Cambridge: Cambridge University Press, 1995), p. 894.

3   Yasmin Khan, "Wars of Displacement: Exile and Uprooting in the 1940s" in Geyer and Tooze, *The Cambridge History of the Second World War*, Vol. III, pp. 277–278.

4   "A Holocaust Survivor Tells of Auschwitz at 18 and, Again, at 90" in *New York Times*, 14 March 2015, p. A11.

5   Czeslaw Milosz, "Preparation" in *New York Review of Books*, 26 September 1985.

6   Quoted by Roger Cohen in "Syria's White Rose," *New York Times*, 20 February 2016, p. A19.

7   Sabina de Werth Neu, *A Long Silence: Memories of a German Refugee Child, 1941–1958* (Amherst, NY: Prometheus, 2011), p. 15.

    In late January 2015, Anna Sauerbrey, an editor attached to the opinion page of *Der Tagesspiegel*, wrote: "I am a patriot. Being German, those words don't come easily . . . particularly not now, just a few days before we commemorate the 70th anniversary of the liberation of Auschwitz." See Sauerbrey, "Germany Is Not Turning Backward," *New York Times*, 23 January 2015, p. A25. A few months after Sauerbrey testified, Andreas Wirsching, director of the Institute of Contemporary History (in Munich) observed: "The Nazi period will remain a thorn in Germany's side." To this, he added: "We will continually be confronted with the question of how it could be that such a highly civilized country plunged into such an abyss of transgression, into a regime of injustice and murder." See "Tracing Nazism's Rise Where the Perpetrators Plotted Their Crimes," *New York Times*, 2 May 2015, p. A7.

8   Hata Tsuneo, *Atomic Bomb and a Soldier: A Diary of the Chronicle of the Emperor Hirohito* (private printing in author's possession, n.d., translated from the Japanese by Lisa Shinohara), p. 178; email to author from Hata Gohei, 2 January 2015.

9   Primo Levi, "The Child-Girl of Pompei" in *Collected Poems* (London: Faber and Faber, 1988), p. 34.

10 Grace Fox, "The Origins of UNRRA," *Political Science Quarterly*, December 1950, pp. 566–567.

11 Herbert Hoover to Lehman, 25 November 1942; Hoover to Cordell Hull, 24 April 1941; Hull to Hoover, 10 May 1941; Hoover to Hull, 3 June 1941; Hull to Hoover, 28 June 1941, Box 157, Herbert Lehman Papers; Nevins, *Herbert H. Lehman and His Era*, pp. 222, 225.

12 Jessica Reinisch, "Internationalism in Relief: The Birth (and Death) of UNRRA" in Mark Mazower et al., Eds., *Post-War Reconstruction in Europe: International Perspectives, 1945–1949* (Oxford: Oxford University Press, 2011), p. 263.

13 Winston Churchill, *Never Give In! The Best of Winston Churchill's Speeches* (New York, NY: Hyperion, 2003), "The Few," 20 August 1940, pp. 240–241; Mary Kinnear, *Woman of the World: Mary McGeachy and International Cooperation* (Toronto: University of Toronto Press, 2004), p. 105.

14 Lehman to FDR, 30 August 1943, Box 157, Herbert Lehman Papers; Dan Plesch, *America, Hitler and the UN: How the Allies Won World War II and Forged a Peace* (London: I.B. Tauris, 2011), p. 122; Nevins, *Herbert H. Lehman and His Era*, pp. 227–228; Fox, "The Origins of UNRRA," p. 565.

15 Andrew Williams, "Reconstruction Before the Marshall Plan," *Review of International Studies*, July 2005, p. 551; Dean Acheson, *Present at the Creation* (New York, NY: W.W. Norton, 1969), pp. 68–71.

16 William Hitchcock, *The Bitter Road to Freedom: The Human Cost of Allied Victory in World War II Europe* (New York, NY: Free Press, 2008), p. 219.

17 Fox, "The Origins of UNRRA," p. 584.

18 Acheson's proposals regarding UNRRA's financing of relief operations sprang from his consultations with Harry Dexter White of the Treasury Department, Britain's John Maynard Keynes and Richard Law (later Lord Coleraine), and Herbert Lehman. See Acheson, *Present at the Creation*, p. 77.

19 See www.bls.gov/data/inflation_calculator.htm.

20 Plesch, *America, Hitler and the UN: How the Allies Won World War II and Forged a Peace*, p. 125; Hitchcock, *The Bitter Road to Freedom: The Human Cost of Allied Victory in World War II Europe*, p. 220.

21 Herbert Lehman, Oral History, p. 747, Columbia University.

22 Reinisch, "Internationalism in Relief: The Birth (and Death) of UNRRA," pp. 271–272; Stephen Porter, "Humanitarian Politics and Governance: International Responses to the Civilian Toll in the Second World War" in Geyer and Tooze, *The Cambridge History of the Second World War*, Vol. III, pp. 516–517.

23 Herbert Lehman, Oral History, p. 758.

24 Dwight Eisenhower to Lehman, 15 November 1945, Box 149, Herbert Lehman Papers; Herbert Lehman, Oral History, p. 738.

25 George Woodbridge, *UNRRA: The History of the United Nations Relief and Rehabilitation Administration* (New York, NY: Columbia University Press, 1950), Vol. III, p. 428.

26 Ben Shephard, *The Long Road Home: The Aftermath of the Second World War* (New York, NY: Alfred A. Knopf, 2011), p. 52; Reinisch, "Internationalism in Relief: The Birth (and Death) of UNRRA," pp. 282–283; Fox, "The Origins of UNRRA," pp. 571, 578–579. For a detailed explanation of UNRRA organization, assorted committees, and financing see Woodbridge, *UNRRA: The History of the United Nations Relief and Rehabilitation Administration*, Vol. I, parts 1–2.

27 Adult leaders of the American Girl Scouts worked with UNRRA personnel to help displaced children and train people in the "techniques of youth leadership." Mrs. Marshall Simpson to La Guardia, 28 June 1946, Box 23D4, File 1, Fiorello La Guardia Papers. CARE cooperated with UNRRA in

providing food relief in Europe. CARE = Cooperative for American Remittances to Europe.

28 Woodbridge, *UNRRA: The History of the United Nations Relief and Rehabilitation Administration*, Vol. II, p. 541.

29 Hitchcock, *The Bitter Road to Freedom: The Human Cost of Allied Victory in World War II Europe*, p. 222; Shephard, *The Long Road Home: The Aftermath of the Second World War*, p. 311.

30 Lehman was also the father of an airman, Peter, a Distinguished Flying Cross awardee, killed in 1944 and buried in the U.S. military cemetery at Cambridge (England).

31 Lehman to Ernest Bevin, regarding Jackson: "There was no part of the world to which he was not willing to go and no work seemed too much for him." 11 December 1947, Box 141, Herbert Lehman Papers.

32 Shephard, *The Long Road Home: The Aftermath of the Second World War*, pp. 310–311. On McGeachy, see section two of Susan Armstrong-Reid and David Murray, *Armies of Peace: Canada and the UNRRA Years* (Toronto: University of Toronto Press, 2008) and Kinnear, *Woman of the World: Mary McGeachy and International Cooperation*, p. 148.

33 Fox, "The Origins of UNRRA," p. 561. La Guardia asserted in November 1946 that "UNRRA has given the first lesson in applied world cooperation." See La Guardia, "How Should Food Be Distributed After UNRRA Expires?" Town Meeting, p. 4, 28 November 1946, Box 23D4, File 1, Fiorello La Guardia Papers.

34 Woodbridge, *UNRRA: The History of the United Nations Relief and Rehabilitation Administration*, Vol. II, pp. 551–552. President Truman labeled UNRRA, as of November 1945, "the greatest and most difficult humanitarian effort ever undertaken." Truman to Lehman, 8 November 1945, Box 182, Herbert Lehman Papers. La Guardia felt that UNRRA "operated in the spirit of the Sermon on the Mount." See "How Should Food Be Distributed After UNRRA Expires?", p. 6.

35 David Mayers, *FDR's Ambassadors and the Diplomacy of Crisis* (Cambridge: Cambridge University Press, 2013), p. 96.

36 H.H. Kung to Lehman, 7 March 1946; Lehman to Kung, 3 April 1946, Box 161, Herbert Lehman Papers.

37 Woodbridge, *UNRRA: The History of the United Nations Relief and Rehabilitation Administration*, Vol. II, pp. 451–452.

38 Ibid., p. 453.

39 Lehman to Dean Acheson, 14 January 1950, Box 137, Herbert Lehman Papers. Chiang Kai-shek's government conferred the *Auspicious Star, Grand Cordon* upon Lehman for UNRRA's "great humanitarian work" in China—Wellington Koo file, 31 July 1947, Box 160, Herbert Lehman Papers.

40 Carlos Romulo Speech, 10 November 1958, Box 175, Herbert Lehman Papers.

41 Woodbridge, *UNRRA: The History of the United Nations Relief and Rehabilitation Administration*, Vol. II, pp. 454–465.

42 Ira A. Hirschmann, *The Embers Still Burn* (New York, NY: Simon & Schuster, 1949), p. 185.

43 Woodbridge, *UNRRA: The History of the United Nations Relief and Rehabilitation Administration*, Vol. II, pp. 229–230.

44 Timothy Snyder, *Bloodlands: Europe Between Hitler and Stalin* (New York, NY: Basic, 2010), pp. 162–163, 168.

45 Woodbridge, *UNRRA: The History of the United Nations Relief and Rehabilitation Administration*, Vol. II, p. 256.

46 Ibid., p. 188.

47 Czech tribute to Lehman, 7 January 1947, Box 140, Herbert Lehman Papers; Woodbridge, *UNRRA: The History of the United Nations Relief and Rehabilitation Administration*, Vol. II, p. 199.

48 Tony Judt, *Postwar: A History of Europe Since 1945* (New York, NY: Penguin, 2006), p. 52; Woodbridge, *UNRRA: The History of the United Nations Relief and Rehabilitation Administration*, Vol. II, p. 320, #122.

49 James Byrnes to Lehman, 22 March 1946, Box 143, Herbert Lehman Papers; Hitchcock, *The Bitter Road to Freedom: The Human Cost of Allied Victory in World War II Europe*, pp. 227–233, 239–243.

50 Woodbridge, *UNRRA: The History of the United Nations Relief and Rehabilitation Administration*, Vol. II, p. 294. Also see Hitchcock, *The Bitter Road to Freedom: The Human Cost of Allied Victory in World War II Europe*, pp. 233–239.

51 Herbert Lehman, Oral History, p. 759.

52 Kinnear, *Woman of the World: Mary McGeachy and International Cooperation*, p. 162.

53 Keith Lowe, *Savage Continent: Europe in the Aftermath of World War II* (New York, NY: St. Martin's Press, 2012), p. 27.

    One displaced American was La Guardia's sister, Gemma. She survived internment at Ravensbruck. Afterward she experienced the vicissitudes of life in a DP center but won passage back to America in May 1947. See H. Paul Jeffers, *The Napoleon of New York: Mayor Fiorello La Guardia* (New York, NY: John Wiley and Sons, 2002), pp. 372–373; Thomas Kessner, *Fiorello H. La Guardia and the Making of Modern New York* (New York, NY: McGraw-Hill, 1989), pp. 562–564.

54 Milton Winn to Dear Sy, 1 March 1946, Box 23D4, File 1, Fiorello La Guardia Papers.

55 Shephard, *The Long Road Home: The Aftermath of the Second World War*, pp. 305–327; Plesch, *America, Hitler and the UN: How the Allies Won World War II and Forged a Peace*, p. 137.

56 As of September 1946, roughly 355,000 Polish DPs still resided in Germany. To encourage their return to Poland, UNRRA pledged to provide each one with sixty-day food rations.

57 Mayers, *FDR's Ambassadors and the Diplomacy of Crisis*, pp. 240–241.

58 Lowe, *Savage Continent: Europe in the Aftermath of World War II*, p. 94.

59 Nevins, Herbert H. *Lehman and His Era*, p. 286. Philip Noel-Baker, a Labour MP, said in 1960: "Without UNRRA, Europe would have gone to complete disaster in 1945–46." Quoted from his letter to Mrs. Lehman, 15 February 1960, Box 171, Herbert Lehman Papers.

60 Porter, "Humanitarian Politics and Governance: International Responses to the Civilian Toll in the Second World War," pp. 519–520.

61 Herbert Lehman, Oral History, p. 736.

62 Shephard, *The Long Road Home: The Aftermath of the Second World War*, p. 57; Robert Ingalls, *Herbert H. Lehman and New York's Little New Deal* (New York, NY: New York University, 1975), pp. 2, 17–18; Herbert Lehman, Oral History, p. 748.

63 Woodbridge, *UNRRA: The History of the United Nations Relief and Rehabilitation Administration*, Vol. II, pp. 543–544. Lehman once confessed: "So the first group of people we recruited, in some of the foreign countries, did not measure up to the job, and we had to get rid of them." Cited in Herbert Lehman, Oral History, p. 737. La Guardia was also troubled by reported inefficiency in UNRRA services and "bent" to improve matters. Director General's Statement, Record of Meeting on Displaced Persons, 14/15 August 1946, p. 2, Myer Cohen File, UNRRA, 1, 1946, Fiorello La Guardia Papers.

64 Hitchcock, *The Bitter Road to Freedom: The Human Cost of Allied Victory in World War II Europe*, pp. 218–219, 223; Lowe, *Savage Continent: Europe in the Aftermath of World War II*, p. 108; Nevins, *Herbert H. Lehman and His Era*, p. 226; Porter, "Humanitarian Politics and Governance: International Responses to the Civilian Toll in the Second World War," p. 518.

65 Personal Diary September 1945–August 1946, Entries 6 April 1946 and 25 August 1946, Lieutenant General Sir Frederick Morgan Papers.

66 Report on Visit to Germany, 21 June 1946, Myer Cohen File, UNRRA 1, 1946, and Sidney Morell interview, 1 October 1985, pp. 6–12, Fiorello La Guardia Papers.

67 Personal Diary September 1945–August 1946, Entry 1 August 1946, Lieutenant General Sir Frederick Morgan Papers.

68 Ibid., Entries 23 March 1946 and 1 August 1946; Morgan to Under Secretary of State, 14 September 1946 and Morgan to Major General G.W.R. Templer,

4 July 1946, Folders containing papers related to UNRRA, 6/1, Lieutenant General Sir Frederick Morgan Papers.

69   Hirschmann, *The Embers Still Burn*, pp. 10–11, 144; Shephard, *The Long Road Home: The Aftermath of the Second World War*, p. 241; Lieutenant General Sir Frederick Morgan, *Peace and War: A Soldier's Life* (London: Hodder and Stoughton, 1961), pp. 218–262; Ira Hirschmann, *Caution to the Winds* (New York, NY: David McKay, 1962), pp. 204–206.

70   Cohen, a published author specializing on the Supreme Court, earned a Ph.D. at Yale University. He also worked in the western United States to assist migrant workers ("Oakies" and "Arkies") displaced by dust storms and farm closings.

71   Morgan to Major General E.D. Fanshawe, 1 April 1947, Folders containing papers related to UNRRA, 6/3, Lieutenant General Sir Frederick Morgan Papers.

72   Lehman to Stewart Alsop, 14 May 1958, Box 137, Herbert Lehman Papers.

73   Nevins, *Herbert H. Lehman and His Era*, pp. 275, 277–278; La Guardia, "How Should Food Be Distributed After UNRRA Expires?" p. 13.

74   Shephard, *The Long Road Home: The Aftermath of the Second World War*, pp. 155–157; Herbert Lehman, Oral History, pp. 738, 761, 763.

75   Thomas Reynolds to Lehman, 20 February 1943, Box 157, Herbert Lehman Papers; Richard Norton Smith, *An Uncommon Man: The Triumph of Herbert Hoover* (New York, NY: Simon & Schuster, 1984), pp. 319–320; Gary Dean Best, *Herbert Hoover: The Postpresidential Years 1933–1964* (Stanford, CA: Hoover Institution Press, 1983), Vol. I, pp. 218, 268–269.

76   Joan Hoff Wilson, *Herbert Hoover: Forgotten Progressive* (Boston, MA: Little, Brown, 1975), p. 256; William Leuchtenburg, *Herbert Hoover* (New York, NY: Times Books, 2009), p. 157.

77   Best, *Herbert Hoover: The Postpresidential Years 1933–1964*, Vol. II, pp. 288–290.

78   Hirschmann, *The Embers Still Burn*, p. 147.

79   Shephard, *The Long Road Home: The Aftermath of the Second World War*, p. 260.

80   Best, *Herbert Hoover: The Postpresidential Years 1933–1964*, Vol. II, p. 295.

81   Speech to UNRRA Council Meeting, 6 August 1946 and The European Crisis, 31 May 1947, Box 60, William Clayton Papers; Acheson, *Present at the Creation*, p. 231.

82   Acheson to Bernard Baruch, 18 April 1950, Box 29, Dean Acheson Papers, Harry S. Truman Presidential Library; Acheson, *Present at the Creation*, p. 201; Robert Beisner, *Dean Acheson: A Life in the Cold War* (New York, NY: Oxford University Press, 2006), p. 46.

83 William Hitchcock, "The Marshall Plan and the Creation of the West" in Melvyn Leffler and Odd Arne Westad, Eds., *The Cambridge History of The Cold War* (Cambridge: Cambridge University Press, 2011), Vol. I, p. 154.

84 La Guardia, "How Should Food Be Distributed After UNRRA Expires?" p. 22.

85 The first Bikini test (Able) was by airdrop, the second (Baker) underwater. Truman had hesitated before authorizing these two atomic tests. Truman to Carl Hatch, 6 July 1946, Box 1, Atomic Bomb Collection.

86 David Holloway, "Nuclear Weapons and the Escalation of the Cold War, 1945–1962" in Leffler and Westad, *The Cambridge History of the Cold War*, Vol. I, pp. 376–377; James Chace, *Acheson: The Secretary of State Who Created the American World* (New York, NY: Simon & Schuster, 1998), p. 128.

87 Andrei Sakharov, *Memoirs* (New York, NY: Alfred A. Knopf, 1990), p. 164.

88 Petition by scientists of the Metallurgical Laboratory of University of Chicago, 17 July 1945. Also notable was O.C. Brewster, an engineer with the Kellex Corporation and involved with the Manhattan Project since February 1942. He wrote to Truman before the atomic bomb was a reality: "This thing [atomic bomb] must not be permitted on this earth. We must not be the most hated and feared people on earth however good our intent may be." Brewster to Truman, 24 May 1945, Box 2, Atomic Bomb Collection.

   Franck's colleagues in favor of a demonstration explosion were D.J. Hughes, J.J. Nickson, Eugene Rabinowitch, Glenn Seaborg, J.C. Stearns, and Leo Szilard.

89 Stuart Rice and Joshua Jortner, *James Franck 1882–1964* (Washington, DC: National Academy of Sciences, 2010), p. 16.

90 Martin Sherwin, *A World Destroyed: The Atomic Bomb and the Grand Alliance* (New York, NY: Vintage, 1977), pp. 210–219.

91 A young California woman allowed herself this confusion on contemplating the atomic attacks: "It sank in. Seventy thousand or a hundred thousand or two hundred thousand civilians? It came as a shock . . . to see women, children, and old innocent civilians burned. And Nagasaki! Two of them?"

   Herbert Hoover declared in 1945: "The use of the Atomic bomb, with its indiscriminate killing of women and children, revolts [me]." Hoover and the California woman were closer than they realized to India's Mohandas Gandhi, when in July 1946 he speculated on whether use of the bombs had destroyed the soul of the United States. The same year, John Hersey published in *The New Yorker* his *Hiroshima* that humanized the victims and recounted horrid scenes.

   See Studs Terkel, *The Good War* (New York, NY: New Press, 1984), p. 560; Best, *Herbert Hoover: The Postpresidential Years, 1933–1964*, Vol. I, p. 277; Mohandas Gandhi, "The Atom Bomb, America and Japan" in

John Vasquez, Ed. *Classics of International Relations* (Englewood Cliffs, NJ: Prentice Hall, 1990), p. 50.

92 Henry Stimson and McGeorge Bundy. *On Active Service in Peace and War* (New York, NY: Harper and Brothers, 1948), p. 645.

93 Ibid., p. 644.

94 Acheson did not doubt the need to use the atomic bombs against Japan in August 1945 and endorsed Stimson's public defense of the actions. Acheson to Henry Stimson, 23 January 1947, Reel 19, Dean Acheson Papers, Yale University.

95 Beisner, *Dean Acheson: A Life in the Cold War*, p. 45. In summer 1949, with the Cold War under way but before the Soviets tested their first atomic weapon, Acheson still held that the matter of atomic energy should be resolved. Acheson to Louis Johnson, 22 July 1949, Box 32, Dean Acheson Papers, Harry S. Truman Presidential Library.

96 Oppenheimer was esteemed by Lilienthal and colleagues. Of Oppenheimer, Lilienthal once testified: "He is worth living a life-time just to know that mankind has been able to produce such a being—even if we may have to wait another 100 years for the second one off the line." David Lilienthal to "Dear Herb," 14 January 1948, Box 46, J. Robert Oppenheimer Papers.

97 Peter Goodchild, *J. Robert Oppenheimer: Shatterer of Worlds* (Boston, MA: Houghton Mifflin, 1981), p. 180. On Truman, see: John Blum, Ed., *The Price of Vision: The Diary of Henry A. Wallace 1942–1946* (Boston, MA: Houghton Mifflin, 1973), entry of 10 August 1945; Matthew Jones, *After Hiroshima: The United States, Race and Nuclear Weapons in Asia, 1945–1965* (Cambridge: Cambridge University Press, 2010), pp. 26–27; Barton Bernstein, "Understanding the Atomic Bomb and the Japanese Surrender: Missed Opportunities, Little-Known Near Disasters, and Modern Memory" in Michael Hogan, Ed., *Hiroshima in History and Memory* (Cambridge: Cambridge University Press, 1996), p. 73.

98 Oppenheimer to David Lilienthal, From a Note, 2 February 1946, Box 262, J. Robert Oppenheimer Papers; J. Robert Oppenheimer to Lilienthal, 24 May 1946, Box 116, David Lilienthal Papers; Gregg Herken, *Brotherhood of the Bomb: The Tangled Lives and Loyalties of Robert Oppenheimer, Ernest Lawrence, and Edward Teller* (New York, NY: Henry Holt, 2002), p. 163; Acheson, *Present at the Creation*, p. 153; Steven Neuse, *David E. Lilienthal: The Journey of an American Liberal* (Knoxville, TN: University of Tennessee Press, 1996), p. 170.

99 State Department, *A Report on the International Control of Atomic Energy* (Washington, DC: Government Printing Office, 1946), pp. 9–10.

100 Ibid., pp. 26, 29, 31–32.

101 Ibid., p. xiii.

To Walter Lippmann, Chester Bernard wrote: "The alternative [to international control] is to try to keep ahead of the rest of the world in an atomic armament race, the end of which would be catastrophic quite beyond the imagination of most people, if not of everybody." Bernard to Lippmann, 20 June 1946, Box 114, David Lilienthal Papers. Similar sentiments larded the Acheson–Vannever Bush interview with Larry Lesueur of CBS on 23 April 1946, Box 134 Dean Acheson Papers, Harry S. Truman Library.

Also see David Holloway, *Stalin and the Bomb: The Soviet Union and Atomic Energy 1939–1956* (New Haven, CT: Yale University Press, 1994), p. 161; Herken, *Brotherhood of the Bomb: The Tangled Lives and Loyalties of Robert Oppenheimer, Ernest Lawrence, and Edward Teller*, pp. 163–164.

102 *A Report on the International Control of Atomic Energy*, p. 61. Also see Fritz Bartel, "Surviving the Years of Grace: The Atomic Bomb and the Specter of World Government, 1945–1950," *Diplomatic History*, April 2015, pp. 288–293.

103 David Lilienthal, *The Journals: The Atomic Energy Years 1945–1950* (New York, NY: Harper and Row, 1964), p. 35; Susan Butler, *Roosevelt and Stalin: Portrait of a Partnership* (New York, NY: Alfred A. Knopf, 2015), pp. 318–319.

104 Margaret Coit, *Mr. Baruch* (Boston, MA: Houghton Mifflin, 1957), p. 567; Beisner, *Dean Acheson: A Life in the Cold War*, p. 34.

105 Jordan Schwarz, *The Speculator: Bernard M. Baruch in Washington, 1917–1965* (Chapel Hill, NC: University of North Carolina Press, 1981), p. 494; Lilienthal, *The Journals: The Atomic Energy Years*, pp. 69–70.

106 Baruch recruited to his team these men: Herbert Swope, Ferdinand Eberstadt, John Hancock, and Fred Searls.

107 For Wallace, see Blum's *The Price of Vision: The Diary of Henry A. Wallace 1942–1946*, entry of 23 July 1946.

108 Baruch remained adamant on the subject of punishment, possibly to the point of war, for atomic violators. See, for example, Baruch to Lilienthal, 27 May 1946, Box 114, David Lilienthal Papers; Baruch to Robert Patterson, 1 July 1946, Box 31, Baruch to Lilienthal, 28 April 1947, Box 444, Baruch to John Foster Dulles, 5 October 1948, Box 443, Baruch to James Conant, 24 December 1946, Box 439, Memorandum of Baruch Meeting with Harry Truman and James Byrnes, 7 June 1946, Box 31, Bernard Baruch Papers; Baruch to Oppenheimer, 15 January 1947, Box 19, J. Robert Oppenheimer Papers.

109 *The Baruch Plan*, 14 June 1946, p. 4, www.atomicarchive.com/Docs/Deterrence/BaruchPlan.shtml.

110 Holloway, *Stalin and the Bomb*, p. 162.

111 Ibid., pp. 162, 164, 166; Beisner, *Dean Acheson: A Life in the Cold War*, p. 35.

112 Oppenheimer objected to the Bikini tests, for reasons technical and moral-political. Of the latter and in advance of the explosions, he expressed doubt—as did the American Federation of Scientists—about "the appropriateness of a purely military test of atomic weapons, at a time when our plans for effectively eliminating them from national armaments are in their earliest beginnings." Oppenheimer to Harry Truman, 3 May 1946, Box 373, J. Robert Oppenheimer Papers. The Soviet newspaper, *Pravda* (3 July 1946), excoriated the Bikini explosions as proof of U.S. perfidy and Washington's desire to perfect weapons of mass destruction for blackmail purposes.

113 Schwarz, *The Speculator: Bernard M. Baruch in Washington, 1917–1965*, p. 506.

114 Andrei Vishinsky speech, 10 November 1949, Box 74, J. Robert Oppenheimer Papers; Memorandum of Conversation: Bernard Baruch, Philip Jessup, Acheson, 24 September 1950, Box 29, Dean Acheson Papers, Harry S. Truman Presidential Library.

115 Joel Colton, *Léon Blum: Humanist in Politics* (New York, NY: Alfred A. Knopf, 1966), e-book.

116 Oppenheimer to James Conant, 7 March 1947, Box 27, J. Robert Oppenheimer Papers.

117 www.atomicarchive.com/Movies/Movie8.shtml.

118 Churchill, *Never Given In! The Best of Winston Churchill's Speeches*, "Never Despair," 1 March 1955, p. 496.

119 William Faulkner, "Speech on Acceptance of the Nobel Prize," November 1950, Daniel Boorstin, Ed., *An American Primer* (Chicago, IL: University of Chicago Press, 1966), p. 899.

120 Strobe Talbot, Ed., *Khrushchev Remembers* (Boston, MA: Little, Brown, 1970), p. 435; Holloway, "Nuclear Weapons and the Escalation of the Cold War, 1945–1962," pp. 391–392.

121 "Arsenals and Aspirations" in *The Economist*, 7–13 March 2015, p. 25.

122 Kessner, *Fiorello H. La Guardia and the Making of Modern New York*, p. 584, 585. Radio Broadcast, 18 September 1946, pp. 3–4, Box 23D4, File 1, Fiorello La Guardia Papers; La Guardia to Lehman, 18 April 1947, Box 161, Herbert Lehman Papers.

123 Hirschmann, *The Embers Still Burn*, p. xiii. Lehman said: "We liquidated [UNRRA] . . . at least a year and probably two years before we should have." Cited in Herbert Lehman, Oral History, p. 760. In 2017, the United Nations estimated that the number of forcibly displaced people worldwide exceeded sixty-five million. See www.unhcr.org/en-us/figures-at-a-glance.html.

124 Reinisch, "Internationalism in Relief: The Birth (and Death) of UNRRA," p. 285.

125 I have here borrowed heavily from the language and imagery of Primo Levi. See his *The Reawakening* (New York, NY: Simon & Schuster, 1995),

pp. 16–17. Regarding use of the atomic bombs against Japan, *The Christian Century*, a mainline Protestant magazine, stated on 29 August 1945: "It is our belief that the use of the atomic bomb has placed our nation in an indefensible moral position."

126   Edwin Gault, a seminarian at Yale Divinity School, wrote in December 1950, as Chinese armies were forcing a retreat of UN/U.S. forces in Korea and as the White House contemplated the nuclear option: "I am convinced that the United States dare not, in the face of God, explode another atomic bomb . . . There are many of us here who are still doing penance for Hiroshima, and we cannot bear the guilt of yet another." Gault to Acheson, 7 December 1950, Box 29, Dean Acheson Papers, Harry S. Truman Library.

Chapter 2: Justice

1   Robert Jackson, 21 November 1945: www.roberthjackson.org/speech-and-writing/opening-statement-before-the-international-military-tribunal.

2   Robert Jackson, "Nuremberg in Retrospect," *Canadian Bar Review*, August–September 1949, pp. 780–781.

3   Elizabeth Borgwardt, *A New Deal for the World: America's Vision for Human Rights* (Cambridge, MA: Harvard University Press, 2005), p. 203; Christopher Dodd, *Letters from Nuremberg: My Father's Narrative of a Quest for Justice* (New York, NY: Crown, 2007), pp. 90–92; Airey Neave, *On Trial at Nuremberg* (Boston, MA: Little, Brown, 1978), pp. 42–45; Robert Storey, *The Final Judgment: Pearl Harbor to Nuremberg* (San Antonio, TX: Naylor, 1968), p. 87; Whitney Harris, *Tyranny on Trial: The Evidence at Nuremberg* (Dallas, TX: Southern Methodist University, 1970), p. xiii; Norbert Ehrenfreund, *The Nuremberg Legacy: How the Nazi War Crimes Trials Changed the Course of History* (New York, NY: Palgrave Macmillan, 2007), p. xiii; Eugene Gerhart, *America's Advocate: Robert H. Jackson* (Indianapolis, IN: Bobbs-Merrill, 1958), p. 21.

4   Francis Biddle, *In Brief Authority* (Garden City, NJ: Doubleday, 1962), p. 419.

5   Dan Plesch, *America, Hitler and the UN: How the Allies Won World War II and Forged a Peace* (London: I.B. Tauris, 2011), pp. 101–118.

6   None of the Big Three had a bloody-minded imagination superior to Josef Schmid-Treuenfeld of Vienna. He advised this in July 1946, at the time of atomic bomb tests in the Bikini Atoll: A just punishment for the Nuremberg culprits would be to experience the "suffering, fear and torture" that they had visited upon their victims. "For this purpose, one should expose those guilty war criminals to the world's most terrible weapon, the atom bomb on the target ships of the experimentary (sic) fleet. This would be the greatest satisfaction to the whole world, and perhaps at the same time would serve as

a scientific experiment." Schmid-Treuenfeld to Dodd, 13 July 1946, Series 7, Box 327, Thomas Dodd Papers.

7 Gary Bass, *Stay the Hand of Vengeance: The Politics of War Crimes Tribunals* (Princeton, NJ: Princeton University Press, 2000), p. 153.

8 Stimson, possessed of a type of country club anti-Semitism, privately muttered that Morgenthau's approach to captured Nazis was permeated with Jewish vengeance. See Borgwardt, *A New Deal for the World: America's Vision for Human Rights*, pp. 206, 208.

9 Henry Stimson, and McGeorge Bundy, *On Active Service in Peace and War* (New York, NY: Harper and Brother, 1948), pp. 584–585; William Schabas, "International War Crimes Tribunals and the United States," *Diplomatic History*, November 2011, p. 785; Kai Bird, *The Chairman: John J. McCloy: The Making of the American Establishment* (New York, NY: Simon & Schuster, 1992), p. 258.

10 Telford Taylor, *Nuremberg and Vietnam: An American Tragedy* (New York, NY: Bantam, 1971), p. 14.

11 International Military Tribunal, *Trial of the Major War Criminals before the International Military Tribunal, Nuremberg, 14 November 1945–1 October 1946* (Nuremberg: International Military Tribunal, 1947), Vol. I, pp. 10–16.

12 David Crowe, *War Crimes, Genocide, and Justice: A Global History* (New York, NY: Palgrave Macmillan, 2014), p. 162.

13 Telford Taylor, *The Anatomy of the Nuremberg Trials* (New York, NY: Alfred A. Knopf, 1992), pp. 137, 243, 527; Dodd, *Letters from Nuremberg: My Father's Narrative of a Quest for Justice*, p. 184.

14 G.M. Gilbert, *Nuremberg Diary* (New York, NY: Farrar, Straus, 1947), pp. 22, 30–31.

15 Taylor, *The Anatomy of the Nuremberg Trials*, p. 219.

16 Rebecca West testified in autumn 1946, as Nuremberg wound down, that the trial was "a great machine, by which mankind, in spite of its infirmity of purpose and its frequent desire for death, has defended its life." Cited in Taylor, *The Anatomy of the Nuremberg Trials*, p. 547.

    Howard K. Smith remarked many years after the IMT: "God's judgment is perfect; ours won't be. But we should start, and we started, and I think [Nuremberg] was a glorious effort." Howard K. Smith interview, p. 48, Witnesses to Nuremberg Oral History Project.

17 Ernest Harmon, Personal Memoirs, p. 181, Box 3A, Ernest N. Harmon Papers.

18 Ibid. Also see Statistical Report of Operations, March 1947, Office of the Provost Marshal United States Constabulary, Box 3A, Ernest N. Harmon Papers.

19   Harmon to Major General Hobart "Hap" Gay, 16 May 1945, Box 3A, Ernest N. Harmon Papers.

20   Harmon, Personal Memoirs, p. 181, Box 3A, Ernest N. Harmon Papers.

21   African American soldiers posted in postwar Berlin, and who formed liaisons with local German women, aroused the usual snickering and suspicions. These men were also objects of U.S. Army discipline. On this subject, Nadja Klopprogge has written perceptively—"Intimacy, Histories, and Space: Wannsee Beach and Nuremberg in African American Memories and Experiences," paper presented at Transatlantic Studies Association Annual Conference, 10–12 July 2017, Cork, Ireland.

22   Biddle, *In Brief Authority*, p. 422; Taylor, *The Anatomy of the Nuremberg Trials*, pp. 4, 208, 217.

23   Francine Hirsch, "The Soviets at Nuremberg: International Law, Propaganda, and the Making of the Postwar Order," *American Historical Review*, June 2008, p. 710.

24   Enough feeling existed between Rudenko and Taylor to allow the latter in 1973 to approach his IMT colleague and ask that he intervene on behalf of a young Jewish man who wanted to emigrate from the USSR for Israel. Found guilty of "militant Zionism," he had been sentenced to a psychiatric facility.

       I have been unable to determine whether Rudenko responded to Taylor and I do not know of the imprisoned man's fate. The man's father was Yulius Markovich Krylski, an acquaintance of Taylor; the son was "Yan." See Taylor to General Roman Rudenko, 16 March 1973, Series 14, Subseries 6, Box 11, Folder 232, Telford Taylor Papers.

25   Possible Line of Approach for *New York Times* Article on Lessons of this Trial (written by William E. Jackson), 23 May 1946; Some Lessons of the Nuremberg Trial (written by Robert Jackson), 29 May 1946, p. 6, Box 55, Robert Jackson Papers; Lord Kilmuir, *Political Adventure: The Memoirs of the Earl of Kilmuir* (London: Weidenfeld and Nicolson, 1964), pp. 89, 98. Also see Nuremberg in Retrospect, 24 February 1947, 7/3, Lord Kilmuir Papers.

26   Hirsch, "The Soviets at Nuremberg: International Law, Propaganda and the Making of the Postwar Order," pp. 719–720; Taylor, *The Anatomy of the Nuremberg Trials*, pp. 316–317; Dodd, *Letters from Nuremberg: My Father's Narrative of a Quest for Justice*, pp. 251, 263.

27   Taylor, *The Anatomy of the Nuremberg Trials*, pp. 232, 627.

28   *The Case Against the Nazi War Criminals: Opening Statement for the United States of America by Robert H. Jackson and Other Documents* (New York, NY: Alfred A. Knopf, 1946), pp. 114–115.

29   Ibid., pp. 100–101.

30   Jay Baird, Ed., *From Nuremberg to My Lai* (Lexington, MA: D.C. Heath, 1972), p. x; Ehrenfreund, *The Nuremberg Legacy: How the Nazi War Crimes Trials Changed the Course of History*, p. 54; Michael Bess, *Choices Under Fire: Moral Dimensions of World War II* (New York, NY: Alfred A. Knopf, 2006), pp. 269–275.

31   Another man in Nuremberg detention who killed himself before trial was Dr. Leonardo Conti (head of the Nazi medical association), doing so in October 1945. Colonel-General Johannes Blaskowitz appears also to have been a Nuremberg suicide. He died in February 1948. According to some speculation, though, he might not have committed suicide but was murdered. See Richard Giziowski, *The Enigma of General Blaskowitz* (New York, NY: Hippocrene, 1997).

32   Hirsch, "The Soviets at Nuremberg: International Law, Propaganda, and the Making of the Postwar Order," p. 726.

33   Taylor, *The Anatomy of the Nuremberg Trials*, p. 211.

34   Johannes Morsink, *The Universal Declaration of Human Rights: Origins, Drafting, and Intent* (Philadelphia, PA: University of Pennsylvania Press, 1999), p. 38.

35   See Janet Flanner ("Genêt"), "Letter from Nuremberg," *The New Yorker*, 30 March 1946; Robert Jackson's lawyer son, William, served on his father's staff at Nuremberg and witnessed the Justice's verbal duel with Goering. Decades later, the younger Jackson remembered Goering as "extremely intelligent" and "a person of considerable force." William Jackson interview of 17 July 1995, p. 12, Witnesses to Nuremberg Oral History Project.

36   Crowe, *War Crimes, Genocide, and Justice: A Global History*, pp. 174–176.
        Jackson's mood was not improved when in June 1946, following the death in April of Chief Justice Harlan Stone, Truman appointed Fred Vinson over Jackson to head the Supreme Court. A simmering feud between Jackson and Associate Justice Hugo Black also broke into public view in June 1946, adding to Jackson's distractions and disappointments.

37   As Flanner recounted, Goering's testimony was accompanied by sounds of distant dynamite explosions used to clear piles of debris in rubble-strewn Nuremberg. See Baird, *From Nuremberg to My Lai*, pp. 62, 64.

38   Walter Gorlitz, Ed., *The Memoirs of Field-Marshal Keitel* (New York, NY: Stein and Day, 1966), p. 238.

39   Philippe Sands, *East West Street: On the Origins of "Genocide" and "Crimes Against Humanity"* (New York, NY: Alfred A. Knopf, 2016), p. 299; Gilbert, *Nuremberg Diary*, pp. 19–21; Robert Jackson, "Nuremberg in Retrospect," p. 776.

40   Taylor, *The Anatomy of the Nuremberg Trials*, p. 24.

41   Fyfe to Sylvia, 13 January 1946, Acc. 1485, Box 1, File 4, Lord Kilmuir Papers.

42 Howard K. Smith interview, p. 48, Witnesses to Nuremberg Oral History Project.

43 Sands, *East West Street: On the Origins of "Genocide" and "Crimes Against Humanity,"* p. 297; Taylor, *The Anatomy of the Nuremberg Trials*, pp. 362–363.

44 Biddle, *In Brief Authority*, p. 432.

45 William Bosch, *Judgment on Nuremberg: American Attitudes Toward the Major German War-Crime Trials* (Chapel Hill, NC: University of North Carolina Press, 1970), pp. 102–103.

46 Stephen Holmes, "Is Defiance of Law a Proof of Success? Magical Thinking in the War on Terror" in Karen Greenberg, Ed. *The Torture Debate in America* (Cambridge: Cambridge University Press, 2006), p. 127. Father Edmund Walsh, an adviser to the U.S. prosecution at Nuremberg and founder of the Foreign Service School at Georgetown University, believed that the IMT constituted "a mighty blow for justice and international decency." See Walsh to Dodd, 27 June 1946, Series 7, Box 326, Thomas Dodd Papers.

47 International Military Tribunal, *The Trial of German Major War Criminals: Speeches Chief Prosecutors and Prosecutors 1945–46* (Buffalo, NY: William S. Hein, 2001) "Opening Speeches," p. 88.

48 Ibid., pp. 93–94, 97.

49 Ibid., pp. 3, 5, 46.

50 Ordinary lawyers also disapproved of Nuremberg. One was Clarence Mulligan of Del Mar, California. He told Jackson: "Those proceedings were . . . a farce, undertaken by stung conquerors against the conquered who had paid dearly for their mistakes before you hove in judicial view, baying for their blood . . . let us drop this talk of International Law and its improvement as silly and puerile." Mulligan to Jackson, 28 March 1947, Box 22, Robert Jackson Papers.

51 Biddle, *In Brief Authority*, p. 375; Bass, *Stay the Hand of Vengeance: The Politics of War Crimes Tribunals*, p. 25.

52 Ehrenfreund, *The Nuremberg Legacy: How the Nazi War Crimes Trials Changed the Course of History*, p. 54.

53 Clarence Wunderlin, Ed., *The Papers of Robert A. Taft* (Kent, OH: Kent State University Press, 2003), Vol. III, p. 200.

54 Bosch, *Judgment on Nuremberg: American Attitudes Toward the Major German War-Crime Trials*, pp. 171–172.

55 War and War Crimes Trials (questions and answers), National War College, 6 December 1946, Box 44, Robert Jackson Papers. Also see Robert Jackson, "The Significance of the Nuremberg Trials to the Armed Forces," *Military Affairs*, Winter 1946.

56 The Soviets pressed at the IMT against Germany for the Katyn murders. The IMT refrained from making any finding, however. Only in 1990 did the Soviet leadership (Mikhail Gorbachev) admit Soviet responsibility for Katyn.

57 Dodd, *Letters from Nuremberg: My Father's Narrative of a Quest for Justice*, pp. 129–130; Borgwardt, *A New Deal for the World: America's Vision for Human Rights*, p. 231.

58 International Military Tribunal, *The Trial of German Major War Criminals: Speeches Chief Prosecutors and Prosecutors 1945–46*, "Opening Speeches," pp. 135, 139–140, 168.

59 Dodd, *Letters from Nuremberg: My Father's Narrative of a Quest for Justice*, pp. 336–337.

60 David Mayers, *Dissenting Voices in America's Rise to Power* (Cambridge: Cambridge University Press, 2007), p. 279; Bosch, *Judgment on Nuremberg: American Attitudes Toward the Major German War Crime Trials*, pp. 122–123, 213.

61 Harry Ashmore, *Unseasonable Truths: The Life of Robert Maynard Hutchins* (Boston, MA: Little, Brown, 1989), pp. 250–251.

62 George Kennan, *American Diplomacy 1900–1950* (Chicago, IL: University of Chicago Press, 1951), p. 95.

63 Dodd, *Letters from Nuremberg: My Father's Narrative of a Quest for Justice*, p. 37; Bosch, *Judgment on Nuremberg: American Attitudes Toward the Major German War-Crime Trials*, pp. 118–199.

64 Bosch, *Judgment on Nuremberg: American Attitudes Toward the Major German War-Crime Trials*, p. 109.

65 In the estimation of Taylor in May 1947: "The Judges are a variegated assortment, not notable for youth. Some of them are excellent. It is quite a sight to see sixteen State Court Judges from all over the United States suddenly flung together in Nuremberg to grapple with German history and the other novel problems that the cases here present. As a result, life continues to be full of daily surprises. So far, only one written judgment has come down— that of the Milch case . . . they have scrupulously followed the prevailing practice of multiple opinions . . . At page 26 of the Opinion of the Court in the Milch case . . . they endeavored (accidentally, I am told) to acquit the principal defendant in our Ministry of Justice case, Franz Schlegelberger. I thought I'd seen everything but when I found that in the Judgment, I realized that even the most theoretical and improbable possibilities can suddenly become actualities." Telford Taylor to Jackson, 21 May 1947, Box 20, Robert Jackson Papers.

66 Donald Bloxham, *Genocide on Trial: War Crimes Trials and the Formation of Holocaust History and Memory* (Oxford: Oxford University Press, 2001), pp. 231–232; Kevin Heller, *The Nuremberg Military Tribunals and the Origins of International Criminal Law* (Oxford: Oxford University Press, 2011), pp. 4, 403–464; Crowe, *War Crimes, Genocide, and Justice: A Global History*, pp. 249–251.

67 Bosch, *Judgment on Nuremberg: American Attitudes Toward the Major German War-Crime Trials*, pp. 82–85; Heller, *The Nuremberg Military Tribunals and the Origins of International Criminal Law*, pp. 35–36.

68 Heller, *The Nuremberg Military Tribunals and the Origins of International Criminal Law*, p. 35; Borgwardt, *A New Deal for the World: America's Vision for Human Rights*, pp. 233–234.

69 Bird, *The Chairman: John J. McCloy: The Making of the American Establishment*, p. 331; Heller, *The Nuremberg Military Tribunals and the Origins of International Criminal Law*, pp. 373–374, 400.

70 Arieh Kochavi, *Prelude to Nuremberg: Allied War Crimes Policy and the Question of Punishment* (Chapel Hill, NC: University of North Carolina Press, 1998), p. 244.

71 Elizabeth Borgwardt, "Commerce and Complicity: Human Rights and the Legacy of Nuremberg" in Bruce Schulman, Ed., *Making the American Century: Essays on the Political Culture of Twentieth Century America* (New York, NY: Oxford University Press, 2014), pp. 95–96.

72 Ana Filipa Vrdoljak, "Human Rights and Genocide: The Work of Lauterpacht and Lemkin in Modern International Law," *The European Journal of International Law*, 2009, Vol. 20, No. 4, p. 1186; Sir Elihu Lauterpacht, *The Life of Sir Hersch Lauterpacht* (Cambridge: Cambridge University Press, 2010), pp. 6, 346–348.

73 Taylor to Francis Biddle, 9 April 1951, Series 14, Subseries 4, Box 3, Folder 51, Telford Taylor Papers.

   Also see Taylor to Freda Kirchwey of the *Nation*, 1 February 1951, Series 14, Subseries 4, Box 3, Folder 49 and Taylor to Eleanor Roosevelt, 19 June 1951, Series 14, Subseries 4, Box 3, Folder 1953, Telford Taylor Papers. In his letter to Kirchwey, Taylor explained: "The freeing of the Krupp managers and the restoration of Alfried Krupp's interests in the Krupp plants will, in my judgment, do grave harm to American efforts to strengthen Europe against the menace of Communism. We have handed the Russians a propaganda weapon of inestimable value [that] they will exploit to the full. We have sown distrust of America among the peoples of both Western and Eastern Europe. If this action is an effort to win favor among the Germans it is a losing game which will weaken, not strengthen, our position in Germany."

74 Jackson to Telford Taylor, 1 February 1951, Box 20, Robert Jackson Papers.

75 Heller, *The Nuremberg Military Tribunals and the Origins of International Criminal Law*, pp. 2, 358–360.

76 Nearly 6,000 defendants were charged as class B and C criminals. Almost 1,000 were sentenced to death; about five hundred were given life imprisonment; practically 3,000 were given lesser prison terms. Details and numbers related

to trials conducted by the Soviets are not obtainable. See Madoka Futamura, *War Crimes Tribunals and Transitional Justice: The Tokyo Trial and the Nuremberg Legacy* (London: Routledge, 2008), p. 75. On Chinese trials of alleged Japanese war criminals, see Barak Kushner's *Men to Devils: Japanese War Crimes and Chinese Justice* (Cambridge, MA: Harvard University Press, 2015).

77 Philip Piccigallo, *The Japanese on Trial: Allied War Crimes Operations in the East, 1945–1951* (Austin, TX: University of Texas Press, 1979), pp. 56–57; Michael Walzer, *Just and Unjust Wars: A Moral Argument with Historical Illustrations* (New York, NY: Basic, 2000), pp. 319–322.

78 A. Frank Reel, *The Case of General Yamashita* (Chicago, IL: University of Chicago Press, 1949), p. 241. See also Allan Ryan's *Yamashita's Ghost: War Crimes, MacArthur's Justice, and Command Accountability* (Lawrence, KS: University Press of Kansas, 2012).

79 Elizabeth Kopelman (later Borgwardt), "Ideology and International Law: The Dissent of the Indian Justice at the Tokyo War Crimes Trial," *New York University Journal of International Law and Politics*, Winter 1991, p. 406.

80 The IMTFE judges were, in addition to Webb, the following: Lord William Patrick (UK), Major General Myron Cramer/John Higgins (USA), Major General Mei Ju-ao (China), Major General I.M. Zaryanov (USSR), Radhabinod Pal (India), B.V.A. Roling (Netherlands), Edward Stuart McDougall (Canada), Henri Bernard (France), E.H. Northcroft (New Zealand), Colonel Delfin Jaranilla (Philippines).

81 Alva Carpenter to Keenan, 14 October 1947, Box 1, Joseph Keenan Papers; James Sedgwick, *Inside Justice: Being International in Postwar Tokyo, 1946–1948* (unpublished manuscript, 2013), pp. 55–56; Crowe, *War Crimes, Genocide, and Justice: A Global History*, p. 203.

82 Sedgwick, *Inside Justice: Being International in Postwar Tokyo, 1946–1948*, p. 61.

83 Richard Minear, *Victors' Justice: The Tokyo War Crimes Trial* (Princeton, NJ: Princeton University Press, 1971), pp. 5, 13, 18; Kopelman (Borgwardt), "Ideology and International Law: The Dissent of the Indian Justice at the Tokyo War Crimes Trial," p. 377.

84 Keenan to Hap Flanigan, 18 February 1946, Box 2, Joseph Keenan Papers; Keenan to Dr. Harry Krould, 19 December 1945, Box 2, Joseph Keenan Papers.

85 Arnold Brackman, *The Other Nuremberg: The Untold Story of the Tokyo War Crimes Trials* (New York, NY: William Morrow, 1987), p. 18.

86 Keenan to Charlotte Keenan, 16 December 1947, Box 2, Joseph Keenan Papers.

87 John Dower, *Embracing Defeat: Japan in the Wake of World War II* (New York, NY: W.W. Norton, 1999), p. 460.

88 Futamura, *War Crimes Tribunals and Transitional Justice: The Tokyo Trial and the Nuremberg Legacy*, pp. 54–55, 60; Mickael Ho Foui Sang, "Justice Bernard" in Yuki Tanaka et al. *Beyond Victor's Justice? The Tokyo War Crimes Trial Revisited* (Leiden: Martinus Nijhoff, 2011), pp. 93–102; Piccigallo, *The Japanese on Trial: Allied War Crimes Operations in the East, 1945–1951*, pp. 28–31; Paul Schroeder, *The Axis Alliance and Japanese-American Relations 1941* (Ithaca, NY: Cornell University Press, 1958), pp. 218–219, 228.

89 B.V.A. Roling, *The Tokyo Trial and Beyond: Reflections of a Peacemonger* (Cambridge: Polity Press, 1993), p. 28; Kopelman (Borgwardt), "Ideology and International Law: The Dissent of the Indian Justice at the Tokyo War Crimes Trial," pp. 416–417.

90 Radhabinod Pal, *International Military Tribunal for the Far East: Dissentient Judgment* (Calcutta: Sanyal, 1953), pp. 606–607.

91 Ibid., pp. 63–64, 620–621.

92 Ibid., pp. 697, 700; Crowe, *War Crimes, Genocide, and Justice: A Global History*, pp. 236–241; Kopelman (Borgwardt), "Ideology and International Law: The Dissent of the Indian Justice at the Tokyo War Crimes Trial," p. 431; Dower, *Embracing Defeat: Japan in the Wake of World War II*, pp. 471–473.

93 Cited in Sedgwick, *Inside Justice: Being International in Postwar Tokyo, 1946–1948*, p. 284.

94 John Hersey, *Hiroshima* (New York, NY: Alfred A. Knopf, 1946), p. 117.

95 Kopelman (Borgwardt), "Ideology and International Law: The Dissent of the Indian Justice at the Tokyo War Crimes Trial," p. 402.

96 Bass, *Stay the Hand of Vengeance: The Politics of War Crimes Tribunals*, p. 296; Futamura, *War Crimes Tribunals and Transitional Justice: The Tokyo Trial and the Nuremberg Legacy*, pp. 74; Donald Bloxham and Jonathan Waterlow, "War Crimes Trials" in Richard Bosworth and Joseph Maiolo, Eds., *The Cambridge History of the Second World War* (Cambridge: Cambridge University Press, 2015), Vol. II, p. 199.

97 Keith Lowe, *Savage Continent: Europe in the Aftermath of World War II* (New York, NY: St. Martin's Press, 2012), pp. 159–160; Kurt Riess, "Trial Goes On," *Die Weltwoche*, 14 December 1945; Taylor, *The Anatomy of the Nuremberg Trials*, p. 234; Heller, *The Nuremberg Military Tribunals and the Origins of International Criminal Law*, pp. 372–373.

98 Rebecca Wittmann, *Beyond Justice: The Auschwitz Trial* (Cambridge, MA: Harvard University Press, 2005), p. 271; Bass, *Stay the Hand of Vengeance: The Politics of War Crimes Tribunals*, pp. 295–296. For an analysis of the long-term impact of the Nuremberg trials on German opinion, see Suzanne Karstedt, "The Nuremberg Tribunal and German Society: International Justice and Local Judgment in Post-Conflict Reconstruction" in David Blumenthal and Timothy McCormack, Eds., *The Legacy of Nuremberg: Civilising Influence or Institutionalised Vengeance?* (Leiden: Martinus Nijhoff, 2008), pp. 13–35.

99 Karl Jaspers, *The Question of German Guilt* (New York, NY: Dial, 1947), p. 60.

100 Futamura, *War Crimes Tribunals and Transitional Justice: The Tokyo Trial and the Nuremberg Legacy*, pp. 32–33.

101 Taylor agreed with A. Frank Reel that a "grave injustice was done" to Yamashita. See Taylor to Reel, 16 June 1971, Series 14, Subseries 6, Box 9, Folder 199, Telford Taylor Papers.

102 Taylor, *Nuremberg and Vietnam: An American Tragedy*, p. 143.

103 Roling, *The Tokyo Trial and Beyond: Reflections of a Peacemonger*, p. 59.

104 "Panel Hears Grim Details of V.D. Test on Inmates," *New York Times*, p. A4, 31 August 2011; Futamura, *War Crimes Tribunals and Transitional Justice: The Tokyo Trial and the Nuremberg Legacy*, pp. 62–64; Tsuneishi Kei-ichi, "Reasons for the Failure to Prosecute Unit 731 and its Significance" in Tanaka et al., *Beyond Victor's Justice? The Tokyo War Crimes Trial Revisited*, pp. 177–205; Roling, *The Tokyo Trial and Beyond: Reflections of a Peacemonger*, pp. 47–48.

105 Heller, *The Nuremberg Military Tribunal and the Origins of International Criminal Law*, p. 296; Alan Rosenbaum, *Prosecuting Nazi War Criminals* (Boulder, CO: Westview, 1993), pp. 75–77; Mark Aarons, "Justice Betrayed: Post-1945 Responses to Genocide" in Blumenthal and McCormack, *The Legacy of Nuremberg: Civilising Influence or Institutionalized Vengeance?*, pp. 74–75. For full accounts, see Annie Jacobsen, *Operation Paperclip: The Secret Intelligence Program that Brought Nazi Scientists to America* (Boston, MA: Little, Brown, 2014) and Eric Lichtblau, *The Nazis Next Door: How America Became a Safe Haven for Hitler's Men* (Boston, MA: Houghton Mifflin, 2014).

106 Sands, *East West Street: On the Origins of "Genocide" and "Crimes Against Humanity,"* p. 361.

107 International Military Tribunal, *The Trial of German Major War Criminals, "Opening Speeches,"* p. 27; Taylor, *The Anatomy of the Nuremberg Trials*, p. 169; Heller, *The Nuremberg Military Tribunal and the Origins of International Criminal Law*, p. 372.

108 Lord Kilmuir, *Political Adventure: The Memoirs of the Earl of Kilmuir*, p. 126.

109 Lord Kilmuir once warned an audience against moral self-congratulations: "We are not all faced with the choice between right and wrong action in quite so stark a way as the people of Nazi Germany were faced with it. . . . We may do well to ask ourselves what course we as individuals would choose if we were faced with alternatives that would have faced us as Germans under Hitler." Athenaeum Speech, p. 4, 16 January 1950, 7/2, Lord Kilmuir Papers.

110 Cited in Taylor, *Nuremberg and Vietnam: An American Tragedy*, p. 84.

111 Jackson, "Nuremberg in Retrospect," p. 761.

112 Sands, *East West Street: On the Origins of "Genocide" and "Crimes Against Humanity,"* p. 363.

113 Taylor, *Nuremberg and Vietnam: An American Tragedy*, pp. 95–96; Taylor, *The Anatomy of the Nuremberg Trials*, pp. 4, 637, 641; Stimson and Bundy, *On Active Service in Peace and War*, pp. 590–591; Jackson, Broadcast on Christmas Eve, 24 December 1945, p. 3, Box 43, Robert Jackson Papers.

114 John Duffett, Ed., *Against the Crime of Silence: Proceedings of the International War Crimes Tribunal* (New York, NY: Simon & Schuster, 1970), p. 311.

115 Telford Taylor, "Nuremberg and Vietnam: Who is Responsible for War Crimes?" in *War/Peace Report*, November 1970, pp. 9–10.

116 Andrew Preston, *Sword of the Spirit, Shield of Faith: Religion in American War and Diplomacy* (New York, NY: Alfred A Knopf, 2012), p. 527. Had Drinan known, he doubtless would have approved of a query made in 1968 by Bill Clinton to Telford Taylor. Clinton, then a senior at Georgetown University, asked Taylor, then a law professor at Columbia University, if the Nuremberg principles could be properly cited by young men resisting conscription. Taylor thought not. See Clinton to Taylor, 28 March 1968, Series 14, Subseries 5, Box 7, Folder 156, Telford Taylor Papers.

117 Dodd, *Letters from Nuremberg: My Father's Narrative of a Quest for Justice*, pp. 10–11.

118 From 1949 and cited in Roling, *The Tokyo Trial and Beyond: Reflections of a Peacemonger*, p. 88.

119 Eric Fair, "I Can't Be Forgiven for Abu Graib," *New York Times*, p. A31, 10 December 2014. Also see *The Senate Intelligence Committee Report on Torture: Committee Study of the Central Intelligence Agency's Detention and Interrogation Program* (Brooklyn, NY: Melville House, 2014).

Chapter 3: Humanity

1 *My Day*, 16 February 1946 in Allida Black, Ed., *The Eleanor Roosevelt Papers* (Detroit, MI: Thomson Gale, 2007), Vol. I, p. 252.

2 A careful and full account of Lemkin and his career/ideas is contained in Douglas Irvin-Erikson's *Raphael Lemkin and the Concept of Genocide* (Philadelphia, PA: University of Pennsylvania Press, 2016).

3 Donna-Lee Frieze, Ed., *Totally Unofficial: The Autobiography of Raphael Lemkin* (New Haven, CT: Yale University Press, 2013), pp. 17–19; Raphael Lemkin, "Totally Unofficial Man" in Samuel Totten and Steven Jacobs, Eds., *Pioneers of Genocide Studies* (New Brunswick, NJ: Transaction, 2002), pp. 366–367, 370–371; Philippe Sands, *East West Street: On the Origins of "Genocide" and "Crimes Against Humanity"* (New York, NY: Alfred A. Knopf, 2016), p. 147. Hersh Lauterpacht, slightly older than Lemkin, had also studied law at the University of Lwow. Both men shared various instructors, among whom accomplished Professors Juliusz Makarewicz and Stanislaw Starzynski.

4   Ana Filipa Vrdoljak, "Human Rights and Genocide: The Work of Lauter-pacht and Lemkin in Modern International Law," *The European Journal of International Law*, Vol. 20, No. 4, p. 1186.

5   John Cooper, *Raphael Lemkin and the Struggle for the Genocide Convention* (New York, NY: Palgrave Macmillan, 2008), p. 73.

6   Theodore Roosevelt, *Fear God and Take Your Own Part* (New York, NY: George Doran, 1916), p. 381.

7   Winston Churchill, *Never Give In! The Best of Winston Churchill's Speeches* (New York, NY: Hyperion, 2003), Speech of 24 August 1941, p. 300.

8   From the Editor, "Lemkin Redux: In Quest of a Word," *Journal of Genocide Research*, December 2005, p. 444.

9   Franz Werfel, *The Forty Days of Musa Dagh* (New York, NY: The Modern Library, 1934), p. 136; Lionel Steiman, *Franz Werfel: The Faith of an Exile* (Waterloo: Wilfrid Laurier University Press, 1985), p. 82; Samantha Power, *A Problem from Hell: America and the Age of Genocide* (New York, NY: Basic, 2002), p. 6.

10 Daniel Segesser and Myriam Gessler, "Raphael Lemkin and the International Debate on the Punishment of War Crimes (1919–1948)," *Journal of Genocide Research*, December 2005, p. 463; Norman Naimark, *Stalin's Genocides* (Princeton, NJ: Princeton University Press, 2010), p. 17; Vrdoljak, "Human Rights and Genocide: The Work of Lauterpacht and Lemkin in Modern Law," p. 1193.

11 Lemkin's Memorandum for Telford Taylor, 28 September 1945, Raphael Lemkin Papers, American Jewish Archives (AJA).

12 Kevin Heller, *The Nuremberg Military Tribunals and the Origins of International Criminal Law* (Oxford: Oxford University Press, 2011), pp. 249–250.

13 William Schabas, *Genocide in International Law: The Crimes of Crimes* (Cambridge: Cambridge University Press, 2000), pp. 48–49.

14 Cooper, *Raphael Lemkin and the Struggle for the Genocide Convention*, pp. 70–72, 75; Schabas, *Genocide in International Law: The Crimes of Crimes*, p. 49.

15 Raphael Lemkin, "Genocide as a Crime under International Law," *American Society of International Law*, January 1947, p. 147, # 6; Lemkin, "Totally Unofficial Man," pp. 367–368, 384; Lemkin to Sir David Maxwell Fyfe, 26 August 1946, Box 1, Raphael Lemkin Papers, AJA.

16 Lemkin's language for the Madrid meeting ran as follows and is cited in Lemkin, "Genocide as a Crime under International Law," p. 146:

>   Whosoever, out of hatred towards a racial, religious or social collectivity, or with a view to the extermination thereof, undertakes a punishable action against the life, bodily integrity, liberty, dignity or economic existence of a person belonging to such a collectivity, is liable, for the crime of barbarity,

to a penalty . . . unless his deed falls within a more severe provision of the given code.

Whosoever, either out of hatred towards a racial, religious or social collectivity, or with a view to the extermination thereof, destroys its cultural or artistic works, will be liable for the crime of vandalism, to a penalty . . . unless his deed falls within a more severe provision of the given code.

The above crimes will be prosecuted and punished irrespective of the place where the crime was committed and of the nationality of the offender, according to the law of country where the offender was apprehended.

17 Power, *A Problem from Hell: America and the Age of Genocide*, p. 22.
18 Lemkin did not win assent for his *barbarism* and *vandalism* ideas in subsequent European law conferences (Budapest, Copenhagen, Paris, Amsterdam), where delegates concentrated their attention on aspects of the collapsing Versailles status quo. See Ibid., p. 23.
19 Frieze, *Totally Unofficial: The Autobiography of Raphael Lemkin*, pp. 56–59; Segesser and Gessler, "Raphael Lemkin and the International Debate on the Punishment of War Crimes (1919–1948)," p. 458; Paul Bartrop, *A Biographical Enyclopedia of Contemporary Genocide: Portraits of Good and Evil* (Santa Barbara: ABC-CLIO, 2012), p. 187; Ronald Berger, *The Holocaust, Religion, and the Politics of Collective Memory: Beyond Sociology* (New Brunswick, NJ: Transaction, 2012), p. 213.
20 The Lemkin-McDermott collaboration resulted in *The Polish Penal Code of 1932 and the Law of Minor Offenses* (Durham, NC: Duke University Press, 1939). McDermott remained friendly to Lemkin and wrote encouragingly to him during his UN lobbying career at Lake Success: "What a pitiable plight humanity is in! I hope and pray you men at work on the situation may find some sane solution." Malcolm McDermott to Lemkin, 25 February 1948, Box 1, Raphael Lemkin Papers, American Jewish Historical Society (AJHS).
21 Cooper, *Raphael Lemkin and the Struggle for the Genocide Convention*, pp. 24–25, 40, 54–55; Lemkin, "Totally Unofficial Man," p. 381.
22 Frieze, *Totally Unofficial: The Autobiography of Raphael Lemkin*, p. 78.
23 Lemkin admired the Roma in their uneven struggle against the Third Reich: "The gypsies were fighting their butchers and resisting death to the last moment." See Lemkin to Gypsy Lore Society, 2 August 1949, Reel 1, Raphael Lemkin Papers, New York Public Library (NYPL).
24 Cooper, *Raphael Lemkin and the Struggle for the Genocide Convention*, pp. 50–52; Frieze, *Totally Unofficial: The Autobiography of Raphael Lemkin*, pp. 114–115.
25 Frieze, *Totally Unofficial: The Autobiography of Raphael Lemkin*, p. 80.
26 David Crowe, *War Crimes, Genocide, and Justice: A Global History* (New York, NY: Palgrave Macmillan, 2014), p. 287.

27 Raphael Lemkin, *Axis Rule in Occupied Europe* (Washington, DC: Carnegie Endowment for International Peace, 1944), p. xi.

28 Ibid., p. 79.

29 Ibid.

30 Cooper, *Raphael Lemkin and the Struggle for the Genocide Convention* pp. 120, 134; Michael McDonnell and A. Dirk Moses, "Raphael Lemkin as Historian of Genocide in the Americas," *Journal of Genocide Research*, December 2005, p. 502; Dominik Schaller, "Raphael Lemkin's View of European Colonial Rule in Africa: Between Condemnation and Admiration," *Journal of Genocide Research*, December 2005, pp. 534–535; essays in A. Dirk Moses and Dan Stone, Eds., *Colonialism and Genocide* (London: Routledge, 2007).

31 Lemkin, *Axis Rule in Occupied Europe*, pp. xi–xii.

After Nuremberg, Lemkin elaborated upon ways/methods and the explanatory power of *genocide*. Cited in Lemkin, "Genocide as a Crime under International Law," p. 147:

> The crime of genocide involves a wide range of actions, including not only the deprivation of life but also the prevention of life (abortions, sterilizations) and also devices considerably endangering life and health (artificial infections, working to death in special camps, deliberate separation of families for depopulation purposes and so forth). All these actions are subordinated to the criminal intent to destroy or to cripple permanently a human group. The acts are directed against groups, as such, and individuals are selected for destruction only because they belong to these groups. In view of such a phenomenon the terms previously used to describe an attack upon nationhood were not adequate. Mass murder or extermination wouldn't apply in the case of sterilization because the victims of sterilizations were not murdered, rather a people was killed through delayed action by stopping propagation. Moreover mass murder does not convey the specific losses to civilization in the form of the cultural contributions which can be made only by groups of people united through national, racial or cultural characteristics.

32 Lemkin, *Axis Rule in Occupied Europe*, pp. 90–95; Lemkin, "Genocide as a Crime under International Law," pp. 145, 150.

33 Schabas, *Genocide in International Law: The Crimes of Crimes*, p. 52. Lawrence LeBlanc, *The United States and the Genocide Convention* (Durham, NC: Duke University Press, 1991), p. 25.

34 Cooper, *Raphael Lemkin and the Struggle for the Genocide Convention*, p. 174.

35 Power, *A Problem from Hell: America and the Age of Genocide*, p. 60.

36 Lemkin, "Totally Unofficial Man," p. 391.

37 Mark Mazower, *No Enchanted Palace: The End of Empire and the Ideological Origins of the United Nations* (Princeton, NJ: Princeton University Press, 2009), p. 130.

38 Schabas, *Genocide in International Law: The Crimes of Crimes*, p. 53; Frieze, *Totally Unofficial: The Autobiography of Raphael Lemkin*, pp. 172–173.

39 John Humphrey, *Human Rights and the United Nations: A Great Adventure* (Dobbs Ferry, NY: Transnational, 1984), p. 54.

40 Schabas, *Genocide in International Law: The Crimes of Crimes*, pp. 55, 58; Cooper, *Raphael Lemkin and the Struggle for the Genocide Convention*, pp. 94, 101–104, 138–139; Lemkin, "Totally Unofficial Man," pp. 390–391.

41 Naimark, *Stalin's Genocides*, pp. 21–22.

42 Cooper, *Raphael Lemkin and the Struggle for the Genocide Convention*, p. 96; Meetings of ECOSOC, 26 August 1948, p. 3, Box 1, Raphael Lemkin Papers, AJHS.

43 Frieze, *Totally Unofficial: The Autobiography of Raphael Lemkin*, pp. 150–179.

44 Lemkin, The Genocide Convention Goes Into Force Today, 12 January 1951, Box 6, Raphael Lemkin Papers, AJHS.

45 Cooper, *Raphael Lemkin and the Struggle for the Genocide Convention*, pp. 174, 187, 260, 264; Power, *A Problem from Hell: America and the Age of Genocide*, pp. 63–64.

46 Cooper, *Raphael Lemkin and the Struggle for the Genocide Convention*, p. 199; Carol Anderson, *Eyes Off the Prize: The United Nations and the African American Struggle for Human Rights, 1944–1955* (Cambridge: Cambridge University Press, 2003), pp. 252–253.

47 Michael Ignatieff, Ed. *American Exceptionalism and Human Rights* (Princeton, NJ: Princeton University Press, 2005), p. 22. The international and comparative law section—1,000 enrollees—of the ABA dissented from the majority membership and recommended ratification of the Genocide Convention.

48 Leblanc, *The United States and the Genocide Convention*, pp. 41, 130–131; Power, *A Problem from Hell: America and Age of Genocide*, pp. 67–68.

49 Civil Rights Congress, *We Charge Genocide* (New York, NY: Civil Rights Congress, 1951), pp. 53–54. The petition included this passage, based on Article II of the Genocide Convention:

> We charge the Government of the United States of America ... with responsibility for, and participation in, violation of the Genocide Convention by killing members of the group, causing serious bodily or mental harm to members of the group, deliberately inflicting on the group conditions of life calculated to bring about its physical destruction in whole or in part, conspiracy to commit genocide, direct and public incitement

to commit genocide, complicity in genocide, failure to enact domestic legislation enforcing the Genocide Convention as was contracted by becoming a signatory to it, and violation of international law by its failure to carry out its solemn pledges under the Convention.

For these offenses, the petitioners ask the General Assembly for relief and redress on behalf of the Negro people of the United States now suffering under the crime of genocide.

50   Civil Rights Congress, *We Charge Genocide*, p. 195.

51   William Patterson, *The Man Who Cried Genocide* (New York, NY: International, 1971), pp. 178–179, 191.

52   Tanya Elder, "What You See Before Your Eyes: Documenting Raphael Lemkin's Life by Exploring his Archival Papers, 1900–1959," *Journal of Genocide Research*, December 2005, p. 487. Also see Lemkin, *The Genocide Convention Goes Into Force Today*, where he said: "Discrimination aims at keeping certain people on a different level of existence without the purpose of annihilating them." Along these same lines, Lemkin instructed an inquirer about Japanese colonial policy in pre-World War II Korea, saying that genocide was never the goal, nor more than England in Ireland. Various prohibitions, raw injustice, and imperialism were hard for the oppressed to bear in both instances, but this onerousness did not equal genocide. See Lemkin to Miriam Milliren, 7 July 1947, Reel 1, Raphael Lemkin Papers, NYPL.

53   William Patterson to Du Bois, 15 January 1947, Box 115, W.E.B. Du Bois Papers.

54   Oakley C. Johnson to Lemkin, 24 June, 1953, Box 1, Raphael Lemkin Papers, AJA,

55   Cooper, *Raphael Lemkin and the Struggle for the Genocide Convention*, p. 198; LeBlanc, *The United States and the Genocide Convention*, pp. 19–20.

56   Case in point is Lemkin to Edwin Canham of the *Christian Science Monitor*, 14 June 1949, Box 2, Raphael Lemkin Papers, AJHS: "I do sincerely believe that we do not do enough to counter-act the systematic and almost scientifically organized Soviet propaganda for peace (Pax Sovietica)."

57   Lemkin to Cardinal Francis Spellman, 13 September 1949, Box 2, Raphael Lemkin Papers, AJHS. Also see Anton Weiss-Wendt, "Hostage of Politics: Raphael Lemkin on 'Soviet Genocide,'" *Journal of Genocide Research*, December 2005, pp. 555–556.

58   Lemkin to Gertrude Samuels, 30 March 1949, Box 2, Raphael Lemkin Papers, AJHS; Lemkin to Berle, 5 June 1950, Box 90, Adolf Berle Papers; "Statement by Professor Raphael Lemkin," 10 February 1951, Box 6, Raphael Lemkin Papers, AJHS.

59 James Green, *The United Nations and Human Rights* (Washington, DC: Brookings Institution, 1958), p. 742 and Elizabeth Borgwardt, "Constitution-alizing Human Rights: The Rise and Fall of the Nuremberg Principles" in Akira Iriye et al., Eds., *The Human Rights Revolution: An International History* (New York, NY: Oxford University Press, 2012), p. 449.

60 Lemkin to John Foster Dulles, 11 April 1953, Box 2, Raphael Lemkin Papers, AJA.

61 Richard Walsh (John Day Company) to Lemkin, 16 February 1955, Charles Pearce (Duell, Sloan and Pearce) to Lemkin, 19 August 1958, Naomi Burton to Lemkin, 7 November 1958, Reel 1, Raphael Lemkin Papers, NYPL. Also see Steven Jacobs, Ed., *Raphael Lemkin's Thought on Nazi Genocide: Not Guilty?* (Lewiston, NY: Edwin Mellen, 1992), pp. xxiv–xxv.

62 J. Robert Oppenheimer to Lemkin, 24 October 1947 and Oppenheimer to Lemkin, 17 November 1947, Box 1, Raphael Lemkin Papers, AJHS; Kenneth Thompson to Lemkin, 20 March 1959, Reel 1, Raphael Lemkin Papers, NYPL. In 1957 Lemkin also approached the Ford Foundation for financial support. See Lemkin to Donald Price, 1 December 1957, Box 2, Raphael Lemkin Papers, AJA.

63 Application for research fellowship, p. 4, (n.d.) 1958, Reel 3, Raphael Lemkin Papers, NYPL.

64 Michael Ignatieff, "The Unsung Hero Who Coined the Term Genocide," *The New Republic*, 21 September 2013; Frieze, *Totally Unofficial: The Auto-biography of Raphael Lemkin*, pp. 220–222; Cooper, *Raphael Lemkin and the Struggle for the Genocide Convention*, p. 270.

65 Robert Bartlett, *The Sixth Race* (London: Blackie, 1961), p. 110.

66 Samuel Moyn, *The Last Utopia: Human Rights in History* (Cambridge, MA: Harvard University Press, 2010), p. 82.

One person who respected Lemkin was Herbert Evatt (1894–1965), president of the UN General Assembly in 1948. Evatt wrote of Lemkin:

> He devoted himself with a single-minded purpose to securing international action to outlaw genocide and provide effective measures to punish it if it ever occurred again. He showed indomitable faith and energy both spurring on other people and in making concrete suggestions of a practical nature, and the final adoption of the convention is a great tribute to him.
>
> (Cited in *Frieze, Totally Unofficial: The Autobiography of Raphael Lemkin*, p. 252 #12)

Representative Emanuel Celler (D, New York) was a steadfast admirer. Upon learning of the Genocide Convention's ratification by the necessary number of signatory states, Celler wrote to Lemkin: "While I have not had an opportunity to ransack all historical literature, I doubt that there is one case in which one man accomplished equally worthwhile results, despite the baffling and almost insurmountable [obstacles]." Emanuel Celler to Lemkin, 18 October 1950, Box 1, Raphael Lemkin Papers, AJA. Celler also nominated Lemkin for the Nobel Peace Prize.

The West German government awarded Lemkin its Cross of Merit in 1954, the same year that Bonn ratified the Genocide Convention.

67 Power, *A Problem from Hell: America and the Age of Genocide*, pp. 78–85.

68 Cooper, *Raphael Lemkin and the Struggle for the Genocide Convention*, pp. 268–271; Ignatieff, "The Unsung Hero Who Coined the Term Genocide."

69 The Sovereignty Package emphasized the following: the United States would be subject in any specific case to the jurisdiction of the International Court of Justice only when the Washington government—the Senate above all— via treaty agreed in advance. The Constitution of the United States controlled American obligations and responsibilities, not the Genocide Convention. The matter of intentionality, both in wartime and peacetime, must be central to make determinations of genocide. The question of "mental harm" must correspond to permanent impairment of mental faculties by such methods as drugs and torture. Extradition must not be automatically applied and the domestic laws of the requesting and requested states must be in alignment. For details, see LeBlanc, *The United States and the Genocide Convention*, pp. 11, 144–145, 253–254.

70 See James Martin, *The Man Who Invented "Genocide": The Public Career and Consequences of Raphael Lemkin* (Torrance, CA: Institute for Historical Review, 1984).

71 Lemkin to Robert Taft, 4 June 1949, Box 2, Raphael Lemkin Papers, AJHS.

72 Frieze, *Totally Unofficial: The Autobiography of Raphael Lemkin*, p. 171.

73 Elder, "What You See Before Your Eyes: Documenting Raphael Lemkin's Life by Exploring his Papers, 1900–1959," p. 486; Sir Elihu Lauterpacht, *The Life of Sir Hersch Lauterpacht* (Cambridge: Cambridge University Press, 2010), pp. 259, 261; Hersch Lauterpacht, *International Law and Human Rights* (London: Stevens and Sons, 1950), pp. 416–417, 419; Elihu Lauterpacht, Ed., *International Law: Being the Collected Papers of Hersch Lauterpacht* (Cambridge: Cambridge University Press, 1977), Vol. 3, p. 413; Martti Koskenniemi, *The Gentle Civilizer of Nations: The Rise and Fall of International Law 1870–1960* (Cambridge: Cambridge University Press, 2002), p. 395; Sands, *East West Street: On the Origins of "Genocide" and "Crimes Against Humanity,"* p. 362; Jay Winter and Antoine Prost, *René Cassin and Human Rights: From the Great War to the Universal Declaration* (Cambridge: Cambridge University Press, 2013), p. 249.

74 Lemkin to James Rosenberg, 30 August 1948, Box 1, Raphael Lemkin Papers, AJHS; Berle to James Rosenberg, 22 July 1949, Box 90, Adolf Berle Papers; Lemkin to Max Sorensen, 15 April 1951, Box 2, Raphael Lemkin Papers, AJA; Power, *A Problem from Hell: America and the Age of Genocide*, pp. 74–76, 534 #39.

75 Joseph Lash, *Eleanor: The Years Alone* (New York, NY: W.W. Norton, 1972), p. 79.

76 Mary Ann Glendon, *A World Made New: Eleanor Roosevelt and the Universal Declaration of Human Rights* (New York, NY: Random House, 2001), pp. 32–33; Lash, *Eleanor: The Years Alone*, p. 61. See Charles Malik, "For a Policy of True Humanism," *The Commonweal*, 12 October 1951, p. 8.

77 Lauterpacht, *The Life of Sir Hersch Lauterpacht*, p. 258. See Hersch Lauterpacht, *An International Bill of the Rights of Man* (New York, NY: Columbia University Press, 1945). Although numerous British Jews and Zionists believed that Bevin held anti-Semitic views, his biographer, Alan Bullock, argues to the contrary, albeit admitting that the foreign secretary occasionally misspoke and expressed clumsy or crude ideas. See Bullock's *Ernest Bevin: Foreign Secretary 1945–1951* (New York, NY: W.W. Norton, 1983), pp. 164–170, 182–183, 277–278.

78 Vratislav Pechota, "The Development of the Covenant on Civil and Political Rights" in Louis Henken, Ed. *The International Bill of Rights: The Covenant on Civil and Political Rights* (New York, NY: Columbia University Press, 1981), pp. 39–43.

79 Statement by Mrs. Franklin D. Roosevelt U.S. Representative to the General Assembly, 9 December 1948 in Black, *The Eleanor Roosevelt Papers*, Vol. I, pp. 972–973. See also Eleanor Roosevelt, "The Promise of Human Rights," *Foreign Affairs*, April 1948.

80 Johannes Morsink, *The Universal Declaration of Human Rights: Origins, Drafting, and Intent* (Philadelphia, PA: University of Pennsylvania Press), p. 21.

81 Arvind Sharma, *Are Human Rights Western? A Contribution to the Dialogue of Civilizations* (Oxford: Oxford University Press, 2006), pp. xii, 242.

82 Melville Herskovits, friend of Du Bois and son of Jewish immigrants, founded both the Anthropology Department and African Studies at Northwestern. See Herskovits to Du Bois, 20 February 1948, Box 119, W.E.B. Du Bois Papers.

83 American Anthropological Association (Executive Board), "Statement on Human Rights," *American Anthropologist*, Vol. 49, No. 4, Part 1 (Oct–Dec 1947), pp. 540–541.

84 See the following in ibid., p. 543:

> The rights of Man in the Twentieth Century cannot be circumscribed by the standards of any single culture, or be dictated by the aspirations of any single people. Such a document will lead to frustration, not realization of the personalities of vast numbers of human beings.

85 David Levering Lewis, *W.E.B. Du Bois: The Fight for Equality and the American Century 1919–1963* (New York, NY: Henry Holt, 2001), pp. 521–522. Also see NAACP, *An Appeal to the World: A Statement on the Denial of Human Rights to Minorities in the Case of Citizens of Negro Descent in the United States of America and An Appeal to the United Nations for Redress* (New York, NY: National Association for the Advancement of Colored People, 1947).

86 See John Humphrey to Du Bois, 9 October 1947, Warren Austin to H.H. Smythe, 9 October 1947, Warren Austin to Du Bois, 21 October 1947 in Box 116, and NAACP Petition to the UN Chronology (1 August 1946 to 31 January 1948), Box 121, W.E.B. Du Bois Papers. Mark Mazower, "The Strange Triumph of Human Rights, 1933–1950," *The Historical Journal*, June 2004, p. 395.

87 Black, *The Eleanor Roosevelt Papers*, Vol. I, p. xxxix; Lewis, *W.E.B. Du Bois: The Fight for Equality and the American Century 1919–1963*, pp. 528–529, 531–532; Anderson, *Eyes Off the Prize: The United Nations and the African American Struggle for Human Rights, 1944–1955*, p. 112.

88 Brian Urquhart, *Ralph Bunche: An American Life* (New York, NY: W.W. Norton, 1993), pp. 135, 137.

    Bunche first met Eleanor Roosevelt in May 1940 when he interviewed her in connection with his research on behalf of the Carnegie Council–Gunnar Myrdal study of race relations in the United States and later published as *An American Dilemma: The Negro Problem and Modern Democracy* (New York, NY: Harper and Brothers, 1944), 2 vols. See memorandum of interview with Eleanor Roosevelt, 15 May 1940, Box 33, Ralph Bunche Papers, Schomburg Center for Research in Black Culture.

89 See *To Secure These Rights: The Report of the President's Committee on Civil Rights* (New York, NY: Simon & Schuster, 1947). In keeping with this report, and to the displeasure of Southern Democrats, Truman proposed a civil rights package in early February 1948: the establishment of a federal commission on civil rights, an end to segregated public schools, an end to racial discrimination in employment, prohibitions on lynching.

90 Roosevelt to Walter White, 20 January 1948, Box 1659, Anna Eleanor Roosevelt Papers.

91 Du Bois to Secretary and Board of Directors of the NAACP, Memorandum: The United Nations and the NAACP, 7 September 1948, Box 121, W.E.B. Du Bois Papers.

92 Du Bois to Walter White, Memorandum: Meeting with Mrs. Eleanor Roosevelt—NAACP Petition, 1 July 1948 and Eleanor Roosevelt to Du Bois, 6 July 1948, Box 122, W.E.B. Du Bois Papers. Anderson, *Eyes Off the Prize: The United Nations and the African American Struggle for Human Rights, 1944–1945*, pp. 130, 140–141, 150.

93 On the needs for international renewal and justice, and European unity, see E.H. Carr, *Conditions of Peace* (London: Macmillan, 1942), pp. 5, 29, 102, 110–111, 123, 253, 269, 273–275. Also see Carr, *Nationalism and After* (London: Macmillan, 1945) along with Michael Cox, Ed., *E.H. Carr: A Critical Appraisal* (New York, NY: Palgrave Macmillan, 2000), pp. 206–207.

94 The Carr committee roster also counted: Georges Friedmann, Marxist sociologist and professor at Paris's Conservatoire National des Arts et Metiers; Cheng-shu Lo, a philosopher at West-China University; and Belgian political theorist Luc Sommerhausen. See UNESCO, Ed., *Human Rights: Comments and Interpretations* (New York, NY: Columbia University Press, 1949), p. 272.

95 Alexander Danilovic, *Pragmatism, Philosophy and International Politics: The UNESCO Committee on the Philosophic Principles of the Rights of Man and the Drafting of the Universal Declaration of Human Rights* (University of British Columbia, MA thesis, 2002), pp. 13, 25.

96 M.K. Gandhi, "A letter addressed to the Director-General of UNESCO" in UNESCO, *Human Rights: Comments and Interpretations*, p. 18: "I learnt from my illiterate but wise mother that all rights to be deserved and preserved came from duty well done. Thus the very right to live accrues to us only when we do the duty of citizenship of the world."

97 Jacques Maritain, "Introduction" in UNESCO, *Human Rights: Comments and Interpretations*, p. 17:

> We do know that, though the crisis of civilization which arose with this century has offered to our gaze the gravest violations of human rights, yet simultaneously it has led the public mind to a keener sense of those rights. . . . Pending something better, a Declaration of Human Rights agreed by the nations would be a great thing in itself, a word of promise for the downcast and oppressed throughout all lands, the beginning of changes which the world requires, the first condition precedent for the later drafting of a universal Charter of civilized life.

98 Danilovic, *Pragmatism, Philosophy and International Politics: The UNESCO Committee on the Philosophic Principles of the Rights of Man and the Drafting of the Universal Declaration of Human Rights*, pp. 39–42.

99 Eleanor Roosevelt, *On My Own* (London: Hutchinson, 1959), p. 77; Lash, *Eleanor: The Years Alone*, p. 61; Humphrey, *Human Rights and the United Nations: A Great Adventure*, p. 29.

100 A.J. Hobbins, Ed. *On the Edge of Greatness: The Diaries of John Humphrey, First Director of the United Nations Division of Human Rights* (Montreal: McGill University Libraries, 1994), Vol. I, pp. 66–67, 88.

101 Jay Winter, *Dreams of Peace and Freedom: Utopian Moments in the Twentieth Century* (New Haven, CT: Yale University Press, 2006), pp. 100, 114; Winter

and Prost, *René Cassin and Human Rights: From the Great War to the Universal Declaration*, pp. 304–305, 321, 323, 326, 335, 346.

102 Clinton Timothy Curle, *Humanité: John Humphrey's Alternative Account of Human Rights* (Toronto: University of Toronto Press, 2007), pp. 36–38; Humphrey, *Human Rights and the United Nations: A Great Adventure*, pp. 31–32.

103 Humphrey long entertained this conviction: "Human rights without economic and social rights have little meaning for most people, particularly on empty bellies." See his *Human Rights and the United Nations: A Great Adventure*, p. 2.

104 Morsink, *The Universal Declaration of Human Rights: Origins, Drafting and Intent*, p. 6.

105 Steve Neal, Ed., *Eleanor and Harry: The Correspondence of Eleanor Roosevelt and Harry S. Truman* (New York, NY: Scribner, 2002), p. 131.

106 Morsink, *The Universal Declaration of Human Rights: Origins, Drafting, and Intent*, pp. 21–28; Humphrey, *Human Rights and the United Nations: A Great Adventure*, pp. 54–55, 72–73.

107 Glendon, *A World Made New: Eleanor Roosevelt and the Universal Declaration of Human Rights*, p. 170; Black, *The Eleanor Roosevelt Papers*, Vol. I, p. 974, #10.

108 Roosevelt said this on the first anniversary of the UN's endorsement of the UDHR:

> Naturally since people in different areas have reached different levels of development, [the UDHR] will not be understood in the same way in every area, but the mere fact that we all of us are working in the same direction and that we do take appreciable steps in recognizing the value of the human personality and the dignity of the human being and grow in respect for his rights and freedoms, is of immense importance.
>
> (Exact date not indicated, Box 1419,
> Anna Eleanor Roosevelt Papers)

109 Anderson, *Eyes Off the Prize: The United Nations and the African American Struggle for Human Rights, 1944–1955*, p. 218.

110 Allida Black, Ed., *Courage in a Dangerous World: The Political Writings of Eleanor Roosevelt* (New York, NY: Columbia University Press, 1999), p. 188.

111 Roosevelt wrote this to René Cassin about Mary Pillsbury Lord: "She is a fine young woman but she will need all the help you can give her." Roosevelt to Cassin, 16 February 1953, Box 1682, Anna Eleanor Roosevelt Papers.

112 Anderson, *Eyes Off the Prize: The United Nations and the African American Struggle for Human Rights, 1944–1955*, p. 237.

113 Article 2.7 of the UN Charter includes these words:

> Nothing contained in the present Charter shall authorize the United Nations to intervene in matters which are essentially within the domestic jurisdiction of any State or shall require the Members to submit such matters to settlement under the present Charter.

114 Lauterpacht, *International Law: Being the Collected Papers of Hersch Lauterpacht*, Vol. 3, p. 412.

115 Koskenniemi, *The Gentle Civilizer of Nations: The Rise and Fall of International Law 1870–1960*, p. 394.

   The 1950 European Convention on Human Rights provided for a Commission on Human Rights to which individual persons could register complaints against their governments.

116 Lauterpacht, *International Law and Human Rights*, p. 425.

117 Humphrey, *Human Rights and the United Nations: A Great Adventure*, pp. 74–75; Hobbins, *On the Edge of Greatness: The Diaries of John Humphrey, First Director of the United Nations Division of Human Rights*, Vol. I, pp. 81–82.

118 Julius Lester, Ed. *The Seventh Son: The Thought and Writings of W.E.B. Du Bois* (New York, NY: Random House, 1971), Vol. II, pp. 616–618.

119 Du Bois believed that the Chinese communist revolution amounted to a momentous advance in history and progress toward a radiant future. At ninety-one, touring in Mao's China, Du Bois exclaimed: "I have seen the world. But never so vast and glorious a miracle as China." He said this in 1959 just as the Great Leap Forward and related human-made famine were inaugurated. Had Du Bois lived long enough (d. 1963) to understand what was starting in 1959 China, he would certainly have revised his original enthusiasm. The above quotation is from Lester, *The Seventh Son: The Thought and Writings of W.E.B. Du Bois*, Vol. II, p. 666.

120 Ibid., p. 551.

121 Anderson, *Eyes Off the Prize: The United Nations and the African American Struggle for Human Rights, 1944–1955*, p. 132.

122 Sharma, *Are Human Rights Western? A Contribution to the Dialogue of Civilizations*, p. 242.

123 Winter and Prost, *René Cassin and Human Rights: From the Great War to the Universal Declaration*, pp. 274–278. In 1953, Roosevelt and Cassin strongly disagreed over French actions to suppress Moroccan moves for independence. Cassin's defense of France is in his letter to Roosevelt, 3 February 1953, Box 1682, Anna Eleanor Roosevelt Papers.

124 Sharma, *Are Human Rights Western? A Contribution to the Dialogue of Civilizations*, p. 258.

125 Ibid., p. 269.

126   An Encyclical Letter of His Holiness Pope John XXIII, *Peace On Earth* (New York, NY: Ridge Press/Golden Press, 1964), p. 152.

127   Glendon, *A World Made New: Eleanor Roosevelt and the Universal Declaration of Human Rights*, pp. 214, 228; Brownlie, *Basic Documents in International Law* (Oxford: Oxford University Press, 1983), p. 76.

128   Apologies to Mary Ann Glendon for my close paraphrase of her formulation: "[The UDHR's] nonbinding principles, carried far and wide by activists and modern communications, have vaulted over the political and legal barriers that impede efforts to establish international enforcement mechanisms." See Glendon, *A World Made New: Eleanor Roosevelt and the Universal Declaration of Human Rights*, p. 236. Also see for similar language/imagery, from which I have again borrowed much, Schabas, *Genocide in International Law: The Crimes of Crimes*, p. 544:

> The Universal Declaration laid the groundwork for steady progress in both standard-setting and a growing recognition of the right of the international community in general and United Nations bodies such as the Commission on Human Rights in particular to breach the wall of the *domaine reservé* by which States historically sheltered atrocities from international scrutiny.

The reference to Mandela is from Mary Robinson, "The Universal Declaration of Human Rights: The International Keystone of Human Dignity" in Barend van der Heijden and Bahia Tahzib-Lie, Eds., *Reflections on the Universal Declaration of Human Rights: A Fiftieth Anniversary Anthology* (The Hague: Martinus Nijhoff, 1998), p. 256.

129   Winter and Prost, *René Cassin and Human Rights: From the Great War to the Universal Declaration*, p. 261.

130   Robinson, "The Universal Declaration of Human Rights: The International Keystone of Human Dignity," p. 254.

131   Paul Kennedy, *The Parliament of Man: The Past, Present, and Future of the United Nations* (New York, NY: Vintage, 2006), p. 183; Morsink, *The Universal Declaration of Human Rights: Origins, Drafting, and Intent*, pp. xi–xii, 20.

132   Paul Gordon Lauren, *The Evolution of International Human Rights: Visions Seen* (Philadelphia, PA: University of Pennsylvania Press, 2011), pp. 273–274.

133   Three people involved in formulating the Responsibility to Protect idea of 2005 were Australia's Gareth Evans, Canada's Michael Ignatieff, and Algeria's Mohamed Sahnoun.

134   Cited in Koskenniemi, *The Gentle Civilizer of Nations: The Rise and Fall of International Law 1870–1960*, p. 389.

135   John Hope Franklin, *Mirror to America* (New York, NY: Farrar, Straus and Giroux, 2005), p. 92.

136 See Schabas, *Genocide in International Law: The Crimes of Crimes*, p. 9, where he writes:

> While genocide is a crime that is, fortunately, rarely committed, it remains a feature of contemporary society. It has become apparent that there are undesirable consequences to enlarging or diluting the definition of genocide. This weakens the terrible stigma associated with the crime and demeans the suffering of its victims. It is also likely to enfeeble whatever commitment States may believe they have to prevent the crime. The broader and more uncertain the definition, the less responsibility States will be prepared to assume. This can hardly be consistent with the new orientation of human rights law, and of the human rights movement, which is aimed at the eradication of impunity and assurance of human security.

137 See, for example, Mark Levene, *Genocide in the Age of the Nation State* (London: I.B. Tauris, 2005), especially Vol. 1, and his two volume study, *The Crisis of Genocide* (New York, NY: Oxford University Press, 2013). Also see A. Dirk Moses, "Genocide," *Australian Humanities Review*, November 2013 and Rouben Adalian, "Finding the Words" in Totten and Jacobs, *Pioneers of Genocide Studies*, p. 11. In support of a precise meaning of genocide, Adalian writes:

> There are five elements that I find necessary to identify a specific atrocity as genocide: the commissioning party is the state, or any institution acting as an instrument of the state, proceeding in the avowed interest of the state; the objects of the policy, the victims, are civilians incapable of mounting an organized defense of their lives, families, and properties; the atrocity is on a scale to indicate a scheme by its architects for the wholesale extermination of a sizable segment of a population, if not an entire people, defined or self-defined as a distinct social community; that the objective is a permanent alteration of the demographic characteristics and composition of a defined geographic space; and that all of the above occur or are implemented over, historically speaking, a short period of time.

See also the discussions in Naimark, *Stalin's Genocides*, pp. 1–8. On post-World War II genocides and rates of civilian fatality, see LeBlanc, *The United States and the Genocide Convention*, see p. 84.

138 *My Day*, 6 December 1948 in Black, *The Eleanor Roosevelt Papers*, Vol. I, p. 964; Roosevelt, *On My Own*, p. 108.

139 In a 1950 radio interview, Roosevelt confessed: "I have a sense of shame . . . that we have not ratified the genocide convention. . . . We can't possibly, as a nation, want to be classed as a nation that believes in mass murder." Mrs. Roosevelt Irate at U.S. Snub of UN Covenant, 3 June 1950, Box 90, Adolf Berle Papers.

140 Jean-Paul Sartre, *On Genocide* (Boston, MA: Beacon, 1968), pp. 23, 53, 73, 83.

141 Perhaps Lemkin would have turned his mind to this comment made in March 1950 by the writer Gouverneur Paulding: "Genocide is difficult to legislate, because in war even democracies might find themselves involved in something terribly close to it." Gouverneur Paulding, "Genocide and Mercy Killing," *The Reporter*, 14 March 1950.

142 Lemkin to Gertrude Samuels, 12 January 1948, Box 1, Raphael Lemkin Papers, AJHS. In this letter to Samuels, Lemkin also observed: "More human lives were lost in the genocide case of India (about 500,000) than in all the cases of so-called threats to peace which have been treated by the [UN] Security Council."

143 Totten and Jacobs in their *Pioneers of Genocide Studies*, p. 399.

144 John Stuart Mill, *Considerations on Representative Government*, Chapter III, cited in Edward Hallett Carr, *Conditions of Peace* (New York, NY: Macmillan, 1943), p. xxi. For full citation, see John Robson, Ed., *The Collected Works of John Stuart Mill* (Toronto: University of Toronto Press, 1977), Vol. XIX, "Considerations on Representative Government," Chapter III: "That the Ideally Best Form of Government is Representative Government."

145 Lemkin once wrote this on the physical and psychological toll exacted by his *genocide* campaign: "Whoever fights for an ideal must risk his life. . . . Ideals like ancient gods, demand constant sacrifices." See Frieze, *Totally Unofficial: The Autobiography of Raphael Lemkin*, p. 217. At the same time, Lemkin was impatient with ivory-tower intellectuals who sought tranquility and shunned political engagement. See Eugene Rostow to Lemkin, 31 December 1948, Box 1, Raphael Lemkin Papers, AJHS.

146 Moyn, *The Last Utopia: Human Rights in History*, p. 62.

147 In March 2014 a French court sentenced Pascal Simbikangwa to twenty-five years in prison. A Hutu intelligence officer in the Rwandan government in 1994, he was charged with genocide against the Tutsi and crimes against humanity. French prosecutors took this action in compliance with provisions of the Genocide Convention that permit a country to exercise criminal jurisdiction over a person who has committed genocide regardless of where the crime occurred. Belgian, Swedish, and Norwegian authorities had earlier convicted Rwandan figures per the Genocide Convention. See "France Convicts Rwandan of Genocide," *New York Times*, p. A7, 15 March 2014.

See also Alex Bellamy's "The Responsibility to Protect Turns Ten" in *Ethics and International Affairs*, Summer 2015; Beth Simmons, *Mobilizing for Human Rghts: International Law in Domestic Politics* (Cambridge: Cambridge University Press, 2009), p. 380; Mark Bradley, "Making Peace as a Project of Moral Reconstruction" in Michael Geyer and Adam Tooze, Eds., *The Cambridge*

History of the Second World War (Cambridge: Cambridge University Press, 2015), Vol. III, p. 551: "The power of the post-war imagination continues to shape contemporary human rights thought and practice as the central moral language through which we articulate our common humanity."

Chapter 4: United Nations

1   Ralph Bunche, Address to American Association for the United Nations, 9 May 1949, Box 343, Ralph Bunche Papers, UCLA.

2   Wilfred Jenks, "Hersch Lauterpacht—The Scholar as Prophet," *British Year Book of International Law*, 1960, p. 56.

3   Mark Mazower, *Governing the World: The History of an Idea, 1815 to the Present* (New York, NY: Penguin, 2012), pp. 198–199.

4   Cordell Hull, *Memoirs* (New York, NY: Macmillan, 1948), Vol. II, pp. 1662, 1664.

5   Evan Luard, *A History of the United Nations* (New York, NY: St. Martin's Press, 1982), Vol. I, p. 33.

6   Brian Urquhart, *A Life in Peace and War* (New York, NY: Harper and Row, 1987), pp. 98–99.

7   Luard, *A History of the United Nations*, Vol. I, pp. 84–85; David Bosco, *Five to Rule Them All: The UN Security Council and the Making of the Modern World* (Oxford: Oxford University Press, 2009), pp. 63–67; Urquhart, *A Life in Peace and War*, pp. 111–112.

8   Mazower, *Governing the World: The History of an Idea, 1815 to the Present*, p. 217.

9   Thomas Campbell and George Herring, Eds., *The Diaries of Edward R. Stettinius, Jr., 1943–1946* (New York, NY: New Viewpoints, 1975), p. 474.

10   John Barros, *Trygve Lie and the Cold War: The UN Secretary-General Pursues Peace, 1946–1953* (DeKalb, IL: Northern Illinois University Press, 1989), pp. 5–6.

11   Philip Jessup, *The Birth of Nations* (New York, NY: Columbia University Press, 1974), pp. 43–92, 261.

12   Andrew Cordier and Wilder Foote, Eds., *Public Papers of the Secretaries-General of the United Nations* (New York, NY: Columbia University Press, 1969), Vol. I, *Trygve Lie 1946–1953*, p. 449–450; Townsend Hoopes and Douglas Brinkley, *FDR and the Creation of the U.N.* (New Haven, CT: Yale University Press, 1997), pp. 208–209; Abba Eban, *The New Diplomacy: International Affairs in the Modern Age* (New York, NY: Random House, 1983), pp. 265–266.

13   Seymour Finger, *Your Man at the UN: People, Politics, and Bureaucracy in Making Foreign Policy* (New York, NY: New York University Press, 1980), pp. 53–54.

14 Dan Plesch, *America, Hitler and the UN: How the Allies Won World War II and Forged a Peace* (London: I.B. Tauris, 2011), p. 167; Finger, *Your Man at the UN: People, Politics, and Bureaucracy in Making Foreign Policy*, p. 17.

15 The "Memorandum of Points for Consideration in the Development of a Twenty-Year Program for Achieving Peace Through the United Nations" is here reproduced from Trygve Lie, *In the Cause of Peace: Seven Years with the United Nations* (New York, NY: Macmillan, 1954), pp. 279–282.

Inauguration of periodic meetings of the Security Council, attended by foreign ministers, or heads or other members of governments, as provided by the United Nations Charter and the rules of procedure; together with further development and use of other United Nations machinery for negotiations, mediation, and conciliation of international disputes.

A new attempt to make progress toward esablishing an international control system for atomic energy that will be effective in preventing its use for war and promoting its use for peaceful purposes.

A new approach to the problem of bringing the armaments race under control, not only in the field of atomic weapons, but in other weapons of mass destruction and in conventional armaments.

A renewal of serious efforts to reach agreement on the armed forces to be made available under the Charter to the Security Council for the enforcement of its decisions.

Acceptance and application of the principle that it is wise and right to proceed as rapidly as possible toward universality of membership.

A sound and active progam of technical assistance for economic development and encouragement of broadscale capital investment, using all appropriate private, governmental, and intergovernmental resources.

More vigorous use by all Member Governments of the Specialized Agencies of the United Nations, to promote, in the words of the Charter, "higher standards of living, full employment, and conditions of economic and social progress."

Vigorous and continued development of the work of the United Nations for wider observance and respect for human rights and fundamental freedoms throughout the world.

Use of the United Nations to promote, by peaceful means instead of by force, the advancement of dependent, colonial, or semi-colonial peoples toward a place of equality in the world.

Active and systematic use of all the powers of the Charter and all the machinery of the United Nations to speed up the development of international law toward an eventual enforceable world law for a universal world society.

16 Lawrence Kaplan, *NATO and the UN: A Peculiar Relationship* (Columbia, MO: University of Missouri Press, 2010), pp. 2, 13–14, 24–25.

17 Harry Truman, "Working in the UN—A Challenge to Better Human Relations," *The Department of State Bulletin*, 31 October 1949, p. 645.

18 Bosco, *Five to Rule Them All: The UN Security Council and the Making of the Modern World*, p. 32; Stephen Schlesinger, *Act of Creation: The Founding of the United Nations* (Boulder, CO: Westview, 2003), pp. 5–6.

19 Acheson to Harry Truman, 3 February 1954, Reel 19, Dean Acheson Papers, Yale University; Jessup, *The Birth of Nations*, pp. 8, 87.

20 Dean Acheson, *Present at the Creation* (New York, NY: W.W. Norton, 1969), pp. 111–112.

21 Memorandum of [Acheson's] Conversation with the President and Mr. Lie, p. 2, 20 April 1950, United Nations, Box 53, Warren Austin Papers.

22 Anna Kasten Neson, Ed., *The State Department Policy Planning Staff Papers* (New York, NY: Garland, 1983), Vol. III, United Nations, 14 November 1949, pp. 187–198; Giles Harlow and George Maerz, Eds., *Measures Short of War: The George F. Kennan Lectures at the National War College 1946–47* (Washington, DC: National Defense University Press, 1991), pp. 11, 196; Frank Costigliola, Ed., *The Kennan Diaries* (New York, NY: W.W. Norton, 2014), p. 364.

23 "Social Scientists Told U.N. Record Hollow," *Christian Science Monitor*, 19 April 1947.

24 That the UN work load exhausted Austin is evidenced in this comment to a onetime United Nations colleague: "Really, this work is getting tougher and tougher, and I do not know in what it will end. We did not finish until 2:20 A.M. a few nights ago, and I got to bed about 3:30 in the morning." Austin to Quo Tai-chi, 22 April 1948, Correspondence, Box V, Warren Austin Papers.

25 Austin to Herschel Johnson, 1 December 1948, Correspondence, Box V, Warren Austin Papers; Finger, *Your Man at the UN: People, Politics, and Bureaucracy in Making Foreign Policy*, p. 45.

26 George Mazuzan, *Warren R. Austin at the UN 1946–1953* (Kent, OH: Kent State University Press, 1977), pp. 34, 38, 49, 56–58, 67–68, 79, 92, 94, 128, 134–135, 185.

27 Warren Austin to Keenan, 16 August 1946, Box 1, Joseph Keenan Papers.

28 Journal entries, 21 November 1952 and 8 January 1953, Box 23, Henry Cabot Lodge, Jr. Papers; William Miller, *Henry Cabot Lodge* (New York, NY: James Heineman, 1967), p. 257; Forrest Pogue, *George C. Marshall: Statesman 1945–1959* (New York, NY: Viking, 1987), p. 410.

29 Bosco, *Five to Rule Them All: The UN Security Council and the Making of the Modern World*, pp. 59–60.

30 Jessup appreciated Austin of whom he recollected in 1957: "I look back with the greatest pleasure and satisfaction to my service under him at the [UN] mission." Jessup to Henry Cabot Lodge, 21 May 1957, Series II, Box 18, Philip Jessup Papers. Jessup also was cleared-eyed about the United Nations, which he readily admitted "serves to condense and to present in most distasteful form some of the weaknesses and troubles of the international community." Jessup to Dean Acheson, 20 November 1953, Series II, Box 3, Philip Jessup Papers.

31 Lie, *In the Cause of Peace: Seven Years with the United Nations*, p. 334.

32 Itamar Rabinovich and Jehuda Reinharz, Eds., *Israel in the Middle East: Documents and Readings on Society, Politics, and Foreign Relations, Pre-1948 to the Present* (Waltham: Brandeis University Press, 2008), pp. 571–572. The question of Palestine/Israel demographics is fraught with controversy. See Bernard Wasserstein, *Israelis and Palestinians: Why Do They Fight? Can They Stop?* (New Haven, CT: Yale University Press, 2004), pp. 5–30.

33 David Motadel, *Islam and Nazi Germany's War* (Cambridge, MA: Harvard University Press, 2014), pp. 41–44.

34 Ibid., p. 97.

35 Steven Spiegel, *The Other Arab–Israeli Conflict: Making America's Middle East Policy, from Truman to Reagan* (Chicago, IL: University of Chicago Press, 1985), p. 13.

36 Ben Shephard, *The Long Road Home: The Aftermath of the Second World War* (New York, NY: Alfred Knopf, 2011), p. 195.

37 "Zionism from the Standpoint of Its Victims" in Moustafa Bayoumi and Andrew Rubin, Eds., *The Edward Said Reader* (New York, NY: Vintage, 2000), p. 128.

38 Jo Roberts, *Contested Land, Contested Memory: Israel's Jews and Arabs and the Ghosts of Catastrophe* (Toronto: Dundurn, 2013), pp. 38–39.

39 Ibid., pp. 46–47.

40 Ibid., p. 41.

41 Abba Eban, *An Autobiography* (New York, NY: Random House, 1977), p. 97.

42 Shephard, *The Long Road Home: The Aftermath of the Second World War*, p. 365.

43 "Zionism from the Standpoint of Its Victims" in Bayoumi and Rubin, *The Edward Said Reader*, p. 118.

44 Bernard Baruch complained about what he labeled as American "weather-vaning." Baruch to Austin, 5 April 1948, Correspondence, Box V, Warren Austin Papers.

45 Clark Clifford, *Counsel to the President: A Memoir* (New York, NY: Random House, 1991), p. 12; Pogue, *George C. Marshall: Statesman 1945–1959*, p. 364.

46 President Barack Obama said during a round of fighting between Hamas forces in Gaza versus Israel: "It is amazing to see what Israel has become over the last several decades. To have scratched out of rock this incredibly vibrant, incredibly successful, wealthy and powerful country is a testament to the ingenuity, energy and vision of the Jewish people." See Thomas Friedman, "Obama on the World," *New York Times*, p. A19, 9 August 2014.

47 Pogue, *George C. Marshall: Statesman 1945–1959*, pp. 336–378.

48 Irene Gendzier, *Dying to Forget: Oil, Power, Palestine, and the Foundations of U.S. Policy in the Middle East* (New York, NY: Columbia University Press, 2015), pp. 57–58.

49 Alonzo Hamby, *Man of the People: A Life of Harry S. Truman* (New York, NY: Oxford University Press, 1995), p. 411.

50 Spiegel, *The Other Arab–Israeli Conflict: Making America's Middle East Policy from Truman to Reagan*, p. 18; Edward Maffitt's Memorandum: General Howard Kennedy (UNPRA)—Meetings with Near East Oil Companies and Relief Societies, 22 June 1950, Correspondence, Box V, Warren Austin Papers.

51 Karl Twitchell to Senator Aiken (R, Vermont), 8 March 1948, United Nations, Box 62, Warren Austin Papers.

52 Karl Twitchell to Austin, 9 November 1944, United Nations, Box 62, Warren Austin Papers.

53 Harry Truman, *Memoirs* (New York, NY: Doubleday, 1956), Vol. II, Chapter 12.

54 Ilya Gaiduk, *Divided Together: The United States and the Soviet Union in the United Nations, 1945–1965* (Stanford, CA: Stanford University Press, 2012), pp. 136–137.

55 Mazuzan, *Warren R. Austin at the U.N. 1946–1953*, p. 99.

56 Lie, *In the Cause of Peace: Seven Years with the United Nations*, p. 171.

57 Hamby, *Man of the People: A Life of Harry S. Truman*, pp. 416–417.

58 Jessup, *The Birth of Nations*, pp. 281–283, 286.

59 Robert Donovan, *Conflict and Crisis: The Presidency of Harry S. Truman, 1945–1948* (New York, NY: W.W. Norton, 1977), p. 385; Lie, *In the Cause of Peace: Seven Years with the United Nations*, p. 173.

60 Lellen Ravndal, "The First Major Test: The UN Secretary-General and the Palestine Problem, 1947–49" in *International History Review*, January 2016, pp. 203–204; Lie, *In the Cause of Peace: Seven Years with the United Nations*, pp. 166, 174.

61 Peter Kenez, *The Coming of the Holocaust: From Antisemitism to Genocide* (Cambridge: Cambridge University Press, 2013), p. 214.

62 Lie, *In the Cause of Peace: Seven Years with the United Nations*, p. 159.

63 Bunche's mediation efforts were difficult in the extreme. At one point in March 1949, Bunche allowed to his wife: "You can't imagine what it takes to hold these monkeys together long enough to squeeze agreement out of them. . . . I swear by all that's Holy, I will never come anywhere near the Palestine problem once I liberate myself from this trap." Cited in Elad Ben-Dror, *Ralph Bunche and the Arab–Israeli Conflict: Mediation and the UN, 1947–1949* (London: Routledge, 2016), p. 207.

64 Brian Urquhart, *Ralph Bunche: An American Life* (New York, NY: W.W. Norton, 1993), p. 230. Also see Ben-Dror, *Ralph Bunche and the Arab–Israeli Conflict: Mediation and the UN, 1947–1949*, p. 140.

65 Urquhart, *Ralph Bunche: An American Life*, p. 211. Also see Eban, *An Autobiography*, p. 137; Ben-Dror, *Ralph Bunche and the Arab–Israeli Conflict: Mediation and the UN, 1947–1949*, pp. 242–267.

66 On the Occasion of the Presentation of the Nobel Peace Prize, 10 December 1950, Box 415, Ralph Bunche Papers, UCLA. Also on Bernadotte see Nobel Lecture, 11 December 1950, Box 14, Ralph Bunche Papers, Schomburg Center for Research in Black Culture.

67 On the Occasion of the Presentation of the Nobel Peace Prize, 10 December 1950.

68 William Stueck, "The Korean War" in Melvyn Leffler and Odd Arne Westad, Eds., *The Cambridge History of the Cold War* (Cambridge: Cambridge University Press, 2010), Vol. I, p. 283–284; Allan Millett, *The War for Korea, 1945–1950: A House Burning* (Lawrence, KS: University Press of Kansas, 2005), p. 5; William Stueck, *Rethinking the Korean War: A New Diplomatic and Strategic History* (Princeton, NJ: Princeton University Press, 2002), p. 1; Bruce Cumings, *The Origins of the Korean War* (Princeton, NJ: Princeton University Press, 1981), Vol. I, p. xix.

69 The number of UN casualties (killed, wounded, captured, missing), outside of those suffered by the United States and South Korea, totaled 17,260. See James Matray, Ed., *Historical Dictionary of the Korean War* (New York, NY: Greenwood, 1991), p. 553.

70 Lie, *In the Cause of Peace: Seven Years with the United Nations*, p. 261.

71 The Security Council's decision to act in Korea pleased Truman, sparing his administration from taking the United States "alone" into the conflict. Harry Truman to Acheson, 19 July 1950, Reel 19, Dean Acheson Papers, Yale University.

72 Paul Gordon Lauren, "The Diplomats and Diplomacy of the United Nations" in Gordon Craig and Francis Lowenheim, Eds., *The Diplomats 1939–1979* (Princeton, NJ: Princeton University Press, 1994), pp. 466–469.

73 Cordier and Foote, *Public Papers of the Secretaries-General of the United Nations*, Vol. I, *Trygve Lie 1946–1953*, p. 391.

74 Milton Leitenberg, "New Russian Evidence on the Korean War Biological Warfare Allegations: Background and Analysis," *Cold War International History Project Bulletin*, Winter 1998, p. 192.

75 Lie, *In the Cause of Peace: Seven Years with the United Nations*, p. 366. Also see Statement by the Secretary-General on the World Situation and the United Nations, 29 September 1952, p. 9, Box 53, United Nations, Warren Austin Papers.

76 F[elix] Edward Hébert to Austin, 3 May 1948, and resolution adopted by the general membership of the Young Men's Business Club, 28 April 1948, Correspondence, Box V, Warren Austin Papers.

77 Richard Winslow to Victor Schiro, 14 May 1948, Correspondence, Box V, Warren Austin Papers.

78 Inis Claude, *Swords into Plowshares: The Problems and Progress of International Organization* (New York, NY: Random House, 1971), p. 203; Luard, *A History of the United Nations*, Vol. I, p. 355; Finger, *Your Man at the UN: People, Politics and Bureaucracy in Making Foreign Policy*, p. 64; Acheson, *Present at the Creation*, pp. 698, 713.

79 Claude, *Swords into Plowshares: The Problems and Progress of International Organization*, p. 204; Luard, *A History of the United Nations*, Vol. I, pp. 355–356; Lie, *In the Cause of Peace: Seven Years with the United Nations*, p. 399; Barros, *Trygve Lie and the Cold War: The UN Secretary-General Pursues Peace, 1946–1952*, pp. 66–67, 311–320.

80 Lodge to Joseph McCarthy, 2 February 1953, Alexander Wiley to Lodge, 4 February 1953, Joseph McCarthy to Lodge, 6 February 1953, Lodge to Donald Lourie, 7 April 1953, Box 24, Lodge to William Harrison, 20 March 1953, Box 29, Henry Cabot Lodge Papers; Statement by the Honorable Henry Cabot Lodge in Plenary Session on the Report of the Secretary General on Personnel Policy, 28 March 1953, United Nations, Box 53, Warren Austin Papers; *Congressional Record*, 15 September 1954, p. A6709.

81 Testimony of Ambassador Henry Cabot Lodge, 23 July 1953, *Hearing Before the Committee on Foreign Relations, United States Senate, Eighty-Third Congress, First Session* (Washington, DC: Government Printing Office, 1953), p. 5.

82 Feller once worked as General Counsel of UNRRA. Herbert Lehman regarded him as not only an admirable colleague but also valued his friendship. Lehman to Mrs. Abraham Feller, 20 November 1952, Box 151, Herbert Lehman Papers.

83 Cordier and Foote, *Public Papers of the Secretaries-General of the United Nations*, Vol. I, *Trygve Lie 1946–1953*, p. 486; Urquhart, *A Life in Peace and War*, pp. 122–123.

84 David Greenberg, "Washington Gone Crazy: Nativist Son," 31 October 2004, NYTimes.com; "UN Has A Bad Week," *Life*, 24 November 1952, p. 35.

85 Luard, *A History of the United Nations*, Vol. I, pp. 356–357; Brian Urquhart, *Hammarskjold* (New York, NY: Harper Colophon, 1972), pp. 63–64.

86 Acheson identified Bunche as "one of the world's great citizens who give us confidence in the future." Acheson to Ralph Bunche, 16 January 1951, Box 29, Dean Acheson Papers, Harry S. Truman Library.

87 Bunche wrote four lengthy research reports for the Carnegie Corporation-sponsored Myrdal study: "A Brief and Tentative Analysis of Negro Leadership," "Conceptions and Ideologies of the Negro Problem," "The Political Status of the Negro," and "The Programs, Ideologies, Tactics and Achievements of Negro Betterment and Interracial Organizations."

88 Dean Rusk, long an acquaintance of Bunche, said of him in 1973: "He was one of the great human beings of our time." Rusk to Jessup, 26 June 1973, Series II, Box 13, Philip Jessup Papers; Charles Henry, Ed., *Ralph J. Bunche: Selected Speeches and Writing* (Ann Arbor, MI: University of Michigan Press, 1995), p. 10.

89 A. Philip Randolph, president of the Brotherhood of Sleeping Car Porters, also resigned his membership from the National Negro Congress. He did so after delivering (April 1940) an impassioned oration against its capture by communist activists.

90 Annotated reply to interrogatory, (n.d.) February 1954, Box 100, Ralph Bunche Papers, UCLA.

91 Pierce Cerety to John Foster Dulles, 28 May 1954, and United Nations Bureau of Personnel to Bunche, 1 July 1954, Box 100, Ralph Bunche Papers, UCLA; Urquhart, *Ralph Bunche: An American Life*, pp. 247–256.

92 On his experiences in America, see Bunche's Address to the Forty-Second Annual Conference of the NAACP. In it, he said: "I feel a sense of personal insult whenever I see a sign reading 'For Colored' or 'White Only.'" Box 14, Ralph Bunche Papers, Schomburg Center for Research in Black Culture.

93 Annotated reply to interrogatory, (n.d.) February 1954, Box 100, Ralph Bunche Papers, UCLA.

94 Presidential Address to the American Political Science Association, p. 20, 9 September 1954, Box 14b, Ralph Bunche Papers, Schomburg Center for Research in Black Culture.

95 Lodge explained to Philip Young, chair of the Civil Service Commission, whose agency was aggressively used with the FBI to screen American employees of the UN: "The President is anxious that the United Nations be a success and that American confidence in it be restored. This question of personnel is basic to the restoration of American confidence and speed is really a vital factor." Lodge to Philip Young, 15 April 1953, Box 24, Henry Cabot Lodge Papers.

96 Henry Cabot Lodge, *The Storm Has Many Eyes: A Personal Narrative* (New York, NY: W.W. Norton, 1973), p. 252.

97 Member governments in the United Nations in 1945 numbered 51; in the year 2000 the number had reached 189; in 2017 the number exceeded 200.

98 The General Assembly in December 1991, with substantial U.S. support, revoked the 1975 Zionist/racism resolution.

99 Hoopes and Brinkley, *FDR and the Creation of the UN*, p. 213.

100 See William Keylor, "The United Nations' Record as the Guardian of Global Cooperative Security" in Vojtech Mastny and Zhu Liqun, Eds., *The Legacy of the Cold War: Perspectives on Security, Cooperation, and Conflict* (Lanham, MD: Lexington, 2014), pp. 81–122.

101 UNRWA = United Nations Relief and Works Agency for Palestine Refugees in the Near East. WHO = World Health Organization. UNICEF = United Nations International Children's Emergency Fund. UNHCR = United Nations High Commission for Refugees. UNESCO = United Nations Educational, Scientific and Cultural Organization.

102 Lodge, *The Storm Has Many Eyes: A Personal Narrative*, p. 153.

103 Collective Security Through the United Nations, p. 4, 10 May 1951, Correspondence, Box VI, Warren Austin Papers.

104 Jessup to Dean Acheson, 14 January 1957, Series II, Box 3, Philip Jessup Papers.

Chapter 5: Empires

1 Senate Floor Speech, 13 December 1967, Series 71, Box 33, J. William Fulbright Papers.

On the seventy-second anniversary of Nazi Germany's surrender to the Allies, Senator John McCain (R, Arizona), a critic of President Donald Trump's "America first" notion, issued this warning, reminiscent in tone and substance of Fulbright in 1967:

> Our values are our strength and greatest treasure. We are distinguished from other countries because we are not made from a land or tribe or particular race or creed, but from an ideal that liberty is the inalienable right of mankind and in accord with nature and nature's Creator.
>
> To view foreign policy as simply transactional is more dangerous than its proponents realize. Depriving the oppressed of a beacon of hope could lose us the world we have built and thrived in. It could cost our reputation in history as the nation distinct from all others in our achievements, our identity and our enduring influence on mankind. Our values are central to all three.

Were they not, we would be one great power among the others of
history. We would acquire wealth and power for a time, before receding
into the disputed past.
John McCain, "We Must Support Human Rights,"
New York Times, p. A21, 8 May 2017.

2   Rudyard Kipling, *Recessional*, Christopher Ricks, Ed., *The Oxford Book of English Verse* (Oxford: Oxford University Press, 1999), p. 533.

3   Niall Ferguson, *Colossus: The Rise and Fall of the American Empire* (New York, NY: Penguin, 2004), pp. xii, 14.

4   Charles Maier, *Among Empires: American Ascendency and Its Predecessors* (Cambridge, MA: Harvard University Press, 2006), pp. 75–77.

5   Lord Curzon, British secretary of state for foreign affairs during 1919–1924, referred to the "unmixing" of peoples. See Jane Burbank and Frederick Cooper, *Empires in World History: Power and the Politics of Difference* (Princeton, NJ: Princeton University Press, 2010), p. 381.

6   Dean Acheson, Oral History, p. 5, Harry S. Truman Presidential Library.

7   Marilyn Young, *The Vietnam Wars 1945–1990* (New York, NY: Harper Perennial, 1991), pp. 12, 14.

8   Senator Mike Gravel edition, *The Pentagon Papers: The Defense Department History of United States Decisionmaking on Vietnam* (Boston, MA: Beacon, 1971), Vol. I, p. 54.

9   Fredrik Logevall, "The Indochina Wars and the Cold War, 1945–1975" in Melvyn Leffler and Odd Arne Westad, Eds., *The Cambridge History of the Cold War* (Cambridge: Cambridge University Press, 2011), Vol. II, p. 284.

10 Ibid., p. 288; Gravel, *The Pentagon Papers*, Vol. I, p. 54; Irwin Wall, *France, the United States, and the Algerian War* (Berkeley, CA: University of California, Press, 2001), p. 262.

11 Dwight Eisenhower to Hazlett, 18 March 1954, and Eisenhower to Hazlett, 27 April 1954, in Box 2, Edward Hazlett Papers.

12 Fredrik Logevall, *Embers of War: The Fall of an Empire and the Making of America's Vietnam* (New York, NY: Random House, 2012), p. xiv.

13 Ibid., p. 712; Logevall, "The Indochina Wars and the Cold War 1945–1975," p. 289.

14 Wall, *France, the United States, and the Algerian War*, p. 261.

15 See Frantz Fanon with Jean-Paul Sartre's preface, *The Wretched of the Earth* (New York, NY: Grove, 1963). Fanon's book was originally published in France: *Les Damnes de la Terre* (Paris: Francois Maspero, 1961).

16 Wall, *France, the United States, and the Algerian War*, pp. 2–3.

17 Odd Arne Westad, *The Global Cold War: Third World Interventions and the Making of Our Times* (Cambridge: Cambridge University Press, 2007), p. 115; A.W. Brian Simpson, *Human Rights and the End of Empire: Britain and the*

Genesis of the European Convention (Oxford: Oxford University Press, 2001), pp. 833–834; Burbank and Cooper, *Empires in World History: Power and the Politics of Difference*, p. 418.

18 Fanon, *The Wretched of the Earth*, p. 78; Caroline Elkins, *Imperial Reckoning: The Untold Story of Britain's Gulag in Kenya* (New York, NY: Henry Holt, 2005), pp. xv–xvi.

19 Elkins, *Imperial Reckoning: The Untold Story of Britain's Gulag in Kenya*, pp. 91, 93, 281–282; Simpson, *Human Rights and the End of Empire: Britain and the Genesis of the European Convention*, pp. 834–835.

20 Homer Jack, *Bandung: An on-the-spot Description of the Asian-African Conference, Bandung, Indonesia, April 1955* (Chicago, IL: Toward Freedom, 1955), pp. 5, 33; Carlos Romulo, *The Meaning of Bandung* (Chapel Hill, NC: University of North Carolina Press, 1956), p. 35; Richard Wright, *The Color Curtain: A Report on the Bandung Conference* (Cleveland, OH: World Publishing, 1956), pp. 132–133, 149; Carl Rowan, *Breaking Barriers: A Memoir* (Boston, MA: Little Brown, 1991), p. 129; See Seng Tan and Amitav Acharya, Eds. *Bandung Revisited: The Legacy of the 1955 Asian-African Conference for International Order* (Singapore: National University of Singapore, 2008), pp. 3, 14; *FRUS, 1955–1957*, Vol. XXII, pp. 268–273; UK High Commissioner in Ceylon to Foreign Office, 2 May 1955, FO371/115049/1041/828, National Archives, (Kew) London; Audrey R. and George McT. Kahin, *Subversion as Foreign Policy: The Secret Eisenhower and Dulles Debacle in Indonesia* (New York, NY: New Press, 1995), p. 44.

21 President Soekarno (Sukarno), speech of 18 April 1955, *Vital Speeches of the Day* (New York, NY: City News Publishing, 1 June 1955), p. 1252.

22 Final Communiqué of the Asian-African Conference, 24 April 1955, reproduced in George McT. Kahin, *The Asian-African Conference: Bandung, Indonesia, April 1955* (Ithaca, NY: Cornell University Press, 1956), pp. 70, 76–85; Wright, *The Color Curtain: A Report on the Bandung Conference*, p. 138.

The Bandung communiqué endorsed these ten principles:

Respect for fundamental human rights and for the purposes and principles of the Charter of the United Nations.

Respect for the sovereignty and territorial integrity of all nations.

Recognition of the equality of all races and of the equality of all nations large and small.

Abstention from intervention or interference in the internal affairs of another country.

Respect for the right of each nation to defend itself singly or collectively, in conformity with the Charter of the United Nations.

(a) Abstention from the use of arrangements of collective defense to serve the particular interests of any of the big powers. (b) Abstention by any country from exerting pressures on other countries.

Refraining from acts or threats of aggression or the use of force against the territorial integrity or political independence of any country.

Settlement of all international disputes by peaceful means, such as negotiation, conciliation, arbitration or judicial settlement as well as other peaceful means of the parties' own choice, in conformity with the Charter of the United Nations.

Promotion of mutual interests and cooperation.

Respect for justice and international obligations.

23 Washington Embassy telegram No. 1007 to Foreign Office, 29 April 1955, FO371/115049/1041/807, National Archives, (Kew) London; Lorenz Luthi, *The Sino-Soviet Split: Cold War in the Communist World* (Princeton, NJ: Princeton University Press, 2008), p. 36.

24 244th Meeting of the National Security Council, 7 April 1955, NSC Series, Box 6, Papers as President (Ann Whitman File), Dwight D. Eisenhower Papers.

25 John Foster Dulles memorandum for Governor Sherman Adams, 31 March 1955, Box 503, White House Central Files; John Foster Dulles memorandum of conversation with the President, 11 April 1955, JFD Chronological Series, General Correspondence and Memoranda Series, Box 11, John Foster Dulles Papers; Mr. Villard to Mr. Staats, Status Report on the Asian-African Conference, 28 March 1955, OCB Central File Series, Box 85, White House Office, National Security Council; Westad, *The Global Cold War: Third World Interventions and the Making of Our Times*, p. 103; Charles Hamilton, *Adam Clayton Powell, Jr.: The Political Biography of an American Dilemma* (New York, NY: Athenaeum, 1991), p. 241.

26 Peter Grose, *Gentleman Spy: The Life of Allen Dulles* (Boston, MA: Houghton Mifflin, 1994), p. 411.

27 Sir Alexander Grantham to Secretary of State for Colonies, 23 June 1956 and P.M. (56)4, 7 January 1956. Also see Foreign Office to UK Embassy in Washington, 27 April 1955: "We [British] must also bring home to them [Americans] the mischief that is likely to result from these Nationalist activities." See PREM 11/1309, National Archives, (Kew) London. See, too, these extensive files in the National Archives, (Kew) London: DO35/4977, DO35/4978, DO35/4979.

Hard evidence did not implicate Americans in the *Kashmir Princess* episode. Still, other explanation exists as a matter of theoretical possibility, bearing in mind that U.S. covert operations were conducted in ways that allowed

Washington to disclaim plausibly any responsibility for them. See James Lay in Note by the Executive Secretary to the National Security Council on Covert Operations, p. 2, 15 March 1954, NSC Series, Policy Papers Subseries, White House Office, Office of the Special Assistant for National Security Affairs.

28 Wright, *The Color Curtain: A Report on the Bandung Conference*, pp. 12, 177–178, 207. On Wright and his perception of racial matters at Bandung, see Robert Vitalis, *White World Order: Black Power Politics: The Birth of American International Relations* (Ithaca, NY: Cornell University Press, 2015), pp. 127, 164.

29 Rowan, *Breaking Barriers: A Memoir*, pp. 128–131.

30 Jack, *Bandung: An on-the-spot Description of the Asian-African Conference, Bandung, Indonesia*, April 1955, p. 29; Richard Lamb, *The Failure of the Eden Government* (London: Sidwick and Jackson, 1987), p. 125; Speech by Premier Chou En-lai (Zhou Enlai) to the Political Committee of the Asian-African Conference, 23 April 1955, reproduced in Kahin, *The Asian-African Conference, Bandung, Indonesia, April 1955*, p. 62.

31 Adam Clayton Powell, Jr., *Adam by Adam* (New York, NY: Dial, 1971), pp. 108–109; Wil Haygood, *King of the Cats: The Life and Times of Adam Clayton Powell, Jr.* (Boston, MA: Houghton Mifflin, 1993), pp. 202–203; Hamilton, *Adam Clayton Powell, Jr.: The Political Biography of an American Dilemma*, pp. 242–243.

32 Appointment of Congressman Adam Clayton Powell, Jr. with the President (submitted by Maxwell Rabb), 11 May 1955, Box 503, White House Central Files, Official File; Powell, *Adam by Adam*, pp. 115–117; Hamilton, *Adam Clayton Powell, Jr.: The Political Biography of an American Dilemma*, pp. 245–246.

33 Audry and George Kahin, *Subversion as Foreign Policy: The Secret Eisenhower and Dulles Debacle in Indonesia*, pp. 76–77.

34 *FRUS 1955–1957*, Vol. IX, p. 532. Also see Jackson to Henry Luce, 23 April 1955, Box 71, C.D. Jackson Papers; Results of the Bandung Conference: A Preliminary Analysis, OIR No. 6903, 27 April 1955, OCB Central File Series, Box 85, White House Office, National Security Council Staff: "The pro-Western nations, in part from genuine conviction, in part in the expectation of future U.S. aid, spoke up forcefully against Communist colonialism and in defense of their alignment in defense pacts."

35 Nasser's speech, 18 April 1955 at Bandung, *Vital Speeches of the Day*, 1 June 1955, p. 1257.

36 André Beaufre, *The Suez Expedition 1956* (New York, NY: Frederick A. Praeger, 1969), pp. 14, 141.

37 Kahin, *The Asian-African Conference, Bandung, Indonesia, April 1955*, pp. 12–13, 18–21.

38 Mohammad Fadhil Jamali's speech, 18 April 1955 at Bandung, *Vital Speeches of the Day*, 1 June 1955, p. 1261.

39 Carlos Romulo's speech, 18 April 1955 in Ibid., p. 1274.

40 Final Communiqué of the Asian-African Conference, 24 April 1955, reproduced in Kahin, *The Asian-African Conference, Bandung, Indonesia, April 1955*, p. 81.

41 Under Allied occupation since 1945, Austria became independent on 12 May 1955. Until that date, American, British, French, and Soviet authorities had exercised joint responsibility for the country. Each occupying power had a zone of its own in Vienna and in the country at large. The Soviet zone was located in the eastern part of the country. The population there endured the stringencies of Moscow rule and hardships, horrendous during the first months when Red Army personnel drove up the rape and plunder rates. By late October 1955, all Allied occupation forces—Soviet included—had vacated Austria.

42 Czeslaw Milosz, *The Captive Mind* (New York, NY: Vintage, 1981), p. 165.

43 Christian Ostermann, "Keeping the Pot Simmering: The United States and the East German Uprising of 1953," *German Studies Review*, February 1996, p. 64; Rainer Hildebrandt, *The Explosion: The Uprising Behind the Iron Curtain* (Boston, MA: Little, Brown, 1955), p. 197; Arnulf Baring, *Uprising in East Germany: June 17, 1953* (Ithaca, NY: Cornell University Press, 1972), pp. xxiii–xxiv.

44 Ostermann, "Keeping the Pot Simmering: The United States and the East German Uprising of 1953," pp. 80, 83 #17; 150th meeting of the NSC, 18 June 1953, NSC Series, Papers as President (Ann Whitman File), Dwight D. Eisenhower Papers.

45 C.D. Jackson to Frank Wisner, 15 March 1954, OCB Central File Series, Box 85, White House Office, National Security Council Staff.

46 Tony Judt, *Postwar: A History of Europe Since 1945* (New York, NY: Penguin, 2005), p. 177. Also see Torsten Diedrich, *Der 17 Juni 1953: Bewaffnete Gewalt gegen das Volk* (Berlin: Dietz Verlag, 1991) and Martin McCauley, *The German Democratic Republic Since 1945* (New York, NY: St. Martin's Press, 1983).

47 Judt, *Postwar: A History of Europe Since 1945*, p. 177.

48 Strobe Talbott, Ed. *Khrushchev Remembers* (Boston, MA: Little, Brown, 1970), p. 417.

49 Sergei Khrushchev, *Rozhdenie sverkh derzhavy. Kniga ob otse* (Moscow: Vremia, 2000), pp. 172–174. Nikita Khrushchev recalled of Soviet decision-making on whether to act in Hungary: "I don't know how many times we changed our minds back and forth." Talbott, *Khrushchev Remembers*, p. 418.
    Nagy praised Bandung's adoption of these principles: "national independence, sovereignty, equality, noninterference in internal affairs, and the

assurance of self-determination." Imre Nagy, *On Communism: In Defense of the New Course* (New York, NY: Frederick A. Praeger, 1957), pp. 20–23.

50 The "secret speech" is reproduced in Talbott, *Khrushchev Remembers*, pp. 559–618.

51 Csaba Bekes, "East Central Europe, 1953–1956" in Melvyn Leffler and Odd Arne Westad, Eds., *The Cambridge History of the Cold War* (Cambridge: Cambridge University Press, 2011), Vol. I, pp. 341, 345, 347.

To Secretary of State Dulles, the outbreak of violence in Poland indicated that Moscow's empire was stretched thin: "It shows if we will stay firm and solid, cracks will begin to open up because they [the Soviets] are overextended." Dulles's telephone call to Senator Joseph O'Mahoney, 29 June 1956, Telephone Conversation Series, Box 5, John Foster Dulles Papers.

52 Charles Gati, *Failed Illusions: Moscow, Washington, Budapest, and the 1956 Hungarian Revolt* (Stanford, CA: Stanford University Press, 2006), p. 4.

Nagy's devotion to Stalin was apparent in 1953 when, upon Stalin's death, Nagy eulogized him in ceremony at the Hungarian parliament: "the great leader of humanity." Cited in Bill Lomax, *Hungary 1956* (New York, NY: St. Martin's Press, 1976), p. 53.

53 Peter Kenez, "Khrushchev and Hungary in 1956," n.d., unpublished essay in author's possession; United Nations, *Report of the Special Committee on the Problem of Hungary* (New York, NY: General Assembly, Official Records, Eleventh Session, Supplement No, 18, A/3592, 1957), p. 255.

54 Bekes, "East Central Europe, 1953–1956," p. 350.

55 Paul Lendvai, *One Day That Shook the Communist World: The 1956 Hungarian Uprising and Its Legacy* (Princeton, NJ: Princeton University Press, 2008), p. 185; Gyorgy Litvan, Ed., *The Hungarian Revolution of 1956: Reform, Revolt and Repression 1953–1963* (London: Longman, 1996), pp. 102–103.

56 Judt, *Postwar: A History of Europe Since 1945*, pp. 317–318; Bekes, "East Central Europe, 1953–1956," p. 351; Litvan, *The Hungarian Revolution of 1956: Reform, Revolt and Repression 1953–1963*, pp. 143–144.

57 Gati, *Failed Illusions: Moscow, Washington, and the 1956 Hungarian Revolt*, p. 192.

58 A member of the peasant party (Petofi), Bibo appealed to Washington during the crisis and invoked the "ten year old American liberation policy." Cited in Bibo statement, 4 November, Dulles-Herter Papers, Box 8, Papers as President (Ann Whitman File), Dwight D. Eisenhower Papers.

59 Lendvai, *One Day that Shook the Communist World: The 1956 Hungarian Uprising and Its Legacy*, pp. 185–186, 190–191; Litvan, *The Hungarian Revolution of 1956: Reform, Revolt and Repression 1953–1963*, p. 103; Tamas Szabo, *Boy on the Rooftop* (Boston, MA: Little, Brown, 1958), p. 113; Miklos Molnar, *Budapest 1956: A History of the Hungarian Revolution* (London:

George Allen and Unwin, 1971), p. 216; Gati, *Failed Illusions: Moscow, Washington, Budapest, and the Hungarian Revolt*, p. 207.

60 Victor Sebestyen, *Twelve Days: The Story of the 1956 Hungarian Revolution* (New York, NY: Pantheon, 2006), p. xxv.

61 Judt, *Postwar: A History of Europe Since 1945*, pp. 321–322.

62 See James Michener, *The Bridge at Andau* (New York, NY: Random House, 1957), p. 247. He wrote: "Russia has suffered a staggering defeat in the world battle for men's minds."

63 Litvan, *The Hungarian Revolution of 1956: Reform, Revolt and Repression 1953–1963*, p. 154.

64 Ibid., p. 155.

In 1956 the prime ministers of the five sponsoring states of Bandung—Burma, Ceylon, India, Indonesia, Pakistan—roundly condemned Soviet violence against Hungary. See John Thomson, "Burma: A Neutral in China's Shadow," *The Review of Politics*, July 1957, pp. 330–331.

65 For a treatment of empire skeptics in the United States, see David Mayers, *Dissenting Voices in America's Rise to Power* (Cambridge: Cambridge University Press, 2007). Of related interest, see John A. Thompson, *A Sense of Power: The Roots of America's Global Role* (Ithaca, NY: Cornell University Press, 2015).

66 The United States via war and purchase acquired the Philippines from Spain in 1898, but recognized the country as independent on 4 July 1946.

67 Cited in Andrew Bacevich, *American Empire: The Realities and Consequences of U.S. Diplomacy* (Cambridge, MA: Harvard University Press, 2002), p. 244.

68 Mossadegh, a secular and liberal-minded nationalist, was pictured (4 June 1951) on the cover of *Time*. The editors of that magazine, as well as U.S. and British diplomats with whom he dealt, tended to dismiss him as fickle, given to childlike outbursts, and sartorially odd (sometimes wearing pajamas when conducting state business). The verdict: he was plainly unfit to exercise high office in a country crucial to the energy needs of the West. See Mary Ann Heiss, "Real Men Don't Wear Pajamas: Anglo-American Cultural Perceptions of Mohammed Mossadeq and the Iranian Oil Nationalization Dispute" in Peter Hahn and Mary Ann Heiss, Eds., *Empire and Revolution: The United States and the Third World since 1945* (Columbus, OH: Ohio State University Press, 2001), pp. 183–185. Lieutenant Colonel Vernon Walters—later Lieutenant General, inductee in the Military Intelligence Hall of Fame, ambassador to West Germany, and ambassador to the United Nations—referred to Mossadegh's "imponderable Oriental mind." See Vernon Walters to General Gruenther, 9 November 1951, NATO Series, Box 1, Alfred Gruenther Papers.

The U.S. ambassador to Iran in 1953, Loy Henderson, respected Mossadegh more than did most Americans and British, thinking him a serious person, accomplished orator, and an idealist, though not a skillful administrator or natural leader. See Loy Henderson Oral History, OH-191, Dwight D. Eisenhower Presidential Library.

69 David Collier, *Democracy and the Nature of American Influence in Iran, 1941–1979* (Syracuse, NY: Syracuse University Press, 2017), pp. 119, 131.

70 See John Cable, *Intervention at Abadan: Plan Buccaneer* (New York, NY: St. Martin's Press, 1991).

71 David Wilber, *Regime Change in Iran: Overthrow of Premier Mossadeq of Iran November 1952–August 1953* (Nottingham: Spokesman, 2006), pp. 13–18. Also see Ervand Abrahamian, *The Coup: 1953, the CIA, and the Roots of Modern U.S.-Iranian Relations* (New York, NY: New Press, 2013).

72 Wilber, *Regime Change in Iran: Overthrow of Premier Mossadeq of Iran November 1952–August 1953*, pp. 15–16.

73 Tim Weiner, *Legacy of Ashes: The History of the CIA* (New York, NY: Doubleday, 2007), pp. 81–92; James Bill, "America, Iran, and the Politics of Intervention, 1951–1953" in James Bill and Wm. Roger Louis, Eds., *Mussaddiq, Iranian Nationalism, and Oil* (Austin, TX: University of Texas, 1988), p. 285.

74 Stephen Kinzer, *All the Shah's Men: An American Coup and the Roots of Middle East Terror* (Hoboken, NJ: John Wiley and Sons, 2003), p. 193.

75 Dulles's remarks in cabinet meeting, 27 August 1953, Cabinet Series, Box 2, Papers as President (Ann Whitman File), Dwight D. Eisenhower Papers. Under Secretary of State Walter Bedell Smith was most emphatic on 17 September 1953 in a meeting of the National Security Council. The administration, he said, "had snatched victory from the jaws of death." See *FRUS, 1952–1954*, Vol. X, p. 796.

76 William Stivers, "Eisenhower and the Middle East" in Richard Melanson and David Mayers, Eds., *Reevaluating Eisenhower: American Foreign Policy in the Fifties* (Urbana, IL: University of Illinois Press, 1989), p. 206; Wilber, *Regime Change in Iran: Overthrow of Premier Mossadeq of Iran November 1952–August 1953*, p. 18.

77 Kinzer, *All the Shah's Men: An American Coup and the Roots of Middle East Terror*, pp. 195–196; Collier, *Democracy and the Nature of American Influence in Iran, 1941–1979*, p. 157.

78 The numbers on Guatemalan population and Maya percentage are from a 1950 census cited in Jim Handy, *Revolution in the Countryside: Rural Conflict and Agrarian Reform in Guatemala, 1944–1954* (Chapel Hill, NC: University of North Carolina Press, 1994), p. 14.

79 Richard Immerman, *The CIA in Guatemala: The Foreign Policy of Intervention* (Austin, TX: University of Texas Press, 1982), p. 197.

80 Stephen Schesinger and Stephen Kinzer, *Bitter Fruit: The Story of the American Coup in Guatemala* (Cambridge, MA: Harvard University Press, 1999), p. 73.

81 Handy, *Revolution in the Countryside: Rural Conflict and Agrarian Reform in Guatemala, 1944–1954*, p. 94.

82 Ibid., pp. 172–173.

83 Walter LaFeber, *Inevitable Revolutions: The United States in Central America* (New York, NY: W.W. Norton, 1983), pp. 118–120.

84 Walter B. Smith to Eisenhower, Memorandum for the President: Visit of Guatemalan Ambassador Toriello, (n.d.) January 1954, International Series, Papers as President (Ann Whitman File), Dwight D. Eisenhower Papers; Immerman, *The CIA in Guatemala: The Foreign Policy of Intervention*, p. 155; Schlesinger and Kinzer, *Bitter Fruit: The Story of the American Coup in Guatemala*, p. 61; Stephen Kinzer, *Overthrow: America's Century of Regime Change from Hawaii to Iraq* (New York, NY: Henry Holt, 2006), pp. 204–205; LaFeber, *Inevitable Revolutions: The United States in Central America*, pp. 114–115.

85 Immerman, *The CIA in Guatemala: The Foreign Policy of Intervention*, p. 171; CIA report—Situation in Guatemala as of 20 June 1954, Administration Series, Box 13, Papers as President (Ann Whitman File), Dwight D. Eisenhower Papers.

86 Handy, *Revolution in the Countryside: Rural Conflict and Agrarian Reform in Guatemala, 1944–1954*, p. 179; Kinzer, *Overthrow: America's Century of Regime Change from Hawaii to Iraq*, p. 145; Grose, *Gentleman Spy: The Life of Allen Dulles*, p. 383.

87 LaFeber, *Inevitable Revolutions: The United States in Central America*, p. 125.

88 Dulles-Henry Cabot Lodge telephone conversation, 24 June 1954, Telephone Conversation Series, Box 2, John Foster Dulles Papers; Immerman, *The CIA in Guatemala: The Foreign Policy of Intervention*, pp. 170–172.

89 Daniel Yergin, *The Prize: The Epic Quest for Oil, Money, and Power* (New York, NY: Simon & Schuster, 1991), p. 480.

90 Wall, *France, the United States, and the Algerian War*, pp. 33–34.

91 David Reynolds, *Britannia Overruled: British Policy and World Power in the Twentieth Century* (London: Longman, 1991), p. 203; Tony Shaw, *Eden, Suez and the Mass Media: Propaganda and Persuasion During the Suez Crisis* (London: I.B. Tauris, 1996), p. 193.

92 Dwight Eisenhower to Hazlett, 3 August 1956, Box 2, Edward Hazlett Papers.

93 Robert Schulzinger, "The Impact of Suez on United States Middle East Policy, 1957–1958" and Alfred Atherton, "The United States and the Suez Crisis: The Uses and Limits of Diplomacy" in Selwyn Troen and Moshe Shemesh, Eds., *The Suez-Sinai Crisis 1956: Retrospective and Reappraisal* (New York, NY:

Columbia University Press, 1990), pp. 253, 269; Hermann Eilts, "Reflections on the Suez Crisis: Security in the Middle East" in William Louis and Roger Owen, Eds., *Suez 1956: The Crisis and its Consequences* (Oxford: Oxford University Press, 1989), pp. 356–357.

94 Albert Hourani, "Conclusion" in Louis and Owen, *Suez 1956: The Crisis and its Consequences*, p. 400; Steven Freiberger, *Dawn Over Suez: The Rise of American Power in the Middle East, 1953–1957* (Chicago, IL: Ivan R. Dee, 1992), pp. 148–149.

95 John Foster Dulles's memorandum for the President, 28 March 1955, and Eisenhower to Sir Anthony Eden, 9 May 1956, in Dulles-Herter Series, Box 6, Papers as President (Ann Whitman File), Dwight D. Eisenhower Papers; Dwight Eisenhower to Hazlett, 22 July 1957, Box 2, Edward Hazlett Papers.

96 Embassy London telegram (Ambassador Winthrop Aldrich) to Secretary of State, 26 November 1956 and Embassy Paris telegram (Ambassador C. Douglas Dillon) to Secretary of State, 29 November 1956 in Records as President, White House Central Files (Confidential File), Subject Series, Dwight D. Eisenhower Papers.

97 For a review of attitudes toward Suez of the governments of Indonesia, India, Pakistan, Burma, and Ceylon, see *Indonesia News*, 28 September 1956, Vol. VI, No. 35; Nehru quotation is cited in Sarvepalli Gopal, "India, the Crisis, and the Non-Aligned Nations" in Louis and Owen, *Suez 1956: The Crisis and its Consequences*, p. 185.

98 John Darwin, *Britain and Decolonization: The Retreat from Empire in the Post-War World* (New York, NY: St. Martin's Press, 1988), p. 212; Atherton, "The United States and the Suez Crisis: The Uses and Limits of Diplomacy," p. 270.

99 William Roger Louis, "Dulles, Suez, and the British" in Richard Immerman, Ed., *John Foster Dulles and the Diplomacy of the Cold War* (Princeton, NJ: Princeton University Press, 1990), p. 158.

100 Eisenhower to John Foster Dulles (cablegram), 12 December 1956, Dulles-Herter Series, Box 8, Papers as President (Ann Whitman File), Dwight D. Eisenhower Papers.

101 Dwight Eisenhower to Hazlett, 2 November 1956, Box 2, Edward Hazlett Papers; Eisenhower to John Foster Dulles, 30 October 1956, Dulles-Herter Papers, Box 7, Papers as President (Ann Whitman File), Dwight D. Eisenhower Papers.

102 Donald Neff, *Warriors at Suez: Eisenhower Takes America into the Middle East* (New York, NY: Simon & Schuster, 1981), p. 391.

103 Louis, "Dulles, Suez, and the British," pp. 148–149, 153.

104 Dwight Eisenhower to Guy Mollet, 27 November 1956, State Department Subseries, Box 1, White House Office, Office of the Staff Secretary.

105 Laszlo Borhi, "Containment, Rollback, Liberation or Inaction? The United States in Hungary in the 1950s" in *Journal of Cold War Studies*, Fall 1999, p. 105.

106 Schulzinger, "The Impact of Suez on United States Middle East Policy, 1957–1958," p. 252.

107 Ibid., p. 262.

108 Richard Schlatter, Ed., *Hobbes's Thucydides* (New Brunswick, NJ: Rutgers University Press, 1975), p. 379.

109 See Alastair Buchan, *The End of the Postwar Era: A New Balance of World Power* (London: Weidenfeld and Nicolson, 1974), p. 323: *non-market economies are excluded from the total; **net Material Product at 0.72 roubles = $1; ***net Material Product at 0.72 roubles = $1.

Some simple orders of magnitude, 1952 and 1962: The political size of the major empires

The major powers	GNP ($ billion)	Population (millions)	Military manpower ('000)	Strategic nuclear delivery systems	Exports as a percentage of world exports*
1952					
USA	350	157.5	3550	800	20.6
USSR	113**	184.8	4600	—	—
UK	44	50.7	890	—	10.4
France	29	42.4	645	—	5.2
1962					
USA	560	186.7	2827	1835	17.4
USSR	229***	221.7	3600	865	5.6
UK	81	53.3	445	90	9.1
France	74	47.0	742	—	5.9
EEC	232	173.3	1784	—	27.4

110 Jussi Hanhimaki, *The Rise and Fall of Détente: American Foreign Policy and the Transformation of the Cold War* (Washington, DC: Potomac, 2013), pp. 30, 241 #9.

111 Mikhail Gorbachev, *Perestroika: New Thinking for Our Country and the World* (New York, NY: Harper and Row, 1987), p. 215.

112 Andrei Kozyrev, "Don't Threaten US," *New York Times*, 18 March 1994.

113 Peregrine Worsthorne, "The Bush Doctrine," *Sunday Telegraph*, 3 March 1991.

114 "To Paris, U.S. Looks Like a Hyperpower," *New York Times*, 5 February 1999, www.nytimes.com/1999/02/05/news/05iht-france.t._0.html.

115 "China Turns the Tables, Faulting U.S. on Rights," *New York Times*, 5 March 1997.

116 Samir Amin, *Empire of Chaos* (New York, NY: Monthly Review Press, 1992), pp. 16, 18, 30, 81.

117 Fanon, *The Wretched of the Earth*, p. 313.

118 My dear Dorothy Fisher, 10 March 1956, Margaret Rose Gladney, Ed., *How Am I to Be Heard? Letters of Lillian Smith* (Chapel Hill, NC: University of North Carolina Press, 1993), p. 197. See Timothy Tyson, *The Blood of Emmett Till* (New York, NY: Simon Schuster, 2017).

Chapter 6: America

1 Kennan to Patricia Grady Davies, 22 July 1957, Box 10, George Kennan Papers.

2 To the Editors of the *New York Times*, 22 March 1948, Margaret Rose Gladney, Ed., *How Am I to Be Heard? Letters of Lillian Smith* (Chapel Hill, NC: University of North Carolina Press, 1993), p. 120.

3 On Jefferson's conception, see Robert Tucker and David Hendrickson: *Empire of Liberty: The Statecraft of Thomas Jefferson* (New York, NY: Oxford University Press, 1990).

4 Lillian Smith, *Killers of the Dream* (Garden City, NJ: Doubleday, 1949 and 1961), p. 214.

5 Statement by Senator Herbert Lehman before the Platform Committee of the Democratic National Convention, 10 August 1956, Box 25, Martin Luther King Papers.

6 Allan Nevins, *Herbert H. Lehman and His Era* (New York, NY: Charles Scribner's Sons, 1963), p. 342.

7 Ibid., pp. 345–346, 350.

8 *My Day*, 15 October 1945, *My Day*, 13 August 1947, Allida Black, Ed., *The Eleanor Roosevelt Papers* (Detroit, MI: Thomson, 2007), Vol. I, pp. 118, 605; *My Day*, 30 April 1957, Allida Black, Ed., *Courage in a Dangerous World: The Political Writings of Eleanor Roosevelt* (New York, NY: Columbia University Press, 1999), pp. 277–278.

9 Eleanor and Anna Roosevelt Radio Program, 22 December 1948, Black, *The Eleanor Roosevelt Papers*, Vol. I, p. 976.

10 Eleanor Roosevelt to King, 17 October 1956, and King to Eleanor Roosevelt, 5 November 1956, in Box 95, Martin Luther King Papers; Eleanor Roosevelt to King, 28 March 1961, in Box 109, Martin Luther King Papers.

11 Allida Black, *Casting Her Own Shadow: Eleanor Roosevelt and the Shaping of Postwar Liberalism* (New York, NY: Columbia University Press, 1996), p. 86.

12 Ibid., pp. 87, 136.

13 *My Day*, 29 October 1947, Black, *The Eleanor Roosevelt Papers*, Vol. I, p. 650.

14 *My Day*, 29 August 1952, Black, *Courage in a Dangerous World: The Political Writings of Eleanor Roosevelt*, pp. 266, 283; Black, *Casting Her Own Shadow: Eleanor Roosevelt and the Shaping of Postwar Liberalism*, p. 164.

15 Ralph Bunche (telegram) to King, 22 February 1956, and Ralph Bunche (letter) to King, 21 November 1956, in Box 91, Martin Luther King Papers; Charles Henry, Ed., *Ralph J. Bunche: Selected Speeches and Writings* (Ann Arbor, MI: University of Michigan Press, 1998), pp. 11–12, 279; Benjamin Rivlin, "The Legacy of Ralph Bunche" and Charles Henry, "Civil Rights and National Security: The Case of Ralph Bunche" in Benjamin Rivlin, Ed., *Ralph Bunche: The Man and His Times* (New York, NY: Holmes and Meier, 1990), pp. 23, 61–62, 236.

16 Charles Henry, *Ralph Bunche: Model Negro or American Other?* (New York, NY: New York University Press, 1999), p. 158.

17 NAACP Convention Address 1951 in Henry, *Ralph J. Bunche: Selected Speeches and Writings*, p. 238.

18 Brian Urquhart, *Ralph Bunche: An American Life* (New York, NY: W.W. Norton, 1993), p. 235.

19 Carol Anderson, *Bourgeois Radicals: The NAACP and the Struggle for Colonial Liberation, 1941–1960* (Cambridge: Cambridge University Press, 2015), p. 289; Beverly Lindsay, "Educational and Diplomatic Influences at Public Research Universities" in Beverly Lindsay, Ed., *Ralph Johnson Bunche: Public Intellectual and Nobel Peace Laureate* (Urbana, IL: University of Illinois Press, 2007), p. 80; Charles Henry, "Civil Rights and National Security: The Case of Ralph Bunche" and Ralph Bunche, "The Attack on the UN," June 1953, Benjamin Rivlin, Ed. *Ralph Bunche: The Man and His Times* (New York, NY: Holmes and Meier, 1990), pp. 56–57, 249.

20 Telford Taylor, *Dangerous Common Sense in Politics*, 1 April 1954, pp. 2–3, 10, Box 20, Robert H. Jackson Papers.

21 Telford Taylor, *Grand Inquest: The Story of Congressional Investigations* (New York, NY: Simon & Schuster, 1955), p. xiii.

22 Ibid., p. 273.

23 In her Declaration of Conscience, 1 June 1950, Senator Smith said: "I don't want to see the Republican Party ride to political victory on the Four Horsemen of Calumny—Fear, Ignorance, Bigotry, and Smear." Other Republican senators who sided with Smith were Charles Tobey (New Hampshire), George Aiken (Vermont), Wayne Morse (Oregon), Irving Ives (New York), Edward Thye (Minnesota), and Robert Hendrickson (New Jersey). See Declaration

of Conscience, pp. 15–16 and Statement of Seven Republican Senators, pp. 17–18 in William Lewis, Ed., *Declaration of Conscience: Margaret Chase Smith* (Garden City, NJ: Doubleday, 1972).

24 Taylor, *Dangerous Common Sense in Politics*, p. 12.

25 Taylor, *Grand Inquest: The Story of Congressional Investigations*, pp. xii, xv, 280–281.

26 Ibid., p. 276.

27 George Kennan to John Paton Davies, 16 October 1961, Box 4, John Paton Davies Papers.

28 George Kennan to Patricia Grady Davies, 9 August 1975, Box 6, John Paton Davies Papers and Box 10, George Kennan Papers.

29 "In a 1,600-Word Missive, Fidel Castro Criticizes Obama's Efforts in Cuba," *New York Times*, 29 March 2016, p. A8.

30 On whether to revive torture, so-called enhanced interrogation techniques, President Donald Trump said this in January 2017: "I want to do everything within the bounds of what you're allowed to do legally. But do I feel it works? Absolutely, I feel it works." See "Leaked Draft of Executive Order Risks a Divide Over National Security," *New York Times*, p. A18, 26 January 2017.

31 Gunnar Myrdal, *An American Dilemma: The Negro Problem and Modern Democracy* (New York, NY: Harper and Brothers, 1944), Vol. II, p. 1021.

32 President Barack Obama to the United Nations General Assembly, 28 September 2015. See www.whitehouse.gov/the-press-office/2015/09/28/remarks-president-obama-united-nations-general-assembly.

BIBLIOGRAPHY

Manuscript collections

Acheson, Dean, 1893–1971. Harry S. Truman Presidential Library (Independence, MO); Yale University (New Haven, CT).

Atomic Bomb Collection. Harry S. Truman Presidential Library.

Austin, Warren, 1877–1962. University of Vermont (Burlington, VT).

Baruch, Bernard, 1870–1965. Princeton University (Princeton, NJ).

Berle, Adolf, 1895–1971. Franklin D. Roosevelt Presidential Library (Hyde Park, NY).

Bunche, Ralph, 1904–1971. Schomburg Center for Research in Black Culture (New York City, NY); University of California at Los Angeles (UCLA).

Clayton, William, 1880–1966. Harry S. Truman Presidential Library.

Davies, John Paton, 1908–1999. Harry S. Truman Presidential Library.

Dodd, Thomas Joseph, 1907–1971. University of Connecticut (Storrs, CT).

Du Bois, W.E.B., 1868–1963. University of Massachusetts (Amherst, MA).

Dulles, John Foster, 1888–1959. Dwight D. Eisenhower Presidential Library (Abilene, KS).

Dwight D. Eisenhower Presidential Library. Central Files, General File; Oral Histories; White House Central Files, Official File; White House Office, National Security Council Staff, OCB [Operations Coordinating Board] Central Files Series; White House Office, Office of the Special Assistant for National Security Affairs, Policy Papers Subseries; White House Office, Office of the Staff Secretary, Subject Series, White House Subseries.

Eisenhower, Dwight David, 1890–1969. Dwight D. Eisenhower Presidential Library. Papers as President (Ann Whitman File): Dulles-Herter Series; NSC Series; Records as President, White House Central Files (Confidential File), Subject Series.

Fulbright, J. William, 1905–1995. University of Arkansas (Fayetteville, AK).

Gruenther, Alfred Maximilian, 1899–1983. Dwight D. Eisenhower Presidential Library.

Harmon, Ernest Nason, 1894–1979. U.S. Army Military History Institute (Carlisle Barracks, PA).

Hazlett, Edward E. "Swede," 1892–1958. Dwight D. Eisenhower Presidential Library.

Herter, Christian, 1895–1966. Dwight D. Eisenhower Presidential Library.

Jackson, C.D. (Charles Douglas), 1902–1964. Dwight D. Eisenhower Presidential Library.

Jackson, Robert H., 1892–1954. Library of Congress (Washington, DC).

Jessup, Philip, 1897–1986. Library of Congress.

Keenan, Joseph Berry, 1888–1954. Harvard University Law School (Cambridge, MA).

Kennan, George Frost, 1904–2005. Princeton University.

Kilmuir, Lord (David Patrick Maxwell Fyfe), 1900–1967. Churchill College, Cambridge University (Cambridge, England).

King, Martin Luther, 1929–1968. Boston University (Boston, MA).

La Guardia, Fiorello, 1882–1947. La Guardia Community College (New York City, NY).

Lehman, Herbert, 1878–1963. Columbia University (New York City, NY).

Lemkin, Raphael, 1900–1959. American Jewish Archives (Cincinnati, OH); American Jewish Historical Society (New York City, NY); Columbia University; New York City Public Library.

Lodge, Henry Cabot, 1902–1985. Massachusetts Historical Society (Boston, MA).

Lilienthal, David, 1899–1981. Princeton University.

Morgan, Lieutenant General Sir Frederick, 1894–1967. Imperial War Museum (London).

National Archives (Kew, London). Dominions and Commonwealth Relations Office; Foreign Office; Prime Minister's Office.

Oppenheimer, J. Robert, 1904–1967. Library of Congress.

Roosevelt, Anna Eleanor, 1881–1962. Franklin D. Roosevelt Presidential Library.

Taylor, Telford, 1908–1998. Columbia University.

United Nations Relief and Rehabilitation Administration. Columbia University (microfilm reels).

Warren, George, 1890–1981. Harry S. Truman Presidential Library.

Witnesses to Nuremberg Oral History Project. University of Connecticut.

Published documents

American Anthropological Association (Executive Board), "Statement on Human Rights," *American Anthropologist*, Vol. 49, No. 4, Part 1 (October–December, 1947).

An Encyclical Letter of His Holiness Pope John XXIII, *Peace on Earth* (New York, NY: Ridge Press/Golden Press, 1964).

Bekes, Csaba, Malcolm Byrne, and Janos Rainer, Eds. *The 1956 Hungarian Revolution: A History in Documents* (Budapest: Central European Press, 2002).

Boorstin, Daniel, Ed. *An American Primer* (Chicago, IL: University of Chicago Press, 1966).

Brownlie, Ian, Ed. *Basic Documents on Human Rights* (Oxford: Oxford University Press, 1983).

Department of State. *A Report on the International Control of Atomic Energy* (Washington, DC: Government Printing Office, 1946).

Foreign Relations of the United States (Washington, DC: Government Printing Office, series): *FRUS*.

Gravel (edition), Senator Mike. *The Pentagon Papers: The Defense Department History of United States Decisionmaking on Vietnam* (Boston, MA: Beacon, 1971), Vol. I.

Greenberg, Karen and Joshua Dratel, Eds. *The Torture Papers: The Road to Abu Ghraib* (Cambridge: Cambridge University Press, 2005).

Grenville, J.A.S., Ed. *The Major International Treaties 1914–1973* (London: Methuen, 1974).

International Military Tribunal. *Trial of the Major War Criminals before the International Military Tribunal, Nuremberg, 14 November 1945–1 October 1946* (Nuremberg: International Military Tribunal, 1947), 42 vols.

Jackson, Robert. *The Case Against the Nazi War Criminals* (New York, NY: Alfred A. Knopf, 1946).

Marrus, Michael, Ed. *The Nuremberg War Crimes Trial 1945–46: A Documentary History* (Boston, MA: Bedford, 1997).

NAACP. *An Appeal to the World: A Statement on the Denial of Human Rights to Minorities in the Case of Citizens of Negro Descent in the United States of America and An Appeal to the United Nations for Redress* (New York, NY: National Association for the Advancement of Colored People, 1947).

National Negro Congress. *A Petition to the United Nations on Behalf of Thirteen Million Oppressed Negro Citizens of the United States of America* (New York, NY: National Negro Congress, 1946).

Nazi Conspiracy and Aggression (Washington, DC: United States Government Printing Office, 1947).

Nelson, Anna Kasten, Ed., *The State Department Policy Planning Staff Papers 1947–1949* (New York, NY: Garland, 1983), 3 vols.

Pal, Radhabinod. *International Military Tribunal for the East: Dissentient Judgment* (Calcutta: Sanyal, 1953).

Patterson, William, Ed. *We Charge Genocide* (New York, NY: Civil Rights Congress, 1951).

Senate Select Committee on Intelligence. *The Senate Intelligence Committee Report on Torture: Committee Study of the Central Intelligence Agency's Detention and Interrogation Program* (Brooklyn, NY: Melville House, 2014).

Smith, Bradley, Ed. *The American Road to Nuremberg: The Documentary Record 1944–1945* (Stanford, CA: Hoover Institution Press, 1982).

Taylor, Telford. *Final Report to the Secretary of the Army on the Nuremberg War Crimes Trials under Control Council Law, No. 10* (New York, NY: William Hein, 1997).

The Baruch Plan. Presented to the United Nations Atomic Energy Commission, 14 June 1946, www.atomicarchive.com/Docs/Deterrence/BaruchPlan.shtml.

The Charter and Judgment of the Nuremberg Tribunal: History and Analysis (Lake Success, NY: United Nations General Assembly, International Law Commission, 1949).

The Trial of German Major War Criminals: Speeches, Chief Prosecutors, and Prosecutors 1945–46 (Buffalo, NY: William S. Hein, 2001).

To Secure These Rights: The Report of the President's Committee on Civil Rights (New York, NY: Simon & Schuster, 1947).

UNESCO, Ed. *Human Rights: Comments and Interpretations* (New York, NY: Columbia University Press, 1949).

United Nations. *Report of the Special Committee on the Problem of Hungary* (New York, NY: General Assembly, Official Records, Eleventh Session, Supplement No, 18, A/3592, 1957).

Autobiographies, diaries, edited collections, memoirs, speeches

Acheson, Dean. *Present at the Creation* (New York, NY: W.W. Norton, 1969).

Baruch, Bernard. *My Own Story* (New York, NY: Henry Holt, 1957).

Biddle, Francis. *In Brief Authority* (Garden City, NJ: Doubleday, 1962).

Black, Allida, Ed. *Courage in a Dangerous World: The Political Writings of Eleanor Roosevelt* (New York, NY: Columbia University Press, 1999).

Black, Allida, Ed. *The Eleanor Roosevelt Papers* (Detroit, MI: Thomson Gale, 2007), Vol. I.

Blum, John, Ed. *The Price of Vision: The Diary of Henry A. Wallace 1942–1946* (Boston, MA: Houghton Mifflin, 1973).

Campbell, Thomas and George Herring, Eds. *The Diaries of Edward R. Stettinius, Jr., 1943–1946* (New York, NY: New Viewpoints, 1975).

Churchill, Winston. *Never Give In! The Best of Winston Churchill's Speeches* (New York, NY: Hyperion, 2003).

Cliff, Michelle, Ed. *The Winner Names the Age: A Collection of Writings by Lillian Smith* (New York, NY: W.W. Norton, 1978).

Clifford, Clark. *Counsel to the President: A Memoir* (New York, NY: Random House, 1991).

Cordier, Andrew and Wilder Foote, Eds. *Public Papers of the Secretaries-General of the United Nations* (New York, NY: Columbia University Press, 1969), Vol. I. *Trygve Lie 1946–1953*.

Costigliola, Frank, Ed. *The Kennan Diaries* (New York, NY: W.W. Norton, 2014).

Davies, John Paton. *China Hand: An Autobiography* (Philadelphia, PA: University of Pennsylvania Press, 2012).

Dodd, Christopher, Ed. *Letters from Nuremberg: My Father's Narrative of a Quest for Justice* (New York, NY: Crown Publishing, 2007).

Duffett, John, Ed. *Against the Crime of Silence: Proceedings of the International War Crimes Tribunal* (New York, NY: Simon & Schuster, 1970).

Eban, Abba. *An Autobiography* (New York, NY: Random House, 1977).

Ferrell, Robert, Ed. *Off the Record: The Private Papers of Harry S. Truman* (New York, NY: Harper and Row, 1980).

Ferrell, Robert, Ed. *The Eisenhower Diaries* (New York, NY: W.W. Norton, 1981).

Franklin, John Hope. *Mirror to America* (New York, NY: Farrar, Straus and Giroux, 2005).

Frieze, Donna-Lee, Ed. *Totally Unofficial: The Autobiography of Raphael Lemkin* (New Haven, CT: Yale University Press, 2013).

Gilbert, G.M. *Nuremberg Diary* (New York, NY: Farrar, Straus, 1947).

Gladney, Margaret Rose, Ed. *How Am I to Be Heard? Letters of Lillian Smith* (Chapel Hill, NC: University of North Carolina Press, 1993).

Gorlitz, Walter, Ed. *The Memoirs of Field-Marshal Keitel* (New York, NY: Stein and Day, 1966).

Hata, Tsuneo. *Atomic Bomb and a Soldier: A Diary of the Chronicle of the Emperor Hirohito* (private printing, translated from the Japanese manuscript by Lisa Shinohara, author's possession).

Henry, Charles, Ed. *Ralph J. Bunche: Selected Speeches and Writings* (Ann Arbor, MI: University of Michigan Press, 1998).

Hirschmann, Ira. *Caution to the Winds* (New York, NY: David McKay, 1962).

Hobbins, A.J. *On the Edge of Greatness: The Diaries of John Humphrey, First Director of the United Nations Division of Human Rights* (Montreal: McGill University Libraries, 1994), Vol. I.

Hull, Cordell. *Memoirs* (New York, NY: Macmillan, 1948), Vol. II.

Humphrey, John. *Human Rights and the United Nations: A Great Adventure* (Dobbs Ferry, NY: Transnational, 1984).

Jessup, Philip. *The Birth of Nations* (New York, NY: Columbia University Press, 1974).

Kennan, George. *Memoirs: 1925–1950* (Boston, MA: Little, Brown, 1967).

Khrushchev, Sergei. *Rozhdenie sverkhderzhavy kniga ob otse* (Moscow: Vremia, 2000).

Lauterpacht, Elihu, Ed. *International Law: Being the Collected Papers of Hersch Lauterpacht* (Cambridge: Cambridge University Press, series), 5 Vols.

Lester, Julius, Ed. *The Seventh Son: The Thought and Writings of W.E.B. Du Bois* (New York, NY: Random House, 1971), Vol. II.

Lewis, William, Ed. *Declaration of Conscience: Margaret Chase Smith* (New York, NY: Doubleday, 1972).

Lie, Trygve. *In the Cause of Peace: Seven Years with the United Nations* (New York, NY: Macmillan, 1954).

Lilienthal, David. *The Journals: The Atomic Energy Years 1945–1950* (New York, NY: Harper and Row, 1964).

Lodge, Henry Cabot. *The Storm Has Many Eyes* (New York, NY: W.W. Norton, 1973).

Kilmuir, Lord (David Patrick Maxwell Fyfe). *Political Adventures: The Memoirs of the Earl of Kilmuir* (London: Weidenfeld and Nicolson, 1964).

Morgan, Lieutenant General Sir Frederick. *Peace and War: A Solider's Life* (London: Hodder and Stoughton, 1961).

Neal, Steve, Ed. *Eleanor and Harry: The Correspondence of Eleanor Roosevelt and Harry S. Truman* (New York, NY: Scribner, 2002).

Neave, Airey. *On Trial at Nuremberg* (Boston, MA: Little, Brown, 1978).

Neu, Sabina de Werth. *A Long Silence: Memories of a German Refugee Child, 1941–1958* (Amherst, NY: Prometheus, 2011).

Papen, Franz von. *Memoirs* (New York, NY: E.P. Dutton, 1953).

Patterson, William. *The Man Who Cried Genocide: An Autobiography* (New York, NY: International, 1971).

Powell, Jr., Adam Clayton. *Adam by Adam* (New York, NY: Dial, 1971).

Ricks, Christopher, Ed. *The Oxford Book of English Verse* (Oxford: Oxford University Press, 1999).

Roling, B.V.A. *The Tokyo Trial and Beyond: Reflections of a Peacemonger* (Cambridge: Polity, 1993).

Roosevelt, Eleanor. *On My Own* (London: Hutchinson, 1959).

Rowan, Carl. *Breaking Barriers: A Memoir* (Boston, MA: Little, Brown, 1991).

Rumulo, Carlos. *Forty Years: A Third World Solider at the UN* (New York, NY: Greenwood, 1986).

Said, Edward. *Out of Place: A Memoir* (Alfred A. Knopf, 1999).

Sakharov, Andrei. *Memoirs* (New York, NY: Alfred A. Knopf, 1990).

Smith, Alice Kimball and Charles Weiner, Eds. *Robert Oppenheimer: Letters and Recollections* (Cambridge, MA: Harvard University Press, 1980).

Speer, Albert. *Inside the Third Reich* (London: Weidenfeld and Nicolson, 1970).

Speer, Albert. *Spandau: The Secret Diaries* (New York, NY: Macmillan, 1976).

Stimson, Henry and McGeorge Bundy. *On Active Service in Peace and War* (New York, NY: Harper and Brothers, 1948).

Storey, Robert. *The Final Judgment? Pearl Harbor to Nuremberg* (San Antonio, TX: Naylor Company, 1968).

Talbot, Strobe, Ed. *Khrushchev Remembers* (Boston, MA: Little, Brown, 1970).

Taylor, Telford. *The Anatomy of the Nuremberg Trials* (New York, NY: Alfred A. Knopf, 1992).

The Asian-African Conference (New York, NY: Vital Speeches of the Day, 1 June 1955).

Truman, Harry. *Memoirs* (New York, NY: Doubleday, 1956), 2 vols.

Urquhart, Brian. *A Life in Peace and War* (New York, NY: Harper and Row, 1987).

Wunderlin, Clarence, Ed. *The Papers of Robert A. Taft* (Kent, OH: Kent State University Press, 2003), Vol. III.

Books, journal articles, unpublished manuscripts

Abrahamian, Ervand. *Iran between Two Revolutions* (Princeton, NJ: Princeton University Press, 1982).

Abrahamian, Ervand. *The Coup: 1953, the CIA, and the Roots of Modern U.S.-Iranian Relations* (New York, NY: New Press, 2013).

Albert, David, Ed. *Tell the American People: Perspectives on the Iranian Revolution* (Philadelphia, PA: Movement for a New Society, 1980).

Amin, Samir. *Empire of Chaos* (New York, NY: Monthly Review Press, 1992).

Ampiah, Kweku. *The Political and Moral Imperatives of the Bandung Conference of 1955: The Reactions of the U.S., U.K. and Japan* (London: Global Oriental, 2007).

Anderson, Carol. *Bourgeois Radicals: The NAACP and the Struggle for Colonial Liberation, 1941–1960* (Cambridge: Cambridge University Press, 2015).

Anderson, Carol. *Eyes Off the Prize: The United Nations and the African American Struggle for Human Rights, 1944–1955* (Cambridge: Cambridge University Press, 2003).

Anderson, Carol. "The Moral Arc of the Universe Bends Long but It Bends toward Justice: The Search for Justice in International Law," *Diplomatic History*, November 2011.

Armitage, David. *Foundations of Modern International Thought* (Cambridge: Cambridge University Press, 2013).

Armstrong-Reid, Susan and David Murray. *Armies of Peace: Canada and the UNRRA Years* (Toronto: University of Toronto Press, 2008).

Ashmore, Harry. *Unseasonable Truths: The Life of Robert Maynard Hutchins* (Boston, MA: Little, Brown, 1989).

Bacevich, Andrew. *American Empire: The Realities and Consequences of U.S. Diplomacy* (Cambridge, MA: Harvard University Press, 2002).

Baird, Jay, Ed. *From Nuremberg to My Lai* (Lexington, MA: D.C. Heath, 1972).

Baring, Arnulf. *Uprising in East Germany: June 17, 1953* (Ithaca, NY: Cornell University Press, 1972).

Barrett, John. "Katherine B. Fite: The Leading Female Lawyer at London and Nuremberg, 1945," lecture to the International Humanitarian Dialogs, Chautauqua, New York, 31 August 2009.

Barros, James. *Trygve Lie and the Cold War: The UN Secretary-General Pursues Peace, 1946–1953* (DeKalb: Northern Illinois University Press, 1989).

Bartel, Fritz. "Surviving the Years of Grace: The Atomic Bomb and the Specter of World Government, 1945–1950," *Diplomatic History*, April 2015.

Bartlett, Robert. *The Sixth Race* (London: Blackie, 1961).

Bass, Gary. *Stay the Hand of Vengeance: The Politics of War Crimes Tribunals* (Princeton, NJ: Princeton University Press, 2000).

Battini, Michele. *The Missing Italian Nuremberg: Cultural Amnesia and Postwar Politics* (New York, NY: Palgrave Macmillan, 2007).

Bayandor, Darioush. *Iran and the CIA: The Fall of Mosaddeq Revisited* (New York, NY: Palgrave Macmillan, 2010).

Beaufre, André. *The Suez Expedition 1956* (New York, NY: Frederick A. Praeger, 1969).

Beisner, Robert. *Dean Acheson: A Life in the Cold War* (New York, NY: Oxford University Press, 2006).

Bell, Duncan. *Reordering the World: Essays on Liberalism and Empire* (Princeton, NJ: Princeton University Press, 2016).

Bellamy, Alex. "The Responsibility to Protect Turns Ten," *Ethics and International Affairs*, Summer 2015.

Ben-Dror, Elad. *Ralph Bunche and the Arab–Israeli Conflict: Mediation and the UN, 1947–1949* (London: Routledge, 2016).

Benhabib, Seyla. "International Law and Human Plurality in the Shadow of Totalitarianism: Hannah Arendt and Raphael Lemkin," *Constellations*, Vol. 16, No. 2, 2009.

Bernstorff, Jochen von. "The Changing Fortunes of the Universal Declaration of Human Rights: Genesis and Symbolic Dimensions of the Turn to Rights in International Law," *The European Journal of International Law*, 2008, Vol. 19 No. 5.

Bess, Michael. *Choices Under Fire: Moral Dimensions of World War II* (New York, NY: Alfred A. Knopf, 2006).

Best, Gary. *Herbert Hoover: The Postpresidential Years 1933–1964* (Stanford, CA: Hoover Institution Press, 1983), 2 vols.

Bill, James and William Roger Louis, Eds. *Musaddiq, Iranian Nationalism, and Oil* (Austin, TX: University of Texas, 1988).

Bird, Kai. *The Chairman: John J. McCloy: The Making of the American Establishment* (New York, NY: Simon & Schuster, 1992).

Black, Allida. *Casting Her Own Shadow: Eleanor Roosevelt and the Shaping of Postwar Liberalism* (New York, NY: Columbia University Press, 1996).

Blackwell, Louise and Frances Clay. *Lillian Smith* (New York, NY: Twayne, 1971).

Bloxham, Donald. *Genocide on Trial: War Crimes Trials and the Formation of Holocaust History and Memory* (Oxford: Oxford University Press, 2001).

Blumenthal, David and Timothy McCormack, Eds. *The Legacy of Nuremberg: Civilizing Influence or Institutionalised Vengeance?* (Leiden: Martinus Nijhoff, 2008).

Borgwardt, Elizabeth. *A New Deal for the World: America's Vision for Human Rights* (Cambridge, MA: Harvard University Press, 2005).

Borhi, Laszlo. "Containment, Rollback, Liberation or Inaction? The United States in Hungary in the 1950s," *Journal of Cold War Studies*, Fall 1999.

Bosch, William. *Judgment on Nuremberg: American Attitudes Toward the Major War-Crime Trials* (Chapel Hill, NC: University of North Carolina Press, 1970).

Bosco, David. *Five to Rule Them All: The UN Security Council and the Making of the Modern World* (Oxford: Oxford University Press, 2009).

Boyd, Andrew. *Fifteen Men on a Powder Keg: A History of the UN Security Council* (New York, NY: Stein and Day, 1971).

Brackman, Arnold. *The Other Nuremberg: The Untold Story of the Tokyo War Crimes Trials* (New York, NY: William Morrow, 1987).

Brands, H.W. *The Specter of Neutralism: The United States and the Emergence of the Third World, 1947–1960* (New York, NY: Columbia University Press, 1989).

Buchan, Alastair. *The End of the Postwar Era: A New Balance of World Power* (London: Weidenfeld and Nicolson, 1974).

Bull, Hedley. *The Anarchical Society: A Study of Order in World Politics* (London: Macmillan, 1977).

Bullock, Alan. *Ernest Bevin: Foreign Secretary 1945–1951* (New York, NY: W.W. Norton, 1983).

Burbank, Jane and Frederick Cooper. *Empires in World History: Power and the Politics of Difference* (Princeton, NJ: Princeton University Press, 2010).

Butler, Susan. *Roosevelt and Stalin: Portrait of a Partnership* (New York, NY: Alfred A. Knopf, 2015).

Cable, James. *Intervention at Abadan: Plan Buccaneer* (New York, NY: St. Martin's Press, 1991).

Calvocoressi, Peter. *Nuremberg: The Facts, the Law and the Consequences* (New York, NY: Macmillan, 1948).

Carr, Edward Hallett. *Conditions of Peace* (New York, NY: Macmillan, 1943).

Carr, Edward Hallett. *Nationalism and After* (London: Macmillan, 1945).

Carr, Edward Hallett. *The Twenty Years' Crisis 1919–1939* (London: Macmillan, 1984 edition).

Cassin, René. *La Pensee et L'Action* (Paris: Editions F. Lalou, 1972).

Chace, James. *Acheson: The Secretary of State Who Created the American World* (New York, NY: Simon & Schuster, 1998).

Claude, Inis. *Swords into Plowshares: The Problems and Progress of International Organization* (New York, NY: Random House, 1971).

Clough, Marshall. *Mau Mau Memoirs: History, Memory, and Politics* (Boulder, CO: Lynne Rienner, 1998).

Cohen, Theodore. *Remaking Japan: The American Occupation as New Deal* (New York, NY: The Free Press, 1987).

Coit, Margaret. *Mr. Baruch* (Boston, MA: Houghton Mifflin, 1957).

Collier, David. *Democracy and the Nature of American Influence in Iran, 1941–1979* (Syracuse, NY: Syracuse University Press, 2017).

Colton, Joel. *Léon Blum: Humanist in Politics* (New York, NY: Alfred A. Knopf, 1966).

Conot, Robert. *Justice at Nuremberg* (New York, NY: Harper and Row, 1983).

Conte, Arthur. *Bandoung tournant de l'Histoire* (Paris: Robert Laffont, 1965).

Cooper, John. *Raphael Lemkin and the Struggle for the Genocide Convention* (New York, NY: Palgrave Macmillan, 2008).

Cordier, Andrew and Wilder Foote, Eds. *The Quest for Peace* (New York, NY: Columbia University Press, 1965).

Cox, Michael, Ed. *E.H. Carr: A Critical Appraisal* (New York, NY: Palgrave Macmillan, 2000).

Craig, Gordon and Francis Loewenheim, Eds. *The Diplomats 1939–1979* (Princeton, NJ: Princeton University Press, 1994).

Crowe, David. *War Crimes, Genocide, and Justice: A Global History* (New York, NY: Palgrave Macmillan, 2014).

Cumings, Bruce. *The Origins of the Korean War* (Princeton, NJ: Princeton University Press, 1981 and 1990), 2 vols.

Curle, Clinton Timothy. *Humanité: John Humphrey's Alternative Account of Human Rights* (Toronto: University of Toronto Press, 2007).

Danilovic, Alexander. *Pragmatism, Philosophy and International Politics: The UNESCO Committee on the Philosophic Principles of the Rights of Man and the Drafting of the Universal Declaration of Human Rights* (University of British Columbia, MA thesis, 2002).

Danner, Mark. "After September 11: Our State of Exception," *The New York Review of Books*, 13 October 2011.

Darwin, John. *Britain and Decolonisation: The Retreat from Empire in the Post-War World* (New York, NY: St. Martin's Press, 1988).

Davidson, Eugene. *The Trial of the Germans* (New York, NY: Macmillan, 1966).

Diedrich, Torsten. *Der 17 Juni 1953 in der DDR* (Berlin: Dietz Verlag, 1991).

Donovan, Robert. *Conflict and Crisis: The Presidency of Harry S. Truman, 1945–1948* (New York, NY: W.W. Norton, 1977).

Dower, John. *Embracing Defeat: Japan in the Wake of World War II* (New York, NY: W.W. Norton, 1999).

Doyle, Michael. *Empires* (Ithaca, NY: Cornell University Press, 1986).

Du Bois, W.E.B. *Black Reconstruction in America: An Essay Toward a History of the Past Which Black Folk Played in the Attempt to Reconstruct Democracy in America, 1860–1880* (New York, NY: Harcourt, Brace, 1935).

Eban, Abba. *The New Diplomacy: International Affairs in the Modern Age* (New York, NY: Random House, 1983).

Ehrenfreund, Norbert. *The Nuremberg Legacy: How the Nazi War Crimes Trials Changed the Course of History* (New York, NY: Palgrave Macmillan, 2007).

Elder, Tanya. "What You See Before Your Eyes: Documenting Raphael Lemkin's Life by Exploring His Archival Papers, 1900–1959," *Journal of Genocide Research*, December 2005.

Elkins, Caroline. *Imperial Reckoning: The Untold Story of Britain's Gulag in Kenya* (New York, NY: Henry Holt, 2005).

Elliott, Lawrence. *Little Flower: The Life and Times of Fiorello La Guardia* (New York, NY: William Morrow, 1983).

Elm, Mostafa. *Oil, Power and Principle: Iran's Nationalization and Its Aftermath* (Syracuse, NY: Syracuse University Press, 1994).

Engle, Karen. "From Skepticism to Embrace: Human Rights and the American Anthropological Association from 1947–1999," *Human Rights Quarterly*, Vol. 23, No. 3, 2001.

Fanon, Frantz. *Peau Noire Masques Blancs* (Paris: Editions du Seuil, 1952).

Fanon, Frantz. *The Wretched of the Earth* (New York, NY: Grove, 1963).

Falk, Richard and Gabriel Kolko and Robert Lifton, Eds. *Crimes of War* (New York, NY: Random House, 1971).

Fasulo, Linda. *Representing America: Experiences of U.S. Diplomats at the UN* (New York, NY: Praeger, 1984).

Ferguson, Niall. *Colossus: The Rise and Fall of the American Empire* (New York, NY: Penguin, 2004).

Ferris, John and Evan Mawdsley, Richard Bosworth, Joseph Maiolo, Michael Geyer, and Adam Tooze, Eds. *The Cambridge History of the Second World War* (Cambridge: Cambridge University Press, 2015), 3 vols.

Finger, Seymour. *Your Man at the UN: People, Politics, and Bureaucracy in Making Foreign Policy* (New York, NY: New York University, 1980).

Fletcher, Luke. *The Grand Area: The Conception, Design and Construction of the American Global Economic Order, 1939–1960* (Ph.D. dissertation, Cambridge University, 2014).

Fox, Grace. "The Origins of UNRAA," *Political Science Quarterly*, December 1950.

Freiberger, Steven. *Dawn Over Suez: The Rise of American Power in the Middle East* (Chicago, IL: Ivan R. Dee, 1992).

Fulbright, J. William. *The Arrogance of Power* (New York, NY: Random House, 1966).

Futamura, Madoka. *War Crimes Tribunal and Transitional Justice: The Tokyo Trial and the Nuremberg Legacy* (London: Routledge, 2008).

Gaddis, John Lewis. *George F. Kennan: An American Life* (New York, NY: Penguin, 2011).

Gaddis, John Lewis. *Strategies of Containment: A Critical Appraisal of Postwar American National Security Policy* (New York, NY: Oxford University Press, 2005).

Gaddis, John Lewis. *The Cold War* (London: Allen Lane, 2005).

Gaddis, John Lewis. *The United States and the End of the Cold War: Implications, Reconsiderations and Provocations* (New York, NY: Oxford University Press, 1992).

Gadney, Reg. *Cry Hungary! Uprising 1956* (New York, NY: Atheneum, 1986).

Gaiduk, Ilya. *Divided Together: The United States and the Soviet Union in the United Nations, 1945–1965* (Stanford, CA: Stanford University Press, 2012).

Gardner, Lloyd and Walter LaFeber and Thomas McCormick, Eds. *Creation of the American Empire: U.S. Diplomatic History* (Chicago, IL: Rand McNally, 1973).

Gasiorowski, Mark. *U.S. Foreign Policy and the Shah: Building a Client State in Iran* (Ithaca, NY: Cornell University Press, 1991).

Gasiorowski, Mark and Malcolm Byrne, Eds. *Mohammad Mosaddeq and the 1953 Coup in Iran* (Syracuse, NY: Syracuse University Press, 2004).

Gendzier, Irene. *Dying to Forget: Oil, Power, Palestine, and the Foundations of U.S. Policy in the Middle East* (New York, NY: Columbia University Press, 2015).

Gendzier, Irene. *Frantz Fanon: A Critical Study* (New York, NY: Grove, 1985).

Gendzier, Irene. *Notes from the Minefield: United States Intervention in Lebanon and the Middle East, 1945–1958* (Boulder, CO: Westview, 1999).

Gerhart, Eugene. *America's Advocate: Robert H. Jackson* (Indianapolis, IN: Bobbs-Merrill Company, 1958).

Gettig, Eric. "Trouble Ahead in Afro-Asia: The United States, the Second Bandung Conference, and the Struggle for the Third World, 1964–1965," *Diplomatic History*, 2015, No. 1.

Ghosh, Ranjan, Ed. *Edward Said and the Literary, Social, and Political World* (New York, NY: Routledge, 2009).

Giziowski, Richard. *The Enigma of General Blaskowitz* (New York, NY: Hippocrene, 1997).

Glendon, Mary Ann. *A World Made New: Eleanor Roosevelt and the Universal Declaration of Human Rights* (New York, NY: Random House, 2001).

Glendon, Mary Ann. *The Forum and the Tower: How Scholars and Politicians Have Imagined the World, from Plato to Eleanor Roosevelt* (Oxford: Oxford University Press, 2011).

Glover, Jonathan. *Humanity: A Moral History of the Twentieth Century* (New Haven, CT: Yale University Press, 2000).

Go, Julian. *Patterns of Empire: The British and American Empires, 1688 to the Present* (Cambridge: Cambridge University Press, 2011).

Goodchild, Peter. *J. Robert Oppenheimer: Shatterer of Worlds* (Boston, MA: Houghton Mifflin, 1981).

Gorbachev, Mikhail. *Perestroika: New Thinking for Our Country and the World* (New York, NY: Harper and Row, 1987).

Gordon, Robert, Ed. *The Cambridge Companion to Primo Levi* (Cambridge: Cambridge University Press, 2007).

Grant, James. *Bernard M. Baruch: The Adventures of a Wall Street Legend* (New York, NY: Simon & Schuster, 1983).

Granville, Johanna. *The First Domino—International Decision Making During the Hungarian Crisis of 1956* (College Station, TX: Texas A&M University Press, 2004).

Green, James. *The United Nations and Human Rights* (Washington, DC: Brookings Institution, 1958).

Greenberg, Karen, Ed. *The Torture Debate in America* (Cambridge: Cambridge University Press, 2006).

Griffin, James. *On Human Rights* (Oxford: Oxford University Press, 2008).

Grose, Peter. *Gentleman Spy: The Life of Allen Dulles* (Boston, MA: Houghton Mifflin, 1994).

Hahn, Peter and Mary Ann Heiss, Eds. *Empire and Revolution: The United States and the Third World Since 1945* (Columbus, OH: Ohio State University Press, 2001).

Hamby, Alonzo. *Man of the People: A Life of Harry S. Truman* (New York, NY: Oxford University Press, 1995).

Hamilton, Charles. *Adam Clayton Powell, Jr.: The Political Biography of an American Dilemma* (New York, NY: Atheneum, 1991).

Handy, Jim. *Revolution in the Countryside: Rural Conflict and Agrarian Reform in Guatemala, 1944–1954* (Chapel Hill, NC: University of North Carolina Press, 1994).

Hanhimaki, Jussi. *The Rise and Fall of Détente: American Foreign Policy and the Transformation of the Cold War* (Washington, DC: Potomac Books, 2013).

Harbutt, Fraser. *Yalta: Europe and America at the Crossroads* (Cambridge: Cambridge University Press, 2010).

Harris, Whitney. *Tyranny on Trial: The Evidence at Nuremberg* (Dallas, TX: Southern Methodist University Press, 1970).

Haslam, Jonathan. *The Vices of Integrity: E.H. Carr, 1892–1982* (London: Verso, 2000).

Haywood, Wil. *King of the Cats: The Life and Times of Adam Clayton Powell, Jr.* (Boston, MA: Houghton Mifflin, 1993).

Heijden, Barend van der and Bahia Tahzib-Lie, Eds. *Reflections on the Universal Declaration of Human Rights: A Fiftieth Anniversary Anthology* (The Hague: Martinus Nijhoff, 1998).

Heiss, Mary Ann. *Empire and Nationhood: The United States, Great Britain, and Iranian Oil, 1950–1954* (New York, NY: Columbia University Press, 1997).

Heller, Kevin. *The Nuremberg Military Tribunals and the Origins of International Criminal Law* (Oxford: Oxford University Press, 2011).

Henkin, Louis, Ed. *The International Bill of Rights: The Covenant on Civil and Political Rights* (New York, NY: Columbia University Press, 1981).

Henry, Charles. *Ralph Bunche: Model Negro or American Other?* (New York, NY: New York University, 1999).

Herken, Gregg. *Brotherhood of the Bomb: The Tangled Lives and Loyalties of Robert Oppenheimer, Ernest Lawrence, and Edward Teller* (New York, NY: Henry Holt, 2002).

Hersey, John. *Hiroshima* (New York, NY: Alfred A. Knopf, 1946).

Hewins, Ralph. *Count Folke Bernadotte: His Life and Work* (Minneapolis, MN: T.S. Denison, 1950).

Heydecker, Joe and Johannes Leeb. *The Nuremberg Trial* (Cleveland, OH: World Publishing, 1958).

Hickey, Neil and Ed Edwin. *Adam Clayton Powell and the Politics of Race* (New York, NY: Fleet, 1965).

Hildebrandt, Rainer. *The Explosion: The Uprising Behind the Iron Curtain* (Boston, MA: Little, Brown, 1955).

Hilderbrand, Robert. *Dumbarton Oaks: The Origins of the United Nations and the Search for Postwar Security* (Chapel Hill, NC: University of North Carolina Press, 1990).

Hirsch, Francine. "The Soviets at Nuremberg: International Law, Propaganda, and the Making of the Postwar Order," *American Historical Review*, June 2008.

Hirschmann, Ira. *The Embers Still Burn* (New York, NY: Simon & Schuster, 1949).

Hitchcock, William. *The Bitter Road to Freedom* (New York, NY: Free Press, 2008).

Hogan, Michael, Ed. *Hiroshima in History and Memory* (Cambridge: Cambridge University Press, 1996).

Hogan, Michael. *The Marshall Plan: America, Britain, and the Reconstruction of Western Europe, 1947–1952* (Cambridge: Cambridge University Press, 1987).

Holloway, David. *Stalin and the Bomb: The Soviet Union and Atomic Energy 1939–1956* (New Haven, CT: Yale University Press, 1994).

Holm, Michael. "Also Present at the Creation: Henry Cabot Lodge, Jr., and the Coming of the Cold War," *Journal of the Historical Society*, June 2010.

Holm, Michael. *The Marshall Plan: A New Deal for Europe* (New York, NY: Routledge, 2017).

Hoopes, Townsend and Douglas Brinkley. *FDR and the Creation of the U.N.* (New Haven, CT: Yale University Press, 1997).

Ignatieff, Michael, Ed. *American Exceptionalism and Human Rights* (Princeton, NJ: Princeton University Press, 2005).

Ikenberry, G. John. *After Victory: Institutions, Strategic Restraint, and the Rebuilding of Order After Major Wars* (Princeton, NJ: Princeton University Press, 2001).

Ikenberry, G. John. *Liberal Leviathan: The Origins, Crisis, and Transformation of the American World Order* (Princeton, NJ: Princeton University Press, 2011).

Immerman, Richard. *Empire for Liberty: A History of American Imperialism from Benjamin Franklin to Paul Wolfowitz* (Princeton, NJ: Princeton University Press, 2010).

Immerman, Richard. *John Foster Dulles and the Diplomacy of the Cold War* (Princeton, NJ: Princeton University Press, 1990).

Immerman, Richard. *The CIA in Guatemala: The Foreign Policy of Intervention* (Austin, TX: University of Texas Press, 1982).

Ingalls, Robert. *Herbert H. Lehman and New York's Little New Deal* (New York, NY: New York University Press, 1975).

Iriye, Akira, Petra Goedde, and William Hitchcock, Eds. *The Human Rights Revolution: An International History* (New York, NY: Oxford University Press, 2012).

Irvin-Erikson, Douglas. *Raphael Lemkin and the Concept of Genocide* (Philadelphia, PA: University of Pennsylvania Press, 2016).

Jack, Homer. *Bandung: an on-the-spot description of the Asian-African Conference, Bandung, Indonesia April 1955* (Chicago, IL: Toward Freedom, 1955).

Jackson, Robert. "Nuremberg in Retrospect," *Canadian Bar Review*, August–September 1949.

Jackson, Robert. "Our Number One International Problem," *Society for the Prevention of World War III*, June–September 1947.

Jackson, Robert. "The Law Under Which Nazi Organizations Are Accused of Being Criminal," *Temple Law Quarterly*, April 1946.

Jackson, Robert. "The Significance of the Nuremberg Trials to the Armed Forces," *Military Affairs*, Winter 1946.

Jackson, Robert Harry. *The Global Covenant: Human Conduct in a World of States* (Oxford: Oxford University Press, 2000).

Jacobs, Steven, Ed. *Raphael Lemkin's Thoughts on Nazi Genocide* (Lampeter: Edwin Mellen, 1992).

Jacobsen, Annie. *Operation Paperclip: The Secret Intelligence Program that Brought Nazi Scientists to America* (Boston, MA: Little, Brown, 2014).

Jaspers, Karl. *The Question of German Guilt* (New York, NY: Dial, 1947).

Jeffers, H. Paul. *The Napoleon of New York: Mayor Fiorello La Guardia* (New York, NY: John Wiley and Sons, 2002).

Jenks, Wilfred. "Hersch Lauterpacht—The Scholar as Prophet," *British Year Book of International Law*, 1960.

Jones, Joseph. *The Fifteen Weeks* (New York, NY: Viking, 1955).

Jones, Matthew. "A Segregated Asia?: Race, the Bandung Conference, and Pan-Asianist Fear in American Thought and Policy, 1954–1955," *Diplomatic History*, 2005, No. 5.

Jones, Matthew. *After Hiroshima: The United States, Race and Nuclear Weapons in Asia, 1945–1965* (Cambridge: Cambridge University Press, 2010).

Judis, John. *Genesis: Truman, American Jews, and the Origins of the Arab–Israeli Conflict* (New York, NY: Farrar, Straus, and Giroux, 2014).

Judt, Tony. *Postwar: A History of Europe Since 1945* (New York, NY: Penguin, 2006).

Kahin, Audrey and George Kahin. *Subversion as Foreign Policy: The Secret Eisenhower and Dulles Debacle in Indonesia* (New York, NY: New Press, 1995).

Kahin, George. *The Asian-African Conference: Bandung, Indonesia, April 1955* (Ithaca, NY: Cornell University Press, 1956).

Kaplan, Lawrence. *NATO and the UN: A Peculiar Relationship* (Columbia, MO: University of Missouri Press, 2010).

Katznelson, Ira. *Desolation and Enlightenment: Political Knowledge After Total War, Totalitarianism, and the Holocaust* (New York, NY: Columbia University Press, 2003).

Kearney, James. *Anna Eleanor Roosevelt: The Evolution of a Reformer* (Boston, MA: Houghton Mifflin, 1968).

Kecskemeti, Paul. *The Unexpected Revolution: Social Forces in the Hungarian Uprising* (Stanford, CA: Stanford University Press, 1961).

Keenan, Joseph Berry and Brendan Francis Brown. *Crimes Against International Law* (Washington, DC: Public Affairs Press, 1950).

Kenez, Peter. "Khrushchev and Hungary in 1956," n.d., essay in author's possession.

Kenez, Peter. *The Coming of the Holocaust: From Antisemitism to Genocide* (Cambridge: Cambridge University Press, 2013).

Kennan, George. *American Diplomacy 1900–1950* (Chicago, IL: University of Chicago, 1951).

Kennedy, Paul. *The Parliament of Man: The Past, Present, and Future of the United Nations* (New York, NY: Vintage, 2006).

Kennedy, Paul. *The Rise and Fall of the Great Powers: Economic Change and Military Conflict from 1500 to 2000* (New York, NY: Random House, 1987).

Kessner, Thomas. *Fiorello H. La Guardia and the Making of Modern New York* (New York, NY: McGraw-Hill, 1989).

Kinnear, Mary. *Woman of the World: Mary McGeachy and International Cooperation* (Toronto: University of Toronto Press, 2004).

Kinzer, Stephen. *All the Shah's Men: An American Coup and the Roots of Middle East Terror* (Hoboken, NJ: John Wiley and Sons, 2003).

Kinzer, Stephen. *Overthrow: America's Century of Regime Change from Hawaii to Iraq* (New York, NY: Henry Holt, 2006).

Kiraly, Bela and Paul Jonas. *The Hungarian Revolution in Retrospect* (New York, NY: Columbia University Press, 1978).

Klopprogge, Nadja. "Intimacy, Histories, and Space: Wannsee Beach and Nuremberg in African American Memories and Experiences," paper presented at Transatlantic Studies Association Annual Conference, 10–12 July 2017, Cork, Ireland.

Kochavi, Arieh. *Post-Holocaust Politics: Britain, the United States and Jewish Refugees, 1945–1948* (Chapel Hill, NC: University of North Carolina Press, 2001).

Kochavi, Arieh. *Prelude to Nuremberg: Allied War Crimes Policy and the Question of Punishment* (Chapel Hill, NC: University of North Carolina Press, 1998).

Kopelman (later Borgwardt), Elizabeth. "Ideology and International Law: The Dissent of the Indian Justice at the Tokyo War Crimes Trial," *New York University Journal of International Law and Politics*, Winter 1991.

Korey, William. *An Epitaph for Raphael Lemkin* (New York, NY: Jacob Blaustein Institute for the Advancement of Human Rights, 2001).

Koskenniemi, Martti. *The Gentle Civilizer of Nations: The Rise and Fall of International Law 1870–1960* (Cambridge: Cambridge University Press, 2002).

Kramer, Paul. "Power and Connection: Imperial Histories of the United States in the World," *American Historical Review*, December 2011.

Kumar, Krishan. *Visions of Empire: How Five Imperial Regimes Shaped the World* (Princeton, NJ: Princeton University Press, 2017).

Kushner, Barak. *Men to Devils: Japanese War Crimes and Chinese Justice* (Cambridge, MA: Harvard University Press, 2015).

Lael, Richard. *The Yamashita Precedent: War Crimes and Command Responsibility* (Wilmington, DE: Scholarly Resources, 1982).

LaFeber, Walter. *Inevitable Revolutions: The United States in Central America* (New York, NY: W.W. Norton, 1983).

Lamb, Richard. *The Failure of the Eden Government* (London: Sidgwick and Jackson, 1987).

Lash, Joseph. *Eleanor: The Years Alone* (London: Andre Deutsch, 1973).

Lauren, Paul Gordon. *The Evolution of International Human Rights: Visions Seen* (Philadelphia, PA: University of Pennsylvania Press, 2011).

Lauterpacht, Elihu. *The Life of Sir Hersch Lauterpacht* (Cambridge: Cambridge University Press, 2010).

Lauterpacht, Hersch. *An International Bill of the Rights of Man* (New York, NY: Columbia University Press, 1945).

Lauterpacht, Hersch. *International Law and Human Rights* (London: Stevens and Sons, 1950).

LeBlanc, Lawrence. *The United States and the Genocide Convention* (Durham, NC: Duke University Press, 1991).

Leffler, Melvyn. *A Preponderance of Power: National Security, the Truman Administration, and the Cold War* (Stanford, CA: Stanford University Press, 1992).

Leffler, Melvyn and Odd Arne Westad, Eds. *The Cambridge History of the Cold War* (Cambridge: Cambridge University Press, 2010), 3 vols.

Leifer, Michael. *Dilemmas of Statehood in Southeast Asia* (Vancouver: University of British Columbia Press, 1972).

Lemkin, Raphael. *Axis Rule in Occupied Europe* (Washington, DC: Carnegie Endowment for International Peace, 1944).

Lemkin, Raphael. "Genocide as a Crime under International Law," *The American Journal of International Law*, January 1947.

Lemkin, Raphael and Malcolm McDermott. *The Polish Penal Code of 1932 and the Law of Minor Offenses* (Durham, NC: Duke University Press, 1939).

Lendvai, Paul. *One Day that Shook the Communist World: The 1956 Hungarian Uprising and its Legacy* (Princeton, NJ: Princeton University Press, 2008).

Leuchtenburg, William. *Herbert Hoover* (New York, NY: Henry Holt, 2009).

Levene, Mark. *Genocide in the Age of the Nation State* (London: I.B. Tauris, 2005), 2 vols.

Levene, Mark. *The Crisis of Genocide* (New York, NY: Oxford University Press, 2013), 2 vols.

Levi, Primo. *Collected Poems* (London: Faber and Faber, 1988).

Levi, Primo. *If This is a Man* (London: Orion, 1959).

Lewis, David Levering. *W.E.B. Du Bois: The Fight for Equality and the American Century 1919–1963* (New York, NY: Henry Holt, 2000).

Lichtblau, Eric. *The Nazis Next Door: How America Became a Safe Haven for Hitler's Men* (Boston, MA: Houghton Mifflin Harcourt, 2014).

Lindsay, Beverly, Ed. *Ralph Johnson Bunche: Public Intellectual and Nobel Peace Laureate* (Urbana, IL: University of Illinois Press, 2007).

Litvan, Gyorgy, Ed. *The Hungarian Revolution of 1956: Reform, Revolt and Repression 1953–1963* (London: Longman, 1996).

Loescher, Gil. *The UNHCR and World Politics: A Perilous Path* (Oxford: Oxford University Press, 2001).

Logevall, Fredrik. *Embers of War: The Fall of an Empire and the Making of America's Vietnam* (New York, NY: Random House, 2012).

Lomax, Bill. *Hungary 1956* (New York, NY: St. Martin's Press, 1976).

Louis, William and Roger Owen, Eds. *Suez 1956: The Crisis and its Consequences* (Oxford: Clarendon Press, 1989).

Loveland, Ann. *Lillian Smith: A Southerner Confronting the South* (Baton Rouge, LA: Louisiana State University Press, 1986).

Lowe, Keith. *Savage Continent: Europe in the Aftermath of World War II* (New York, NY: St. Martin's Press, 2012).

Luard, Evan. *A History of the United Nations* (New York, NY: St. Martin's Press, 1982), Vol. I.

Luthi, Lorenz. *The Sino-Soviet Split: Cold War in the Communist World* (Princeton, NJ: Princeton University Press, 2008).

Maier, Charles. *Among Empires: American Ascendency and Its Predecessors* (Cambridge, MA: Harvard University Press, 2006).

Malik, Charles. "For a Policy of True Humanism," *The Commonweal*, 12 October 1951.

Malik, Habib Charles. "The Universal Declaration of Human Rights at Sixty," delivered at United Nations Headquarters, 10 December 2008.

Mann, Michael. *Incoherent Empire* (London: Verso, 2005).

Martin, James. *The Man Who Invented "Genocide": The Public Career and Consequences of Raphael Lemkin* (Torrance, CA: Institute for Historical Review, 1984).

Maser, Werner. *Nuremberg: A Nation on Trial* (New York, NY: Charles Scribner's Sons, 1979).

Mastny, Vojtech and Zhu Liqun, Eds. *The Legacy of the Cold War: Perspectives on Security, Cooperation, and Conflict* (Lanham, MD: Lexington, 2014).

May, Larry and Andrew Forchehimes, Eds. *Morality, Jus Post Bellum, and International Law* (Cambridge: Cambridge University Press, 2012).

Mayers, David. *Dissenting Voices in America's Rise to Power* (Cambridge: Cambridge University Press, 2007).

Mayers, David. *FDR's Ambassadors and the Diplomacy of Crisis* (Cambridge: Cambridge University Press, 2013).

Mayers, David. *George Kennan and the Dilemmas of U.S. Foreign Policy* (New York, NY: Oxford University Press, 1988).

Mazower, Mark. *Governing the World: The History of an Idea, 1815 to the Present* (New York, NY: Penguin, 2012).

Mazower, Mark. *Hitler's Empire: How the Nazis Ruled Europe* (New York, NY: Penguin, 2008).

Mazower, Mark. *No Enchanted Palace: The End of Empire and the Ideological Origins of the United Nations* (Princeton, NJ: Princeton University Press, 2009).

Mazower, Mark. "The Strange Triumph of Human Rights, 1933–1950," *The Historical Journal*, June 2004.

Mazower, Mark, Jessica Reinisch, and David Feldman. *Post-War Reconstruction in Europe: International Perspectives, 1945–1949* (Oxford: Oxford University Press, 2011).

Mazuzan, George. *Warren R. Austin at the U.N. 1946–1953* (Kent, OH: Kent State University Press, 1977).

McCauley, Martin. *The German Democratic Republic since 1945* (New York, NY: St. Martin's Press, 1983).

McDonnell, Michael and Dirk Moses. "Raphael Lemkin as Historian of Genocide in the Americas," *Journal of Genocide Research*, December 2005.

McDougall, Walter. *Promised Land, Crusader State: The American Encounter with the World Since 1776* (Boston, MA: Houghton Mifflin, 1997).

McGuinness, Margaret. "Peace v. Justice: The Universal Declaration of Human Rights and the Modern Origins of the Debate," *Diplomatic History*, November 2011.

Mearsheimer, John. *The Tragedy of Great Power Politics* (New York, NY: W.W. Norton, 2001).

Melanson, Richard and David Mayers, Eds. *Reevaluating Eisenhower: American Foreign Policy in the Fifties* (Urbana, IL: University of Illinois Press, 1989).

Mendelsohn, John. *Trial by Document: The Uses of Seized Records in the United States Proceedings at Nuremberg* (New York, NY: Garland, 1988).

Mettraux, Guenael, Ed. *Perspectives on the Nuremberg Trial* (Oxford: Oxford University Press, 2008).

Michener, James. *The Bridge at Andau* (New York, NY: Random House, 1957).

Miller, William. *Henry Cabot Lodge* (New York, NY: James H. Heineman, 1967).

Millett, Allan. *The War for Korea, 1945–1950: A House Burning* (Lawrence, KS: University Press of Kansas, 2005).

Milne, David. *Worldmaking: The Art and Science of American Diplomacy* (New York, NY: Farrar, Straus and Giroux, 2015).

Milosz, Czeslaw. *The Captive Mind* (New York, NY: Vintage, 1981).

Milward, Alan. *The Reconstruction of Western Europe 1945–51* (Berkeley, CA: University of California Press, 1984).

Minear, Richard. *Victors' Justice: The Tokyo War Crimes Trial* (Princeton, NJ: Princeton University Press, 1971).

Mishra, Pankaj. *Age of Anger: A History of the Present* (New York, NY: Farrar, Straus and Giroux, 2017).

Molnar, Miklos. *Budapest: A History of the Hungarian Revolution* (London: George Allen and Unwin, 1971).

Morsink, Johannes. *The Universal Declaration of Human Rights* (Philadelphia, PA: University of Pennsylvania Press, 1999).

Moses, A. Dirk. "Genocide," *Australian Humanities Review*, November 2013.

Moses, A. Dirk and Dan Stone, Eds. *Colonialism and Genocide* (London: Routledge, 2007).

Motadel, David. *Islam and Nazi Germany's War* (Cambridge, MA: Harvard University Press, 2014).

Moyn, Samuel. *Christian Human Rights* (Philadelphia, PA: University of Pennsylvania Press, 2015).

Moyn, Samuel. *The Last Utopia: Human Rights in History* (Cambridge, MA: Harvard University Press, 2010).

Myrdal, Gunnar. *An American Dilemma: The Negro Problem and Modern Democracy* (New York, NY: Harper and Brothers, 1944), 2 vols.

Nagy, Imre. *On Communism: In Defense of the New Course* (New York, NY: Frederick A. Praeger, 1957).

Naimark, Norman. *Stalin's Genocides* (Princeton, NJ: Princeton University Press, 2010).

Neff, Donald. *Warriors at Suez: Eisenhower Takes America into the Middle East* (New York, NY: Simon & Schuster, 1981).

Neuse, Steven. *David E. Lilienthal: The Journey of an American Liberal* (Knoxville, TN: University of Tennessee Press, 1996).

Nevins, Allan. *Herbert H. Lehman and His Era* (New York, NY: Charles Scribner's Sons, 1963).

Niebuhr, Reinhold. *The Irony of American History* (Chicago, IL: University of Chicago Press, 2008).

Nolde, O. Frederick. *Free and Equal: Human Rights in Ecumenical Perspective: With Reflections on the Origin of the Universal Declaration of Human Rights by Charles Habib Malik* (Geneva: World Council of Churches, 1968).

Oakeshott, Michael, Ed., Thomas Hobbes, *Leviathan or the Matter, Forme and Power of a Commonwealth Ecclesiasticall and Civil* (New York, NY: Collier, 1973).

Offner, Arnold. *Another Such Victory: President Truman and the Cold War, 1945–1953* (Stanford, CA: Stanford University Press, 2002).

Ostermann, Christian. "Keeping the Pot Simmering: The United States and the East German Uprising of 1953," *German Studies Review*, February 1996.

Pagden, Anthony. *The Burdens of Empire: 1539 to the Present* (Cambridge: Cambridge University Press, 2015).

Parker, Jason. "Cold War II: The Eisenhower Administration, the Bandung Conference, and the Reperiodization of the Postwar Era," *Diplomatic History*, 2006, No. 5.

Paulding, Gouverneur. "Genocide and Mercy Killing," *The Reporter*, 14 March 1950.

Persico, Joseph. *Nuremberg: Infamy on Trial* (New York, NY: Viking, 1994).

Piccigallo, Philip. *The Japanese on Trial: Allied War Crimes Operations in the East, 1945–1951* (Austin, TX: University of Texas Press, 1979).

Plesch, Dan. *America, Hitler and the UN: How the Allies Won World War II and Forged a Peace* (London: I.B. Tauris, 2011).

Plummer, Brenda, Ed. *Window on Freedom: Race, Civil Rights, and Foreign Affairs, 1945–1988* (Chapel Hill, NC: University of North Carolina Press, 2003).

Pogue, Forrest. *George C. Marshall: Statesman 1945–1959* (New York, NY: Viking, 1987).

Power, Samantha. *A Problem from Hell: America and the Age of Genocide* (New York, NY: Basic, 2002).

Preston, Andrew. *Sword of the Spirit, Shield of Faith: Religion in American War and Diplomacy* (New York, NY: Alfred A. Knopf, 2012).

Price, Harry. *The Marshall Plan and Its Meaning* (Ithaca, NY: Cornell University Press, 1955).

Rabinovich, Itamar and Jehuda Reinharz, Eds. *Israel in the Middle East: Documents and Readings on Society, Politics, and Foreign Relations, Pre-1948 to the Present* (Waltham, MA: Brandeis University Press, 2008).

Radvanyi, Janos. *Hungary and the Superpowers: The 1956 Revolution and Realpolitik* (Stanford, CA: Hoover Institution Press, 1972).

Ravndal, Ellen. "The First Major Test: The UN Secretary-General and the Palestine Problem, 1947–49" in *International History Review*, January 2016.

Reel, A. Frank. *The Case of General Yamashita* (Chicago, IL: University of Chicago Press, 1949).

Reynolds, David. *Britannia Overruled: British Policy and World Power in the Twentieth Century* (London: Longman, 1991).

Rice, Stuart and Joshua Jortner. *James Franck 1882–1964: A Biographical Memoir* (Washington, DC: National Academy of Sciences, 2010).

Richard, Guy, Ed. *L'Histoire Inhumaine, Massacres et Genocides des Origins a Nos Nours* (Paris: Armand Collin, 1992).

Rivlin, Benjamin, Ed. *Ralph Bunche: The Man and His Times* (New York, NY: Holmes and Meier, 1990).

Roberts, Jo. *Contested Land, Contested Memory: Israel's Jews and Arabs and the Ghosts of Catastrophe* (Toronto: Dundurn, 2013).

Romulo, Carlos. *The Meaning of Bandung* (Chapel Hill, NC: University of North Carolina Press, 1956).

Roosevelt, Eleanor. "The Promise of Human Rights," *Foreign Affairs*, April 1948.

Roosevelt, Theodore. *Fear God and Take Your Own Part* (New York, NY: George Doran, 1916).

Rosenbaum, Alan. *Prosecuting Nazi War Criminals* (Boulder, CO: Westview, 1993).

Rusk, Dean. "The Place of the Genocide Convention in the General Pattern of U.S. Foreign Relations," *Department of State Bulletin*, 30 January 1950.

Russell, Ruth. *A History of the United Nations Charter: The Role of the United States 1940–1945* (Washington, DC: Brookings Institution, 1958).

Ryan, Allan. *Yamashita's Ghost: War Crimes, MacArthur's Justice, and Command Accountability* (Lawrence, KS: University Press of Kansas, 2012).

Ryan, David and Victor Pungong, Eds. *The United States and Decolonization: Power and Freedom* (London: Macmillan, 2000).

Sands, Philippe. *East West Street: On the Origins of "Genocide" and "Crimes Against Humanity"* (New York, NY: Alfred A. Knopf, 2016).

Sartre, Jean-Paul. *On Genocide* (Boston, MA: Beacon, 1968).

Schabas, William. *Genocide in International Law: The Crimes of Crimes* (Cambridge: Cambridge University Press, 2000).

Schabas, William. "International War Crimes Tribunals and the United States," *Diplomatic History*, November 2011.

Schaller, Dominik. "Raphael Lemkin's View of European Colonial Rule in Africa: Between Condemnation and Admiration," *Journal of Genocide Research*, December 2005.

Schaller, Dominik and Jurgen Zimmerer. "From the Guest Editors: Raphael Lemkin: The 'Founder of the United Nation's Genocide Convention' as a Historian of Mass Violence," *Journal of Genocide Research*, December 2005.

Schaller, Michael. *The American Occupation of Japan: The Origins of the Cold War in Asia* (New York, NY: Oxford University Press, 1985).

Schlatter, Richard, Ed. *Hobbes's Thucydides* (New Brunswick, NJ: Rutgers University Press, 1975).

Schlesinger, Stephen. *Act of Creation: The Founding of the United Nations* (Boulder, CO: Westview, 2003).

Schlesinger, Stephen and Stephen Kinzer. *Bitter Fruit: The Story of the American Coup in Guatemala* (Cambridge, MA: Harvard University Press, 1999).

Schroeder, Paul. *The Axis Alliance and Japanese-American Relations 1941* (Ithaca, NY: Cornell University Press, 1958).

Schulman, Bruce, Ed. *Making the American Century: Essays on the Political Culture of Twentieth Century America* (New York, NY: Oxford University Press, 2014).

Schwarz, Jordan. *The Speculator: Bernard M. Baruch in Washington, 1917–1965* (Chapel Hill, NC: University of North Carolina Press, 1981).

Sebestyen, Victor. *Twelve Days: The Story of the 1956 Hungarian Revolution* (New York, NY: Pantheon, 2006).

Sedgwick, James. "A People's Court: Emotion, Participant Experiences, and the Shaping of Postwar Justice at the International Military Tribunal for the Far East, 1946–1948," *Diplomacy and Statecraft*, September 2011.

Sedgwick, James. *Inside Justice: Being International in Postwar Tokyo, 1946–1948* (unpublished manuscript, 2013).

Segesser, Daniel and Myrian Gessler. "Raphael Lemkin and the International Debate on the Punishment of War Crimes, 1919–1948," *Journal of Genocide Research*, December 2005.

Sharma, Arvind. *Are Human Rights Western? A Contribution to the Dialogue of Civilizations* (Oxford: Oxford University Press, 2006).

Shaw, Tony. *Eden, Suez and the Mass Media: Propaganda and Persuasion During the Suez Crisis* (London: I.B. Tauris, 1996).

Shawcross, William. *Justice and the Enemy: Nuremberg, 9/11, and the Trial of Khalid Sheikh Mohammed* (New York, NY: Public Affairs, 2011).

Shephard, Ben. *The Long Road Home: The Aftermath of the Second World War* (New York, NY: Alfred A. Knopf, 2011).

Sherwin, Martin. *A World Destroyed: The Atomic Bomb and the Grand Alliance* (New York, NY: Vintage, 1977).

Simmons, Ruth. *Mobilizing for Human Rights: International Law in Domestic Politics* (Cambridge: Cambridge University Press, 2009).

Simpson, A.W. Brian. *Human Rights and the End of Empire: Britain and the Genesis of the European Convention* (Oxford: Oxford University Press, 2001).

Smith, Lillian. *Killers of the Dream* (Garden City, NJ: Doubleday, 1949 and 1961).

Smith, Richard Norton. *An Uncommon Man: The Triumph of Herbert Hoover* (New York, NY: Simon & Schuster, 1984).

Snyder, Timothy. *Bloodlands: Europe Between Hitler and Stalin* (New York, NY: Basic, 2010).

Snyder, Timothy. *On Tyranny: Twenty Lessons from the Twentieth Century* (New York, NY: Tim Duggan, 2017).

Southern, David. *Gunnar Myrdal and Black-White Relations: The Use and Abuse of An American Dilemma, 1944–1969* (Baton Rouge, LA: Louisiana State University Press, 1987).

Spiegel, Steven. *The Other Arab–Israeli Conflict: Making America's Middle East Policy, from Truman to Reagan* (Chicago, IL: University of Chicago Press, 1985).

Stahn, Carsten and Jann Kleffner, Eds. *Jus Post Bellum: Towards a Law of Transition from Conflict to Peace* (The Hague: Asser, 2008).

Steil, Benn. *The Battle of Bretton Woods: John Maynard Keynes, Harry Dexter White, and the Making of a New World Order* (Princeton, NJ: Princeton University Press, 2013).

Steiman, Lionel. *Franz Werfel: The Faith of an Exile* (Waterloo: Wilfrid Laurier University Press, 1985).

Stone, Dan. "Raphael Lemkin on the Holocaust," *Journal of Genocide Research*, December 2005.

Stueck, William. *Rethinking the Korean War: A New Diplomatic and Strategic History* (Princeton, NJ: Princeton University Press, 2002).

Suganami, Hidemi, Madeline Carr, and Adam Humphreys, Eds. *The Anarchical Society at 40: Contemporary Challenges and Prospects* (Oxford: Oxford University Press, 2017).

Szabo, Tamas. *Boy on the Rooftop* (Boston, MA: Little, Brown, 1958).

Tan, See Seng, and Amitav Acharya, Eds. *Bandung Revisited: The Legacy of the 1955 Asian-African Conference for International Order* (Singapore: National University of Singapore, 2008).

Tanaka, Yuki, Tim McCormack, and Gerry Simpson, Eds. *Beyond Victor's Justice? The Tokyo War Crimes Trial Revisited* (Leiden: Martinus Nijhoff, 2011).

Taylor, Telford. *Grand Inquest: The Story of Congressional Investigations* (New York, NY: Simon & Schuster, 1955).

Taylor, Telford. *Nuremberg and Vietnam: An American Tragedy* (New York, NY: Bantam, 1971).

Taylor, Telford. "Nuremberg and Vietnam: Who is Responsible for War Crimes?" *War/Peace Report*, November 1970.

Terkel, Studs. *The Good War* (New York, NY: New Press, 1984).

Thakur, Ramesh. *The United Nations, Peace and Security: From Collective Security to the Responsibility to Protect* (Cambridge: Cambridge University Press, 2006).

Thomas, Martin. *Fight or Flight: Britain, France, and their Roads from Empire* (Oxford: Oxford University Press, 2014).

Thompson, John. *A Sense of Power: Roots of America's Global Role* (Ithaca, NY: Cornell University Press, 2015).

Thomson, John. "Burma: A Neutral in China's Shadow," *The Review of Politics*, July 1957.

Totten, Samuel and Steven Jacobs, Eds. *Pioneers of Genocide Studies* (New Brunswick, NJ: Transaction, 2002).

Trachtenberg, Marc. *A Constructed Peace: The Making of the European Settlement, 1945–1963* (Princeton, NJ: Princeton University Press, 1999).

Troen, Selwyn and Moshe Shemesh, Eds. *The Suez-Sinai Crisis 1956: Retrospective and Reappraisal* (New York, NY: Columbia University Press, 1990).

Tucker, Robert and David Hendrickson. *Empire of Liberty: The Statecraft of Thomas Jefferson* (New York, NY: Oxford University Press, 1990).

Tusa, Ann and John Tusa. *The Nuremberg Trial* (New York, NY: Atheneum, 1984).

Tyson, Timothy. *The Blood of Emmett Till* (New York, NY: Simon & Schuster, 2017).

Urquhart, Brian. *Hammarskjold* (New York, NY: Harper and Row, 1984).

Urquhart, Brian. *Ralph Bunche: An American Life* (New York, NY: W.W. Norton, 1993).

Vik, Hanne Hagtvedt. "How Constitutional Concerns Framed the U.S. Contribution to the International Human Rights Regime from Its Inception, 1947–53," *International History Review*, December 2012.

Vitalis, Robert. *White World Order, Black Power Politics: The Birth of American International Relations* (Ithaca, NY: Cornell University Press, 2015).

Vrdoljak, Ana Filipa. "Human Rights and Genocide: The Work of Lauterpacht and Lemkin in Modern International Law," *The European Journal of International Law*, 2009, Vol. 20, No. 4.

Wall, Irwin. *France, the United States, and the Algerian War* (Berkeley, CA: University of California Press, 2001).

Walzer, Michael. *Arguing About War* (New Haven, CT: Yale University Press, 2004).

Walzer, Michael. *Just and Unjust Wars: A Moral Argument with Historical Illustrations* (New York, NY: Basic, 2000).

Wasserstein, Bernard. *Israelis and Palestinians: Why Do They Fight? Can They Stop?* (New Haven, CT: Yale University Press, 2004).

Weinberg, Gerhard. *A World at Arms: A Global History of World War II* (Cambridge: Cambridge University Press, 1995).

Weiner, Tim. *Legacy of Ashes: The History of the CIA* (New York, NY: Doubleday, 2007).

Weisbrode, Kenneth. *The Year of Indecision, 1946: A Tour Through the Crucible of Harry Truman's America* (New York, NY: Viking, 2016).

Weiss-Wendt, Anton. "Hostage of Politics: Raphael Lemkin on 'Soviet Genocide,'" *Journal of Genocide Research*, December 2005.

Weitz, Eric. "The Human Rights Surges of the 1940s and 1990s: A Commentary on Margaret E. McGuinness and William A. Schabas," *Diplomatic History*, November 2011.

Werfel, Franz. *The Forty Days of Musa Dagh* (New York, NY: The Modern Library, 1934).

Wested, Odd Arne. *The Cold War: A World History* (New York, NY: Basic, 2017).

Wested, Odd Arne. *The Global Cold War: Third World Interventions and the Making of Our Times* (Cambridge: Cambridge University Press, 2007).

Wilber, Donald. *Regime Change in Iran: Overthrow of Premier Mossadeq of Iran, November 1952–August 1953* (Nottingham: Spokesman, 2006).

Williams, Andrew. *Liberalism and War: The Victors and the Vanquished* (London: Routledge, 2006).

Williams, Andrew. "Reconstruction Before the Marshall Plan," *Review of International Studies*, July 2005.

Williams, William Appleman. *Empire as a Way of Life: An Essay on the Causes and Character of America's Present Predicament Along with a Few Thoughts About an Alternative* (New York, NY: Oxford University Press, 1980).

Willis, James. *Prologue to Nuremberg: The Politics and Diplomacy of Punishing War Criminals of the First World War* (Westport, CT: Greenwood, 1982).

Wilson, Joan Hoff. *Herbert Hoover: Forgotten Progressive* (Boston, MA: Little, Brown, 1975).

Winter, Jay. *Dreams of Peace and Freedom: Utopian Moments in the Twentieth Century* (New Haven, CT: Yale University Press, 2006).

Winter, Jay and Antoine Prost. *René Cassin and Human Rights: From the Great War to the Universal Declaration* (Cambridge: Cambridge University Press, 2013).

Wittmann, Rebecca. *Beyond Justice: The Auschwitz Trial* (Cambridge, MA: Harvard University Press, 2005).

Woodbridge, George. *UNRRA: The History of the United Nations Relief and Rehabilitation Administration* (New York, NY: Columbia University Press, 1950), 3 vols.

Wooley, Wesley. *Alternatives to Anarchy: American Supranationalism since World War II* (Bloomington, IN: Indiana University Press, 1988).

Wright, Richard. *The Color Curtain: A Report on the Bandung Conference* (Cleveland, OH: World Publishing, 1956).

Yergin, Daniel. *The Prize: The Epic Quest for Oil, Money, and Power* (New York, NY: Simon & Schuster, 1991).

Young, Marilyn. *The Vietnam Wars 1945–1990* (New York, NY: HarperPerennial, 1991).

Zimmerer, Jurgen and Joachim Zeller, Eds. *Volkermord in Deutsch-Sudwestafrika: Der Kolonialkrieg 1904–1908 in Namibia und seine Folgen* (Berlin: Links, 2003).

Zolo, Danilo. *Victors' Justice: From Nuremberg to Baghdad* (London: Verso, 2009).

INDEX